Invisible Reconstruction

FRINGE

Series Editors
Alena Ledeneva and Peter Zusi, School of Slavonic
and East European Studies, UCL

The FRINGE series explores the roles that complexity, ambivalence and immeasurability play in social and cultural phenomena. A cross-disciplinary initiative bringing together researchers from the humanities, social sciences and area studies, the series examines how seemingly opposed notions such as centrality and marginality, clarity and ambiguity, can shift and converge when embedded in everyday practices.

Alena Ledeneva is Professor of Politics and Society at the School of Slavonic and East European Studies of UCL.

Peter Zusi is Associate Professor at the School of Slavonic and East European Studies of UCL.

Invisible Reconstruction

Cross-disciplinary responses to natural, biological and man-made disasters

Edited by

Lucia Patrizio Gunning and Paola Rizzi

First published in 2022 by
UCL Press
University College London
Gower Street
London WC1E 6BT

Available to download free: www.uclpress.co.uk

Collection © Editors, 2022
Text © Contributors, 2022
Images © Contributors and copyright holders named in captions, 2022

The authors have asserted their rights under the Copyright, Designs and Patents Act 1988 to be identified as the authors of this work.

A CIP catalogue record for this book is available from The British Library.

Any third-party material in this book is not covered by the book's Creative Commons licence. Details of the copyright ownership and permitted use of third-party material is given in the image (or extract) credit lines. If you would like to reuse any third-party material not covered by the book's Creative Commons licence, you will need to obtain permission directly from the copyright owner.

This book is published under a Creative Commons Attribution-Non-commercial Non-derivative 4.0 International licence (CC BY-NC-ND 4.0). This licence allows you to share, copy, distribute and transmit the work for personal and non- commercial use provided author and publisher attribution is clearly stated. Attribution should include the following information:

Gunning, L. P., and Rizzi, P. (eds). 2022. *Invisible Reconstruction: Cross-disciplinary responses to natural, biological and man-made disasters*. London: UCL Press. https://doi.org/10.14324/111.781800083493

Further details about Creative Commons licences are available at
http://creativecommons.org/licenses/

ISBN: 978-1-80008-351-6 (Hbk.)
ISBN: 978-1-80008-350-9 (Pbk.)
ISBN: 978-1-80008-349-3 (PDF)
ISBN: 978-1-80008-352-3 (epub)
DOI: https://doi.org/10.14324/111.9781800083493

Contents

List of figures	viii
List of tables	xvi
List of contributors	xvii
Series editors' preface	xxiii
Foreword Florian Mussgnug	xxv
Acknowledgements	xxxi

Introduction: The Invisible Reconstruction project and its aims   1
Lucia Patrizio Gunning and Paola Rizzi

Part I Reconstruction and society

1   L'Aquila 2009–2019: back to the future. Cultural heritage
and post-seismic reconstruction challenges   11
Alessandra Vittorini

2   Invisible recovery: physical reconstruction versus social
reconstruction. The case of Central Italy   29
Donato Di Ludovico and Lucia Patrizio Gunning

3   Revealing the vulnerable in society: Contradictions between
victims' intentions and housing provision   45
Haruka Tsukuda and Yasuaki Onoda

4   Invisible hands: institutional resilience and tsunami risk.
The case of Kochi City in Japan   62
Sarunwit Promsaka Na Sakonnakron,
Paola Rizzi and Satoshi Otsuki

5   L'Aquila: from old to new castles: Rediscovering poles and
networks to rebuild a community   84
Simonetta Ciranna and Patrizia Montuori

Part II Public space, a human right

6   Post-crisis masterplanning: A new approach to public spaces.
Italy (2009–2021)   107
Quirino Crosta

7   Rethinking inequality and the future: The pre-Hispanic past in
post-disaster Lima, Peru   123
Rosabella Alvarez-Calderon and Julio Sanchez

8   (Re)-constructing the contemporary city in Latin America   140
Maria Andrea Tapia

9   Invisible regeneration: The communities of Shahjahanabad in
times of pandemic   156
Abhishek Jain

Part III Communication, prevention and protection

10   Rebuilding engagement with social media and
consumer technologies   173
Barnaby Gunning and Lucia Patrizio Gunning

11   The Great East Japan Earthquake and COVID-19: Through the
lenses of gender and age   189
Miwako Kitamura

12   Disaster risk management, social participation and geoethics   203
*Francesco De Pascale, Piero Farabollini and
Francesca Romana Lugeri*

13   Soundscapes of non-reality: Alternative approach to post-
disaster reconstruction   218
Paola Rizzi, Nora Sanna and Anna Porębska

Part IV Tourism, culture and economy

14   Atmospheric images: Photographic encounters in L'Aquila's
historic centre   235
Federico De Matteis and Fatima Marchini

15   Providing disaster information to inbound tourists:
Case study for the historical city of Kyoto, Japan   250
Kohei Sakai and Hideiko Kanegae

16 Landscape as a post-earthquake driver of resilience:
The intangible multiple values of territory 268
Fabio Carnelli and Paola Branduini

17 Heritage assets, fairs and museums: Places of encounter and
presence in times of pandemic 283
Franca Zuccoli, Alessandra De Nicola and Pietro Magri

Part V Schools, social integration and rights

18 Dimensions of educational poverty and emergencies:
What are the protective factors for wellbeing? 299
Nicoletta Di Genova

19 Existential and identity displacement in catastrophic events.
Teacher training: skills and strategies for coping 313
Antonella Nuzzaci

20 Intercultural relations and community development:
education in L'Aquila among earthquake and COVID-19
emergencies 328
Alessandro Vaccarelli and Silvia Nanni

Index 341

List of figures

Note
Figures without a credit are author images.

1.1 L'Aquila in the Antonio Vandi plan (1753). 14
1.2 The basilica of Santa Maria di Collemaggio: view from the outside. 21
1.3 Santa Maria di Collemaggio: the post-earthquake collapse (2009). 22
1.4 Santa Maria di Collemaggio: the dismantled pillars during the restoration works. 22
1.5 Santa Maria di Collemaggio: the discovery of the original gildings in the Celestine Chapel. 23
1.6 The Basilica of Santa Maria di Collemaggio after the restoration (2017). 23
1.7 Santa Maria di Collemaggio: the restored baroque organ. 24
1.8 L'Aquila, Palazzo Morini Cervelli: the *Pietà* found within sixteenth-century masonry. 26
1.9 L'Aquila, Palazzo dell'Emiciclo: the underground spaces of the ancient monastery of Saint Michael found during the restoration works, excavated and repurposed to host the public library. 27
2.1 Schematic representation of a social structure and related bonds, and its modifications following a disaster. From left to right: the pre-disaster community, the suspension/interruption of bonds following the disaster, the re-bonding process and the state of fusion, the interruption of the fusion and the differentiation of the post-disaster community (according to the Wraith and Gordon scheme). 36
2.2 Resilience Scale for Adults (RSA) profiles in response to the COVID-19 pandemic, with variance for four age groups. Design: Rodolfo Rossi. 38

3.1	The main choices of housing reconstruction.	49
3.2	Registration status for each household based on the number of members therein.	51
3.3	Registration status for each household and house type before the disaster.	52
3.4	Movement of residence and desired place of disaster public housing.	53
3.5	The organisational structure for supporting vulnerable victims' recovery in Ishinomaki.	56
3.6	The exterior of the collective-type public housing for mutual assistance in Ishinomaki.	58
3.7	The inside of the collective-type public housing for mutual assistance in Ishinomaki.	58
4.1	Nankai Earthquake and Kochi city: the effects in 1946 and the forecast of effects of next Nankai. Source: authors. Graphic by Irene Friggia.	64
4.2	The development of national spatial planning and disaster management system in Japan after World War II. Source: authors. Graphic by Irene Friggia.	65
4.3	Structural Process of the Spatial Planning System in Japan. Source: Introduction of Urban Land Use Planning System in Japan, City Bureau, Japanese Ministry of Land, Infrastructure and Transport (2003). Graphic by Irene Friggia.	66
4.4	Concept of urban land use planning. Source: Introduction of Urban Land Use Planning System in Japan, City Bureau, Japanese Ministry of Land, Infrastructure and Transport (2003).	67
4.5	Resilience schemes and key performance indicators.	69
4.6	Results of in-depth interview of local government officers of Kochi. Source: Sarunwit Promsaka N.S., 2015. Graphic by Irene Friggia.	70
4.7	A conceptual model of urban resilience transformation. Source: Sarunwit Promsaka N.S., Paola Rizzi. Graphic by Lorenzo Cotti.	71
4.8	Kochi's tsunami resilience profile in terms of urban planning.	72
4.9	The urban development category in the web portal of Kochi City. Source: Kochi City web. Graphic by Irene Friggia.	76
4.10	A model of spatial planning for disaster resilience. Source: Sarunwit Promsaka N.S., Paola Rizzi. Graphic by Lorenzo Cotti.	79

5.1	Map of L'Aquila by Pico Fonticulano, 1575, Biblioteca Provinciale dell'Aquila ms 57, 176r part of the *Breve descrittione di sette città illustri d'Italia di Messer Ieronimo Pico Fonticulano dell'Aquila,* Aquila: Giorgio Dagano e Compagni 1582 (critical edition: Centofanti 1996, 93).	86
5.2	L'Aquila: the market square in a photo taken before the earthquake of 2009.	87
5.3	L'Aquila: the Corso on a day of 'youth movida', before March 2009.	88
5.4	L'Aquila: Piazza Paganica in July 2020 – on the left is Palazzo Ardinghelli, location of MAXXI L'Aquila: on the right, the Santa Maria church. Photo: Francesco Giancola.	89
5.5	L'Aquila: the restored Palazzo dell'Emiciclo, now headquarters of Consiglio Regionale d'Abruzzo. Source: Wikipedia.	90
5.6	L'Aquila: Duomo square during one of the evening shows organised in July 2020 as part of the initiative *Cantieri dell'Immaginario.*	91
5.7	L'Aquila: the courtyard of Palazzo Carli Benedetti during a concert on the occasion of presentation of a book, 26 May 2018. Photo: Carla Bartolomucci.	91
5.8	Design competition for a new students' home in L'Aquila, 2018. Winning project *La Duttilità è nella Memoria* – Ductility is in a Memory: engineers D. Massimo, F. Gabriele, L. Micarelli, M. Paolucci. Source: Giancola 2019, 45, 54.	92
5.9	Design competition for a new students' home in L'Aquila, 2018. Winning project *La Duttilità è nella Memoria* – Ductility is in a Memory: engineers D. Massimo, F. Gabriele, L. Micarelli, M. Paolucci. Source: Giancola 2019, 45, 54..	93
5.10	Onna, L'Aquila: One of the MAP temporary anti-seismic houses built just outside the historic centre. Source: Wikipedia.	95
5.11	View of the CASE in Bazzano in 2015. The buildings rest on seismic-reinforced concrete plates, supported on metal pillars fixed to a foundation, also of reinforced concrete. Photo: Vincenzo Di Florio.	96

5.12 Two of four wall paintings on the façades of the CASE complex in Bazzano made during the 2014 Re_acto Fest, a street art festival organised by the Re_acto Association with the 3e32 committee, sponsored by the Municipality of L'Aquila and the Order of Architects. Wall paintings: Mr.Thoms and v3erbo; photo: Semi Sotto La Pietra.   97

5.13 Onna, L'Aquila: 2010 view of the historic centre, completely destroyed by the 2009 earthquake. Source: Wikipedia.   98

5.14 Onna, L'Aquila: The church of San Pietro Apostolo after the restoration, completed in 2015. The reconstruction plan was promoted and co-financed by the German government in agreement with Onna's municipal administration and the Civil Protection. Source: Wikipedia.   99

5.15 Onna, L'Aquila. Casa Onna, the multifunctional building completed in 2010 at the entrance of the village – a reference point for its inhabitants. Source: Onna Onlus.   100

6.1 Evolutionary process from the public sphere to the integration of new standards.   113

6.2 The historic centre of L'Aquila indicating spaces under examination.   115

6.3 Summary of new research perspectives.   119

7.1 Survivors of the 1950 Cusco earthquake taking shelter in the main plaza. Source: Giesecke Collection, Riva Agüero Institute for Higher Studies, Pontificia Universidad Católica del Perú.   126

7.2 Survivors of the 1950 Cusco earthquake building temporary shelters in the main plaza. Source: Giesecke Collection, Riva Agüero Institute for Higher Studies, Pontificia Universidad Católica del Perú.   127

7.3 The El Paraiso complex (3,500–1,800 BC) in northern Lima, with its blue marker. This well-known site has been mapped and documented, but is still vulnerable to land traffickers. Image: Rosabella Alvarez-Calderón, 2015.   130

7.4 The Maranga Archaeological Complex, most of which is located inside the modern-day Parque de las Leyendas (right), PUCP campus (centre, in yellow) and the Mateo Salado complex (left, in red). The yellow line on the left shows the path that the Inca Road may have followed. Designed by Fabricio Torres, October 2018. Source: Office of Infrastructure, PUCP.   132

7.5	The Inca Road inside the campus of Pontificia Universidad Catolica del Peru (PUCP) is cut off from the pre-Hispanic sites inside Parque de las Leyendas (top) by a modern avenue. The large *huacas* at Parque de las Leyendas are surrounded by several pre-Hispanic and modern plazas and open spaces. Image: Julio Sanchez Garcia, 2019. Source: Office of Infrastructure, PUCP.	132
7.6	Walkability workshop in November 2019, designed to evaluate pedestrian connections between the complex of Mateo Salado, the PUCP campus and the Inca Road, and the Parque de las Leyendas. Organised by the Huaca Fest project and Lima-based *Ocupa tu Calle.* Images: the Estefani Delgado /Huaca Fest project.	134
7.7	Much of the walk between the pre-Hispanic sites in the Maranga area is along narrow sidewalks, with few trees for shade and high fences designed to protect pre-Hispanic sites. Image: Rosabella Alvarez-Calderon.	135
7.8	Pedestrian access between the PUCP campus and the nearby Parque de las Leyendas requires a long, uncomfortable walk along a very narrow sidewalk. Image: Rosabella Alvarez-Calderon.	135
8.1	Exteriors of precarious homes, El Barrio Julián Blanco, Petare, Caracas, Venezuela, 2009.	143
8.2	Informal neighbourhoods, El Barrio Julián Blanco, Petare, Caracas, Venezuela, 2021. Source: Google maps.	144
8.3	Aerial image of the Paraisópolis favela, Sao Paulo, Brazil, 2009.	146
8.4 and 8.5	Public space in Paraisópolis [Sao Paulo, Brazil] – before reconstruction (2009) and afterwards (2011).	149
8.6	Interdependent relationships between the formal neighbourhood and the Toma Las 250 casas. General Roca, Argentina. Image: Luciano Idda (2014).	151
8.7	Toma Las 250 casas house distribution and classification. Images: Luciano Idda (2014).	152
9.1	Map of the city of Shahjahanabad.	159
9.2	Nineteenth-century map of Roshanpura.	160
9.3	Existing map of Roshanpura showing detailed study area of divided *Haveli* in red box.	161
9.4	Plan of transformed grey part shown in Figure 9.3.	162
9.5	The courtyard of Haveli Rai Ji.	163

9.6	Cardboard file making activity has moved to the interior rooms in Haveli Rai Ji.	163
9.7	Connecting terraces allow verbal and visual interaction between people in times of pandemic in Haveli Rai Ji.	165
9.8	Pictures showing residents working in self-created separate zones in Haveli Rai Ji.	165
9.9	Left: a narrow tertiary street where controlled movement of people can be achieved. Right: a longitudinal section showing the benefits of terrace connections.	166
10.1	Come Facciamo: Autoritratto web application, 2010.	176
10.2	Click Days campaign map, 2010.	178
10.3	Click Days work in progress, 2010.	179
10.4	L'Aquila 3d, web application, 2011.	180
10.5	Noi L'Aquila web application, 2011.	181
10.6	Noi L'Aquila Infobox, 2011.	182
10.7	Hello L'Aquila website, 2014.	184
11.1	Gender differences.	196
11.2	Age differences.	196
11.3	Summary of Living Testimony.	198
12.1	Area and municipalities in the so-called seismic crater. Source: https://sisma2016.gov.it.	205
12.2	Abbey of Sant'Eutizio, Preci (PG) Italy. Source: authors.	207
12.3	San Salvatore, Castelluccio, Norcia (PG) Italy. Source: authors.	207
12.4	San Benedetto Abbey, Norcia (PG) Italy. Source: authors.	208
13.1	Urban analysis diagrams regarding main services and points of interest outlined by the citizens of L'Aquila during the survey held in 2017. © Nora Sanna.	223
13.2	Examples of freehand sonographies resulting from soundwalks along Corso Vittorio Emanuele II in L'Aquila that took place during the 2017 International Summer School on Awareness and Responsibility of Environmental Risk. © Federico Puggioni. © Francesco Cherchi.	224
13.3	Participatory process flowchart as applied in the L'Aquila case study. © Nora Sanna.	225
13.4	Results of the survey regarding favourite urban spaces in L'Aquila, 2017. © Nora Sanna.	226
13.5	L'Aquila Old Town's Sonography, 2018. © Francesco Cherchi, Nora Sanna.	227

13.6	Pilot project in San Bernardino Square, L'Aquila, 2018, resulting from the workshop held in March 2018. It consists of two meeting points of light wooden structures with sound-absorbing properties and a walkway inside the park. © Nora Sanna.	229
14.1	The exhibition 'L'Aquila, 6 aprile 2019. Ricordo. Memoria. Futuro' installed on the Corso. Photo: Roberto Grillo.	241
14.2	Roberto Grillo, two photographs from the exhibition series.	241
14.3	Deserted streetscapes in L'Aquila's historic centre. Photo: Fatima Marchini.	244
14.4	Building site at night. Photo: Fatima Marchini.	245
14.5	Ruined building. Photo: Fatima Marchini.	246
15.1	Point of origin of respondents.	255
15.2	Age of respondents.	255
15.3	Gender of respondents.	256
15.4	Number of times respondent has visited Japan.	256
15.5	Natural disasters that the respondents think may occur in Kyoto.	257
15.6	Likelihood of a large-scale earthquake occurring in Kyoto in the next 30 years.	257
15.7	Pictogram used in Japan to indicate an evacuation site.	258
15.8	Ratio of those who had seen 15.7 while sightseeing in Japan.	258
15.9	Impressions of Figure 15.7.	259
15.10	Impression about going to the location indicated by Figure 15.7 after a disaster occurs.	259
15.11	Obtaining information about disasters in Japan before coming to Japan/while in Japan.	260
15.12	Sources of information about disasters in Japan (before arriving in Japan).	260
15.13	Sources of information about disasters in Japan (while in Japan).	260
15.14	Knowledge of websites and apps that provide information during disasters.	261
15.15	Intention to install apps that provide information during disasters.	261
15.16	Important sources of information to be relied upon during disasters.	262
15.17	Post box displaying a QR code for information access. Source: author.	264
16.1	Our actors' map of the study area.	270
16.2	The Castelluccio plain.	272

16.3	The landscape of *marcita* meadows surrounding Norcia.	273
18.1	Teachers' survey question: 'In your opinion, are the social, economic and urban problems caused by the 2009 earthquake still weighing on the wellbeing of the population?'	305
18.2	Parents' survey question.	306
18.3	Word cloud: 'When you think of your city, what are the first three words that come to mind?'	307
19.1	*San Francesco Solano indicates an earthquake next to Saints John the Evangelist and John the Baptist.* Giovanni Battista Tinti, c. 1570. Wikimedia Commons.	314

List of tables

2.1	Comparison of reconstruction planning tools.	32
2.2	Strategies for recovering the social fabric and planning (reworking Gordon's proposal).	37
3.1	The provision period of temporary housing.	55
6.1	Urban case studies.	113
6.2	Dimensions, rights and urban patterns.	114
6.3	New public space management tools.	116
6.4	The toolkit applied to the central axis of L'Aquila.	117
11.1	Coding results.	194
11.2	Categories characteristic of the 65+ age group.	195
11.3	Categories characteristic of men aged 65+.	196
11.4	Categories characteristic of men under age 65.	196
11.5	Characteristics of interviewees.	199
15.1	Summary of questionnaire survey of inbound tourists.	253
15.2	Distance between survey area and sightseeing areas.	254
15.3	Summary of the factual investigation with regard to foreign tourists in the 2018 Kyoto City Tourism Comprehensive Survey.	254
18.1	Research project 'My City'. Brief excerpts of the texts written by the children of L'Aquila in 2012.	301

List of contributors

Rosabella Alvarez-Calderon is an archaeologist, urbanist and Professor at the Department of Architecture of the Pontificia Universidad Católica del Peru, Lima, Peru. She is also a consultant for the Ministry of Culture and the UNESCO-Lima office, for the Heritage Cities project.

Paola Branduini is Assistant Professor in Landscape Conservation, at DAICA, Politecnico di Milano, Italy. She teaches 'Landscape as Heritage' at the School of Architecture, Construction Engineering and Urban Planning of the Politecnico di Milano. Paola is a consultant for the French Ministère de la Transition écologique et solidaire.

Fabio Carnelli is Adjunct Professor at the Politecnico di Milano and EURAC Research, Bolzano, Italy. With a background in cultural anthropology and environmental sociology, he is a member of the editorial board of the book series *Geographies of the Anthropocene* and founding member of the online journal *Il Lavoro Culturale*.

Simonetta Ciranna is Professor in the History of Architecture at the Department of Civil, Construction-Architecture and Environmental Engineering (DICEAA), Università degli Studi, L'Aquila, Italy. She is the representative of the University for the National Museum of 21st Century Art (MAXXI), the European Association for Architectural Education (EAAE) and the Museum Centre of the University of L'Aquila (POMAQ).

Quirino Crosta is an engineer and tutor in Urban Planning and in the Master's in 'Post-disaster technical-administrative management in local authorities' at the DICEAA, Department of Civil, Construction-Architecture and Environmental Engineering, of the Università degli Studi, L'Aquila, Italy. He is a political activist and militant urbanist.

Federico De Matteis is an architect and Associate Professor of Architectural Design at the Università degli Studi, L'Aquila, Italy where he teaches Design. He is Visiting Professor at the Lebanese American University of Beirut and Associate Professor at Xi'an Jiatong-Liverpool University in Suzhou, China. He has a Master's in Architecture from Università degli Studi di Roma 'La Sapienza', one in science from the University of Pennsylvania, and a PhD in Architecture from 'La Sapienza'. His research focuses on urban design and regeneration and the affective dimension of urban and architectural space.

Alessandra De Nicola is a research fellow at the University of Milano-Bicocca. She is Adjunct Professor in Art Education at the Libera Università di Bolzano, Italy. Alessandra collaborates with BiPAC- Interdepartmental Research Centre for Heritage and Arts and the 'Riccardo Massa' Department of Human Sciences for Education in cultural heritage education, interpretation and mediation methodologies.

Francesco De Pascale is a Postdoctoral Research Fellow, at the Italian National Research Council (CNR), Research Institute for Geo-hydrological Protection, Italy. He has a PhD in Geography and Earth Sciences, is a teaching assistant (*Cultore della Materia*) in Geography of Cultural Heritage at the Department of Culture and Society of University of Palermo, Italy. Francesco is Coordinator of the Geo-history, Geographical Education and GIS area at the Institute for the History of the Italian Risorgimento, and of the Provincial Committee of Cosenza, Italy. He is Chair of the 'climate risk' area at the Italian Society of Environmental Geology, Calabria section, Editor-in-Chief of the *Geographies of the Anthropocene* book series and of *Filosofi(e)Semiotiche (Il Sileno Edizioni)*. He is Associate Editor (Geography and Risk section) of *AIMS Geosciences* and, with Piero Farabollini, Francesca Romana Lugeri and Francesco Muto, he is an editor of the topical collection *Ethics in Geosciences.*

Nicoletta Di Genova is a PhD student in the Dipartimento di Psicologia dei Processi di Sviluppo e Socializzazione at Università degli Studi di Roma 'La Sapienza'. She has a degree in Design and Management of Social and Educational Services and Interventions from the University of L'Aquila. Her research fields are poverty, educational wellbeing and resilience in contexts of social and territorial fragility, with particular reference to emergency and post-emergency situations.

Donato Di Ludovico is Associate Professor of Urban Design and Landscape, in the Department of Civil, Construction-Architecture and Environmental Engineering (DICEAA), Università degli Studi, L'Aquila, Italy. His research engages with spatial and strategic planning, urban planning and design (safety, protection and urban and territorial regeneration), civil protection planning, knowledge systems and assessment. Former secretary and vice-president of the National Institute of Urban Planning (INU) Abruzzo and Molise. He is Director of the Urban Planning Laboratory for the reconstruction of L'Aquila – LAURAq of INU/ANCSA, Scientific Director of the AnTeA Laboratory (Territorial and Environmental Analyses) at the University of L'Aquila, member of the university spin-off DRIMS, Diagnostic Retrofitting and Innovation in Material Srl and Coordinator of the 1st level Specialising-Master course in Post-Catastrophe Technical-Administrative Management of Local Authorities.

Piero Farabollini is Professor of Geomorphology and Physical Geography at the University of Camerino, Italy. He is the Former Extraordinary Commissioner for Reconstruction after the Earthquake in Central Italy.

Barnaby Gunning RIBA is an architect, programmer and designer. Barnaby taught degree and diploma units at the Bartlett School of Architecture, University College London. He worked with Norman Foster, Renzo Piano Building Workshop, Atelier One and Ron Arad before setting up his own practice, Barnaby Gunning Studio in 2004. He was the architect of the only house to be built entirely in Lego; the project for *James May's Toy Stories* television programme used crowd sourcing for the construction of the 3.5 million bricks that formed the house. His post-earthquake participatory projects Come Facciamo, L'Aquila 3D and Noi L'Aquila in collaboration with Google were recognised as exemplary by UNESCO in their #Unite4heritage campaign.

Abhishek Jain is a practising architect, specialised in urban regeneration, working on the heritage awareness and documentation of organically grown old cities in India. In 2009, he founded the Shahjahanabadi Foundation. He collaborates with the School of Planning and Architecture, Department of Physical Planning, in the University of New Delhi and with the Faculty of Architecture in Jamia Milia Islamia.

Hideiko Kanegae is Professor in the College of Policy Science of Ritsumeikan University, Osaka, and Research Member of its renowned Institute of Disaster Mitigation for Urban Cultural Heritage (DMUCH). He is specialised in disaster mitigation for urban cultural heritage, environmental policy and social systems; his fields include the study of cultural assets, museology, social systems engineering, safety systems, natural disaster prevention science, economic policy, risk planning, environmental education, disaster mitigation and risk communication.

Miwako Kitamura is a PhD student at the Graduate School of Engineering of Tohoku University, Japan. Her research interests include ageing society and gender perspectives in disaster.

Francesca Romana Lugeri is a geologist, sociologist, geographer. She is a Researcher at ISPRA Institute for Environmental Protection and Research and an Associate Researcher at the University of Camerino, Italy.

Pietro Magri is President of Insieme nelle terre di mezzo ONLUS and Coordinator of the 'Fa' la cosa giusta!' exhibition in Milan, the main Italian fair on responsible consumption and sustainable lifestyle. Pietro coordinated an international centre for young people in France, a Caritas centre for refugees in Varese and is a member of the board of Terre di Mezzo Editore.

Fatima Marchini is a designer in the fields of exhibition design, graphic design, illustration and branding, based in Rome, Italy. With an educational background in architecture and music, Fatima has authored several photography and film projects.

Florian Mussgnug PhD, Scuola Normale Superiore Pisa, teaches Italian and Comparative Literature at University College London. He has published widely on twentieth-and twenty-first-century literature, with a particular focus on literary theory, experimental literature and narrative prose fiction in Italian, English and German. His publications include *Rethinking the Animal-Human Relation: New Perspectives in Literature and Theory* (2019, with Stefano Bellin and Kevin Inston), *The Good Place: Comparative Perspectives on Utopia* (2014, with Matthew Reza), and *The Eloquence of Ghosts: Giorgio Manganelli and the Afterlife of the Avant-Garde* (2010, winner of the 2012 Edinburgh Gadda Prize). He has held visiting and honorary positions at the Universities of Siena, *Roma Tre*, Oxford and Cagliari, and at the British School at Rome. He is co-investigator for the five-year AHRC-funded research project 'Interdisciplinary Italy 1900–2020: Interart/Intermedia' and academic director of the UCL Cities Partnerships Programme in Rome.

Patrizia Montuori is an architect and contract professor in the History of Architecture at the Department of Civil, Construction-Architecture and Environmental Engineering (DICEAA), Università degli Studi, L'Aquila, Italy.

Silvia Nanni is a researcher in General and Social Pedagogy at the Department of Human Sciences (DSU) of the Università degli Studi, L'Aquila, Italy.

Antonella Nuzzaci is Associate Professor of Experimental Pedagogy at the Department of Human Sciences (DSU) of the Università degli Studi, L'Aquila, Italy. She deals with educational experimentalism in the use of cultural heritage by teachers and students in schools, with particular reference to the didactic-methodological renewal of the teaching-learning processes and the strengthening of the cultural profiles of the population through IT. Antonella specialises in teacher training, with particular attention to the role played by methodological, reflective and digital skills as well as evaluation and self-evaluation processes and quality and accreditation systems in higher education.

Satoshi Otsuki is an Associate Professor in the Faculty of Regional Collaboration of Kochi University, Japan.

Lucia Patrizio Gunning is Lecturer (Teaching) at the History Department, University College London, United Kingdom. She is a modern historian specialising in cultural and diplomatic history and on the relationship between cultural heritage, disaster and recovery. Following the devastating 2009 earthquake in her home city of L'Aquila, Lucia has worked to effect change in approaches to reconstruction and disaster preparedness in Europe and Japan. In 2010–2014 Lucia initiated participative projects with Google and the University of L'Aquila to reconnect the city's dispersed population with its cultural heritage and architecture. The projects L'Aquila 3D, Come Facciamo and Noi L'Aquila were recognised as exemplary by UNESCO in their #Unite4heritage campaign.

Anna Porębska is Assistant Professor of Architectural and Urban Design at the Cracow University of Technology, Poland.

Sarunwit Promsaka Na Sakonnakron is Lecturer in the Faculty of Learning Sciences and Education of Thammasat University, Thailand.

Paola Rizzi is Associate Professor at the Department of Architecture, Design and Urban Planning of the University of Sassari, Italy. She is an urban planner and designer, specialising in urban gaming simulation and disaster mitigation. She is Visiting Professor at the Urban Design and Development International Programme (UDDI) at TDS, Thamassat University in Thailand and Visiting Scholar at the Institute of Disaster Mitigation for Urban Cultural Heritage (DMUCH), Kyoto, Japan. Paola is a member of ACRI/Automi Cellulari nella Ricerca e nell'Industria (Cellular Automata into Research and Industry) and sits on the advisory board of directors of CUPUM – (Computers in Urban Planning and Urban Management). She is on the editorial board of the *Journal of Applied Environmental Research*.

Kohei Sakai is Senior Researcher in the Research Organization of Open Innovation and Collaboration of Ritsumeikan University, Osaka, Japan.

Julio Sanchez is campus archaeologist at the Pontificia Universidad Catolica del Peru. With Rosabella Alvarez-Calderon, he is co-director of the *Huaca Fest* Project in Lima.

Nora Sanna is an architect in the Diver S City UrbLab at the University of Sassari, Italy.

Maria Andrea Tapia is Vice-Rector of the National University of Rio Negro. She is Professor of Territorial Urban Project at the National University of Rio Negro in Patagonia, Argentina.

Haruka Tsukuda is Associate Professor in the Department of Architecture of Tohoku University, Japan.

Alessandro Vaccarelli is Professor of General and Social Pedagogy at the Department of Human Sciences (DSU) of the Università degli Studi, L'Aquila, Italy.

Alessandra Vittorini is Director of the Fondazione Scuola Beni Attività Culturali in Rome. She was the Superintendent for Archaeological, Artistic and Architectural Heritage and Landscape for L'Aquila and its Seismic Crater between 2012 and 2020. She is an architect with a PhD in Urban Planning.

Onoda Yusuaki is Professor in the Department of Architecture and at the International Research Institute of Disaster Science of Tohoku University, Japan. He received his PhD (Policy Science) from the Graduate School of Ritsumeikan University. He is an Associate Professor at the College of Policy Science, Ritsumeikan University. He is a steering committee member of Institute of Disaster Mitigation for Urban Cultural Heritage and Research and Development Institute of Regional Information (DMUCH). He is engaged in study and practice for making communities resilient against natural disasters. His special interests are community-based disaster management and disaster education for future generations, making use of simulation and gaming.

Franca Zuccoli is Associate Professor at the Riccardo Massa Department of Human Sciences for Education, Professor of Image Education and General Teaching Approach. She has conducted numerous heritage education projects with museums and schools. She is currently working with the Triennale Museum and Fondazione Arnaldom Pomodoro. She is the Rector's Delegate for Museums and President of the Opera Pizzigoni.

Series editors' preface

The UCL Press FRINGE series presents work related to the themes of the UCL FRINGE Centre for the Study of Social and Cultural Complexity.

The FRINGE series is a platform for cross-disciplinary analysis and the development of 'area studies without borders'. 'FRINGE' is an acronym standing for Fluidity, Resistance, Invisibility, Neutrality, Grey zones, and Elusiveness – categories fundamental to the themes that the Centre supports. The oxymoron in the notion of a 'FRINGE CENTRE' expresses our interest in (1) the tensions between 'area studies' and more traditional academic disciplines; and (2) social, political and cultural trajectories from 'centres to fringes' and inversely from 'fringes to centres'.

The series pursues an innovative understanding of the significance of fringes: rather than taking 'fringe areas' to designate the world's peripheries or non-mainstream subject matters (as in 'fringe politics' or 'fringe theatre'), we are committed to exploring the patterns of social and cultural complexity characteristic of fringes and emerging from the areas we research. We aim to develop forms of analysis of those elements of complexity that are resistant to articulation, visualisation or measurement.

We are accustomed to think of 'repair' as a process measured by visible results: the healing of damage through development, the mending of ruins through reconstruction. Yet especially in events as traumatic and complex as major urban disasters, the physical destruction, as horrific as it may be, is only part of the story. Much that is destroyed is invisible, difficult to measure; the loss of buildings and infrastructure brings with it a loss of historical heritage, communal identity and social bonds. This interdisciplinary volume brings together perspectives drawn from cultural history and urban design to question how one should account for such invisible damage, how one should go about repairing such intangible losses and how one should best prepare for the hidden cost of such disasters. The authors make a compelling case for the role of education in these processes: culture and communication are as important as cranes and concrete.

Alena Ledeneva and Peter Zusi
School of Slavonic and East European Studies, UCL

Foreword
Learning from L'Aquila: catastrophe and the importance of care

Florian Mussgnug, UCL

I was in Rome when the earthquake hit central Italy. From my second-floor apartment, I could feel the ground shake in the early hours of 6 April 2009. Shortly afterwards, the news showed pictures of the catastrophic destruction of L'Aquila, a historic city some 50 miles northeast of Rome, and the capital of the Abruzzo region. I struggled to make sense of those images. Five years earlier, in February 2004, I had visited L'Aquila, and had returned from that trip with vivid memories of the city's understated, little-known magnificence: the quiet elegance of its narrow, medieval streets; the elegant façades of Romanesque churches; the unexpected grandeur of majestic, snow-covered palazzi. The thought that much of that beauty had been destroyed in a few instants seemed inconceivable, just like the unbearable suffering of the people of L'Aquila. Hundreds had died during the night of the earthquake, and many more had lost their homes and livelihoods. Thinking about the destruction of L'Aquila, I asked myself questions that now, 13 years later, feel sadly familiar. In an age shaped by violent conflict, pandemic disease and escalating environmental collapse, these questions have become part of our daily lives. They have come to guide our thinking about disaster and our emotional response to it. How could *this* catastrophe have happened *here*? Why didn't anybody see it coming? Why were we not better prepared? Who are the victims? Who will take care of the survivors? What can I do to help? If this had happened to *me*, what would I have done? What can we learn from the disaster?

Invisible Reconstruction is a timely book that offers important answers to many of these questions. Edited by two scholars who are intimately familiar with the catastrophe of L'Aquila, the volume brings together specialists from a wide range of disciplines: architecture; social and cultural history; urban planning; systems engineering; sustainable development; social anthropology; risk and disaster studies and education science. The contributors focus on different regions and case studies, but share some key assumptions. First, they agree that the social importance of reconstruction cannot be stated in purely economic, material or institutional terms. Rather, it relates to the wellbeing of human and more-than-human communities, not only at the moment of the catastrophe or during its immediate aftermath, but also in the long term. More specifically, the contributors claim that risk analysis, disaster management and reconstruction must be imagined and planned with deliberate attention to the least privileged and most vulnerable members of such communities. In other words, *Invisible Reconstruction* highlights the irreducible complexity of political, social and cultural situations. This complexity, the contributors suggest, requires strategies that are not centred on the short term or on neat solutions, but that are shaped by resourcefulness, generosity and kindness. Consequently, the book affirms the positive value of methodological and disciplinary pluralism. Instead of championing a single approach to disaster and reconstruction, *Invisible Reconstruction* calls for reasoned and respectful dialogue across academic disciplines, between institutions and communities and in wider political and cultural exchanges.

The authors' demand for generosity and inclusion must not be mistaken for a lack of political clarity. By underlining the importance of long-term perspectives, cultural diversity, collective memory, education and site-specific knowledge, the contributors position themselves firmly *against* a widespread, simplistic but influential tradition, which considers disaster in apocalyptic terms. According to this familiar narrative, cataclysmic events are moments of radical and complete renewal. Old structures crack and break, communities sever their ties with the past and new social contracts are stipulated. Western modernity's dark fascination with catastrophe has been shaped by this assumption for centuries. Consider, for example, the events of 1 November 1755, when a great earthquake shook south-west Europe and northern Africa. Its most destructive damage centred on Lisbon, a city that was then an important centre of international commerce and one of Europe's most majestic capitals. The so-called 'Earthquake of Lisbon' etched itself deeply into European consciousness. It reshaped philosophical and religious debates for decades and spelt an abrupt end to Enlightenment optimism. As literary scholar Robert K. Weninger has pointed out, paraphrasing philosopher of history Karl Löwith, 'The earthquake of Lisbon […] marks the watershed moment in European intellectual history when God and nature finally, and once and for all, part ways'.[1]

Two well-known and emblematic reactions to the Earthquake of Lisbon exemplify the cultural influence of apocalyptic thinking and the widespread tendency to imagine the aftermath of catastrophe as *tabula rasa*. There is, of course, Voltaire's famous response to the earthquake. In his ferociously uncompromising *Poem on the Disaster of Lisbon* (1755–56), the French philosopher launches a devastating attack against Gottfried Wilhelm Leibniz's maxim that ours is 'the best of all possible worlds' and against Alexander Pope's *An Essay on Man* (1733–34), one of the most effective literary codifications of Leibnizian optimism. *'Philosophes trompés, qui criez, "tout est bien"*, writes Voltaire, with fierce urgency, *'Accouréz: contemplez ces ruines affreuses, / Ces débris, ces lambeaux, ces cendres malheureuses'* ['Come, ye philosophers, who cry "All's well" / And contemplate this ruin of a world. / Behold these shreds and cinders of your race'].[2] Voltaire finds no solace in the philosophical and religious traditions of the past. The earthquake, he contends, has shattered the possibility of naïve religious faith. Modern individuals can no longer base their actions on the idea of divine providence, but must respond to disaster by making an effort to comprehend and control a world that is indifferent to human wellbeing.

At the opposite end of the ideological spectrum, Protestants and Pietists saw the Lisbon earthquake as a divine warning and as God's punishment of (Catholic) sinfulness. British Methodist John Wesley, for example, composed a hymn that describes the earthquake as an ominous harbinger of Apocalypse:

> The mighty Shock seems now begun,
> Beyond Example great,
> And lo! the World's Foundations groan
> As in their instant Fate!
> JEHOVA shakes the shatter'd Ball,
> Sign of the general Doom!
> The Cities of the Nations fall,
> And Babel's Hour is come.[3]

It is difficult to image a greater contrast than the philosophical divergence between Voltaire's indignant critique of religious hypocrisy and Wesley's moralising celebration of a (Protestant) God, meting out just punishment to a sinful Catholic city. And yet, both authors share the same understanding of natural catastrophe as a radical break with the past – the dawn of a new world. For the English minister, the Earthquake of Lisbon anticipates the sublime rupture of biblical Apocalypse. Similarly, Voltaire treats the event as a watershed moment in human history: a dark revelation that introduces us to the idea of a universe without intrinsic meaning.[4]

What makes these attitudes problematic? In his recent, masterful reflection on colonial and environmental violence, *The Nutmeg's Curse: Parables for a Planet in Crisis* (2021), Indian novelist Amitav Ghosh urges his readers to consider the devastating consequences of apocalyptic thinking. For centuries, Ghosh explains, European elites have fantasised about perfect societies that would emerge from a cataclysmic destruction of the 'old', known world. Religious believers considered historical time as a mere interlude, and saw Earth not as 'a nurturer or life-giver, but as a dead weight whose enveloping ties must be escaped if Man is to rise to a higher stage of being'.[5] Similarly, secular thinkers focused on the pursuit of utopia. A purely mechanistic understanding of Earth-as-resource underpinned both Western, colonial fantasies of mastery and 'the emergence of a new economy based on extracting resources from a desacralized, inanimate Earth'.[6] As Ghosh points out, apocalyptic thinking – in both its conventionally religious and modern secular forms – has remained largely indifferent to colonial and ecological violence. From the perspective of religious apocalypse, the cataclysmic destruction of habitats, communities and human lives appeared like the instrument of a higher purpose. Indeed, Ghosh writes: 'This worldview goes much further than either ecocide or genocide: it envisions and welcomes the prospect of "omnicide", the extermination of everything – people, animals and the planet itself'.[7] Many contemporary social attitudes, according to Ghosh, can be read as expressions of this millenarian disregard for the known world, and of the attendant desire for transcendence and spiritual cleansing:

> Signs of this substrate are everywhere around us: in the evangelical Christian idea of the 'Rapture'; in the apocalyptic visions of ecofascists; in the dreams of those who yearn for a world 'cleansed' of humanity; and in the fantasies of the billionaires who, having grown tired of this surly Earth and its sullen inhabitants, aspire to create a tamer version of it by terraforming some other planet.[8]

Modern, secular attitudes to non-human nature, according to Ghosh, have been similarly shaped by apocalyptic thinking. In his study, the Indian novelist pays specific attention to terraforming and geoengineering, which he describes as ways of treating the planet as raw material for human industriousness. Tragically, in an age of unfolding environmental catastrophe, this human disregard for Earth has already triggered multiple, connected natural disasters: cascading catastrophes which, from a human perspective, appear like self-fulfilling prophecies. As Ghosh points out:

> What the Earth is really exhausted of is not its resources; what it has lost is *meaning*. Conquered, inert, supine, the Earth can no longer ennoble, nor delight, nor produce new aspirations. All it can inspire in its would-be-conqueror's mind is the kind of contempt that arises from familiarity. Over time, this contempt has come to be planted so deep within cultures of modernity that it has become a part of its unseen foundations.[9]

In sum, apocalyptic thinking is focused on catastrophe-as-event. It lacks attention to cultural complexity, entanglement and human and more-than-human vulnerabilities that are best understood in diachronic terms. Ecocritic Timothy Morton makes the same point. 'All those apocalyptic narratives of doom about the "end of the world",' he writes, are 'part of the problem, not part of the solution'.[10] For Morton, this is especially evident in the context of the climate catastrophe. Environmental activists and authors of climate fiction have sketched countless versions of dystopian and apocalyptic futures, but have struggled to convey to the public that environmental catastrophe is already happening all around us. In this way, imaginative engagement with future catastrophe, according to Morton, can easily become a distraction or a form of escapism: 'a way for us to try to install ourselves at a fictional point in time before global warming happened. We are trying to anticipate something inside which we already find ourselves'.[11]

Where Morton calls for a diachronic engagement with the climate catastrophe – 'like realizing for some time you have been conducting your business in the expanding sphere of a slow-motion nuclear bomb' – the authors of *Invisible Reconstruction* apply the same lens and logic to disastrous events such as the L'Aquila earthquake.[12] They call for individual and institutional responses to catastrophe that are not exclusively focused on the experience of collapse, but adopt long-term perspectives. 'Invisible reconstruction', for them, is not a finite process but a constitutive openness, or, in Claudia Castañeda's words, a *figuration*: 'a potentiality rather than an actuality, a becoming rather than a being'.[13] Where market-based recovery plans and textbook definitions of resilience and adaptation focus on just one temporal vector – the progressive human triumph over natural disaster – the contributors to this collection imagine versatile communities of reciprocal care that are capable of diachronic attention. These communities are capable of facing catastrophe and collapse without losing sight of communal traditions (past), diverse ways of being (present) and speculative possibilities (future). In this way, *Invisible Reconstruction* may be read as a celebration of the deep aesthetic and affective ties that Rob Nixon associates with what he has called 'vernacular landscapes': 'historically textured maps that communities have devised over generations, maps replete with names and routes, maps alive to significant ecological and surface geological features'.[14] At the heart of the book, then, lies an emphasis on care, which shapes the contributors' engagement with the complex, syncopated temporalities of catastrophe and recovery.

Notes

1 Robert K. Weninger, *Sublime Conclusions: Last Man Narratives from Apocalypse to Death of God* (Cambridge: Legenda, 2017), p. 17. Weninger refers to Karl Löwith, *Meaning in History: The Theological Implications of the Philosophy of History* (Chicago: University of Chicago Press, 1949).

2 Voltaire, 'Poème sur le désastre de Lisbonne', critical edition by David Adams and Haydn T. Mason, in *Les Œuvre Completes de Voltaire*, vol. 45A (Oxford: Voltaire Foundation, 2009), pp. 269–358: p. 335. English translation by Joseph McCabe, cited in Weninger, *Sublime Conclusions*, p. 12.

3 'Rev. xvi, xvii, etc. Occasion'd by the Destruction of LISBON', in anon., *Hymns occasioned by the Earthquake, March 8, 1750. To which are added an Hymn upon the pouring out of the Seventh Vial, Rev., xvi, xvii, etc. Occasioned by the destruction of Lisbon*, Part 2, 2nd ed (Bristol: E Farley, 1756), pp. 10–12, strophe 10. No author is given on the title page. My decision to attribute the text to Charles Wesley is informed by Weninger's discussion of the hymn in Weninger, *Sublime Conclusions*, 29–30.

4 On the philosophical significance of the Lisbon earthquake, see in particular Susan Neiman, *Evil in Modern Thought: An Alternative History of Philosophy* (Princeton: Princeton University Press, 2002); Helena Carvalhão Buescu and Gonçalo Cordeiro (eds), *O Grande Terramoto de Lisboa: Ficar Diferente* (Lisbon: Editorial Gradiva, 2005); Svend Erik Larsen, 'The Lisbon Earthquake and the Scientific Turn in Kant's Philosophy,' *European Review*, 14, 3 (2006), pp. 359–367.

5 Amitav Ghosh, *The Nutmeg's Curse: Parables for a Planet in Crisis* (London: John Murray, 2021), p. 82.

6 Ghosh, *The Nutmeg's Curse,* p. 38.

7 Ghosh, *The Nutmeg's Curse,* p. 38.

8 Ghosh, *The Nutmeg's Curse,* p. 38.

9 Ghosh, *The Nutmeg's Curse,* p. 77.

10 Timothy Morton, *Hyperobjects: Philosophy and Ecology after the End of the World* (Minneapolis: University of Minnesota Press, 2013), p. 103.

11 Timothy Morton, *Being Ecological* (Cambridge, Massachusetts: MIT Press, 2018), xxiii.

12 Morton, *Hyperobjects*, p. 103.

13 Claudia Castañeda, *Figurations: Child, Bodies, Worlds* (Durham and London: Duke University Press 2002), p. 10.

14 Rob Nixon, *Slow Violence and the Environmentalism of the Poor* (Cambridge, MA, and London: Harvard University Press, 2011), p. 17.

Acknowledgements

The seeds of this publication were sown during a series of conversations held while organising a conference supported by the UCL Rome Fund and the University of L'Aquila in the 10th anniversary year of the 2009 L'Aquila earthquake. At the suggestion of the host university's Provost Paola Inverardi, historian Lucia met urbanist Paola and we found ourselves discussing the failings of a technically excellent reconstruction programme that had completely disregarded the social aspects and psychological impact of the earthquake. We became determined that, in an increasingly unpredictable and volatile world, there must be a better way to face disaster.

The multidisciplinary international conference examined themes of reconstruction, recovery and resilience in historic cities around the world. In the context of the host city, it offered significant and varied perspectives on the problems of physical reconstruction without economic and social planning and without care for the needs of citizens. The themes resonated with participants, one of whom commented that in Japan, the response to disaster is fixed; each problem has its own, separate answer. Yet, he remarked, the interdisciplinary mix that we had chosen for the conference had made him understand that the solution to post-disaster reconstruction is necessarily multifaceted, and that attention to invisible, intangible aspects is just as important as physical reconstruction.

A conference round table that we organised on the theme of education and educational safety had brought academics together with institutional representatives, politicians and parents. Its outcome was the creation of a policy document for safer schools. After the conference we decided to keep working to provoke policy changes and to highlight the importance of institutional transparency and civic participation.

Occasional encounters as conference co-organisers turned into a more structured collaboration and we decided to create the Invisible Reconstruction initiative, an informal, multidisciplinary and cross-institutional collaboration. The initiative brings together academics and practitioners, activists and volunteers, all sharing expertise and experience to change how recovery is measured following a natural, biological or man-made disaster, and to promote understanding of the benefits of prevention and before-the-event action.

As the COVID-19 pandemic emerged, it became increasingly clear to us that this global biological emergency shared many characteristics with the man-made and natural disasters that had been the focus of the conference. Disproportionately affecting the poor and vulnerable, the pandemic has demonstrated the need for public space, for more equitable education and the exponentially negative impact of poor communication.

When we sent out the call for papers for this publication, we were keen to include studies that looked at how societies already affected by disaster were dealing with the ongoing COVID emergencies as well as to gather and compare cultural perspectives from Asia, South America and Europe.

In 2021 we held a second conference, hosted in Kyoto via L'Aquila. The presentations and round table discussion that followed have reinforced our conviction in the need to promote the latent, hidden networks, processes and affinities that can reduce the impact of and promote recovery from disaster.

The Invisible Reconstruction project and this volume would have not been possible without the help of a number of people and institutions. The University of L'Aquila and its former Provost Professor Paola Inverardi who supported the conference via the Provost's Fund, opening the doors of her institution to an alumna who had returned with the proposal to hold a conference for the 10th anniversary of the earthquake in L'Aquila. Her suggestion of creating institutional connections with Professors Paola Rizzi and Alessandro Vaccarelli turned into deep friendships which have inspired our interdisciplinary work and, ultimately, this book. Paola had previously introduced Lucia to Massimo Prosperococco, the indefatigable head of communication at the University of L'Aquila, an invaluable and incredibly positive force within the university and now a dear friend. Professor Edoardo Alesse, the current Provost of the University of L'Aquila has continued to sustain the Invisible Reconstruction initiative, including last-minute assistance to virtualise the conference when travel to Kyoto became impossible in 2021. Through challenging circumstances, Professor Antonella Nuzzaci has been a constant source of tangible and very human support.

At UCL, we are particularly grateful to the Provost Dr Michael Spence for his inspirational opening remarks at the 2021 Invisible Reconstruction conference. None of this would have been possible without the support of the UCL Global Engagement Office and Rome Fund and the personal encouragement of Professor Florian Mussgnug, through the 2019 and 2021 conferences. Similarly, the Development Planning Unit at the Faculty of the Built Environment were fundamental to the success of the first conference – especially the enthusiasm and friendship of Professor Julio Davila. The History Department at UCL has continuously provided institutional support and help with the conference organisation and we are particularly indebted to Claire Morley for her kind, positive support and for successfully managing the complicated organisation between different countries, universities, departments and administrators.

Both conferences were enabled and financially supported by the DICEAA Department at the University of L'Aquila, whose incredible administrator Flavio Grimaldi was key to their success and to enabling the creation of this book. Professor Donato Di Ludovico played a crucial role in the coordination of the second conference within DICEAA. At the DSU Department of Social Science and the *Dipartimento di Eccellenza* at the University of L'Aquila, Professor Massimo Fusillo listened supportively to our early ideas about the conference and encouraged us to apply for funds without which neither the conference nor the work for this volume would have been possible.

No conference would have been possible without the expertise and patient support of the technicians at the University of L'Aquila or the dedication of volunteer students who worked tirelessly throughout the first conference making over 100 guests feel at home in a town still suffering the effects of a major earthquake. Equally, we have benefitted immensely from the administrative help of Francesca Larocchia and her colleagues at the Provost's Office, at the DSU and at the DICEAA departments.

Georgina Phillips copy-edited this volume helping us navigate the process with tremendous diligence, patience and professionalism. Similarly, Chris Penfold and the Fringe Series editors Alena Ledeneva and Peter Zusi have carefully and gently steered us through the path to publication of this volume. Finally we are grateful to our husbands Barnaby Gunning and Lorenzo Cotti, both opinionated architects, for the innumerable conversations, reading, cajoling, constant encouragement and design of the conference websites and posters. Without their help, our projects may have had very different outcomes.

This book is dedicated to the memory of Lucia's father, Professor Serafino Patrizio, whose positive, inclusive and forward-looking approach throughout his life demonstrated the importance of interdisciplinary work and of reaching out to make the world a better place.

Introduction: The Invisible Reconstruction project and its aims

Lucia Patrizio Gunning and Paola Rizzi

What does it really mean to reconstruct a city after a natural, biological or man-made disaster? Is the repair and reinstatement of buildings and infrastructure sufficient without the mending of social fabric? After all, a city without people is no city at all. This disconnection between the hardware of physical rebuilding and the software of social repair typifies approaches to disaster response worldwide. Despite individual initiatives and occasional examples of best practice, institutionally the connection of the visible 'bricks and mortar' of construction with the intangible threads of memory, knowledge, education, wellbeing and the invisible networks of society are exceptionally rare.

Invisible Reconstruction is an interdisciplinary and international initiative aimed at provoking policy change through the entire cycle of disaster from preparedness, through response and to repair, using the instruments of engagement, education and participation to reduce risk, increase institutional transparency and improve outcomes. Our goals with this volume are to change how recovery is measured and to promote awareness of the benefits of building resilience through before-the-event action.

The unwelcome presence of COVID-19 in all of our lives has revealed the same patterns in response to the biological emergency as are seen in other forms of disaster. Disproportionately impacting the most exposed elements of society, increasing vulnerability and social fragility, the pandemic has demonstrated universally how, while physical solutions such as social distancing are vital, these are easily undermined by weak understanding of risk and poor communication.

Interdisciplinary discourse is at the core of this publication, which is deliberately multifaceted, reflecting the complexity and interconnectedness of different aspects of prevention and preparedness as well as reconstruction and recovery. Disastrous events rupture all aspects of normality and, while disaster response can be categorised by typology of disaster, geographic location or by methodology, we have chosen to organise this book in five thematic parts comparing approaches to the protection, reinforcement and mending of social fabric.

The shared premise of all the chapters in the first part of the book is that, even after a pandemic, reconstruction should put communities first. This approach increases the likelihood of successful outcomes and supports the psychological wellbeing of individuals and communities. Conversely, the failure of institutions to pay attention to community needs increases social unease and cultural fragility, leaving citizens themselves to try and rebuild broken links with their cultural heritage. For physical reconstruction to be effective, it must be combined with community outreach and re-engagement. Indeed identity, memory and tradition all require the kind of close attention that is normally only afforded to the techniques of restoration and physical repair. In the opening chapter, Vittorini explains how the artefacts and monuments of a historic city are closely linked to its civic identity and to its citizens' sense of self. Disaster injures the social body, breaking its tissues and interrupting its normal operation. Immediate, temporary reorganisation of social bonds begins the healing process, eventually leading to the growth of new networks. But healing requires careful attention to the nature of the wound, protection of fragile tissue, and diligent, continuous monitoring. Failure to do this prolongs or undermines the process, risks the creation of secondary problems and leaves permanent scarring. Presenting the results of a study on reconstruction following three seismic sequences in central Italy, Patrizio Gunning and Di Ludovico expose how disregard for social aspects have left the populace with lasting insecurities and reduced confidence in their future. Equally, institutional inattention and superficiality can lead to misdiagnosis and incorrect treatment. Tsukuda and Onoda examine how the elderly and vulnerable were left out of housing provision following the Great East Japan Earthquake of 2011, leaving their lives in suspense and preventing social recovery. Generic, one-size-fits-all approaches tend to miss out the marginalised who are most likely to be disproportionately affected. Promsaka, Rizzi and Otsuki set out the steps taken by local and national authorities to educate the citizens of Kochi in order to reduce vulnerability and increase urban resilience in one of the Japanese cities most at risk of earthquake and tsunami. Returning to L'Aquila, Ciranna and Montuori explain how purely physical responses to the 2009 emergency have led to isolated, fragmented and vulnerable communities and broken the deep relationship between inhabitants, their city and its territory. The social body desires healing and in the absence of institutional care, spontaneous processes arose to recreate a sense of community in these post-earthquake housing projects.

Sorely missing from much post-disaster planning, public space provides a network of physical and social connections that are vital to the wellbeing of communities. The second part of this book focuses on how access to public space should be understood as a fundamental human right. Recognising how public space is intrinsically and deeply linked to the public sphere of political thought, Crosta presents an evolving methodology for diagnosis and treatment to respond to citizens' needs and rights. Exacerbating disparities between rich and poor, the pandemic has highlighted the urgent need for safe spaces to gather, for shelter, for vaccination and to distribute and obtain supplies. From Lima, through the Brazilian *favelas* to Delhi, the COVID-19 emergency is forcing reimagination of how to provide public spaces. Alvarez-Calderon and Sanchez argue that archaeological sites, community heritage fundamental to Lima's pre-Hispanic cultural identity, could and should be made accessible as public open space. Tapia explains how the pandemic has triggered discussion not only of the need for adequate domestic space but also of the absolute necessity of public space for all and of the role that these places have to engender a sense of citizenship and to support basic human needs. In the densely inhabited traditional *mahalas* of Shahjahanabad, internal courtyards and narrow alleys reflect the close-knit social structure of communities united by trade. Jain reflects on how, in the absence of public space, the interconnected rooftops of private buildings have created a parallel set of protected connections, suggesting solutions to further protect their uniqueness and enhance resilience.

Part three investigates how participation, consultation and communication, vital elements of democracy, play an important role in raising awareness of risk, mitigating the impact of disaster and improving recovery. In a globally-connected society, when politicians and institutions ignore calls from below to have input on reconstruction, people find increasingly creative ways to make their voices heard. Social media and free or cheap software provide marginalised and disenfranchised communities with powerful tools to organise and protest as well as to map, model, photograph, film and publish to a global audience. Gunning and Patrizio recount four such projects and reflect on the strengths and limitations of these ground-up citizen-driven initiatives and the long-term viability of independent, fast-response and crowd-sourced post-disaster projects. Giving voice to the marginalised requires more than providing a platform; this is particularly true for the elderly and fragile. Analysing survivor testimony from the Great East Japan Earthquake and accounts of life in the period before the tsunamis, Kitamura illustrates the fragility of women and the elderly at the time of the disaster and the paucity of risk awareness among the most exposed. Their lived experience of disaster appears to have modified their attitude to risk in the pandemic, mitigating the impact of the first wave of COVID-19.

As climate change provokes increased numbers of natural disasters, communication of risk has become one of the most complex and pressing issues of the emerging Anthropocene. Good practice leads to improved understanding and positive outcomes in emergency, including during the COVID-19 pandemic. De Pascale, Farabollini and Lugeri point out that successful risk management must adopt multiple strategies, identifying the nature and extent of public concerns, structuring and responding to public debate and reaction and educating communities to understand systems and policies related to public health and safe environments. Closer engagement with the built environment is one key to improved understanding of risk and safety and to improving the resilience of communities living with risk. The creation of safe public spaces and their adoption as dual spaces for both everyday life and for emergency response is explored by Rizzi, Sanna and Porebska. Adopting the techniques of soundscape design, acoustic engineering and sonography, they reconsider how sound, a powerful part of the urban experience, can be used to shape and design public space and provide security.

Tourism and culture can be important, interlinked stimulants to economic and social recovery, but they are also both exposed to especially heavy impact from disaster. Culture binds the material physical context and landscape to the immaterial emotional sphere and can form the basis for sustainable tourism. In the fourth part of the book, anthropologists, conservators, exhibition designers, museum professionals and education theorists look at how culture and tourism can be protected and how they can help overcome the trauma of disaster. When a reconstructed city feels soulless, art can provide the means to inject emotion, rebuild affective connections and reconnect its citizens. De Matteis and Marchini describe how photography can elucidate the emptiness beneath the apparently perfect restoration of a historic centre and reveal the inadequacy of a purely physical approach. When the primary rationale of reconstruction is the resolution of technical aspects and functional requirements, it can leave both citizens and visitors with the sense that a city is a cold, unreal, distant and characterless facsimile of what it had been before the catastrophe.

Analysing the provision of disaster-prevention information to tourists in Kyoto, Sakai and Kanegae note that while tourists may have a high awareness of disaster risk, they remain ill-informed about safety or evacuation measures. Creation of a more resilient tourist industry requires improving direct communication and raising institutional awareness of the issues faced by tourists during disaster. Culture, including intangible heritage, is a key contributor to sustainable tourism. In this context, territory – the broader environment that encompasses both urban and rural heritage – can play a fundamental role. Landscape, often seen by its inhabitants as a key source of identity, is at risk of damage from reconstruction processes that focus on buildings and infrastructure. Branduini and Carnelli suggest a new model for recovery based on the vast intangible repertoire of heritage, which encompasses local food-production techniques, traditions, religious practices and ways of life that can drive resilience by creating a circular and more sustainable economy. The pandemic has, however, challenged the cultural sector to its limits. In the context of the closure of museums and other cultural institutions, Zuccoli, De Nicola and Magri look at how a major national exhibition on ethical consumption and sustainable lifestyles was forced to adapt to the challenging circumstances of the first wave of COVID-19.

Education shapes understanding of risk and is the basis for building deep connections between people and their cultural habitat. Yet at the same time it is shaped by emergency, as disaster amplifies and exacerbates educational poverty. The contributors to the final part of the book have a deep understanding of how catastrophes, including the pandemic, affect all aspects of teaching, impacting equality, or more specifically equity, of access to quality educational experiences. Di Genova explains the factors that contribute to educational poverty and that are related to emergency situations, placing them in the perspective of their long-term consequences. Reflecting on the safety of school buildings, the need for fair accessibility to cultural meeting places and on protective measures for the wellbeing of children involved in emergencies, the author focuses on resilience as an educational goal. But educational resilience requires that educators themselves be given the tools to impart confidence to their pupils. Indeed, the right to education should apply not only to students but also to their teachers, yet this need is often overlooked, leaving teachers fragile and vulnerable and requiring them to provide support

INTRODUCTION   **5**

and healing when they themselves are equally victims of trauma. Disasters can lead to a displacement that undermines the identity, behaviour, attitudes and professional ability of teachers. Nuzzaci suggests strategies to create resilience and provide teachers in areas of high fragility with internal resources to deal with unexpected emergencies and to protect them from being deeply affected by catastrophic events. Vaccarelli and Nanni describe instead how, in culturally-mixed communities, acceptance and integration are the real constructors of social cohesion, particularly in the face of disaster. Yet this social cohesion is particularly vulnerable to hostile political decisions that can further exacerbate underlying inequalities. Foreign-origin citizens who experienced the 2009 L'Aquila earthquake were more exposed to its consequences, and competition dynamics caused by the housing crisis stoked attitudes of hostility and intolerance. Education plays a key role in building reciprocal relations, filling and animating the interstices between individuals and communities, supporting cultural integration and recreating broken social bonds.

In all scenarios, and across all these approaches, disaster exposes pre-existing fragilities and has the greatest impact on the individuals, sectors and environments least equipped to deal with it. Disaster preparedness, response and reconstruction therefore need to account for disparities and provide equity; they must be iterative processes which monitor outcomes and can respond to gaps in provision. Indeed, these processes need to be inclusive and transparent, balancing the needs of communities as a whole with those of marginalised and vulnerable individuals. Top-down and institutional policy should be able to benefit from, rather than compete with, ground-up citizen initiatives. Physical and social reconstruction are inseparable. Social reconstruction is impossible without the repair of buildings and infrastructure, yet recovery and resilience are equally impossible without care and attention to social, cultural, political, psychological and educational needs. Supplementing physical repair with a focus on people and communities should allow reconstruction to become a vehicle for social aggregation and for the creation of sustainable, equitable and resilient societies.

This introduction was first drafted in the summer of 2021, in the middle of the third wave of the COVID-19 pandemic and revised in March 2022 almost a month into the Russian invasion of Ukraine. Many of the papers in this book deal with the superimposition of a global biological disaster on pre-existing natural disasters and vulnerabilities; the imposition of man-made catastrophe onto the pandemic is incomprehensibly irresponsible and cruel, yet sadly not an unusual scenario.

It is hard to avoid reflecting that, more than two years since the declaration of the pandemic, we are still firmly in the emergency phase of this universal disaster. Gradually, but inconsistently, societies around the world are beginning to see the outline of what may be the recovery phase, though we have little idea of how the pandemic will have permanently altered the contours of our social landscape or of its geopolitical ramifications.

We are accustomed to seeing disaster in two ways: locally, and at a distance. When disaster occurs, we are either consumed by it or we observe it unfolding remotely, as somebody else's problem. The narrative of disaster reporting reinforces this perception. Stories of individual or community tragedy and the hope of rescue are paralleled by news of the extraordinary nature of the catastrophe. This firmly places disaster at arm's length. Anniversary events and commemorations create an artificial sense of closure that may cover long-term social damage.

Climate change and the exacerbating impact of human activity are increasing our exposure to disaster with little improvement in our understanding of risk or of how to mitigate it. There is a fatalism in how humans have approached disaster historically – it is unlikely to be coincidental that many of the most superstitious societies are those most at risk of disaster, but we rarely address how our actions can increase risk or how we can change our approach in order to reduce it.

The COVID-19 pandemic should force us as a global society to reconsider our attitudes to disaster. Yet even though a pandemic is, by definition, a worldwide phenomenon, its impact, like all forms of disaster, is disproportionally borne by the poorest and most vulnerable. Inevitably as this emergency recedes from the foreground of our lives, it will become, once more, 'someone else's problem'.

But we do have the tools to change this. Our sophisticated online social networks are universal solutions but with the granular ability to respond to the likes and desires of the individual. We can target political advertising increasingly accurately to change electoral outcomes and information technology has the capacity to inflate the local and personal to global and universal, to tie us together for common benefit, just as it can sow and fertilise the seeds of division.

This publication presents a spectrum of perspectives on how disaster affects the invisible threads from which our societies are woven, and it reflects on different approaches to disaster preparedness and recovery. It is but a beginning, though one that hopes to provoke a paradigm shift in how we approach risk and disaster and how we can build and sustain more resilient societies in an ever more interconnected world.

Part I
Reconstruction and society

1
L'Aquila 2009–2019: back to the future
Cultural heritage and post-seismic reconstruction challenges

Alessandra Vittorini

The artefacts of a historic city are closely linked to its sense of self and civic identity. For physical reconstruction and reinstatement of cultural fabric to be effective, it must be combined with outreach and re-engagement of the community. In the face of widespread cultural destruction, identity, memory and tradition all require attention. Reconstruction needs to focus not just on rebuilding monuments, houses and urban fabric, but also on the connections between people and their relationship with their heritage. This is a process that requires shared commitment to common goals and the contribution of all players in the game to return cities to their citizens and restore identity and history to the community. The ongoing post-earthquake reconstruction of L'Aquila has required an extraordinary combination of innovation, management, protection and restoration of cultural heritage. It saw the creation of the Superintendence for L'Aquila and its seismic crater, the first such entity in Italy with combined powers in monumental, historical, artistic, archaeological and landscape fields. This chapter explains how this organisation developed an integrated approach – defining the governance and legal framework of reconstruction, as well as the planning and technical-economic evaluations of interventions – that is allowing the city to regain control of its future.

L'Aquila, 2009

The devastating earthquake of 2009 shook a vast area inhabited by more than 140,000 people, including a regional capital and several municipalities with historical centres and hamlets. That territory has been dramatically damaged physically, and also in its precious historic image and cultural heritage: a large important historic centre and many small ancient villages (270 or more) with a widespread heritage and ancient traces of a great past.

The post-earthquake reconstruction that began in 2010 represents an extraordinary experience of management, protection and restoration of cultural heritage, fully supported by public funds. This process was further complicated from 2016 by the subsequent earthquakes which devastated nearby Amatrice, Norcia and a large part of central Italy.

The definition of the governance and the legal framework of the reconstruction, the challenging tasks of restoring cultural heritage and the planning and technical-economic evaluations of interventions are some of the main elements managed through the integrated approach assigned to the L'Aquila Superintendence.

This has given us an extraordinary overview of a complex process, due to the importance of the cultural heritage, the severity of the damage and the solutions found. It has also been a very strong opportunity for study, research and scientific discussion on the post-earthquake recovery of cultural heritage.

The 2009 seismic crater includes the large territory of the Municipality of L'Aquila and 56 other small surrounding municipalities. After the 2016 earthquake, another 'seismic crater' has been defined very near, much wider and partly overlapping the previous crater. Their territories have strong geographic, historical, economic and social affinities and most of their problems are the same, as well as their governances, tools, issues and methodologies. For this reason, from the outset it seemed necessary to share the experiences and best practices around restoration and heritage protection that were applied and developed to an advanced stage in the post-2009 reconstruction and make them available for the new reconstruction after the nearby 2016 earthquake.

History and landscape

Since 2012, L'Aquila's historic centre has been a huge, hard-working, busy construction site of masons and labourers, trucks and cranes, with some cafés, restaurants, shops and offices opening gradually, but few inhabitants. Those who used to live here have been, since 2009, spread out in 19 districts known colloquially as 'new towns', and those who chose that name probably didn't know that L'Aquila was already a 'new town – a city founded in the thirteenth century that kept its shape for centuries. A city that, after the earthquake, has become a city to be refounded. A city that, with its past, also contains an extraordinary lesson in urban and civil history, useful for its reconstruction and its future.

The original foundation was a strong and shared response to a widespread need from the communities, finding in their aggregation a way to increase their social and political strength. A great project shared by 99 castles, the result of which was not only a 'new town' but also the creation of an extraordinary and unique relationship between each founding castle and its double in town, between the new city and its wider countryside.

L'Aquila was settled where the 99 founding communities identified the most suitable site for the new city. The whole countryside was then divided into four quarters, crossing at the exact point where the new city would be built. The city was, in turn, divided into four quarters (*quarti*) – areas designed to host the communities from the corresponding territorial quarter. Each of them was then divided into small areas (*locali*), with the same name as the founding castles, where the future residents would have to build their own homes.

Indeed, new inhabitants could move to the city only after having provided for the construction of their square, their church and their fountain, the places representing and symbolising the quarter's common assets: the civil aggregation (the square), the religious community (the church) and the common resources (the fountain). Today we would call these 'public works'. There is an extraordinary lesson of civil engagement of communities in that shared project of the foundation of a new town. In every *locale* the church kept the name of the corresponding church, and sometimes even the name of the castle. So, each founding castle had its 'double' in the new city and the new city was strictly linked to its territory.

Just a few years later, the inhabitants of the new city committed themselves to the realisation of the L'Aquila's greatest common works, such as the large market square of Piazza Duomo, the Basilica di Santa Maria Collemaggio, and the majestic Fontana delle 99 Cannelle. In that

Figure 1.1   L'Aquila in the Antonio Vandi plan (1753).

way they built, together, a square, a church and a fountain for the benefit of every citizen. Finally, this new city was enclosed by five kilometres of impressive city walls, still completely preserved. In the following centuries, the historic centre was enriched with many important buildings, such as the basilica church of San Bernardino, the dominating Spanish Fortress, as well as numerous monumental churches and palaces.

An ancient medieval foundation town, many other ancient villages, castles, churches, monasteries, palaces, ancient routes, all set in a stunning landscape of valleys and mountains – this is the cultural heritage that was devastated by the 2009 earthquake. Almost one thousand privately owned monuments, largely concentrated in L'Aquila, and also many other public monuments (over 1500) are protected by law. That is why reconstructing cultural heritage in L'Aquila means reconstructing L'Aquila.

Earthquakes, symbolic values and identity

Italy has always been a country of earthquakes. And L'Aquila, since its foundation in 1254, has always been a city defined by earthquakes. After the major tremors of 1359 and 1461, another strong earthquake in 1703 completely destroyed the city and the villages. The subsequent reconstruction gave L'Aquila a new baroque image, bestowing on the city the most precious churches and palaces that still compose its image today. At that time almost all the existing medieval churches were seriously damaged and their interiors were rebuilt in the latest architectural style. And for that reason, for almost eight centuries, this continuous process of building and collapsing and rebuilding due to the earthquakes has been one of the main characteristics of L'Aquila's history, its historical-artistic evolution and its restoration, giving us new discoveries and surprises every day that feed a never-ending resilience.

In that history of earthquakes, cultural-heritage destruction has been always one of the major problems of reconstruction. A problem that forces all of us to ensure safety, structural and technological improvement, energy efficiency, urban regeneration, landscape protection and, at the same time, enhance conservation and restoration methodology.

We presented the experience of L'Aquila in the 2016 ICOMOS International Meetings in Paris and Istanbul,[1] focusing particularly on post-trauma and post-disaster reconstruction. During heated debate at the discussion groups, especially during the Paris Colloquium, it became evident that, in all countries that face natural or human destruction – earthquakes, floods, tsunami or wars, air raids and terrorist attacks – many issues require the utmost attention: identity and memory, tradition and innovation and the balance between conservation and living heritage. So, buildings that may have had little interest to the community can suddenly become highly symbolic – and that is what's happening in L'Aquila right now.

Therefore reconstruction means, above all, reconstructing identity and relations. The same applies to the history and memories of local communities. Where, after a trauma, people have developed a fear of old buildings and construction methods and may demand only new ways to rebuild, restore and reinforce buildings, this can mean trying to renew confidence in ancient and durable technologies. In turn, this can create a strengthened relationship with cultural heritage and a city's memory.

Strengthening identity and the relationship between heritage and communities are also the goals of the Faro Convention on the Value of Cultural Heritage for Society, which emphasises the important connections between cultural heritage, human rights and democracy; it promotes a wider understanding of heritage and its relationship to communities and society and encourages us to recognise that objects and places are important because of the meanings and uses that people attach to them and the values they represent.

Reconstruction, a shared commitment

In 2012, the Italian government decided to end the emergency phase after three years of commissarial management and to establish new special offices for the reconstruction. One was dedicated to the capital city (Special Office for the Reconstruction of L'Aquila – USRA) and the other to the remaining territory of the seismic crater (Special Office for the Reconstruction of the seismic crater – USRC). Since then, an important funding programme based on the annual and multiannual economic planning has been launched, and started a huge shared commitment in post-seismic cultural heritage reconstruction. The complex framework of all the players and stakeholders involved in the reconstruction process includes all the local authorities. These are the 57 municipalities, the regional and provincial administrations, two Special Offices, other national offices operating in the management of public works and, especially, the local offices of the Ministry of Cultural Heritage and Activities (MiBAC), responsible for carrying out the conservation and restoration programmes for most of the cultural heritage damaged by the earthquake (with the Regional Directorate of Abruzzo as contracting authority, and the three Superintendences charged with the protection and conservation of the archaeological, architectonic and artistic heritage, and of the landscape). This framework was further expanded when, after the 2016 earthquake, offices managing the new emergency were established as the new regional Special Office for the 2016 reconstruction in Abruzzo and the new Office of the Special Superintendent for the 2016 earthquake, created by the MiBAC.

This widened context was supported by many representatives of civil society and the professions: citizens, companies, universities and schools, associations, professionals and technicians, workers and artisans.

The reconstruction began to have an impact on L'Aquila's old centre from 2011, with construction sites and works in progress. Many of them have been completed since 2015, with buildings, streets and places returning, day by day, to an urban image which is discovering itself, waiting to become a living city again. Twelve years after the earthquake there are already extensive works in progress or concluded. More than 36 public monuments (30 in L'Aquila) have been restored – 3 are nearly finished and 12 are ongoing. Private cultural heritage – most of the old town centre – represents the greater part of the Superintendence's job. In the first 10 years of reconstruction it has examined and approved restoration projects for almost 320 blocks in L'Aquila and in the territory, including more than 350 private monuments and buildings. In terms of costs, that is the value of the public contributions approved, this amounts to about €1.3 billion. Of this, less than €400 million, has been calculated by the Special Offices using a parametric system. This means that the remaining €900 million of public contributions has been calculated, verified and approved only by the Superintendence office. That is an effective indicator of our work and, most of all, of its positive effects and impact on the whole reconstruction process, easily visible when walking around the old town. A significant piece of work that instantly produced significant results and important economic and social outcomes.

But since 2015, the L'Aquila Superintendence was also impacted by an unprecedented experimentation resulting from the 2014 structural reform of the MiBAC, which made it the first such Superintendence in Italy with combined powers in monumental, historical, artistic, archaeological and landscape fields, charged with an integrated approach to the conservation and protection mission. This new role was complicated and expanded after the 2016 earthquake by the overlapping of the two seismic craters, which has further increased the daily workload and responsibilities of the always understaffed Superintendence.

Sharing experiences to build resilience

The achievements of our work in the first 10 years of reconstruction have been presented at several scientific meetings in Italy and abroad, with the aim of sharing experiences and best practices to make these available to the scientific community and to decision makers across Italy and Europe.

Since the beginning we have also tried to activate a constant and sustained dialogue with universities, masters and postgraduate schools, in Italy and abroad, to offer case studies and to activate discussions and research. With these other players, and even more so with communities, we promoted informative activity around the communication of cultural-heritage reconstruction. This meant participating in every public event to present results and works in progress to provide information and ensure accountability. It also involved organising public events about restoration in progress and in restored places and sharing our experiences, both good and bad.

The 2018 European Year of Cultural Heritage saw the launch of the European Framework for Action on Cultural Heritage, with its five areas of action for an inclusive, sustainable, resilient and innovative Europe, and for stronger global partnerships. In that context, the European Quality

Principles for EU-funded interventions on cultural heritage were also promoted. In the 2018 presentation in Venice, the restored Basilica di Collemaggio in L'Aquila was displayed on the screen behind the speakers, representing all the post-seismic reconstruction of cultural heritage being carried out in L'Aquila as a good example of recovery. And after the devastating 2019 fire of Notre-Dame de Paris, sharing knowledge and capabilities around cultural protection has become a collective and common need for European countries, as clearly declared by the office of President Macron.[2] So, Italian experience in post-earthquake recovery of cultural heritage and community resilience can now be of strategic importance.

In this regard, the experience of L'Aquila after the earthquake is an interesting case study. In fact, in the abandoned historical centre – garrisoned by the army, with roads closed, homes inaccessible to the people who lived there, and an extensive forbidden 'red zone' – nothing happened for two years. The 19 new towns were an immediate response to help and support homeless people, but they produced non-places – scattered, devoid of any urban character, hosting 'people without cities' – while in the historic centres lay abandoned houses, empty squares, forbidden streets. Cities without people. And those keys, hanging provocatively on the metal fences that surrounded the red zone until 2013, were a reminder of the sense of deep deprivation that the inhabitants of the centre suffered throughout these years, losing all ties with their places and their houses, of which nothing more remained than a useless – and unusable – bunch of keys. That's why the case of L'Aquila has so much to say about resilience – because of its origins, its history and for its unfortunate centuries-old familiarity with earthquakes. A single story is impressed into this town – into its squares, streets, urban shape, monuments and also in the very masonry of the buildings. It is an extraordinary lesson coming from the past – a lesson of urban planning and a lesson of resilience.

Reclaiming Collemaggio

One of the most interesting and symbolic cases in the whole reconstruction has been the restoration of the Basilica of Santa Maria di Collemaggio: an important and symbolic monument that, according to many, exemplifies the most beautiful medieval architecture of Central Italy. It has been, since 1294, the site of the Perdonanza Celestiniana, the first real Christian jubilee, which preceded and anticipated the first Roman plenary jubilee held by Pope Boniface VIII in 1300.

The Basilica also plays an important role in defining the self-identity of the community of L'Aquila. Construction began in 1275, a few years after the foundation of the city, then its walls were raised while L'Aquila was rebuilt after the destruction carried out by Manfredi di Svevia. Such indissoluble links between the city and its Basilica were enshrined by Pietro Angelerio, a hermit who in 1294 was crowned Pope in Collemaggio with the name Celestine V. One month later, and only four months before abdicating, he established the Perdonanza. For its extraordinary cultural value, this popular manifestation of devotion was inscribed on the UNESCO Representative List of Intangible Cultural Heritage of Humanity in 2019.

The Basilica was one of the monuments most damaged in the 2009 earthquake; it completely collapsed between the aisle and the transept. But only eight months later, after the emergency works of scaffolding, buttresses and underpinning, Christmas mass was celebrated under a temporary shelter.

Thus, around the restoration of Santa Maria di Collemaggio, an original and unprecedented experiment of synergy and institutional collaboration was carried out, starting with the Ripartire da Collemaggio protocol, signed in 2013 between the Municipality of L'Aquila, owner of the Basilica, with ENI S.p.a., a major Italian energy company, as sponsor. This agreement sealed the active participation of the MiBAC with the local Superintendence of L'Aquila and three important Italian universities (Sapienza University of Rome, the Politecnico of Milan and the University of L'Aquila). The Superintendence carried out the project with a selected team of distinguished experts from the universities and supervised the complex two-year restoration works. ENI S.p.a. fully financed the planning and implementation of the restoration intervention and also provided technical-managerial support.

The Superintendence, thanks to the expertise of its technicians (architects and art historians), led the complex phases of study, planning, direction and management of the restoration works while engaged in controlling and supervising the ongoing restoration of all the damaged cultural heritage in the city and the surrounding territory and in carrying out direct works on the public monuments entrusted to the Ministry of Culture.[3] The project was concluded in 2015 and the works started in January 2016.

The restoration project necessitated not only the application of the most advanced methodologies of conservation of built heritage, but also consideration of the paramount symbolic and universal value of the monument. The works began with the structural reinforcement of the aisle pillars, half of which were completely dismantled and reassembled to check resistance and structural integrity. The next step was reinforcement of the walls and reconstruction of the two big pillars that had collapsed with the whole transept and the destroyed vaults. Other work involved the apse with its important chapels. Next came the infinitely delicate restoration of plasterworks, sculptures, marbles and the famous red and white stones of the floor and façade. The frescoes, dating from the thirteenth to fifteenth centuries, have been consolidated and restored, as well as the baroque marble altars and the stucco work of the side chapels. One of the most amazing surprises was to discover original baroque colours and gildings in the Celestine Chapel.

On 20 December 2017, after just two years, the reborn Basilica of Santa Maria di Collemaggio was returned to the community of L'Aquila. Just a few weeks after the opening, it was included in an important tourism website as the main reason to visit L'Aquila in 2018.

The Collemaggio project has become an example of good practice in the case of a post-earthquake restoration project. In spite of the huge challenges that had to be addressed, the project was designed so that the Basilica could keep performing its social function, even when the possibility of it being 'inhabited' had to be temporarily suspended. Restoration, in the case of Collemaggio, was intended as an opportunity for knowledge and cooperation – an act of social reconstruction. The meticulous study underpinning the project was intended as a process that found in the form, history and materials of the building itself the justification for the technical choices made, and in its symbolic meaning the reason for the procedures adopted. This approach made it possible to return Collemaggio to its own community in just two years. The true quality of this project is that this result has been achieved by ensuring that the community never felt left out of its Basilica, or without the possibility of recognising in it what it has always meant for L'Aquila: a testimony of beauty, resilience and rebirth.

On 9 May 2020 the restoration received the European Heritage Award/Europa Nostra Award 2020 – the only Italian project to win an award in the conservation category.[4] Six months later, Mariya Gabriel, the European Commissioner for Innovation, Research, Culture, Education and Youth, also awarded the restoration project the prestigious Grand Prix for the best 2020 European conservation project, as 'a model of best practice in the conservation'.

As the jury observed:

> this intervention truly represents the rebirth of a city. The strong sense of spirituality and the participation of the community in this

project must be considered as an integral piece of the whole. The entire project is based on a public–private partnership and involved the collaboration of three different universities. It has been carried out with an exemplary scientific basis relating to the seismic vulnerability of the building. The comprehensive approach taken to address the consequences of a natural disaster … is exemplary. It is also notable that the programme includes the maintenance and monitoring of the building. The project is a model of best practice in the conservation of critically damaged sites all over the world.[5]

After the reopening, in the summer of 2018, work at the offices of the Ministry of Culture continued with the relocation of the monumental and precious gilded baroque organ that had been completely destroyed by the collapse in 2009. In 2020, a programme began to restore many of the Basilica's artworks, including the precious cycle of Bartholomaeus Ruthart paintings that will soon grace its walls once again, and Saturnino Gatti's extraordinary sixteenth-century *Madonna con Bambino*, temporarily displayed in L'Aquila's MUNDA museum.

Figure 1.2 The Basilica of Santa Maria di Collemaggio: view from the outside.

Figure 1.3 Santa Maria di Collemaggio: the post-earthquake collapse (2009).

Figure 1.4 Santa Maria di Collemaggio: the dismantled pillars during the restoration works.

Figure 1.5 Santa Maria di Collemaggio: the discovery of the original gildings in the Celestine Chapel.

Figure 1.6 The Basilica of Santa Maria di Collemaggio after the restoration (2017).

Figure 1.7 Santa Maria di Collemaggio: the restored baroque organ.

Discovering the past, for our future

Many other restoration works, carried out during the cultural heritage recovery, forced us to open countless unknown pages of history, discovering amazing surprises, often related to previous earthquakes: old anti-seismic devices concealed inside the masonry, ancient structures and sculptures hidden in the walls, painted wooden ceilings above more recent vaults and many wonderful unknown paintings and frescoes masked by plaster and decorations.

The Superintendence also collaborated with the Regional Secretary of the Ministry of Cultural Heritage on the extraordinary projects of the recovery of Palazzo Ardinghelli, an interesting baroque palace restored and transformed into contemporary art museum (MAXXI L'Aquila); the restoration of the Fontana delle 99 Cannelle, of the churches of Santa Maria del Suffragio, Santa Maria del Soccorso and San Silvestro; the reconstruction and recovery of L'Aquila's city walls; and many others.

Wonderful work such as this always presents difficult problems to solve and diverse challenges to overcome in order to ensure safety and good reconstruction, social reporting and accountability of public funds. Therefore, we are – all together – responsible for giving back to every city its people while returning to each community its identity, also represented by the places of its history and its memory.

Monuments, churches, historic buildings, streets and squares are finally coming back to life; rebuilt, restored, safe and beautiful and better than before. But reconstruction also means creating new identities and new relationships. And it must focus on rebuilding not only stones, houses and cities, but also the connections between people and their spaces.

So, giving the city centre its social life back is now the most important and the most difficult mission to conclude the reconstruction, restoring to L'Aquila's communities the keys of their city and of their lives and, at the same time, giving each community back its identity and its history, giving the city back its memory and, finally, bringing it back to its future.

In 1975, more than 40 years ago, the headline of the European Year of the Architectural Heritage was 'A Future for Our Past'. That's the key of our mission and can also be inverted as 'a past for our future'; a key for the resilience of our territories and societies that need a future, but cannot forget their past, especially if it's so wonderfully present.

Figure 1.8 L'Aquila, Palazzo Morini Cervelli: the Pietà found within sixteenth-century masonry.

Figure 1.9 L'Aquila, Palazzo dell'Emiciclo: the underground spaces of the ancient monastery of Saint Michael found during the restoration works, excavated and repurposed to host the public library.

Notes

1. ICOMOS International Colloquium, *Post-Trauma Reconstruction,* 4 March 2016, Paris Charenton-le-Pont, France; ICOMOS International Scientific Symposium, *Post-disaster reconstruction,* 20 October 2016, Istanbul, Turkey.

2. *'Comme le patrimoine n'est pas une compétence européenne, le Président a pris l'initiative d'écrire à ses homologues pour leur proposer de créer un mécanisme de coopération pour le patrimoine européen en péril, visant à se prêter assistance, à partager des compétences et des savoir-faire. Car nos partenaires, qui comprennent notre émotion, souhaitent pouvoir contribuer à notre cotés. Eux-memes on été confronté à des situations de mise en péril de leur patrimoine. Le Britanniques ont par examples enduré de grands incendies de batiments publics; le Italiens connaissent bien les conséquences des tremblements de terre. ...',* M.me Amèlie de Montchalin, Secretary of State for the European Affairs, 'Le Journal du Dimanche', 20 April 2019.

3. The Superintendence team included: Alessandra Vittorini and Antonello Garofalo (architectonic project), Biancamaria Colasacco, Fabrizio Magani, Lucia Arbace (artistic project) and a collaborative group for the technical, administrative and safety aspects. The Universities team included groups from Politecnico di Milano (coordinator, Stefano Della Torre), Università 'Sapienza' di Roma (coordinator, Giovanni Carbonara) and Università degli Studi dell'Aquila (coordinator, Dante Galeota). Supervision of the restoration was by Antonello Garofalo and Biancamaria Colasacco; construction site management by Eniservizi S.p.A

4. For more information: https://www.europeanheritageawards.eu/winner_year/2020/ (18 April 2021).

5. For more information: https://www.europeanheritageawards.eu/winner_year/2020/ (18 April 2021).

2
Invisible recovery: physical reconstruction versus social reconstruction
The case of Central Italy

Donato Di Ludovico and Lucia Patrizio Gunning

Introduction

This chapter presents the results of a study by the DICEAA Department at University of L'Aquila and the History Department at UCL and concerns the reconstruction process underway in central Italy, which was strongly affected by three sequences of earthquakes. The first of these was the 6.3Mw[1] 2009 L'Aquila earthquake, which affected 57 municipalities and displaced 67,000 people. The subsequent 5.9Mw 2012 Emilia Romagna region earthquake affected 59 municipalities and displaced 15,000 people. The third Central Italian sequence with a maximum measured magnitude of 6.5Mw affected a much larger but less populous area in the Abruzzo, Lazio, Umbria and Marche regions covering 140 municipalities and resulted in the displacement of 40,000 individuals. In particular, we describe the first results of research that compares invisible or social reconstruction in these contexts with their visible physical reconstruction.

In Italy there is no single model of post-disaster intervention, but the approach is to determine the rules and methods of post-disaster reconstruction on a case-by-case basis. Consequently, reconstruction processes are extremely varied. Despite this diversity, all these methods share a tendency to background, or even entirely neglect, the processes of social reconstruction, as well as the related study and observation of social changes. The results of this neglect are often evident. Our research therefore aims to understand the evolution of reconstruction models in Italy over the last decade and to articulate a critique of the social reconstruction planning methods adopted in the three earthquakes mentioned above. At a preliminary level, it proposes social recovery strategies to be integrated into a holistic reconstruction planning model that sees social and physical reconstruction as equal and interdependent.

In scientific literature, the theme of the transformation of society following disasters was already addressed in the early twentieth century,[2] but it became fully developed in the 1970s and 1980s, for example in the research of Bates and Peacock[3] on social changes after a disaster, and in the studies of Quarantelli and Dynes that dealt with mental-health implications for communities and their structures.[4] Kreps's work from the same period critically reviewed studies of hazards and disasters from a general sociological perspective.[5] Rob Gordon's studies described and attempted to understand the transformations of societies after a disaster, specifically their disintegration, with the aim of pointing the way to developing strategies to manage the social environment during recovery.[6] There are also studies based on the concept of community innovation, which is studied across the three disaster phases: pre-impact, trans-impact and post-impact.[7] The attention given to community recovery methods in the collation of case studies by Hales, Walzer and Calvin is interesting,[8] as are the numerous manuals on the subject of procedures to be followed for community recovery. 'Manual 10: Recovery', produced by Emergency Management Australia, for instance, addresses the range of community recovery services such as information, community, personal and psychological support, community development and resources.[9] These studies show that the issue of community recovery is an integral part of recovery planning. For example, 'Manual 10: Recovery' states that the planning process should 'facilitate the recovery of affected individuals, communities and infrastructure as quickly and practicably as possible'.[10] This aspect is also found in the documentation of the Federal Emergency Management Agency.[11] In the scientific literature however, there is no evidence of such integration of reconstruction planning. Moreover, in Italian reconstruction planning, social-recovery activities are disconnected from the physical recovery of the city. Post-disaster planning is instead seen as a bricks-and-mortar reconstruction, which generally concerns building and urban planning and does not introduce the theme of social recovery, because it does not consider it a component of the general theme of reconstruction. Tools such as the Minimum Urban Structure, which deal with the maintenance and recovery of ordinary urban and socio-economic activities after a disaster,[12] are integrated into urban planning but do not address the issue of social change and recovery. This chapter seeks to fill this gap, using the experience of both pre-disaster and post-disaster recovery planning.

Methodology

Our research on 'invisible' post-disaster social recovery is centred on the territory of the three most recent and significant Italian earthquake sequences. In all three contexts, reconstruction planning has concentrated essentially on damaged buildings and structures, and on physical recovery of the wider urban context. Our research compares the different processes of physical and social reconstruction adopted, with the aim of tracing the imbalance between the two, both in planning and implementation. All three cases demonstrate neglect of the intangible aspects, which we consider the most important.

In addition, we sought to understand how societies that had already been affected by disaster reacted to the COVID-19 emergency. Thus we looked at the psychological and social impact of the pandemic in the same territories, to see whether there are cascading effects from those caused by the earthquakes.

Physical and social reconstruction

Analysis of the physical and social reconstruction processes cannot be separated from a brief description of the reconstruction planning tools adopted. Table 2.1 briefly describes the contents of these tools, which essentially concern different models of post-disaster intervention.

Table 2.1 shows very clearly the imbalance between the space dedicated by the planning tools to physical as opposed to social reconstruction. Where social reconstruction is envisaged, it is described and understood only in terms of community participation in the preparation of the reconstruction plan or programme, or in the general strategic choices. However, even where the input of the community is allowed, this ends with the contribution to the first post-disaster phase, that of planning, because Italian laws and ordinances do not provide for the activation of community recovery tools. These planning processes are in fact practically and effectively concentrated on building work. This is evident looking at financial data relating to reconstruction in the Abruzzo region following the 2009 earthquake. In the city of L'Aquila, €5.2 billion

Table 2.1 Comparison of reconstruction planning tools.

EARTH QUAKE	LAWS, COMMISSIONER ORDINANCES	PLANNING TOOL	PHYSICAL RECONSTRUCTION	SOCIAL RECONSTRUCTION
Abruzzo 2009	Law No 77 of 24 June 2009	Reconstruction Plan (PdR) for the historic centre	The PdR contains the strategic guidelines to ensure the socio-economic recovery and redevelopment of the built-up area.	--
	Law No. 134 of 7 August 2012	Integrated Programme (PI)	The PI covers interventions in large neighbourhoods where unified actions are needed.	--
Emilia-Romagna 2012	Regional Law no. 16 of 21 December 2012	Reconstruction Plan (PdR)	The PdR concerns the urban transformations to be carried out in the context of reconstruction, the actions to favor the rapid and complete implementation of the interventions of reconstruction and qualification of the urban structure by the private interested.	The PdR is drawn up through a broad process of consultation and active participation of the citizens concerned.
Italia Centrale 2016/17	Decree Law No 189 of 17 October 2016	Implementation Plan (PA) for the historic centres and urban and rural centres	The PA defines actions for the reconstruction of damaged buildings and intervenes in town planning.	--
	Law No 156 of 12 December 2019 Ordinance no. 36 of 8 September 2017 Ordinance no. 107 of 22 August 2020	Extraordinary Reconstruction Programme (PSR)	The PSR defines the framework of activities related to reconstruction and may also contain urban planning choices.	In the elaboration of the strategic choices for reconstruction and the PSR, the participation of citizens and communities shall be ensured.

has been allocated for the reconstruction of private buildings and, at the time of writing, 82 per cent of the construction sites have been completed; €1.5 billion has been allocated to public buildings and of these, 49 per cent have currently been completed. In the earthquake crater, which is the territory affected beyond the city of L'Aquila itself, €1.3 billion has been granted for the reconstruction of private buildings and 76 per cent of the sites have been completed; €140 million has been granted for public buildings with 63 per cent completed.[13] As can be seen, private reconstruction has been prioritised and is much more advanced than public work. However, this has affected community recovery, because it is precisely the reconstruction of public buildings that helps and re-encourages social cohesion and interaction. Furthermore, there have been no significant and relevant processes of participation in preparation of the Reconstruction Plan (PdR). Together with the absence of community recovery tools or community involvement in the reconstruction, and the exclusion of citizens from all decision-making processes, these imbalances are the causes of persistent social fragmentation and psychological stress.

The same imbalance noted in the reconstruction after the L'Aquila 2009 earthquake can be found to a lesser extent in reconstruction following the 2012 Emilia-Romagna earthquake. In this case, €2.5 billion has been granted for private buildings with 99 per cent of the construction sites currently funded; €245 million has been granted for public buildings, funding 76 per cent of the construction sites.[14] While citizens were at least involved in the preparation phase of the Reconstruction Plan, the theme of community recovery was, again, not addressed in any way.

Finally, reconstruction following the 2016–17 central Italian earthquakes is only just beginning in the Abruzzo, Lazio, Umbria and Marche regions. The imbalance between public and private reconstruction is also apparent in this case: €709 million has been disbursed for private buildings and currently about 20 per cent of the planned construction sites have been completed; €266 million has been expended for public buildings and currently 7.5 per cent of the planned construction sites have been started.[15] An extraordinary reconstruction programme is currently still in preparation.

Invisible recovery: social dynamics and reconstruction

We have highlighted the lack of community-recovery approaches in both planning and managing post-disaster reconstruction for all three cases.[16] However, for the case of the 2009 post-earthquake reconstruction of the Abruzzo Region – and in particular of the city of L'Aquila[17] – there are a number of studies that describe the changes and criticalities related to social transformation after the disaster. Analysis of their results allows us to identify themes useful in defining actions to be included in future community-recovery planning processes. Research into the effects on communities focuses on the psychological effects of post-traumatic stress,[18] on quality of life and on the mental wellbeing of citizens.[19] Mazza in 2014 and Valenti in 2013 showed that the lack of information about the work of government structures caused dissatisfaction among citizens who felt that they were not well informed about the reconstruction of the city. The scientific literature does, however, display a dearth of sociological studies, an absence of investigation into the transformation processes of society after a disaster, and a lack of appraisal of the societal characteristics that emerge in the post-reconstruction period.

In L'Aquila, the exclusion of citizens from decision-making and participation continues to the present day, and the city shows persistent signs of social dysfunction, especially among younger generations. As reconstruction in the city centre continues to focus on the restoration of buildings, the primary economic activity has been hospitality, and in particular the opening of bars and restaurants. The post-earthquake generation have been rediscovering the city primarily as a backdrop to the consumption of alcohol and, with nightclubs and indoor venues largely closed due to COVID-19, this has resulted in uncontrolled mass gatherings, vandalism and the use of fountains and back streets as public latrines. Residents of newly rebuilt houses in the city centre are severely affected by this nocturnal social disorder and deeply dissatisfied by the rapid worsening of the urban environment. At the same time, young people who have been almost wholly excluded from the entire reconstruction process, who have been educated in deteriorating temporary school structures and who have been provided with no social stimuli are drawn to an unpoliced city centre where they can find an outlet for their own frustrations.

Residents' appeals to the city administration fall on deaf ears, even though this social disorder should be seen as a signal to the whole administrative structure that it needs to improve educational settings, create positive social stimuli and institute social and economic policies to encourage more diverse, safe and compatible use of the city centre. The state of affairs in L'Aquila constitutes an almost textbook example of a local administration not understanding that social policies are critical for the successful reconstruction and rebirth of the city. The political system is a key point of reference and its decisions deeply affect every individual. When its actions do not meet the needs of citizens, satisfaction with the quality of their lives drops, leaving insecurity and a perception that they lack internal resources.[20] In his research, Stratta found resilient mechanisms in the immediate post-earthquake period, but foresaw major dangers to mental health in the medium to long term specifically due to the long duration of daily difficulties and the disintegration of the social fabric.[21]

Various initiatives have tried to find stimuli that can help wellbeing after a disaster. Chapter 10 of this publication describes how social media and consumer software were used by an author of this chapter to stimulate engagement and participation. Observing the benefits of digital social networks in the post-disaster period in L'Aquila, Masedu noted that their use halved the risk of depression and post-traumatic stress disorders (PTSD). Masedu's study found that 'both men and women using online social networks had significantly higher quality Of life (QOL) scores in the psychological and social domains of the WHOQOL-BREF'.[22] Online social networks had a measurable positive impact on mental health in the years following the earthquake, indeed they can be a tool to repair the damage caused to real-world social fabric by the displacement of people following catastrophe. Grappasonni also reported the perception of the quality of life of citizens in L'Aquila who were rehoused, such as those relocated to temporary wooden houses or to the purpose-built anti-seismic apartment blocks of the Progetto CASE.[23] A study by Calandra, quoted in Grappasonni's work, noted that 'it is one thing to live in a house in which you have chosen to stay, as part of its social fabric; another is to live in a house where you did not choose to stay, away from one's main memories, residential and planning references, and detached from social bonds'.[24] None of these studies directly address social changes and invisible recovery, nor do they give a complete picture of the post-disaster society that is emerging after the 2009 earthquake. We thus describe here ongoing changes articulating a reflection on the case of the city of L'Aquila and providing elements to integrate community recovery strategies in reconstruction planning.

Social dynamics basis after disaster

A series of nine articles on the psychosocial effects of calamities published by psychologists Rob Gordon and Ruth Wraith in the late 1980s highlighted a community's response to a natural disaster and changes in its social behaviour. Figure 2.1 describes this response. In the pre-disaster phase, the community is described as a set of units made up of individuals, families, interest groups and neighbourhoods, linked together in a complex network of social bonds as the basis of support and identity networks. When disaster occurs, this ordinary structure is suspended in favour of survival-oriented activities: social bonds are broken and redirected to survival and therefore to interpersonal relationships. Immediately after disaster, a reorganisation of social bonds takes place as people need the support of systematic structures. This rebonding process creates a new network, different from the pre-disaster structure, that can be described as a tightly bonded and undifferentiated fusion of different social groups where community needs predominate over those of the individual. Further changes to social bonds occur as the state of emergency ends and the long-term needs of the community emerge. Cooperative social fusion is short-lived, but it provides an intermediate step from which new social structures emerge that differ profoundly from those pre-disaster. The rupture of disaster, the cohesive state of emergency and the changed post-disaster needs of both the community and its individual members represent a three-stage transformation of underlying social structures.[25]

The previously mentioned research studies on quality of life and psychology show that the first two steps of this process can be seen to have

Figure 2.1 Schematic representation of a social structure and related bonds, and its modifications following a disaster. From left to right: the pre-disaster community; the suspension/interruption of bonds following the disaster; the re-bonding process and the state of fusion; the interruption of the fusion; and the differentiation of the post-disaster community (according to the Wraith and Gordon scheme).

occurred in L'Aquila. Yet, at the time of writing, 12 years after the earthquake, social bonds are still reorganising themselves and their structures remain illegible. Fragmented and dispersed, the civic community continues to be excluded from the process of reconstruction planning which, in turn, continues to ignore social aspects and has consequently been incapable of activating the process of reorganisation towards a balanced system. Instead, the post-disaster construction of emergency housing caused an explosive physical expansion of the city beyond its suburbs and into the surrounding territory and villages, but without attention to connective or social infrastructure. This secondary dispersion of the population has extended the second step of the process identified by Gordon and Wraith and allowed what would ordinarily be a transition stage to become the new normality of the city. Persistent examples of social discomfort in the younger generations are becoming an increasing cause of concern but the absence of social policy appears to demonstrate the intention, even if involuntary, of the administrative structure of L'Aquila to maintain the current status quo with the hope that matters will simply resolve themselves. This course of inaction is unlikely to work – the most effective strategy would be to develop a new vision for the future of the city that overcomes the tendency to cling to the past and escapes the conflict (sheer stress) generated by the re-emergence of old social structures.[26]

Strategies for recovering the social fabric and planning

In 2004, Rob Gordon defined a number of community-recovery strategies that can help build a social system geared towards reconnecting the social fabric. 'They involve reorienting emergency management and recovery strategies to prioritize social fabric, including communication, information and interaction opportunities. They also involve creating communication systems and information to form normative assumptions that define, interpret and evaluate the disaster experience.' [27] In table 2.2 we have reworked Gordon's strategies to include a column of pre- and post-disaster planning actions derived from academic analyses and reflections on the reconstruction of L'Aquila from 2009 to the present day. On one hand, these analyses concern institutions that have failed to define the principles of adequacy/subsidiarity and participation/responsibility that underlie intervention following a disaster. On the other, they highlight the inadequacies of urban planning and related disciplines, which were unprepared to respond to the demands of a society undergoing rapid change and were inadequate to cope with the sudden dynamics of the earthquake.[28]

Table 2.2 Strategies for recovering the social fabric and planning (reworking Gordon's proposal).

PHASES	STRATEGIES	PRE AND POST-DISASTER PLANNING ACTIONS
Rebonding	Discourage people from withdrawing or isolating themselves and losing contact with the affected community.	(1) Inclusion in the Municipal Urban Plan of collective services and facilities, such as Civic Centres with a mixed social function, as community reference centres located throughout the city and networked. Civic Centres can also manage emergency and post-emergency services, such as those of operational or command and control centres.
Community formation	Convene the community of interest as early as possible, ensuring that they form shared representations of their situation and needs.	
Facilitate social bonds through communication	Establishing communication systems that unify the affected community and allow for the acquisition of useful information to calibrate the recovery process.	
Normalise communication about the disaster and its effects	As early as possible, make sure that anecdotes are told that encourage people to communicate their experiences with each other and with the recovery system.	(2) Inclusion in pre and post-disaster planning of a specific Community Recovery tool, dynamic and flexible (updatable at any time).
Form disaster-related social representations and facilitate reference groups	Encouraging the communication of experiences and forming informal and formal groups with similar problems by integrating them into the recovery system, facilitating and financing them.	(3) Activate after the disaster, at the Civic Centres of point (1), a network of services to support the community, both psychological and social and participatory. These services should remain active throughout the phases described in this table.
Form a common reality	Providing facts and information about the event, its causes, consequences and current situation to limit uncertainty and correct misunderstandings.	
Preserve differences and complexity, boundaries and identities	Combat homogenising fusion trends as soon as possible by ensuring the expression of differences and preserving personal privacy.	(4) Activate digital platforms and mobile applications dedicated to information and communication. Follow and analyse the flow of information generated on social networks, also using Artificial Intelligence techniques to analyse Big Data.
Integrate services	Linking the introduction of services and assistance measures in a way that supports social representations of the disaster.	
Form a frame of reference	Establishing a body of information to form the basis for making informed assessments of the event and their responses.	(5) Involvement, in the formation of the Frame of Reference, of public institutions, such as the University, and of organisations, such as the voluntary sector, in the activities of points (2) and (3). These form a Reference Committee.
Facilitate social representations of post-disaster life	Promoting community-based cultural events to represent the disaster and its aftermath, including rituals, symbols and art forms.	(6) Integration in the functions of the services and facilities of point (1) of those aimed at leisure time. (7) The Reference Committee of point (5) together with the municipality establishes and animates a programme of events for all phases involving neighbourhoods throughout the city.

Earthquakes and COVID-19: a new complexity of social dynamics

The COVID-19 pandemic has superimposed its effects onto the social and psychological impact of earthquake in all three contexts. A longitudinal study called CORONA[29] examined the psychological response of the Italian population to lockdown during the COVID-19 pandemic. Data was collected through online dissemination of a questionnaire between the end of March and the beginning of April 2020, with follow-up data collection one year later. The questionnaire received around 20,000 responses. Among the measures used was the Resilience Scale for Adults (RSA),[30] an 11-point questionnaire designed to measure the resilience levels of the population. Resilience as measured by the RSA includes both elements of personal resilience, such as positive and effective self-perception, ability to plan for the future, interpersonal social competence and lifestyle organisation, and elements of contextual resilience, specifically family cohesion and social connectedness.[31]

Figure 2.2 shows three graphs describing the profiles of these RSA resilience indicators with variance for three age groups, comparing the responses from Italy as a whole with those from L'Aquila, which represented a significant sample of the study.

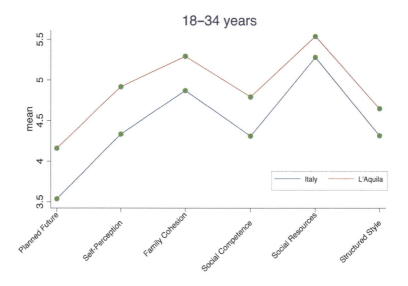

Figure 2.2 Resilience Scale for Adults (RSA) profiles in response to the COVID-19 pandemic, with variance for four age groups. Design: Rodolfo Rossi

38   INVISIBLE RECONSTRUCTION

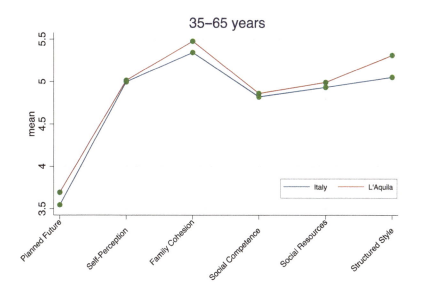

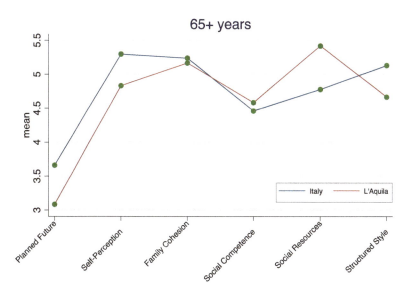

The graphs in Figure 2.2 show a significant increase in all resilience indicators for the 18–34 age group in L'Aquila compared to the national average. At the time of the earthquake, this group would have been between 7 and 23 years old. No such variance is observable in the older age cohorts of 35–65 years and the over-65s. The data supports the thesis that, as a result of their experience with the earthquake, the younger generation seem to have acquired a greater ability to respond to the effects of disaster and a stronger capacity for recovery. This does not seem to be the case with people in the older age groups, who appear, 12 years after the earthquake, to have recovered a good capacity of response in line with the national average.

Conclusions

Comparing the approaches to the last three major earthquake sequences in Italy, we have shown that, with the exception of a brief period following the Emilia Romagna earthquake, institutions have consistently left citizens out of decision-making processes. In all three cases, commitment to physical approaches predominated, with reconstruction planning neglecting social reconstruction and community recovery tools. Where participatory activities existed, all too often these were either citizen initiatives or restricted to providing information.

The research that we have conducted during the gradual reopening of the historic centre of L'Aquila has allowed us to analyse the outcomes of an approach to reconstruction that uniquely favoured the physical aspects. One curiosity has been the apparent resilience to the COVID-19 emergency of the 18–34 cohort in L'Aquila. The pandemic has coincided in L'Aquila with the opening-up of many activities in the city centre, providing new opportunities for social aggregation that were previously missing. However, this has been an unplanned and disorganised process creating significant social friction. Our findings support the thesis that physical reconstruction of the built environment is insufficient without attention to the invisible processes of participation, engagement, communication and education. Social reconstruction and community recovery must go hand in hand with the reopening of the city and its buildings. This additionally requires a refocusing of the physical-reconstruction planning to include, and indeed prioritise, public buildings and public space. In all three of the cases studied, the local, regional and national political system has failed to meet the social needs of the affected populations and to this day these administrations continue to ignore the new dynamics emerging as a result of the reconstruction, leading to further disintegration of real-world social networks.

Our direct experience has shown that where institutions remain ignorant of citizens' needs and where they fail to communicate effectively about the future of their city, it leaves residents with just two insufficient courses of action. Either they can seek to provoke change through grassroots organisation and civic action, or, more probably, they will resign themselves to a loss of faith in those institutions, a lost sense of security in their newly rebuilt city, and a loss of confidence in its future. At the time of writing, L'Aquila is at a crossroads: the reopening of its city centre and responses to the COVID-19 emergency offer the opportunity to redress the balance through consultation, participation and engagement with its citizens to create a well-communicated programme of social recovery. Continued ignorance of emerging social problems and avoidance of political initiative will instead render the costly physical reconstruction ineffective. The case of L'Aquila finds direct parallels in the more recent seismic disasters of Emilia Romagna and central Italy, where the adoption of holistic strategies for invisible reconstruction could avoid a repeat of the same errors.

Acknowledgement

The data used in Section 5 were collected in the Territori Aperti project of the University of L'Aquila (https://territoriaperti.univaq.it/), funded by Fondo Territori Lavoro e Conoscenza CGIL CISL UIL.

Notes

1 Moment magnitude scale.
2 Prince, *Catastrophe and social change based upon a sociological study of the Halifax disaster*, 1920.
3 Bates and Peacock, 'Disaster and social change', 1987.
4 Quarantelli and Dynes, 'Community response to disasters', 1985.
5 Kreps, 'Sociological inquiry and disaster research', 1984.
6 Gordon, 'The social system as site of disaster impact and resource for recovery', 2004; Wraith and Gordon, 'Human responses to natural disaster', 1988.
7 Kendra and Wachtendorf, 'Community innovation and disasters', 2007
8 Hales, Walzer and Calvin, 'Community responses to disasters: a foundation for recovery', 2012.
9 EMA, 'Manual 10: Recovery', 2002.
10 EMA, 'Manual 10: Recovery', 2002.
11 FEMA, 'Pre-Disaster Recovery Planning Guide for Local Governments', 2017; FEMA, 'Long-Term Community Recovery Planning Process', 2005.
12 RegUmb, 'Linee guida per la definizione della Struttura Urbana minima nel Prg', 2010.
13 Gran Sasso Science Institute, 'Open Data ricostruzione'.
14 Regione Emilia Romagna, 'Open Ricostruzione'
15 Commissario Straordinario Ricostruzione Sisma 2016, 'La Ricostruzione dell'Italia Centrale, 2020'.
16 Kendra and Wachtendorf, 'Community Innovation and Disasters', 2007.
17 Di Ludovico, D'Ovidio, Santilli, 'Post-earthquake reconstruction as an opportunity for a sustainable reorganisation of transport and urban structure', 2019; Di Ludovico, Dominici, 'How to combine the Smart City and the historic centre: suggestions from a case study', 2019.
18 Piccardi et al., 'Neuro-functional alterations due to PTSD after environmental disasters: fMRI evidence and clinical suggestions', 2016; Gigantesco, 'Psychopathological chronic sequelae of the 2009 earthquake in L'Aquila', 2013.
19 Grappasonni et al., 'Psychological symptoms and quality of life among the population of L'Aquila's "new towns" after the 2009 earthquake', 2017; Mazza et al., 'Investigation on quality of life and psychological well-being of citizens of L'Aquila after earthquake on April 6, 2009', 2014; Valenti et al., 'A longitudinal study of quality of life of earthquake survivors in L'Aquila, Italy', 2013.
20 Mazza et al., 'Investigation on quality of life and psychological well-being of citizens of L'Aquila after earthquake on April 6, 2009', 2014; Valenti et al., 'A longitudinal study of quality of life of earthquake survivors in L'Aquila, Italy', 2013.
21 Stratta et al., 'Mental health in L'Aquila after the earthquake', 2012.
22 Masedu et al., 'Facebook, quality of life, and mental health outcomes in post-disaster urban environments: the L'Aquila earthquake experience', 2014.
23 Grappasonni et al., 'Psychological symptoms and quality of life among the population of L'Aquila's "new towns" after the 2009 earthquake', 2017.
24 Complessi Antisismici Sostenibili Ecocompatibili or Sustainable Environmentally-Friendly Anti-Seismic Settlements Programme.
25 Wraith and Gordon, 'Human responses to natural disaster', 1988; Kates, 'Natural Hazard in Human Ecological Perspective: Hypotheses and Models', 1971.
26 Wraith and Gordon, 'Human responses to natural disaster', 1988; Kates, 'Natural Hazard in Human Ecological Perspective: Hypotheses and Models', 1971.
27 Gordon, 'The social system as site of disaster impact and resource for recovery', 2004.
28 Properzi and Di Ludovico, 'Il governo del territorio alla prova del terremoto: imparare dagli errori', 2018.
29 Rossi et al., 'Mental Health Outcomes Among Healthcare Workers and the General Population During the COVID-19 in Italy', 2020b; Rossi et al., 'COVID-19 Pandemic and Lockdown Measures Impact on Mental Health Among the General Population in Italy', 2020c.
30 Capanna et al., 'The Italian validation study of the Resilience Scale for Adults (RSA)', 2015.
31 Rossi et al., 'Personal and contextual components of resilience mediate risky family environment's effect on psychotic-like experiences', 2020a.

Bibliography

Bates, F.L. and Peacock, W.G. 'Disaster and social change'. In *Sociology of Disaster, contribution of sociology to disaster research*, edited by R.R. Dynes, B. De Marchi, and C. Pelanda, 291–330. Milano: FrancoAngeli, 1987.

Capanna, C., Stratta, P., Hjemdal, O., Collazzoni, A. and Rossi, A. 'The Italian validation study of the Resilience Scale for Adults (RSA)'. *Applied Psychology Bulletin*, 272(63) (2015): 16–24.

Commissario Straordinario Ricostruzione Sisma 2016. 'La Ricostruzione dell'italia Centrale, 2020'. Accessed 01 July 2021, https://sisma2016.gov.it/wp-content/uploads/2021/03/R2020_rev-1.pdf

Di Ludovico, D., D'Ovidio, G. and Santilli, D. 'Post-earthquake reconstruction as an opportunity for a sustainable reorganisation of transport and urban structure.' *Cities*, 96 (2019) https://doi.org/10.1016/j.cities.2019.102447.

Di Ludovico, D. and Dominici, D. 'How to combine the Smart City and the historic centre: suggestions from a case study'. In *A set of Good Practices and Recommendations for Smart City Resilience Engineering and Evaluation*, edited by S. Bologna , 36–45. AIIC, 2019.

EMA. Manual 10: Recovery. Canberra: National Capital Printing, 2002 . Accessed 16 April 2021: https://doms.csu.edu.au/csu/file/78a6c5d7-fd8b-ff7e-fff3-2ffb78764ebe/1/resources/manuals/Manual-10.pdf.

FEMA. 'Pre-Disaster Recovery Planning Guide for Local Governments', 2017. Accessed 18 April 2021. https://www.fema.gov/sites/default/files/2020-07/pre-disaster-recovery-planning-guide-local-governments.pdf

FEMA. 'Long-Term Community Recovery Planning Process', 2005. Accessed 18 April 2021. https://www.fema.gov/pdf/rebuild/ltrc/selfhelp.pdf

Gigantesco, A., Mirante, N., Granchelli, C., Diodati, G., Cofini, V., Mancini, C., Carbonelli, A., Tarolla, E., Minardi, V., Salmaso, S. and D'Argenio, P. 'Psychopathological chronic sequelae of the 2009 earthquake in L'Aquila, Italy'. *Journal of Affective Disorders*, 148 (2013): 265–271. http://dx.doi.org/10.1016/j.jad.2012.12.006.

Gordon, R. 'The social system as site of disaster impact and resource for recovery'. *The Australian Journal of Emergency Management,* 19 (4) (2004): 16–22.

Gran Sasso Science Institute. 'Open Data Ricostruzione'. Accessed 1 July 2021. https://opendataricostruzione.gssi.it/home

Grappasonni, I., Petrelli, F., Traini, E., Grifantini, G., Mari, M. and Signorelli, C. 'Psychological symptoms and quality of life among the population of L'Aquila's "new towns" after the 2009 earthquake'. *Epidemiology Biostatistics and Public Health*, 14, (2) (2017): 1–13. Accessed 3 June 2022 https://www.researchgate.net/publication/322528550

Hales, B., Walzer, N. and Calvin, J. 'Community responses to disasters: a foundation for recovery'. *Community Development*, 43(5) (2012): 540–549. https://doi.org/10.1080/15575330.2012.731417.

Kates, R. W. Natural hazard in human ecological perspective: hypotheses and models. *Economic Geography*, 47(3) (1971): 438–451.

Kendra, J.M. and Wachtendorf, T. 'Community innovation and disasters'. In *Handbook of Disaster Research*, edited by Rodríguez, H.M., Quarantelli, E.L., Dynes R.R. New York: Springer, 2007.

Kreps, G.A. 'Sociological inquiry and disaster research'. *Annual Review of Sociology*, 10 (1984): 309–330. https://doi.org/10.1146/annurev.so.10.080184.001521.

Masedu, F., Mazza, M., Di Giovanni, C., Calvarese, A., Tiberti, S., Sconci, V. and Valenti, M. 'Facebook, quality of life, and mental health outcomes in post-disaster urban environments: the L'Aquila earthquake experience'. *Frontiers in Public Health*, 2 (2014): 286. https://doi.org/10.3389/fpubh.2014.00286.

Mazza, M., Pacitti, F., Pino, M.C., Peretti, S. and Mazzarelli, E. 'Investigation on quality of life and psychological well-being of citizens of L'Aquila after earthquake on April 6, 2009', *Riv Psichiatr*, 49–3(2014) 145–151. http://dx.doi.org/10.1708/1551.16913.

Piccardi, L., Boccia, M., Colangeli, S., Bianchini, F., Marano, A., Giannini, A.M., Palmiero, M. and D'Amico, S. 'Neuro-functional alterations due to PTSD after environmental disasters: fMRI evidence and clinical suggestions', *Journal of Psychopathology*, 22 (2016): 165–171.

Prince, S.H. *Catastrophe and social change based upon a sociological study of the Halifax disaster*, Ulan Press, 2012.

Properzi, P. and Di Ludovico, D. 'Il governo del territorio alla prova del terremoto: imparare dagli errori'. In *Sviluppare, rigenerare, ricostruire città. Questioni e sfide contemporanee*, edited by Moccia, F.D. and Sepe, M., 236–254. Roma: Accademia, INU Edizioni 2018.

Quarantelli, E.L. and Dynes, R.R. 'Community response to disasters'. *Disasters and Mental Health Selected Contemporary Perspectives* (1986): 158–168.

Regione Emilia Romagna, 'Open Ricostruzione'. Accessed 1 July 2021. https://openricostruzione. regione.emilia-romagna.it

RegUmb, 'Linee guida per la definizione della Struttura Urbana minima nel Prg', 2010. Accessed 18 April 2021. http://www.regione.umbria.it/documents/18/1590324/Linee+guida+Stru ttura+Urbana+Minima/926a4077-a0f9-43f5-adfe-4f8fe9770486

Rossi, R., Collazzoni, A., Talevi, D., Gibertoni, D., Quarta, E., Rossi, A., Stratta, P., Di Lorenzo, G. and Pacitti, F. 'Personal and contextual components of resilience mediate risky family environment's effect on psychotic-like experiences'. *Early Intervention in Psychiatry*, December (2020a). eip.13111. https://doi.org/10.1111/eip.13111.

Rossi, R., Socci, V., Pacitti, F., Mensi, S., Di Marco, A., Siracusano, A. and Di Lorenzo, G. 'Mental health outcomes among healthcare workers and the general population during the COVID-19 in Italy'. *Frontiers in Psychology*, 11 (2020b): 3332. https://doi.org/10.3389/ fpsyg.2020.608986.

Rossi, R., Socci, V., Talevi, D., Mensi, S., Niolu, C., Pacitti, F., Di Marco, A., Rossi, A., Siracusano, A. and Di Lorenzo, G. 'COVID-19 pandemic and lockdown measures impact on mental health among the general population in Italy'. *Frontiers in Psychiatry*, 11 (2020c): 790. https://doi. org/10.3389/fpsyt.2020.00790.

Stratta, P., Cataldo, S.D., Bonanni, R., Valenti, M., Masedu, F. and Rossi, A. 'Mental health in L'Aquila after the earthquake'. *Ann Ist Super Sanità*, 48–2 (2012): 132–137. https://doi. org/10.4415/ANN_12_02_05.

Valenti, M., Masedu, F., Mazza, M., Tiberti, S., Di Giovanni, C., Calvarese, A., Pirro, R. and Sconci, V. 'A longitudinal study of quality of life of earthquake survivors in L'Aquila, Italy'. *BMC Public Health*, 13, (2013): 1143. https://doi.org/10.1186/1471-2458-13-1143.

Wraith, R. and Gordon, R. 'Human responses to natural disaster' (series) Part 8: Community Responses to Disaster. *Macedon Digest*, 3(2) (1988).

3

Revealing the vulnerable in society Contradictions between victims' intentions and housing provision

Haruka Tsukuda and Yasuaki Onoda

Just as disaster changes social dynamics and creates new requirements for urban space, it also increases the vulnerability of invisible, marginalised groups for whom complex support measures may be required.

The Great East Japan Earthquake (GEJE) of March 2011 left nearly 400,000 homes unusable. In Ishinomaki, where damage was the greatest, the scale of public housing reconstruction was enormous. Although early surveys were used to determine people's requirements, mismatches in the data meant that the amount and types of housing did not accurately reflect people's actual needs. As a result only 60 per cent of the people who requested public housing in 2012 eventually used it. Additionally, the large-scale displacement of people left the 'invisible' and vulnerable exposed; groups such as the elderly who had previously been sheltered by their families and communities were particularly affected. Furthermore, since the prerequisite for obtaining new housing was having proof of property damage, low-income renters and those who had failed to pay taxes were often left in a temporary housing situation. Ultimately, the construction of homes needed to be supplemented with complex support, with the city easing occupancy requirements, providing information on private rental housing, and creating mutual aid housing to enable the elderly to rebuild their lives.

Introduction

On 11 March 2011, Japan experienced the Great East Japan Earthquake (GEJE) and resulting tsunami, which caused extensive damage to the coastal area facing the Pacific Ocean, mostly in the northern area of Japan – known as the Tohoku region. Specifically, the affected coastal area has fishing villages that have survived since early times and still consist of their traditional homes and multigenerational households of fisherfolk. Although the Tohoku region has been depopulating and ageing since before the earthquake, these trends were particularly noticeable in fishing villages. Since the disaster-stricken area has a unique culture and various issues, it was assumed that the general public-sector housing projects, which were designed for urban areas, would be unsuitable for this region.

Some programmes for housing reconstruction were prepared by the national government, and disaster public housing was one of the most important projects. Almost 400,000 homes were damaged by the GEJE,[1] with damage especially severe in the Iwate, Miyagi and Fukushima prefectures. Furthermore, Fukushima prefecture was damaged by the collapse of the nuclear power plant. In total, approximately 30,000 units will have been constructed in these three prefectures by the end of 2021.[2]

Research relating to the disaster public housing that began construction after the GEJE remains scant because construction of all housing has not been finished. Furthermore, it is incredibly difficult to access governmental information and data, which means that research regarding the process of, and system behind, public reconstruction remains especially scarce. Among the existing research, an important contribution is from Matsumoto, who clarifies the strategic differences for the disaster-hazard areas in each municipality.[3] Also, Onoda shows that the planning process for housing reconstruction targets municipalities in the Iwate and Miyagi prefecture.[4] The character of reconstruction work could be classified by the differences among processes and variations in the type of projects that could be subsidised by the national government. Even in municipalities of the same size, the type of projects and the allocation of manpower are different. Tsukuda clarifies the change that occurred in victims' opinions on housing recovery, explaining that the choices for housing reconstruction and the family type at reconstruction were influenced by the living situations during temporary housing.[5]

Focusing on Ishinomaki

The research presented here focuses on Ishinomaki city, the municipality close to the seismic centre that experienced the most damage from the GEJE. In September 2010, before the disaster, the population was close to 163,000. In the earthquake and tsunami, around 33,000 homes were damaged, corresponding to 9 per cent of the damage in all three of the aforementioned prefectures. By March 2019, Ishinomaki had built 4,456 units as part of the disaster public housing initiative.

This chapter aims to clarify the contradictions in public housing reconstruction projects from two perspectives. The first concerns the process of housing. The local government, which is the main body for reconstruction efforts, conducted a large-scale survey of housing intentions for the victims to determine the housing provision schema. However, various inconsistencies occurred during this process, so the data was analysed to clarify the structure of these mismatches. The second perspective concerns the contradiction that real life poses. For example, the large-scale displacements caused by the housing disaster exposed vulnerable groups, such as the elderly, who were sheltered by their families and communities before the disaster, and therefore 'invisible' to society and governments. By questioning these issues in detail, the contradictions between the implementation of projects and invisible victims' actualities during disaster recovery efforts are clarified.

Method

In section two, positioning of the disaster public housing in Japan is shown from the perspective of law, alongside the actual situation that resulted from both the Hanshin-Awaji Earthquake and GEJE. In section three, the change of victims' opinions regarding housing recovery is clarified by utilising a statistical analysis that is based on questionnaires that were collected by the local government of Ishinomaki.[6] Section four discusses an issue that emerged regarding the transfer from temporary housing to disaster public housing. Specifically, it delves into how some people experience challenges that are too complicated and multilayered for them to move into disaster public housing.

The Japanese public reconstruction scheme for housing

Public Housing Act

Japan's Public Housing Act was established in 1951 when the country was undergoing reconstruction after the Second World War. Public housing was called one of 'the three pillars of post-war housing policy', along with housing by the Japan Housing Corporation and the subsidy of the Japan Finance Corporation. The act's purpose was for the national and local governments to cooperate in creating a public housing system that would contribute to stabilising people's lives and promote social welfare by developing sufficient housing for a healthy, cultural life. These units were meant to be either rented or subleased at low rates to earners with a fixed income who were also in need of housing.[7] Currently, the occupancy income requirement is set by each local government at a monthly income of ¥259,000 (income quintile 50 per cent) as the maximum limit. Furthermore, the rent is established according to the tenant's income, but nearby rental rates are also taken into consideration.

Disaster public housing

Disaster public housing is specified in the Public Housing Act,[8] and another law regarding special financial assistance after a severe disaster stipulates that the national government can subsidise three-quarters of the costs involved. At the time of the GEJE, a national reconstruction grant covered the other quarter. Furthermore, in the case of a severe disaster, there is no income requirement from tenants, but it is a necessary condition that they have lost their homes. Therefore, disaster public housing is not solely for low-income people, but applies to all disaster victims. During the GEJE, each affected local government issued a housing affliction certificate for each household to determine qualification. After moving in, residents paid a reduced rent for a while, but after a certain period – usually 10 years – the rent was collected in full based on income, as per the public housing standard during normal times.

Public settlement supply after disasters

In 1995, the Hanshin-Awaji Earthquake occurred around Kobe. Afterwards, a series of shelters, temporary housing and disaster public housing were accepted as a public settlement supply. This type of reconstruction route was named 'single-track reconstruction'.[9] Under disaster public housing, many units were built in coastal landfills near urban areas that were vacant. Since the elderly and disabled were given priority, they quickly entered the completed housing. The residents in the disaster public housing were separated from their previous neighbourhood and divided from their community, resulting in 'solitary deaths'.

In Japan, subsidies for disaster construction are directly supplied through a single chain of command, from national to local governments of individual prefectures, and then to each municipality.[10] First, the national government decided on a disaster-hazard area policy after the GEJE. Since this was an area that could be potentially affected by another tsunami, the construction of new houses was prohibited. Based on a tsunami simulation, each local government decided on these areas, and in many of them, houses could not be constructed without certain measures. Moreover, the national government established some core projects that could be subsidised, and each local government chose housing reconstruction projects alongside these.

There were four main housing reconstruction choices (Figure 3.1). The primary form of public reconstruction works for people that lived in disaster-hazard areas at the time of the disaster involved establishing disaster public housing and group relocation to higher ground or inland. Otherwise, victims reconstructed houses by themselves at the sites where they had previously lived or at other sites they either bought or rented. With multiple recovery possibilities for rebuilding, this was dubbed 'multi-track reconstruction'.[11]

Speed was the most important issue in public reconstruction work after the GEJE, and housing supply was particularly prioritised because many victims had lost their homes. In each municipality, a significant amount of housing reconstruction was needed after the disaster had struck. The municipalities needed to know the exact number of houses for the public sector to build, so the national government requested that the municipalities confirm the victims' housing recovery intentions. In response, most municipalities used several questionnaires to confirm victims' intentions with high transparency. While some municipalities with lesser damage initiated more in-depth interviews, others only utilised questionnaires, which seemed to result in insufficient communication.[12]

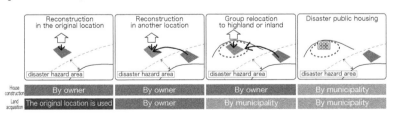

Figure 3.1 The main choices of housing reconstruction.

In summary, disaster public housing in Japan is supplied by the government in the event of a disaster, as set out in the Public Housing Act. Unlike public housing during normal times, victims who have lost their homes to a disaster are eligible for disaster public housing so long as they hold a disaster certificate, which is usually issued by the municipality. Residents have rent reduction measures for a while after they move in, but after a certain period, income-based rent is collected in full, aligning with public housing policies during normal times. After the GEJE, other public housing reconstruction projects, such as group relocation efforts, were established and 'multi-track reconstruction' was realised, but disaster public housing remained an important initiative.

Results of reconstruction

The gap in the plan

In Ishinomaki, the survey for reconstruction primarily followed four steps:

1. In May 2011, to establish the main policy of the reconstruction plan, a questionnaire was conducted and was collected from 9,806 households.
2. In February 2012, a pre-survey of victims' housing recovery opinions targeted 7,113 households and was collected from a total of 5,058 households.
3. In August, November and December 2012, a survey of victims' housing recovery opinions was conducted that targeted 13,433 households and was collected from a total of 9,118 households.
4. In September 2013 and July 2014, registration for disaster public housing, specifying where victims wished to live, was collected from 4,408 households.

The third step involving the 2012 opinion survey was the most important because this data was used for housing planning. After that, at the fourth step, Ishinomaki received registration for disaster public housing. We matched the data from the third and fourth steps, which concerned 7,397 households, and created a database for our analysis.

A change in the number of registrants

In the third step, an opinion survey illustrated that 3,176 households wished to live in disaster public housing. However, at the fourth step only

1,998 of those registered for disaster public housing. So the desired number of disaster public housing units decreased to 62.9 per cent between the third and fourth surveys. The entire amount of target households included was 13,381, after subtracting 52 duplicates from the third step's target number (13,433). Therefore 1,998 is just 14.9 per cent of the whole target. This is because victims considered their housing recovery by comparing multiple choices, and had no responsibility to fulfil their stated opinions. Including the newly registered, a total of 4,408 households registered for disaster public housing at the fourth step. From this, it may be difficult to calculate a definite number for construction based only on the residents' intentions. That raises the question: which households did not register for disaster public housing? If the answer to this question is understood, it may be used as a factor in the decision-making process when creating the formula for calculating the number of units that need to be constructed.

We then went on to analyse the characteristics of victims who did not choose disaster public housing by using the data from 2,085 households, excluding those with missing data. Figure 3.2 shows the registration status for each household based on its number of members. Those with a large number of members tended not to register. The approximate size of disaster public housing after the GEJE has been shown by prefectures. However, the size of units and associated planning were determined by each municipality. For example, the disaster-public-housing construction guidelines by Miyagi prefecture showed 35–50 square metres for a single- or two-person family, 45–60 square metres for a two- or three-person family, 55–70 square metres for a three- or four-person family, and 65–80 square metres for a family that consisted of more than four people.[13] It is important to note that not many households with five or more people were considered in this guideline.

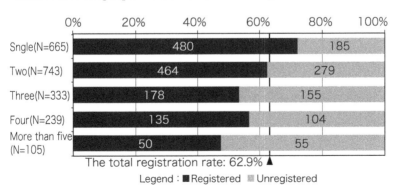

Figure 3.2 Registration status for each household based on the number of members therein.

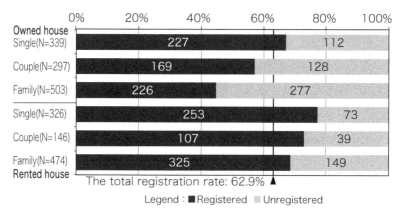

Figure 3.3 Registration status for each household and house type before the disaster.

Figure 3.3 presents the registration status for each household and house type before the GEJE. Households did not register as their household size increased, even where they had owned or rented houses before the GEJE, but households that originally owned houses tended to not register at all. Thus, it is thought that each household's lifestyle had a strong influence on the results. Households that originally rented their homes had no resistance to moving into disaster public housing – a public rented house – as they were accustomed to living in collective housing. However, in the case of homeowners, many had lived in houses and on land that had been inhabited by their ancestors, so it is assumed that they did not want to move into disaster public housing.

Changing opinions about location

Here the change in regard to the location of selected disaster public housing is discussed based on data from 2,011 registered households. Figure 3.4 shows home moves before and after the disaster, and the desired place of residence shown by the surveys. In the 2012 opinion survey, the inland region near the largest group relocation area was the most highly desired location. This was probably because memories of the tsunami remained vivid, and victims wanted to live in a safe place as far away from the coast as possible. However, at the time of registration in 2014, many had changed their opinions about the coastal area they had lived near during the GEJE, especially households that had been living in temporary houses near the coast after the tsunami. At the result of the registration

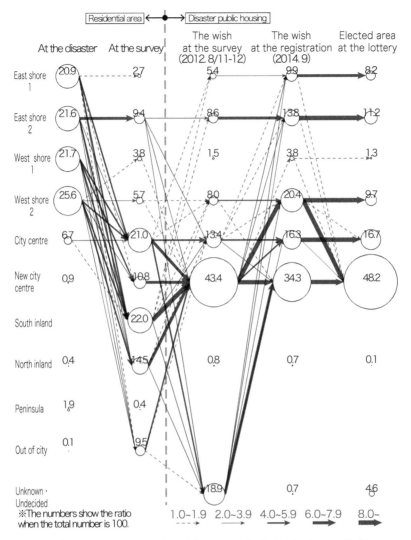

Figure 3.4 Movement of residence and desired place of disaster public housing.

lottery in 2014, many victims found that they could not live in public housing near the area they had lived before the GEJE, because many public housing units were being built inland based on the 2012 opinion survey.

In summary, the opinions of victims in Ishinomaki were collected and reflected upon when considering the recovery plan. Since speed was demanded, the number of disaster public housing units was decided based on residents' intentions as stated in 2012, shortly after the earthquake. At this time, many victims wanted to move inland and wanted disaster public housing. However, many remained in temporary housing near the original settlement on the coast after the disaster and changed their opinion – without communicating this to the municipalities – by acquiring a variety of information before registration. In fact, about 40 per cent of those who had wanted disaster public housing at that time did not end up wanting it. The households that withdrew their hopes for disaster public housing were mainly those who did not match the lifestyle of disaster public housing in terms of the number of members per household and the previous housing type. However, based on the 2012 intention survey, a large amount of housing was supplied inland. As a result, the victims who wanted to stay in the original area had to move.

Transportation from temporary housing to disaster public housing

In Japan, temporary housing is provided after a disaster, as prescribed by the Disaster Relief Act of 1947. After the GEJE, in addition to specially constructed temporary housing, temporary rental assistance was provided, which supported private rental housing. In other words, this latter type of housing was also regarded as 'temporary housing', so the rent was subsidised by the government on a large scale. Under the Disaster Relief Act, the provision of temporary housing was limited to two years in principle, but even in places other than Fukushima prefecture (where long-term evacuation has continued due to the damage from the nuclear power plant), evacuation beyond the assumed residence period for 'temporary construction' has continued due to the large-scale housing damage that was inflicted.

Since the provision period for temporary housing was extended in the areas affected by the GEJE, uniform and specific extensions were also adopted. Uniform extension refers to extending the residence period of temporary housing regardless of each disaster victim's reasons. For specific extensions, it is only permitted to extend temporary housing for households with adequate reasons, such as waiting for the completion of housing or residential land development.

Table 3.1 summarises the provision period for temporary housing with a period of uniform/specific extension adopted by each municipality in Iwate and Miyagi. Ishinomaki is the area with the longest period of temporary housing in terms of provision, particularly for uniform extension. In addition, the provision of temporary housing and decisions on the provision period were led by each prefecture rather than the local government.

Table 3.1 The provision period of temporary housing.

Priod / Prefecture	Until March 2014 (End in 3 years)	Until March 2015 (End in 4 years)	Until March 2016 (End in 5 years)	Until March 2017 (End in 6 years)		Until March 2018 (End in 7 years)		Until March 2019 (End in 8 years)	Until March 2021 (End in 10 years)		
				Specific extension in 6th year	Uniform extension in 6th year	Specific extension in 6th and 7th year	Specific extension from 7th year	Specific extension from 7th year	Specific extension from 7th year	Specific extension from 8th year
Miyagi	Shichigajuku and 2 other municipalities	Shiraishi and 17 other municipalities	Iwanuma and Osaki	Sendai, Watari and Shichigahama	-	Tagajo and Yamamoto	Shiogama	Minamisanriku	Kesennuma and Higashimatsushima	Ishinomaki, Natori and Onagawa
Iwate	Kuzumaki and 5 other municipalities	Hirono and 14 other municipalities	Kuji, Tanohata and Iwaizumi	Oshu and Ichinoseki	Noda	-	-	-	Miyako	Yamada , Otsuchi, Kamaishi, Ofunato and Rikuzentakada

Supporting victims' independence

In Ishinomaki, the peak temporary housing supply reached 7,102 for specially constructed temporary housing in June 2012 and 5,899 for temporary rental assistance in March 2012. This refers to the largest number of units supplied in both Iwate and Miyagi prefectures. At the end of 2017, disaster victims were living in a total of 2,471 units of both types. The authors participated as experts in the study of transition support from temporary housing in the city, examining measures to support victims until March 2019.

Establishing a support system

Japan's administrative organisation is divided vertically, and even during reconstruction projects, different departments are in charge of functions such as providing temporary housing, disaster public housing and welfare support. This can make cooperation difficult when carrying out business initiatives – a problem experienced in Ishinomaki. So, it was necessary to establish a system that would allow the relevant parties to work together when considering support measures for the victims.

In October 2015, a cross-departmental meeting was set up within the government's Working Group on Housing Reconstruction (Figure 3.5). This practical meeting discussed both life recovery and the early elimination of temporary housing. To confirm the intentions of temporary housing residents and formulate a plan for consolidating and removing temporary housing, a survey was conducted among residents. At the meeting, big data was generated by integrating the survey and other relevant information, such as the intention to rebuild and the victims' statistical situation. In Japan, the handling of personal information is strictly regulated by the Act on the Protection of Personal Information. However, in a situation that requires continuous support in reconstruction efforts after a disaster, the system's strict handling hindered this support.

Figure 3.5 The organisational structure for supporting vulnerable victims' recovery in Ishinomaki.

Therefore, Ishinomaki constructed big data that could handle supportive information from multiple sections in an integrated manner.

In June 2016, the programme's final plan for promoting victims' self-recovery was prepared and published. Also in 2016, the Working Group on Supporting Victims' Recovery was established as the city's direct control organisation. As a consultative body, this working group consisted of experts and departments related to rebuilding victims' recovery. By holding cross-departmental meetings, they stay abreast of residents' information and reflect it in the database; establish the status of consolidating and decommissioning temporary housing; support victims who have not yet decided to rebuild; and share the programme's progress.

The programme for promoting self-recovery

This programme is a summary of the temporary housing consolidation and decommissioning schedules, as well as the reconstruction support policies. Upon conducting a detailed survey among residents, it is clear that many households have problems rebuilding their lives on their own. For example, some victims were ineligible for disaster public housing because they failed to pay taxes or could not get certification of their housing damage due to the small scale of the damage. Meanwhile, some others were unemployed, lacked the willingness to work in the future, or had an illness – either physical or mental. Regarding victims who are not eligible to move into disaster public housing, the local government tried to support them moving into other houses by cooperating with private businesses. As for matters related to occupancy requirements, such as tax delinquency, the range of occupancy was partially expanded by imposing conditions, such as pledges for payment. On the other hand, issues concerning the unemployed or those with mental illness not only occur specifically as a response to a disaster, but also require welfare support, even in normal times.

In October 2017, a 'companion-type' victim support project was launched to provide economic and wider support to victims moving into private rental housing, living in poverty and living at home. In doing so, the project provided information consultation services, such as systems for rebuilding homes as well as accompanying welfare services and procedures. Furthermore, it promotes independence and smooth relocation to permanent residences.

Collective-type disaster public housing

Based on various surveys, it was apparent that there are those, such as elderly people who live alone, who need daily watching-over in disaster public housing situations. For these groups, instead of a general housing complex type, collective-type disaster public housing should be constructed where residents can support each other. Thirty units of this type of housing in two single-storey collective buildings were constructed during Phase I (Figure 3.6) in December 2017, while 12 collective-use type units and 20 normal-type units in a three-storey building were completed during Phase I in March 2019. Phase II was the last of all the disaster public housing initiatives to be completed in Ishinomaki. Three years have passed since the first households moved into Phase I of the housing, and a system has been put into place by the residents so they can live together while helping each other. However, as the residents age, the burden on some is increasing. Therefore, it is necessary to consider how mutual assistance can be supported in the future, including through outside organisations.

Figure 3.6 The exterior of the collective-type public housing for mutual assistance in Ishinomaki.

Figure 3.7 The inside of the collective-type public housing for mutual assistance in Ishinomaki.

In summary, since the GEJE caused enormous damage to homes, it took a long time to rebuild them. As a result, residence in temporary housing has been prolonged. Meanwhile, those who were particularly worried about employment and health tended to remain in this housing at the end of the reconstruction period. In Ishinomaki, a self-recovery programme for disaster victims was provided jointly by the department in charge of temporary housing management and reconstruction projects, and the department that carries out welfare projects. In formulating the programme, issues were identified using big data that integrated information, such as surveys of temporary housing residents and people's intention to rebuild. Meanwhile, new support programmes were launched to enhance the existing system and new housing forms were also tackled. The city's last supply units were adopted as a collective-type housing that encourages mutual support among residents who need more watching over. However, it is important to note that three years have passed since residents have moved in, and new issues are beginning to appear due to their ageing. Therefore, it is necessary to consider measures to ensure that residents can continue to live with dignity in the future.

Conclusion

Based on the case of housing reconstruction that was a result of the GEJE, a contradiction occurred between planning to build a large number of houses and the victims' real lives. To resolve this issue, efforts have been made to support disaster victims' recovery. When supplying a large amount of housing, it is necessary to determine the location of housing and the number of units that need to be constructed. In Japan, generally, governments' housing recovery project plans are formulated based on victims' intentions. Of course, victims' intentions are important, but they may instead choose to rebuild their lives in other ways, as they have many options. Thus, their intentions to rebuild their homes may change over time. As the proportion of public housing increases, the financial impact on local governments also increases. Especially in Japan, where the population is declining, this long-term financial burden will also burden citizens. Immediately after the GEJE, the speed of reconstruction projects was emphasised, but to ensure a satisfactory process for disaster public housing in the future, it is necessary to provide appropriate information to the residents and support them in making choices that suit their lifestyle and financial strength. This would help in the proper provision of units, which would also need to be constructed and designed with more consideration for the needs of vulnerable victims who would be living in them.

Furthermore, victims experience a variety of problems, making it difficult for them to rebuild without assistance. In other words, under the existing system, vulnerable groups would not be able to move into disaster public housing. Therefore, it is necessary to consider welfare support in addition to housing during this process. This collaboration, which was difficult due to Japan's vertical organisational structure, could be achieved by a joint meeting system. However, the need remains for vulnerable groups to receive housing and welfare support.

Also, when visible homes and buildings are constructed, it is easy to think that the reconstruction is complete, but to recover the lives of victims, it is also necessary to continue providing careful support in handling the problems that may arise for each victim. While equality was emphasised in the reconstruction after the GEJE, the victims who originally had social problems may find that it is impossible to rebuild their lives with uniform support. It is not just the construction of homes that needs to continue, but the provision of complex support. In summary, it is vital to consider the importance of the long-term recovery of life rather than simply rebuilding a house.

Notes

1 Fire and Disaster Management Agency, '平成23年 (2011年) 東北地方太平洋沖地震 (東日本大震災) について ver. 160', 2020.
2 Reconstruction Agency, '住まいの復興工程表 at March 2020', 2020.
3 Matsumoto et al., 'A Study on Designation Disaster Hazard Areas after the Great East Japan Earthquake', 2015.
4 Onoda et al., 'Implementation of Recovery Plan and Organization Structure of Municipalities', 2015.; Onoda et al., 'Relationships between Work-loads and Organizational Structure of Municipalities in Implementing Housing Reconstruction Program after Large-scale Disasters', 2021.
5 Tsukuda et al., 'A Study on the Change of Housing Recovery Opinions based on Public Housing Registration Data', 2017.; Tsukuda et al., 'The Decision Factors of the Housing Recovery Opinions and the Influence of Temporary Living Conditions after Large-scale Disaster', 2019.
6 We used the data of two opinion surveys by Ishinomaki from 2012 to 2014. These surveys were conducted using paper questionnaires: the 2012 survey covered 13,433 of the affected households that were eligible for reconstruction projects, while the 2013-2014 survey was captured as registration information to 4408 prospective disaster public housing tenants. Tohoku University, to which we belong, has signed a comprehensive agreement with Ishinomaki. As a result, we received various data from the local government and provided the analysis results to support the reconstruction project. This data was provided as part of the agreement.
7 Japanese Diet, 'Act Article 1', 1951.
8 Japanese Diet, 'Act Article 8, paragraph 1', 1951.
9 Shiozaki, 復興 〈災害〉, 9
10 Suzuki et al., 'Fund Distribution and Multi-stakeholder Engagement in the Housing Recovery Programs after Large Scale Disaster', 2019.
11 Shiozaki, 復興 〈災害〉, 159
12 Onoda et al., 'Implementation of Recovery Plan and Organization Structure of Municipalities', 2015.; Tsukuda et al., 'The Decision Factors of the Housing Recovery Opinions and the Influence of Temporary Living Conditions after Large-scale Disaster', 2019.
13 Miyagi Prefecture, '宮城県災害公営住宅整備指針＜ガイドライン＞', 2012.

Bibliography

Davis, I. and Alexander, D. *Recovery from Disaster.* London: Routledge, 2016.

Fire and Disaster Management Agency. '平成23年（2011年）東北地方太平洋沖地震（東日本大震災）について ver. 160', 10 March 2020. Accessed 15 September 2020. https://www.fdma.go.jp/disaster/higashinihon/items/160.pdf

Japanese Diet. Public Housing Act, 1951.

Matsumoto, E. and Ubaura, M. 'A study on designation disaster hazard areas after the Great East Japan Earthquake'. *Journal of the City Planning Institute of Japan*, 50(3) (2015): 1273–1280. (In Japanese) https://doi.org/10.11361/journalcpij.50.1273

Miyagi Prefecture. '宮城県災害公営住宅整備指針＜ガイドライン＞', 18 July 2012. Accessed 15 September 2020. https://www.pref.miyagi.jp/site/ej-earthquake/guidline.html

Onoda, Y., Kato, Y. and Tsukuda, H. 'Implementation of recovery plan and organization structure of municipalities: on the reconstruction procedures in Miyagi prefecture from the Great East Japan Earthquake'. *Journal of Architecture and Planning (Transactions of AIJ),* 80(717) (2015): 2523–2531. (In Japanese) https://doi.org/10.3130/aija.80.2523

Onoda, Y., Tsukuda, H. and Suzuki, S. Complexities and difficulties behind the implementation of reconstruction plans after the Great East Japan Earthquake and Tsunami of March 2011. In *The 2011 Japan Earthquake and Tsunami: Reconstruction and Restoration – Insights and Assessment after 5 years*, edited by Vicente Santiago-Fandino, Shinji Sato, Norio Maki and Kanako Iuchi, 3–20. Berlin: Springer, 2017. https://doi.org/10.1007/978-3-319-58691-5_1

Onoda, Y., Sekine, M. and Tsukuda, H. Relationships between work-loads and organizational structure of municipalities in implementing housing reconstruction program after largescale disasters: reconstruction projects in Miyagi and Iwate Prefecture from the Great East Japan Earthquake. *Journal of Architecture and Planning (Transactions of AIJ),* 86(781)(2021): 849–858. (In Japanese) https://doi.org/10.3130/aija.86.849

Reconstruction Agency. '住まいの復興工程表 at March 2020', 6 June 2020. Accessed 15 September 2020. https://www.reconstruction.go.jp/topics/main-cat1/sub-cat1-12/20200603112502.html

Shiozaki, Y. *復興〈災害〉: 阪神·淡路大震災と東日本大震災.*. Tokyo: Iwanami Shoten Publisher, 2014. (In Japanese)

Suzuki, S., Onoda, Y. and Tsukuda, H. 'Fund distribution and multi-stakeholder engagement in the housing recovery programs after large scale disaster: the case of the Great East Japan Earthquake, Hurricane Katrina, and Indian Ocean Tsunami'. *Journal of Architecture and Planning (Transactions of AIJ),* 84(758) (2019): 925–933. (In Japanese) https://doi.org/10.3130/aija.84.925

Tsukuda, H., Yamanobe, K. and Onoda, Y. 'A study on the change of housing recovery opinions based on public housing registration data'. *Journal of Architecture and Planning (Transactions of AIJ),* 82(731) (2017): 1–9. (In Japanese) https://doi.org/10.3130/aija.82.1

Tsukuda, H., Yokota, S. and Onoda, Y. 'The decision factors of the housing recovery opinions and the influence of temporary living conditions after large-scale disaster: case study on Shichigahama town, Miyagi'. *Journal of Architecture and Planning (Transactions of AIJ),* 84(756) (2019): 311–321. (in Japanese) https://doi.org/10.3130/aija.84.311

Tsukuda, H., Yan, S. and Onoda, Y. 'Support system for the victims moving from temporary to permanent housing after great disasters – case study of Ishinomaki city, Miyagi prefecture'. *Summaries of technical papers of annual meeting of AIJ* (2018): 111–114. (In Japanese).

Tsukuda, H., Hasegawa, K. and Onoda, Y. 'A study on the recovery of local community after a large disaster: case study of damaged areas by the Great East Japan Earthquake in Shichigahama town, Miyagi prefecture'. *Journal of Architecture and Planning (Transactions of AIJ),* 86(781) (2021): 859–868. (In Japanese) https://doi.org/10.3130/aija.86.859

4

Invisible hands: institutional resilience and tsunami risk
The case of Kochi City in Japan

Sarunwit Promsaka Na Sakonnakron,
Paola Rizzi and Satoshi Otsuki

Disasters often highlight weaknesses in social agents and their errors in considering potential natural hazards in their territories. The interconnection between physical features and social components is a determinant factor in urban resilience and vulnerability to natural hazards. This chapter aims to highlight the importance of pre-disaster planning for social learning about how to cope with hazards. The city of Kochi in Japan is used to illustrate how this pre-disaster planning and social learning can increase urban resilience and decrease vulnerability. Kochi is one of the locations in Japan most prone to tsunamis and earthquakes. To explore urban resilience, our study discusses a set of theoretical characteristics of resilient cities, enriched by in-depth interviews and direct observation of relevant sites in Kochi. The qualitative data were then supported by the analysis of spatial policy formation. The study found that national social agents have developed the standards for disaster risk awareness through written laws and policies and unwritten commitments. Local communities in Kochi were also active in performing disaster preparedness activities.

Mapping risk and urban resilience in Japan

The principle of disaster vulnerability and resilience was widely articulated a few decades ago and those theories were translated into practice in the Hyogo Framework of 2005 and UNISDR's 2017 Sendai Framework. These focus not just on physical infrastructure and readiness, but incorporate indicators related to social aspects such as economic and institutional resilience and social capital. Nevertheless, there is no 'one-size-fits-all'. Joerin and Shaw[1] emphasise that the indicators for urban resilience to disaster at different city-regional spatial levels, even within the same country, will need to be readjusted. Various hazards may also require different indicators and criteria to assess urban resilience.[2] Yet, the attempt to assess urban resilience to disaster becomes paradoxical when a single set of indicators cannot define it precisely.

This chapter is partially based on data collected for the first author's dissertation[3] in 2013, with additional up-to-date data collected for this chapter in 2021. We address two distinct questions to help understand the institutional dimension of urban resilience: how is the concept of disaster risk management translated into urban planning standards in the context of Kochi? And how well is disaster risk communicated through urban policies and preparedness in risk management?

Kochi's spatial policy formulation for disaster resilience: tsunami risk

All hazards impact both physical structure and human life. A less severe hazard may not lead to significant changes in terms of social structure and risk management policies, while one of greater severity – such as a tsunami – potentially affects extensive areas and creates thousands of victims, affecting people's perception of risk. Risk awareness triggers how people conduct disaster precautionary measures and formulate risk management policies. Therefore, severe disasters can be considered a potential driving force behind greater social response to risk management strategies, which in turn enhances the urban resilience of the affected area.

The city of Kochi, in the Kochi prefecture, western Japan, is located along the Pacific coast, which is at risk from Nankai Trough tsunamis. The city is expected to face a series of Nankai Earthquakes – tsunami earthquakes which strike repeatedly every 100–150 years. The latest, known as the Showa-Era Nankai Earthquake, was on 21 December 1946. The new urban development of Kochi is concentrated on the river delta of the Kochi coast, on flat land just a few metres above sea level. The 2021 population census counted over 323,000 people living in Kochi, double the population of 1946.

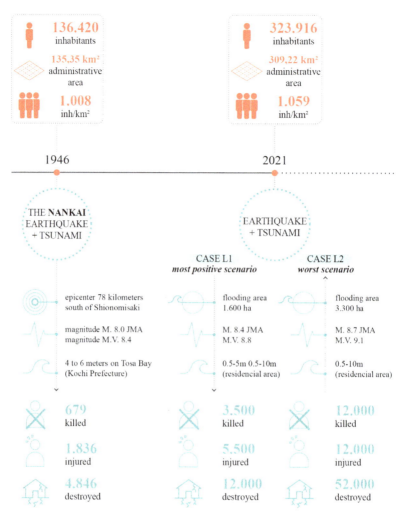

Figure 4.1 Nankai Earthquake and Kochi city: the effects in 1946 and the forecast of effects of next Nankai. Sources: authors. Graphic by Irene Friggia.

The urban density is now greater, which implies that future earthquakes with tsunami waves would have a more significant impact than previous ones. The municipality puts considerable effort into risk management through physical infrastructure and through social measures to raise risk awareness and capability to handle hazards. Local authorities are well aware of the risk, their precautionary measures are perceived as well-prepared risk management by the public, but they have not appraised what needs to be improved.

Japanese national regulations for spatial disaster resilience

One of the foundations of being resilient is the mindset of people and society. Japanese spatial policy formation and enactment cultivates risk awareness and embeds written laws in daily practices. Japan's environmental and disaster concerns have been triggered by the country's rapid urbanisation since the Second World War (Figure 4.2).

Figure 4.2 The development a of national spatial planning and disaster management system in Japan after World War II. Source: authors. Graphic by Irene Friggia.

The Comprehensive National Land Development Act of 1950 stimulated the ideology of spatial planning combined with risk awareness. This conceptualisation of risk translated into policies such as the National Spatial Planning Act of 1950, and the Basic Act for National Resilience Contributing to Preventing and Mitigating Disasters for Developing Resilience in the Lives of the Citizenry.[4] These policies influence social risk awareness and foster spatial precautionary measures such as hazard zoning, vulnerability assessment and the Community Disaster Management Plan (CDMP). The above laws together with the Basic Act for National Resilience of 2013, enable local authorities to designate disaster risk zones in order to limit urban expansion in disaster-prone areas. They also allow precautionary spatial policy using Urban Development Projects for reconstruction of disaster-affected urban areas (Figure 4.3).

Japan's City Planning Act divides urban intervention projects into two types: mega urban facilities and urban development projects. Mega urban facilities and utilities are improved through development plans (Article 11) which are interrelated with other acts, such as the Road Law

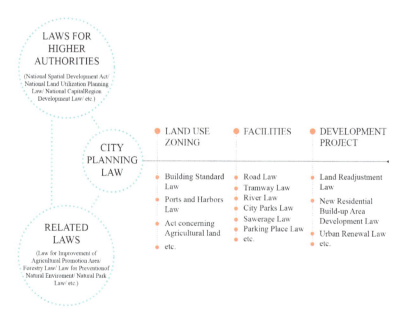

Figure 4.3 Structural process of the spatial planning system in Japan. Source: Introduction of Urban Land Use Planning System in Japan, City Bureau, Japanese Ministry of Land, Infrastructure and Transport (2003). Graphic by Irene Friggia.

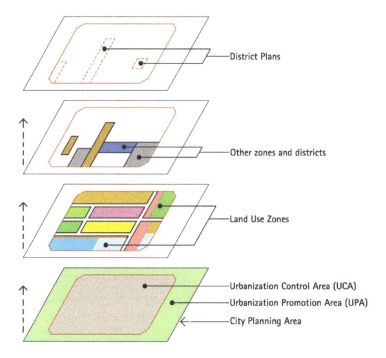

Figure 4.4 Concept of urban land use planning. Source: Introduction of Urban Land Use Planning System in Japan, City Bureau, Japanese Ministry of Land, Infrastructure and Transport (2003).

and City Parks Law. Land readjustment and disaster-prevention zones fall under Urban Development Projects (Article 12).

To define city planning boundaries, the Japanese government applied land use regulations in combination with classification techniques. In disaster recovery, the affected areas within a city planning boundary, or City Planning Areas, can be defined as promotion districts (Figure 4.4) under a district plan which allows urban intervention projects for disaster prevention and recovery.

These measures allow the allocation of financial and human resources to restore both physical and social dimensions. Moreover, Japan's City Planning Law allows local municipalities to bundle disaster risk mitigation and prevention measures through a designation of disaster-prevention districts or disaster-prevention block. With risk awareness shaped by policy, the country's social and cultural milieu results in its society learning to live with precautionary measures to manage the risk of potential natural disasters.

Intangible resilience: the case study of Kochi

There are two major approaches to developing indicators to assess the institutional dimension of urban resilience to disaster. The first approach is quantitative, using statistical data to measure and compare the urban resilience of different spatial areas. For example, Cutter and other authors[5] propose comparing urban–rural resilience quantitatively, using institutional resilience indicators such as average budget spending on mitigation projects and disaster aid experience. The drawback of this approach is that it justifies resilience using historical data rather than reflecting on the real situation. Joerin and Shaw[1] developed the Climate Disaster Resilience Index (CDRI) to assess 15 cities in the Asian region as pilot projects, but highlighted the lack of secondary data as a challenge. Statistical data are insufficient to reflect communities' views on urban resilience.

We applied a qualitative approach. A set of resilience key performances in this study was developed from the model of the US Indian Ocean Tsunami Warning System Program[6] and Twigg.[7] The characteristics of a disaster-resilient community developed by Twigg are regarded as a base concept to identify governance resilience at policy formulation level (Figure 4.5). The guidebook of the US Indian Ocean Tsunami Warning System Program was used to provide the specifics of institutional spatial policy formation. We decided to integrate these works to develop a new set of variables of institutional resilience.

This set was used to create semi-structured interview questions. Using the interpretive research approach, we aimed to clarify the aspect of instructional resilience towards tsunamis and to explore future priorities. Between November 2013 and January 2014, the research team conducted two rounds of direct observation at the site and collected field notes during both visits. A prior interview observation aimed at understanding the physical setting of the city and the situation that we were exploring and assessing helped to identify crucial questions for the interview. We then conducted another round of observation at the sites referred to by the participants. While coding the interviews, the field notes taken during the site observation helped us to make sense of each interview. In December 2013, six Kochi local government officers were purposively selected as the participants for the in-depth interviews: two in the local urban planning department, one in the department of infrastructure planning, one in community planning and two specialists in disaster risk management (Figure 4.6). Aware that interviews alone may not be enough to understand urban resilience, we incorporated literature reviews, GIS data and direct observation.

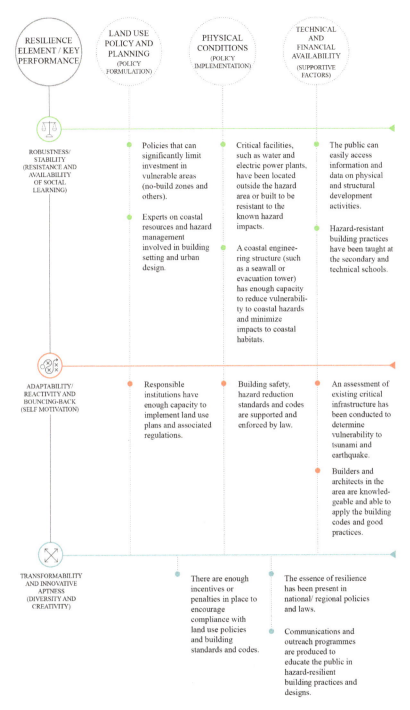

Figure 4.5 Resilience schemes and key performance indicators.

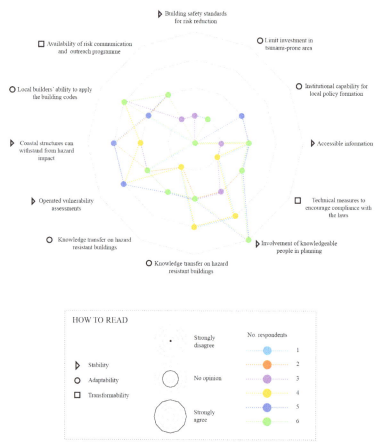

Figure 4.6 Results of in-depth interview of local government officers of Kochi. Source: Sarunwit Promsaka N.S., 2015. Graphic by Irene Friggia.

We then applied a thematic analysis coupled with the conceptual framework of urban resilience to disaster.[8, 9,10] The interviews were transcribed in Japanese and translated into English. The English transcriptions were analysed using two rounds of coding; the first to summarise and describe excerpts, and the second based on a deductive approach using a coding frame, which was predefined in our model of resilience schemes illustrated in Figure 4.5. This model interprets urban resilience as a dynamic state that determines how well a society is able to cope and adapt and its ability to facilitate the disaster-restoration process (Figure 4.7). It highlights a need to focus on effective risk communication to nurture and enhance social learning.

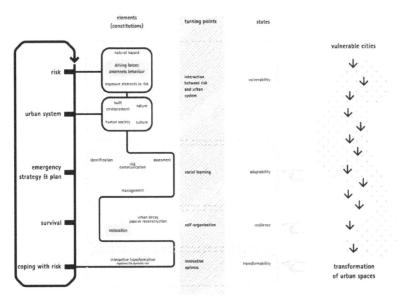

Figure 4.7 A conceptual model of urban resilience transformation. Source: Sarunwit Promsaka N.S., Paola Rizzi. Graphic by Lorenzo Cotti.

This means cultivating risk awareness, encouraging people to take precautionary measures for their household and to acquire the skills and knowledge to self-organise in order to react to disaster in a timely manner. Effective risk communication and the ability to self-organise are fundamental to increasing disaster preparedness and to transforming a vulnerable city into a resilient city.

Exploring institutional resilience

The findings of the in-depth interviews were divided into three main themes: creating urban stability; adaptability and capability to bounce back and transformability (Figure 4.8).

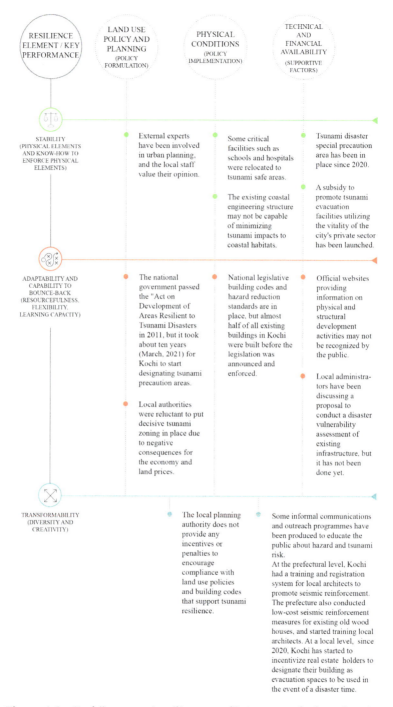

Figure 4.8 Kochi's tsunami resilience profile in terms of urban planning.

Capability to create urban stability

The interviewees are experts in management related to disaster resilience. The city has specialists in civil engineering to construct resilient buildings (structural measures) and in disaster risk management and communication (non-structural measures). Their knowledge is transferred into spatial policy and in the creation of building codes for tsunami-prone areas. They legislate for the prefectural urban planning council[11] and engage in informal consultation with the local urban planning section and seek input from academic experts in the fields of engineering, urban planning and disaster management. These structural risk mitigation and prevention measures are the foundation for stability.

In 2013, some critical facilities like power plants, schools and hospitals were still located in highly tsunami-prone areas in Kochi. Half of the respondents realised this, with one pointing out that 'the area classification of the tsunami-prone coastal zone (UCA: Urban Control Area) was changed a while ago due to the expanded urban fringe and improved infrastructure for disaster prevention'. This means that the city is more exposed to risk due to increased capability and unavoidable urban expansion. Surprisingly, the data from the Geographic Information System (GIS) for 2013 showed that more than half of the critical infrastructures in the tsunami-prone areas were built after the tsunami of 1946. This reflects a dangerous loss of memory of the impact of the tsunami and shows that urban planning measures repeatedly fail to manage potential risk. As a result of the interview, the local authority has suggested a relocation plan for vulnerable schools on a priority basis. The relocation plan can be granted through two types of governmental resources: the grant for infrastructure development – 社会資本整備総合交付金 – or the grant for disaster protection – 防災安全交付金. In 2020, the city started to relocate Kochi's Red Cross Hospital to safer locations, while critical facilities such as the city hall and library were structurally reinforced to withstand tsunami impact and serve as evacuation buildings and emergency shelters. This decision has been criticised by scholars and citizens worried about the possible damage to life and the economy in the event of a tsunami. A proposal to build a billion-yen tidal embankment in the same area was considered too costly by the interviewees. One pointed out that 'building a tidal embankment would decrease the risk of tsunami effectively, but would also create eye-pollution to the beautiful marine scenery of Kochi's coast'. Two believe that the current emergency infrastructure, such as 'escape towers' to provide emergency refuge, is enough to facilitate tsunami evacuation. Two others expressed doubts about the current coastal structure. One, from the department of urban planning, said:

> the existing infrastructure is not enough to prevent a second disaster (as a consequence of the natural disaster). For example the lack of an elevated road or a road that is raised onto an embankment might limit the ability to distribute disaster relief to tsunami victims when the Tohoku earthquake occurs.

After our interviews, the Kochi–Nankoku Road, bridging the airport and the city, was built to serve as a tsunami escape and emergency logistic road. Furthermore, a ¥60 billion triple-protection embankment along the Urado Bay was started in 2018 with a projected conclusion in 2031.[12]

Our experience confirmed that, even if there are legislative options for reducing risk, it takes time for local authorities to adopt national and prefectural opportunities. Innumerable debates have arisen from local government efforts to balance precautionary measures to support the existing urban areas with the huge investment in tsunami embankments.

Adaptability and resilience initiatives

In Japan there are two fundamental spatial regulations: the National Spatial Planning Act and the City Planning Act. They provide a variety of platforms to implement spatial and urban planning measures for disaster prevention and mitigation and enable the prefectural government to designate disaster recovery zones to facilitate the recovery process of affected areas. In addition, thanks to the 2011 Act on the Development of Tsunami-resilient Communities, comprehensive plans and restricted developments were proposed for tsunami-prone areas at a national level.[13] Yet, in 2013 we found hardly any spatial regulation or land use ordinance for Kochi – either to limit investment in highly tsunami-prone areas or to promote resilience. There has been expansion in the landslide-prone northern area of the city and in the coastal area, and local governments were reluctant to designate a risk area in their spatial regulation as this would impact negatively on the economy and land development. As a result, most interviewees pointed out that the local authority 'might' be incapable of limiting investment in these vulnerable areas. However, in March 2021, the Kochi prefecture and city government set up a working group on land classification to designate[14] precautionary areas with two severity levels: a 'yellow zone or tsunami precaution zone' and an 'orange zone or tsunami special precaution zone', a courageous move that will guide future decisions. The interviews shockingly reported that it was unclear whether building safety code and hazard reduction standards were effectively enforced. GIS data of 2013 revealed that nearly 49 per cent of buildings in the Kochi Planning Area were built before the 1981 enactment of Shin-taishin (the New Earthquake Resistant Building Standard). These include wooden houses and concrete offices that may not resist seismic shock, resulting in potential collapses and road blockages during evacuation. Surprisingly, the average rate of such buildings within the Urban Promotion Area (UPA) – where development is encouraged – was higher than in the Urban Control Area (UCA), even though UPAs tend to be more severely affected by earthquakes than UCAs. The larger the physical and economic losses, the more protracted and costly the recovery process will be. An interviewee from the risk management section pointed out that 'Kochi's independent revenue source is relatively small; the city undeniably depends on disaster financial relief from the central government'.

Apart from spatial regulation and ordinances, the skills to facilitate disaster recovery and nurture victims to handle devastating losses become the dominant factor determining resilience – the ability to bounce back. The interviewee from the risk management section shared his experience of the previous disaster:

> Having been involved in disaster prevention activity for almost 10 years, I have realised that the greatest challenge in recovery time is to handle the overwhelming demands of disaster victims who temporarily reside in the shelter-in-place during the recovery process. And those demands change rapidly over time. But surprisingly, what people appreciate is just the kindness of sharing. Once I shared imo-kempi (Japanese sweet snack and vegetable juice).

He pointed out that the ability of local staff to guide disaster victims is necessary to facilitate the recovery process: 'Citizens shall learn how to evacuate safely in a timely manner' while the elderly may need support from their neighbours. In Kochi, the government provides three disaster communication programmes:

1) A Bousaihito-zukurijuku (crash course) programme to educate community leaders and citizens about disaster management. The city government has also promoted the Community Disaster Management Plan (CDMP), supported by the Disaster

Countermeasures Basic Law in June 2013 and the Basic Act on Disaster Management. This led to the formation of the community-based disaster management plan, which was later included in the Kochi City Local Disaster Management Plan, based on the approval of the municipal disaster prevention committee.

2) Since 2017 all municipalities encourage individual communities to make their own community-based shelter management plan and stimulate discussion about risk. This plan covers the whole spectrum of needs, including the elderly or those with different abilities or inabilities.

3) The evacuation planning and route are distributed to the residents in the form of a booklet, with the digital copy uploaded to the website.[15] The city also designed an app – 高知県防災アプリ.

In addition, a programme on 'comprehensive disaster prevention promotion' – 都市防災総合推進事業 – includes various prevention and mitigation activities, such as designing evacuation routes, towers along the coastline, warehouses for emergency goods and outreach programmes for risk communication. This illustrates the wealth of responses in Kochi to the idea of 'good governance' or spatially enabled government (SEG).[16] People are made aware of risk via various channels: web portal, website, a mobile application (Figure 4.9) – unfortunately most are in Japanese so are difficult for non-Japanese speakers to understand.

Figure 4.9 The urban development category in the web portal of Kochi City. Source: Kochi City web. Graphic by Irene Friggia.

Risk and urban transformability

The adaptability of local planning authorities is reflected in the regulations, in activities for enhancing law enforcement and in educating toward hazard-resilient building practices. Yet, half of the respondents were unsure about the incentives or penalties to encourage compliance with land use and building standards policies and codes. Nevertheless, the market encourages developers to comply with building standards as there is increasing demand for hazard-resistant properties, which also attract higher prices.

Although Kochi prefecture and city governments have produced communications and outreach programmes to raise awareness, we found that there is a need for more technical education. The prefecture has good practices in place for building reinforcement and training for local architecture, including low-cost seismic reinforcement measures for vulnerable buildings. The city launched a campaign called 'subsidy for the project to promote tsunami evacuation facilities utilizing the vitality of the city's private sector' – 高知市民間活力活用津波避難施設整備促進事業費補助金 – to incentivise real estate holders to transform their properties into designated evacuation buildings and shelters in case of disaster. The Nankai Earthquakes Countermeasures Special Act was enacted in 2013, legislating that the national government would partially bear the cost for relocating buildings from low to high places. As of 2019, this fund was utilised to create 1,445 tsunami evacuation places and routes, 111 evacuation towers, and one shelter.[17] Critical information, such as signage for tsunami evacuation, uses a prefectural universal design as a symbolic representation of risk communication, however this is being replaced by the national signs to create uniformity and support nationwide recognition.

Bridging a gap

A model of spatial planning for disaster resilience

Japanese policy formation at national and prefectural levels serves as a resilience enabler at a local level. It also supports spatial policy and social outreach communication programmes to make precautionary spatial practices and raise knowledge and awareness among residents and contractors. The use of resilience schemes and key performance indicators (Figure 4.6 and Figure 4.8) helps us understand the efforts to build urban resilience to tsunamis at individual and institutional levels. The cross-sectional data of 2013 and 2021 shows that the efforts of multilevel stakeholders over the years are always accompanied by heated debates on disaster measures. These question potential future directions for Kochi, including enhancing risk communication, relocation plans, building reinforcement, or investing in the tidal embankment to protect the coastal zones. Japanese society also has several social and collective movements on CDMP yet they do not cooperate, while single individuals fear they may be incapable of coping with an enormous Nankai Trough tsunami. We argue here that what needs to be done is to improve social learning and multisectoral cooperation.

1) Social learning improvement: Existing risk communication programmes may be adequate but, in practice, few precautionary measures are aimed at individuals. New housing projects are still being developed in tsunami-prone areas, creating the need to construct thousands of evacuation towers along the coastal area. The absence of individually targeted measures hinders the progress of urban resilience. If personal motivation is not enough, financial incentives and technical support will be needed to facilitate this social transformation towards resilience.

2) Multisectoral cooperation: The initiatives of the Kochi prefecture and city on tsunami precaution and warning zones in 2021 took over 10 years to realise after the 2011 enactment of the national Act on Development of Areas Resilient to Tsunami Disasters. This reflects the limited ability of local authorities to adopt national decisions in a timely manner. In the meantime, Kochi prefecture and city utilised their own resources and involved local experts in a spatial planning and vulnerability assessment to realise its designation criteria for a tsunami warning area – 高知県津波災害警戒区域等の指定基準.

These arguments remind us that urban resilience is not just a technicality or protocol, but a collaboration of different stakeholders. However, although Kochi local authorities put efforts into disaster resilience, their fear of social resistance to the enforcement of a tsunami risk zone made them hesitant. The transformation process took time and involved different levels of decision-making and consultation. Without this cross-sectional study between 2013 and 2021, we would have been unable to capture this dynamic process of the city transforming itself to become more resilient. The lessons learnt from Kochi helped us devise a model of spatial planning for disaster resilience (Figure 4.10).

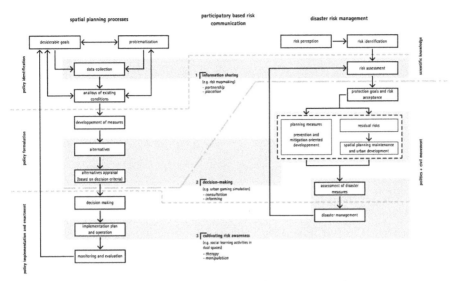

Figure 4.10 A model of spatial planning for disaster resilience. Source: Sarunwit Promsaka N.S., Paola Rizzi. Graphic by Lorenzo Cotti.

In our model, the success of urban planning for tsunami resilience requires greater cross-sectional coordination between spatial policy formulation, urban planning and risk management sectors. The first step is to establish this coordination by promoting a programme of social learning that enables local staff to interpret and analyse data and information to synthesise a comprehensive spatial plan and policies for tsunami resilience. The next step is to think about communications and outreach programmes to educate the public in implementing those policies and plans. Existing neighbourhood associations for disaster risk management should be partially subsidised by the government and by local residents. The national government should enable platforms in which these associations can become part of local spatial planning processes, as they have with local disaster risk management. Engaging them can also alleviate the burden of data collection for the spatial planning process, enhance public understanding and improve the effectiveness of spatial policy enactment.

Conclusions

In this chapter we examined spatial planning for tsunami resilience through three characteristics of resilient systems:

1) the stability and the transformability of physical infrastructure
2) institutional capabilities to self-organise and bounce back
3) social learning capabilities to create adaptive measures for coping with risk.

The study found that despite legislative platforms for integrating risk-mitigation measures into spatial planning, local authorities in Kochi were not sufficiently capable of providing comprehensive and timely integration. Although there were community efforts to build a disaster-resilient city, these were not successfully translated into urban planning. A bundle of spatial policies and plans is not enough to keep residents safe: technical knowledge, skilled professionals and community involvement are also needed. Our model of spatial planning for tsunami resilience highlights the essential role of risk communication and social learning in bridging links between the spatial planning process and risk management procedures. This can serve as a civil platform for the integration of planning and risk management.

The case of Kochi suggests that the journey towards urban resilience involves social learning and self-motivation. Fundamental aspects include individual behaviours and the ever-evolving institutional resilience of the various cross-sectional authorities. We have mentioned that resilience is a dynamic state in an urban system – the system's evolution could make it either more vulnerable or more resilient. This depends on how well institutions can adapt to the changing conditions pre-, during and post-disaster. We are aware that disaster risk management should not limit emergency response in the disaster recovery process. Our case study guides the way in which we explore urban resilience and suggests that a crucial component stems from the capability to initiate proactive measures in the pre-disaster phase. Institutions must provide spatial policies that stimulate the construction of tsunami-resistant buildings, avoid development in tsunami hazard areas and nurture learning environments that foster social risk-awareness at both collective and individual levels. Discussions around disaster resilience measures – which can be problematic due to the differing needs of different stakeholders – can be facilitated by a variety of participatory tools such as social gaming simulations and codesign of urban spaces based on the concept of cocreation architecture. The concept of disaster resilience is not limited to natural disaster, but it can also be applied to pandemic risk. We do not have to change the physical environment, but we need to transform the way it is used. This transformation requires the effective translation of an institutional dimension into social practices by integrating risk awareness in social norms.

Notes

1   Joerin, J. and Shaw, R. *Mapping climate and disaster resilience in cities*, 2011.
2   Sudmeier-Rieux, K., Nehren, U., Sandholz, S. and Doswald, N. *Disasters and Ecosystems, Resilience in a Changing Climate* – Source Book, 2019.
3   Promsaka Na Sakonnakron, S. 'Spatial Planning for Tsunami Resilience: A Case study of Kochi City, Japan', 2015.
4   Ministry of Justice, Japan. 'Basic Act for National Resilience Contributing to Preventing and Mitigating Disasters for Developing Resilience in the Lives of the Citizenry', 2014, Act No. 95 of December 11, 2013.
5   Cutter S.L., Ash K.D., Emrich C.T. 'Urban–Rural differences in disaster resilience', 2016.
6   U.S. Indian Ocean Tsunami Warning System Program. How Resilient Is Your Coastal Community?: *A Guide for Evaluating Coastal Community Resilience to Tsunamis and Other Hazards*, 2007 .
7   Twigg, J. 'Characteristics of a disaster-resilient community: a guidance note', 2009.
8   Promsaka Na Sakonnakron, S. 'Spatial Planning for Tsunami Resilience: A Case study of Kochi City, Japan', 2015.
9   Rizzi, P., Denti, B., Marcia, A., Promsaka Na Sakonnakron, S. 'Dual Space – Resilient Spaces: Risk Awareness and Responsibility', 2016.
10 Rizzi, P., D'Ascanio, F. and Di Lodovico, L. 'From fragile to resilient territories: the reconstruction after earthquakes in Central Italy', 2017.
11 Kochi Prefecture, 'City Planning of Kochi City 2013' *(高知市の都市計画 2013 in Japanese)*, 2013.
12 Kochi Prefecture 'Urado Bay Earthquake and Tsunami Countermeasures' *(浦戸湾の地震・津波対策(三重防護)*.
13 Koshimura, S. and Shuto, N. 'Response to the 2011 Great East Japan earthquake and tsunami disaster', 2015.
14 As described in the Designation criteria for Tsunami Warning Area.
    Kochi Prefecture. 'Designation Criteria for Tsunami Warning Area' (高知県津波災害警戒区域等の指定基準).
15 Kochi Prefecture, 'Disaster Map'.
16 Greiving, S. and Fleischhauer, M. 'Spatial planning response to natural and technological hazards', 2006.
17 Crisis Management Department, Kochi Prefecture, 'Nankai Trough Earthquake Countermeasures in Kochi Prefecture', 2019.

Bibliography

Adger, W.N. 'Vulnerability'. *Global Environmental Change*, 16(3) (2006): 268–281. Accessed 21 June 2021. http://www.gsdrc.org/go/display&type=Document&id=3922

Ando, S. 'City Planning System and the Environment in Japan (2006 Presentation)', Asian Urban Information Center of Kobe. Page no longer available http://www.auick.org/database/training/2006-1/PR/WS2006-1SAndo.pdf

Crisis Management Department, Kochi Prefecture. 'Nankai Trough Earthquake Countermeasures in Kochi Prefecture'. Accessed 21 June 2021. https://www.data.jma.go.jp/svd/eqev/data/nteq/symposium/02/fig/kouen_kochi_2.pdf

Cutter S.L., Ash K.D., Emrich C.T. 2016. Urban–rural differences in disaster resilience. *Annals of the 696 American Association of Geographers*, 106 (2016): 1236–1252.

Dávila, S., Ayala, J.G., Salazar, F. and Ruiz-Vélez, R. A conceptual framework for measuring the exposure to tsunamis of Puerto Rican coastal communities', *Proceedings of the 2014 Industrial and Systems Engineering Research Conference*, 2014.

Greivin S., Fleischhauer, M. and Lückenkötter, J. 'A methodology for an integrated risk assessment of spatially relevant hazards'. *Journal of Environmental Planning and Management*, 49(1) (2006):1–19. DOI: 10.1080/09640560500372800

Holling, C. 'Resilience and stability of ecological systems'. *Annual Review of Ecological System,* 4 (September 1973): 1–23. Accessed 16 June 2022. https://www.annualreviews.org/doi/abs/10.1146/annurev.es.04.110173.000245

IPCC. 'IPCC Fourth Assessment Report: Climate Change'. Intergovernmental Panel on Climate Change – 2007. Accessed 16 June 2022. https://www.ipcc.ch/assessment-report/ar4/

Kobayashi, Y., and Noda, T. 'The methods and approaches used in development planning in Japan'. UNESCO, 1987. Accessed 21 June 2021. http://unesdoc.unesco.org/images/0007/000721/072126EB.pdf

Kochi International Association. 'An information booklet for the international community in Kochi: Preparing for the Nankai Earthquake'. March 2008. http://www.kochi-kia.or.jp/earthquake/english/

Kochi Prefecture. 'Disaster map'. Accessed 21 June 2021. https://bousaimap.pref.kochi.lg.jp

Kochi Prefecture. 'City Planning of Kochi City 2013'高知市の都市計画 2013 (In Japanese). Kochi, 2013.

Kochi Prefecture. 'Urado Bay Earthquake and Tsunami Countermeasures' 浦戸湾の地震・津波対策 (三重防護) *Civil Engineering Department Port and Coast Division*, 2017. Accessed 21 June 2021. https://www.pref.kochi.lg.jp/soshiki/175001/files/2017030200056/file_2017324112337_1.pdf

Kochi Prefecture. 'Designation criteria for Tsunami Warning Area' (高知県津波災害警戒区域等の指定基準), *Nankai Trough Earthquake Countermeasures Division, Crisis Management Department, Kochi Prefecture* , 2021. https://www.pref.kochi.lg.jp/soshiki/010201/files/2021040600041/siteikizyun.pdf

Koshimura, S. and Shuto, N. 'Response to the 2011 Great East Japan earthquake and tsunami disaster'. *Philosophical Transactions of the Royal Society A: Mathematical, Physical and Engineering Sciences*, 373 (2015): 2053.

Kubo, T. 'National Policies for Japanese Cities'. Accessed 6 September 2012. http://blog.mipimworld.com/2012/09/national-policies-for-japanese-cities/

Joerin, J., and Shaw, R. 'Mapping climate and disaster resilience in cities'. In *Climate and Disaster Resilience in Cities*, edited by R. Shaw, and A. Sharma, 47–61. Bingley: Emerald, 2011.

Maguire, B. and Cartwright, S. *Assessing a Community's Capacity to Manage Change: A Resilience Approach to Social Assessment*. Canberra: Commonwealth, 2008.

McCormack, G. and Fieln, N. *The Emptiness of Japanese Affluence.* New York: Routledge, 2001.

McGranahan, G., Marcotullio, P., Bai, X., Balk, D., Braga, T., Douglas, I., Zlotnik, H. 'Urban systems'. In *Ecosystems and Human Well-being: Current State and Trends*, edited by R. Hassan, R. Scholes and N. Ash, 797–821. Washington, DC: Island Press, 2005.

Ministry of Justice, Japan. 'Basic Act for National Resilience Contributing to Preventing and Mitigating Disasters for Developing Resilience in the Lives of the Citizenry' Act No. 95 of December 11, 2013. Japanese Law Translation Database System 2014. http://www.japaneselawtranslation.go.jp/law/detail/?id=2879&vm=04&re=2

Ministry of Land, Infrastructure, Transport and Tourism, Japan. 'The 5th Comprehensive National Development Plan. National and Regional Planning' 2020. Accessed 21 June 2021. https://www.mlit.go.jp/english/nr-planning.html

Phillips, R. *Community Indicators.* American Planning Association, APA Planning Advisory Service, 2003.

Promsaka Na Sakonnakron, S., 'Spatial Planning for Tsunami Resilience: A Case study of Kochi City, Japan'. Doctoral, University of Sassari, Italy, 2015. https://core.ac.uk/download/pdf/33723635.pdf

Rizzi, P. Denti, B., Marcia, A., Promsaka Na Sakonnakron, S. 'Dual Spaces–Resilient Spaces: Risk Awareness and Responsibility', RRRC 2016, November 3–4, I Bucharest.

Rizzi, P., D'ascanio, F., Di Lodovico, L. 'From fragile to resilient territories: the reconstruction after earthquakes in Central Italy', Conference proceeding: *ISOCARP – Smart Communities – 53rd Annual Congress – Session 4: "Natural disaster mitigation"*, Portland, Oregon, 2017.

Sudmeier-Rieux, K., Nehren, U., Sandholz, S. and Doswald, N. *Disasters and Ecosystems, Resilience in a Changing Climate – Source Book*. Geneva, UNEP and Cologne: TH Köln – University of Applied Sciences, 2019.

Twigg, J. *Characteristics of a Disaster-resilient Community: A Guidance Note (version 2)*. Teddington, UK: DFID Disaster Risk Reduction NGO Interagency Group, 2009.

U.S. Indian Ocean Tsunami Warning System Program. *How Resilient Is Your Coastal Community? A Guide for Evaluating Coastal Community Resilience to Tsunamis and Other Hazards*. Bangkok, Thailand: USAID the United States Agency for International Development, 2007. Accessed 21 June 2021. http://www.preventionweb.net/files/2389_CCRGuidelowresatiq.pdf

UNISDR: United Nations Office for Disaster Risk Reduction. *Hyogo Framework for Action 2005–2015: Building the resilience of nations and communities to disasters*. ISRD International Strategy for Disaster Reduction, 2007. Accessed 21 June 2021. http://www.unisdr.org/files/1037_hyogoframeworkforactionenglish.pdf

World Economic Forum. *Building Resilience to Natural Disasters: A Framework for Private Sector Engagement*. Geneva: World Economic Forum, 2008.

5

L'Aquila: from old to new castles Rediscovering poles and networks to rebuild a community

Simonetta Ciranna and Patrizia Montuori

Introduction

L'Aquila is historically configured as a territorial city, founded by the grouping of the castles – 100 according to tradition – that dotted the basin on which it was built. In its continuous and painful constructions and reconstructions, necessitated by cyclic earthquakes, the city has always regenerated itself in its *locali* (the small areas of the city that relate to their founding castles) and in its four *quarti* (quarters), the administrative and urban fabric that goes back to its papal, Swabian and Angevin origins. The different urban sectors are connected by a regular road network and marked by squares, each distinguished by the presence of a church, a fountain and a noble palace. A distant symbol of the intimate relationship between L'Aquila, its inhabitants and the castles of its origin, this system and these poles constitute the tangible fabric of an urban aggregation and help create an intangible but strong sense of belonging together. The 2009 earthquake, which devastated the city, its hamlets and surrounding minor towns, dramatically interrupted the continuity of interactions and the profound relationship between city and territory and between city and inhabitants, many of whom moved to the so-called 'new towns' – new castles that dot the surroundings of L'Aquila and which are almost totally devoid of services and spaces for socialising, and devoid of autonomy from the ancient nucleus and urban centre of reference.

Today L'Aquila is gradually regaining its poles of aggregation by reconstructing buildings and public spaces and also recovering or

84 INVISIBLE RECONSTRUCTION

attributing a specific identity to each as cultural, administrative, scientific, religious and recreational centres. Some examples are: the MAXXI (National Museum of 21st Century Art) in Piazza Santa Maria di Paganica; the Regional Council Building and the *esedra* (exedra) of the Hemicycle – venues for political debate but also for musical events and fairs; San Bernardino with its stairway, the location of the jazz festival; the gardens of the castle with its small auditorium; and also the arcades and the Piazza del Duomo with their café entertainment venues. These events are examples of programmatic strategies, but also spontaneous processes that revive and recompose the material and immaterial, individual and social sense of the city community.

In tandem with these strategies and processes are the difficult and sporadic reconstruction operations of the communities of the smaller centres of the territory through the reappropriation of historical spaces and the creation of new poles of aggregation, such as the House of Culture in Onna, but also the temporary stability of the new towns. In these, even with the lack of services and socialisation spaces, the relationships between the inhabitants and the initiatives of the local associations form the intangible thread that seeks to mend the micro-communities.

Rethinking poles and networks in the old city[1]

In November 2010, Marcello Vittorini emphasised the urgency of reconstructing the city of L'Aquila starting from its historical centre 'with one fundamental priority: begin with the empty spaces, the squares and streets … the basic elements of the city and the life of its inhabitants' and, of these, for example focusing on Piazza grande and the Corso, owing to their central position and symbolic value.[2]

Vittorini was showing his familiarity with and deep attachment to his native city, as well as his convictions about it, understood 'not only as mere physical facts, but as a set of common spaces, the seats of communities, their social relations, their history, their capacity for self-governance'.[3]

From such an observation point, the system of spaces, squares and streets of L'Aquila constitutes an irreversible imprinting. It expresses the specificity of the city's founding process and its capacity for adjustment and resilience to reconstructions and transformations; adjustment and resilience resulting also from the destruction wrought by repeated earthquakes that have marked the story of the city, starting with the seismic swarm that began in December 1315 in the midst of the Anjevin building fervour.[4]

Figure 5.1 Map of L'Aquila by Pico Fonticulano, 1575. Biblioteca Provinciale dell'Aquila ms 57, 176r part of the *Breve descrittione di sette città illustri d'Italia di Messer Ieronimo Pico Fonticulano dell'Aquila,* Aquila: Giorgio Dagano e Compagni 1582 (critical edition: Centofanti 1996, 93).

The checkboard geometry underlying L'Aquila's *forma urbis* (urban structure) – an autocratic expression of planning design, whose metaphorical and representative summary is found in Fonticulano's map – has over the centuries played a connective role in the city's social and productive togetherness. Squares have been sharers and protagonists of the urban life of the city, from those of single *locali* to the public ones of the cathedral and market, of the Palazzo, of San Bernardino and the theatre, along with many others. A 'city of squares', as it is defined in a volume published in 1992,[5] the interpreters [the squares] 'of a polyphony, the multiple voices of an urban structure' revealing, through their architecture, social hierarchies and instances of representation, self-aggrandisement and the search for prestige.[6]

Such physical places are thus a synthesis of social structure and urban spatial articulation, symbolically identifying both ethical and civic values and social and environmental differentiation, from the popular to the merchants' square, from the aristocratic to the middle-class square.[7] A chorus of voices of squares – both intimate and reserved (those of *locali*), counterpointed by animated squares devoted to *capo quarto* (district churches) and, even more so, those hosting public buildings and functions. The symbolic and aggregative force of the latter assumes a particular urban relevance when located along or close to the city's *cardo* and *decumanus,* which intersect at the Quattro Cantoni (four cantons), at which point meet three – Santa Maria, Santa Giusta and San Pietro – of the four *quarti,* the districts into which the historical city was divided. From the fifteenth to the sixteenth century, these routes oriented urban development with the building of the church of the Osservanza di San Bernardino da Siena (at the extreme eastern end of the *decumanus*) and the Spanish fort (to the extreme north of the *cardo*).

Of these various *plateae,* or squares, some are outstanding for their ideological nature and identity – the squares of Santa Maria di Paganica, dominated by the sizeable district church located at the highest point of the city; that of San Francesco, the seat of civic power and also of a small market; and the Maggiore, the historic market square and spiritual centre, owing to the presence of the cathedral dedicated to Saints Massimo and Giorgio.

Figure 5.2 L'Aquila: the market square in a photo taken before the earthquake of 2009.

L'Aquila's urban building plan has seen transformations resulting from the destructive earthquake of 1703 and from renovations after the unification of Italy, when the city became the chief town of the Abruzzo region in the new national state. Such transformations invigorated the financial and dynamic nature of the east–west axis – Corso Federico II and Vittorio Emanuele II – where banks and buildings of the public administration arose behind the new porticos, a sign of the affluent nature of this elegant *passeggio*.[8] This path cuts through the city from its castle to the Giardini dell'Emiciclo, a key space for public recognition of social identity, an area for social gathering where one can enter, find and lose oneself in an individual or collective identity, recognise and be recognised. A space utilised and occupied in different ways throughout the day and week: by employees during the workday, by the youth for nightlife (that is, as a meeting place of university students), as well as by everyone for the rites of consumerism during the daytime.

Eleven years of rebuilding separate L'Aquila before the earthquake from today's city, where the skyline is still pierced by innumerable cranes, with difficulty reclaiming its own spaces in a context marked by profound socio-economic changes – visible even in the almost vanished sites of the banks along the Corso – and almost frozen in the past few months by the COVID-19 epidemic, the most recent social trauma, the impact of which on community forms and rites is still difficult to establish.

Figure 5.3 L'Aquila: the Corso on a day of '*youth movida*', before March 2009.

This last event leads to further reflections as to how the spaces of the rebuilt city, whether already there or prefigured, can accelerate the restart of community life, in an awareness that 'space is always full of presences which, albeit not *things*, occupy and define it with equal – or even greater – force than objects properly so-called'.[9] *Things* through which the binding force that has held the city together over the centuries can be recovered or attributed to the city's streets and squares.

A significant choice made in this direction was the setting up at L'Aquila of a branch of Rome's prestigious National Museum of 21st Century Art – MAXXI L'Aquila. It is located in Piazza Paganica in the eighteenth-century Palazzo Ardinghelli, damaged by the earthquake and restored with contributions by the Russian government.[10] The palazzo faces the superb bulk of the church of Santa Maria, still in its post-seismic state, in a 'condition of grandiose ruin', almost totally roofless after both the dome and barrel vault collapsed. Tackling the restoration of this great *lacuna*, both as a building and as an integral part of a stratified and inseparable ensemble of 'noble' and 'minor' buildings (from the fifteenth century to our own times), will be an exemplary opportunity 'to reflect on the concept of cultural heritage and on the possible choices that may derive from this very concept'[11] to restore a vital and relevant space in the city's urban matrix.

Figure 5.4 L'Aquila: Piazza Paganica in July 2020 – on the left is Palazzo Ardinghelli, location of MAXXI L'Aquila, on the right, the Santa Maria church. Photo: Francesco Giancola.

Other poles of aggregation have settled over the past decade in the network of empty spaces, streets and squares – a melting-pot of relationships. On the eastern stretch of the *decumanus* (Via Andrea Bafile, the continuation of Corso Principe Umberto), the civic essence of the area is being recovered with the ongoing restoration of Palazzo Margherita d'Austria, while the setting up of the Rettorato (Rector's office) in Palazzo Camponeschi and the restoration of the nearby Palazzetto dei Nobili vindicate the central notion – in a symbolic and spatial sense – of knowledge and its divulgation. Awareness of the role of culture as the lifeblood in the recovery of a city has gradually emerged in activities on the three terminals of the *cardo-decumanus* layout: the Emiciclo and the castle on the north–south route; San Bernardino, with its deep stairway; and the nearby National Theatre at the eastern terminal of the *decumanus*. Their architecture and the surrounding open spaces have become lively centres of cultural, stage and musical events, even at an international level. Such events have gradually taken over the new auditorium by Renzo Piano in the castle park; the steep stairway joining the parvis of the Osservanza church with Via di Fortebraccio, the historical medieval path connecting the basilica's Collemaggio to the Quattro Cantoni and the gardens and the Palazzo dell'Emiciclo, which were used for the Regional Exhibition in 1888 and, in the early twentieth century, became a target for urban expansion (Tian project 1917), and later for private speculation and development plans, with blocks of flats and houses invading part of the gardens included in the project.[12] Finally, the cathedral square, still private with its historical daily market, and the cathedral itself, which is still being restored, overlooked by the church of Santa Maria del Suffragio or delle Anima Sante, a symbol of the reconstruction after the earthquakes of 1703 and 2009.[13]

Figure 5.5 L'Aquila: the restored Palazzo dell'Emiciclo, now headquarters of Consiglio Regionale d'Abruzzo. Source: Wikipedia.

Figure 5.6 L'Aquila: Duomo square during one of the evening shows organised in July 2020 as part of the initiative Cantieri dell'Immaginario.

Still performing its historical role as a main arterial road is the *corso largo e stretto*, a unique promenade that binds the city together, running into various cul-de-sacs in the courtyards of noble mansions – some of which are occasionally used as backdrops for dance and musical events, book presentations and such like.

Figure 5.7 L'Aquila: the courtyard of Palazzo Carli Benedetti during a concert on the occasion of the presentation of a book, 26 May 2018. Photo: Carla Bartolomucci.

One example of creating a system of such historical array that it reconnects with new symbolic open spaces and public buildings is the redesign of the area occupied prior to 2009 by the hall of residence of the University of L'Aquila, destroyed by the earthquake with several young lives lost. In 2018, the area became the subject of a competition of ideas among the university's students. This competition has resulted in particularly interesting projects, capable of satisfying not only the need to remember and commemorate a 'painful vacuum', but also to bind together the 'urban and social fabric of a city marked by destruction and reconstruction', by proposing a solution conscious of the material and immaterial, historical and cultural values of its future.[14]

Figures 5.8 Design competition for a new students' home in L'Aquila, 2018. Winning project *La Duttilità è nella Memoria* – Ductility is in a Memory: Engineers D. Massimo, F. Gabriele, L. Micarelli, M. Paolucci. Source: Giancola 2019, 45, 54.

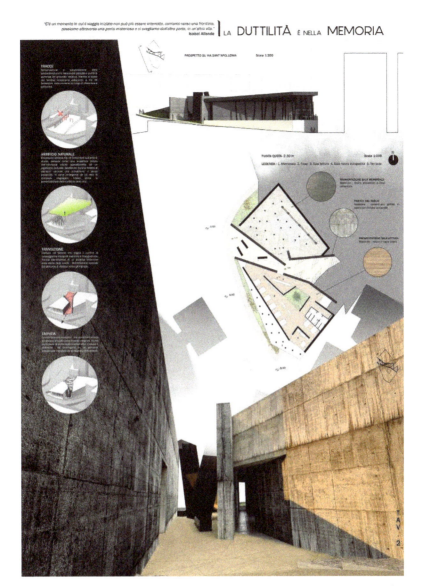

Figures 5.9 Design competition for a new students' home in L'Aquila, 2018. Winning project *La Duttilità è nella Memoria* – Ductility is in a Memory: Engineers D. Massimo, F. Gabriele, L. Micarelli, M. Paolucci. Source: Giancola 2019, 45, 54.

Restoring to L'Aquila its historical set of values, functions and social relations also means establishing it as the focus of its territorial network of over a hundred castles, the participants of its foundation and its continued rebirths.

Rebuilding a community from castles to new towns[15]

> For us who ignore the truth, all the facts are more terrible, especially those whose rarity increases our fear: phenomena familiar to us seem less impressive; unusual ones are more scary ... When terror is general, when cities collapse, peoples are crushed, the earth is shaken, why is it any wonder that the souls, abandoned in pain and fear, are lost?[16]

As Seneca observes, commenting on the earthquake that struck Campania in 62 AD, the effect on the human psyche of a traumatic and unknown event like an earthquake is certainly fear. However, it is also followed by the feeling of *freezing* due to the abrupt interruption of the relationship between people and their city which, unable to continue developing according to its previous model but still without any new perspective, remains suspended on a threshold between a before that no longer exists and an after that is all to be imagined.[17] If, however, following the total or partial destruction of an inhabited centre, the first thought, after assisting the population, is how to restore what has been destroyed, focusing only on material reconstruction one risks losing sight of the need to recover the identity of the places and the population. The deep transformation of areas affected by an earthquake is only the first important upheaval of the living space. It is followed by that, however shocking, of the reconstruction, which involves not only the physical structures, but a wider process of recognition of a place as your own home.[18]

Even before the earthquake of 6 April 2009, the most destructive in Italy in the twentieth century after the earthquakes of Messina (1908), Avezzano (1915), Irpinia (1980) and Friuli (1976), the municipal territory of L'Aquila, the ninth largest in Italy,[19] was very complex. In total, 49 hamlets rise around the city itself, the largest of which[20] are configured either as agglomerations in turn divided into small villages (such as Bagno, Roio and Sassa with Civita di Bagno, Bagno Grande and Piccolo, Roio Piano, Pagliare di Sassa, Sassa Scalo), or as more unified settlements with their own historical centres (such as Paganica, Coppito and Bazzano). Mostly deriving from the ancient castles that participated in the foundation of L'Aquila[21] in the thirteenth century, some of the hamlets were administratively merged with the city only in the twentieth century. After diverse historical events, in fact, the Grande Aquila project, promoted by Royal Decree no. 1,564 on 29 July 1927 by its then Mayor Adelchi Serena,[22] later Secretary of the National Fascist Party and Minister of Public Works in the Mussolini government, aimed to recreate political union between L'Aquila and its countryside, merging with the city eight municipalities of the district (Arischia, Bagno, Camarda, Lucoli, Paganica, Preturo, Roio, Sassa) and the hamlet of San Vittorino di Pizzoli.

This form of 'widespread city' which, historically, already characterised the territory of L'Aquila, was dramatically amplified after the earthquake with the construction of new scattered settlements intended to house the inhabitants, but totally devoid of the identity and autonomy of the ancient castles that founded the city. The reconstruction, in fact, was dealt with largely through the CASE (*Complessi Antisismici Sostenibili Ecocompatibili*) project, that is with the construction of sustainable and eco-compatible anti-seismic complexes[23] in the countryside surrounding L'Aquila – new towns for the earthquake victims of the Abruzzo capital and some of its hamlets. In addition, where CASE project constructions were not desirable or could not be erected, the municipalities of the rest of the seismic crater, but also in the L'Aquila area, also used single-storey MAP (*moduli abitativi provvisori*, or temporary housing modules),[24] potentially capable of being dismantled and located a short distance from some of the destroyed centres, including Onna, San Gregorio, Fossa, San Demetrio Ne' Vestini and Villa Sant'Angelo[25].

Figure 5.10 Onna, L'Aquila: one of the MAP temporary anti-seismic houses built just outside the historic centre. Source: Wikipedia.

This solution, in line with previous experiences in Friuli, Marche and Umbria, aimed to initiate an intermediate phase with temporary accommodation, allowing residents to closely follow the reconstruction of their respective villages and towns.

A counterpoint is the temporary stability of the CASE project, through which 4,449 apartments of various sizes have been built in 19 areas of the Aquila area, distributed across 185 three-storey buildings and using various prefabrication systems (wood, concrete, iron, plasterboard), resting on seismic-reinforced concrete plates, supported on metal pillars fixed to a foundation, also of reinforced concrete.[26]

These settlements were triumphantly baptised as new towns but were actually conceived as simple dormitory neighbourhoods, devoid of services, efficient connections and spaces of socialisation. They favoured an increase of anthropic pressure in areas with a prevalent agricultural intended use prior to the earthquake and, being up to 18 km distant from the city, and with 30 km between them, gave rise to an even more extended widespread city, which has necessitated modification of the pre-existing road system, the construction of new roads and the construction of urban services in previously rural contexts.[27]

Figure 5.11 View of the CASE in Bazzano in 2015. The buildings rest on seismic-reinforced concrete plates, supported on metal pillars fixed to a foundation, also of reinforced concrete. Photo: Vincenzo Di Florio.

The current fragmentation of the L'Aquila territory, in reality, cannot be totally attributed to the anti-seismic settlements, but to a longer urban planning process, which had already begun during fascism with the Grande Aquila project and the consequent construction of the new neighbourhoods outside the city walls. It then continued in the wake of the residential building boom of the 1950s and 1960s which, with the increase in the number of building plots and road layouts, has favoured the construction of shopping centres and sheds for artisans and industries scattered throughout the municipal area. However, after the earthquake, this fragmentation has dramatically increased and today (2021) the inhabitants of L'Aquila find themselves living in an intricate tangle of new neighbourhoods, hybrid spaces and entire centres still to be rebuilt. In the reconstruction of L'Aquila and, in particular, in the anonymous new towns that dot its territory today, the theme of *displacement* is therefore fully applicable, namely the loss of the sense of place 'dependent both on the features of a territory – which together constitute what is defined as the identity of the place – and on the connotation that these features take on in the experience of each individual'.[28] To counter it, where technocratic strategies have struggled to start or are seen to be ineffective, the inhabitants introduced small, everyday gestures such as providing clothes lines, children's games, planters and personal effects along the corridors, anonymous balconies and aseptic terraces of the CASE and MAP units; a timid attempt to adapt these spaces to their own needs and to make them feel their own. They have been accompanied by street art interventions,

Figure 5.12 Two of four wall paintings on the façades of the CASE complex in Bazzano made during the 2014 Re_acto Fest, a street art festival organised by the Re_acto Association with the 3e32 committee, sponsored by the Municipality of L'Aquila and the Order of Architects. Wall paintings: Mr.Thoms and v3erbo; photo: Semi Sotto La Pietra.

such as one in 2014 in the CASE complex of Bazzano, by the Reacto Association in collaboration with the 3e32 committee and with the patronage of the municipality of L'Aquila and the Ordine degli Architetti (Order of Architects), but above all thanks to the voluntary commitment of many young people.[29]

The anti-seismic complexes consequently host scenarios of daily life, with families, students, workers and associations trying to animate the residential units and the undifferentiated spaces between them. However, the absence of any real gathering points, services and an efficient public transport network to connect these satellites to the centre and surrounding urban areas prevents the inhabitants of L'Aquila from rebuilding a true urban community in the anonymous new towns where they have now lived for more than 10 years, but from which they escape daily in search of services or sociability offered by the spaces of the historic centre, partly already recovered.

The outcome of some of the MAPs built in areas adjacent to destroyed towns, such as Onna, is different. Originally part of the municipality of Paganica then, after its suppression in 1927, definitively aggregated to L'Aquila, Onna was a small settlement which, although not distinctive, represented a sound example of a rural village, still substantially intact before the 2009 earthquake. Built in 1,000 CE along the ancient routes connecting Paganica and Monticchio, it featured a compact core around a central square featuring the church of San Pietro

Figure 5.13 Onna, L'Aquila: 2010 view of the historic centre, completely destroyed by the 2009 earthquake. Source: Wikipedia.

Figure 5.14 Onna, L'Aquila: the church of San Pietro Apostolo after the restoration, completed in 2015. The reconstruction plan was promoted and co-financed by the German government in agreement with Onna's municipal administration and the Civil Protection. Source: Wikipedia.

Apostolo. A fine example of Abruzzo Romanesque, believed to be a Cistercian construction, the church was built in the twelfth century then remodelled after the 1461 earthquake, and again between the eighteenth and nineteenth centuries with a massive transformation of the interior in the late baroque style. Almost completely destroyed by the 2009 earthquake, together with the entire village, the church was subject to immediate restoration. This was completed in 2015 as part of a reconstruction plan promoted and co-financed by the German government as a gesture of solidarity and as partial reparation for the terrible massacre perpetrated at Onna by Nazi troops on 11 June 1944. This timely intervention, which also involved the University of Innsbruck, in partnership with the municipal administration of Onna and the Protezione Civile (Civil Protection) allowed a good part of the valuable and still recoverable building heritage to be saved, with a great deal of the initial work focused on protecting and cataloguing the building material. Also welcomed were the suggestions of local residents taking into account the architectural, historical and environmental relevance of the elements analysed.

As part of the same intervention, and welcomed by those residents who have chosen to live in MAPs a short distance from the destroyed centre, Casa Onna was built in 2010. This multifunctional building has a conference and exhibition room, meeting rooms for residents and associations, an internet point, a foyer and more. It is located at the entrance to the village as a new symbolic portal for the small settlement being rebuilt and a reference point for its inhabitants. Also recovered by the project are several symbolic elements of village history and rural identity: the drinking trough, the stone wall built by one of the young victims of the earthquake and a large existing tree which is visible from every point of the town.[30]

Today (2021), compared to the 94 aseismic houses assigned to the inhabitants of Onna, just four or five *aggregati* (blocks consisting of several historic buildings) have been rebuilt out of a total of 21 when work began. Only one family of the almost one hundred who lived in the historic centre has returned to their home, demolished and then rebuilt, with a delay in reconstruction that is common to almost all the historic centres of the hamlets of L'Aquila. Casa Onna, however, remains a positive example and a very active sociocultural reality, partly thanks to the Onna Onlus Association, created in 2009 to support the population during the reconstruction, not only materially but also – and above all – socially; a small but significant step in the intangible reconstruction of the identity of the village and its community.

Figure 5.15 Onna, L'Aquila: Onna, L'Aquila. Casa Onna, the multifunctional building completed in 2010 at the entrance of the village – a reference point for its inhabitants. Source: Onna Onlus.

Notes

1   The author of this section is Simonetta Ciranna.
2   Vittorini, 'Un archivio per il territorio', 47. The text – translated by the author – is taken from a speech by the author at the conference 'Gli archivi per l'urbanistica e per la ricostruzione', Italia Nostra per l'Abruzzo, 19 November 2010. In Italian: 'Ma con una fondamentale priorità: partire dai vuoti, dalle piazze e dalle strade. In sostanza dai luoghi centrali, elementi fondamentali della città e della vita dei suoi cittadini'.
3   Ivi, 48. In Italian: 'non solo come semplici fatti fisici, ma come insieme di spazi collettivi, sede delle comunità, delle loro relazioni sociali, della loro storia, della loro capacità di autogoverno'.
4   Berardi, 'Prestigio e potere nella fondazione e nelle ricostruzioni medievali', 2011.
5   *L'Aquila città di piazze. Spazi urbani e tecniche costruttive*. Ciranna Simonetta. 'Vie e piazze dell'Aquila tra storia, resilienza e reinvenzione'. Montuori, Patrizia. 'Camminando per la città'.
6   Conforti, 'Aquila, città delle piazze', 17–19 (quotation translated by the author).
7   Colapietra, 'Società civile e struttura urbana nella città d'antico regime'.
8   Ciranna, 'L'architettura del potere: il rafforzamento del Corso Vittorio Emanuele II e Federico II tra XIX e XX secolo', 2011.
9   De Matteis, *Vita nello spazio. Sull'esperienza affettiva dell'architettura*, 41. Quotation translated by the author.
10 Due to the pandemic, the opening of this prestigious location was postponed to May 2021. See https://maxxilaquila.art.
11 Bartolomucci, Ciranna, 'Santa Maria Paganica a L'Aquila: la memoria e il futuro', 2019, 45 (quotation translated by the author, in Italian: 'per riflettere sul concetto di eredità culturale e sulle possibili scelte che ne derivano').
12 Montuori, 'Dall'effimero alla permanenza. L'Esposizione di L'Aquila del 1888 e lo sviluppo del "campo di Fossa" tra Ottocento e Novecento'.
13 It was restored also thanks to French intervention and reopened in December 2018 with a ceremony presided over by the President of the Italian Republic, Sergio Mattarella.
14 Giancola, *Tra memoria e futuro. Concorso di idee per la Casa dello Studente a L'Aquila*. The quotations are from Ciranna 2019.
15 The author of this section is Patrizia Montuori.
16 'Nobis autem ignorantibus uerum omnia terribiliora sunt, utique metum raritas auget: leuius accidunt familiaria, at ex insolito formido maior est …. Ubi publice terret, ubi cadunt urbes, populi opprimuntur, terra concutitur, quindmirum est animos, inter dolorem et metum destitutos aberrasse?' See: Seneca, *Naturales Questiones*, lib. VI, 3,2; 29,1.
17 Bertin, 'Città al limite – Per una trattazione urbanistica del disastro', 2014.
18 Pasqualetto, *'Immota manet', Il dopo-terremoto in Abruzzo: dal disastro alle strategie di ricostruzione*.
19 In extent, the territory of L'Aquila is preceded only by that of Rome, Ravenna, Cerignola, Noto, Sassari, Monreale, Gubbio and Foggia.
20 Roio Piano, San Vittorino, Coppito, Collefracido, Sassa, Preturo, Collebrincioni, Aragno, Tempera, Paganica, Bazzano, Onna, Monticchio, Bagno, Pianola, Sant'Elia.
21 Clementi, Piroddi, *L'Aquila*; Roggero, 'Storia demaniale della città dell'Aquila', 2016.
22 Clementi, Piroddi, *L'Aquila*; Cavalli, *La grande Aquila: politica, territorio ed amministrazione all'Aquila tra le due guerre*.
23 The acronym C.A.S.E. was coined following the Law Decree of April 28, 2009, n.39, 'Urgent interventions in favour of the populations affected by the earthquakes in the Abruzzo region in April 2009 and further urgent civil protection interventions.'
24 In the municipality of L'Aquila, 1,414 temporary housing modules were set up, of which 1,113 by the Department of Civil Protection. See: Dipartimento della Protezione Civile – Presidenza del Consiglio dei Ministri, 'Dettaglio Dossier. Terremoto Abruzzo: i Moduli Abitativi Provvisori'.
25 Clementi, Fusero, *Progettare dopo il terremoto. Esperienze per l'Abruzzo*.
26 Ciccozzi, 'Catastrofe e C.A.S.E.'.
27 Cerasoli, 'De L'Aquila non resta che il nome. Racconto di un terremoto', 2009.
28 'dipendente sia dai lineamenti propri di un territorio – che nel loro insieme costituiscono ciò che è definito l'identità del luogo – che dalla connotazione che tali lineamenti assumono nel vissuto di ciascun individuo'. See: De Fanis, *Geografie letterarie: il senso del luogo nell'alto Adriatico*, 38.

29 NewsTown 2014, 'L'Aquila prepares to be invaded by street art with the Re_ActoFest'.
30 Buonamano, Potenza, *Catalogo premio Ad'A 2012*.

Bibliography

Arnone, A. (trans.) *L'Aquila. Una città d'arte da salvare – Saving an Art City*. Pescara: Carsa, 2009.

Bartolomucci, C. *Terremoti e resilienza nell'architettura aquilana. Persistenze, trasformazioni e restauro del palazzo Carli Benedetti*. Roma: Quasar, 2018.

Bartolomucci, C. and Ciranna, S. 'Santa Maria Paganica a L'Aquila: la memoria e il futuro'. *Abitare la Terra* supplement to n. 50, a. XVIII (2019): 45.

Berardi, M.R. 'Prestigio e potere nella fondazione e nelle ricostruzioni medievali'. In Ciranna, Vaquero Piñeiro (eds) 2011: 9–32.

Bertin, M. 'Città al limite – Per una trattazione urbanistica del disastro'. *Cuaderno de Investigación Urbanística*, 94 (2014): 1–73.

Buonamano, O. and Potenza, D. (eds). *Catalogo premio Ad'A 2012*. Pescara: Carsa, 2012.

Bulsei, G.L. and Mastropaolo, A. (eds). *Oltre il terremoto. L'Aquila tra miracoli e scandali*. Rome: Viella, 2011.

Cavalli, E. *La grande Aquila: politica, territorio ed amministrazione all'Aquila tra le due guerre*. L'Aquila: Colacchi, 2003.

Centofanti, M. *L'Aquila città di piazze. Spazi urbani e tecniche costruttive*. Pescara: Carsa, 1992.

Centofanti, M. (ed.). *Breve descrittione di sette città illustri d'Italia*. L'Aquila: Texus. 1996 (critical edition of original from 1582).

Cerasoli, D. 'De L'Aquila non resta che il nome. Racconto di un terremoto', *Meridiana, Rivista di Storia e scienze sociali*, 65–66 (2009), *L'Aquila 2010: dietro la catastrofe*, 35–58.

Ciccozzi, A. 'Catastrofe e C.A.S.E'. In *Il terremoto dell'Aquila. Analisi e riflessioni sull'emergenza*, edited by Osservatorio sul terremoto dell'Università degli Studi dell'Aquila, 1–50. L'Aquila: L'Una, 2011.

Ciranna, S. and Vaquero Piñeiro, M. (eds). 'L'Aquila oltre i terremoti. Costruzioni e ricostruzioni della città'. *Città & Storia* a. VI, 1 (January–June 2011).

Ciranna, S. 'L'architettura del potere: il rafforzamento del Corso Vittorio Emanuele II e Federico II tra XIX e XX secolo'. In Ciranna, Vaquero Piñeiro (eds) 2011: 207–237.

Ciranna, S. 'Risarcire – Ricordare – Ricomporre. L'esperienza del concorso'. In Giancola (ed.) 2019.

Ciranna, S. 'Vie e piazze dell'Aquila tra storia, resilienza e reinvenzione'. In *L'Aquila storia della città e del territorio. Divenire resilienti in un contesto di sviluppo sostenibile*, edited by Andrew Hopkins, 161–166. Roma: Editoriale Anicia.

Clementi, A. and Piroddi, E. L'Aquila. Laterza: Bari, 1986.

Clementi, A. and Fusero, P. (eds) *Progettare dopo il terremoto. Esperienze per l'Abruzzo*. Barcelona: List, 2011.

Colapietra, R. 'Società civile e struttura urbana nella città d'antico regime'. In *L'Aquila città di piazze. Spazi urbani e tecniche costruttive*, 28–47. Pescara: Carsa, 1992.

Conforti, C. 'Aquila, città delle piazze'. In *L'Aquila città di piazze. Spazi urbani e tecniche costruttive*, 10–26. Pescara: Carsa, 1992.

De Fanis, M. *Geografie letterarie: il senso del luogo nell'alto Adriatico*. Roma: Meltemi, 2001.

De Matteis, F. *Vita nello spazio. Sull'esperienza affettiva dell'architettura*. Milano: Mimesis, 2019.

Dipartimento della Protezione Civile – Presidenza del Consiglio dei Ministri. 'Dettaglio Dossier. Terremoto Abruzzo: i Moduli Abitativi Provvisori'. http://www.protezionecivile.gov.it/media-comunicazione/dossier/dettaglio/-/asset_publisher/default/content/terremoto-l-aquila.

Giancola, F. (ed.) *Tra memoria e futuro. Concorso di idee per la Casa dello Studente a L'Aquila*. Ariccia (RM): Aracne, 2019.

Montuori, P. 'Dall'effimero alla permanenza. L'Esposizione di L'Aquila del 1888 e lo sviluppo del "campo di Fossa" tra Ottocento e Novecento'. In *La città palinsesto. Tracce, sguardi e narrazioni sulla complessità dei contesti urbani storici. Primo tomo, Memorie, storie,* edited by Francesca Capano e Massimo Visone. Napoli: Cirice, 2021: 1279–1287.

Montuori, P. 'Camminando per la città'. In *L'Aquila storia della città e del territorio. Divenire resilienti in un contesto di sviluppo sostenibile*, edited by Andrew Hopkins, 166–188. Roma: Editoriale Anicia.

NewsTown 2014. 'L'Aquila prepares to be invaded by street art with the Re_ActoFest', Accessed 21 July 2020. https://news-town.it/cultura-e-societa/4682-l-aquila-si-prepara-ad-essere-invasa-dalla-street-art-con-il-reacto_fest.html.

Nicolin, P. 'Above Ruins', *Lotus* 144 (2010).

Pasqualetto, G. *'Immota manet', Il dopo-terremoto in Abruzzo: dal disastro alle strategie di ricostruzione*, Corso di Laurea magistrale in Antropologia Culturale, Etnologia e Etnolinguistica, Università Cà Foscari, Venezia, Rel. Francesco Vallerani, a.a. 2011–12.

Roggero, F. 'Storia demaniale della città dell'Aquila', *Historia et Ius, rivista di storia giuridica dell'età medievale e moderna* 9 (2016): 1–42.

Cofini, V. and Colonna, F. *Il terremoto dell'Aquila. Analisi e riflessioni sull'emergenza*. L'Aquila: L'Una, 2011.

Turino, R. (ed.). *L'Aquila il progetto C.A.S.E.: complessi Antisismici Sostenibili ed Ecocompatibili: un progetto di ricostruzione unico al mondo che ha consentito di dare alloggio a quindicimila persone in soli nove mesi*. Pavia: IUSS Press, 2010.

Vittorini, M. 'Un archivio per il territorio'. In *Omaggio a Marcello Vittorini. Un archivio per la città*, edited by Angela Marino, Valeria Lupo, 47–50. Roma: Gangemi, 2012.

Part II
Public space, a human right

6
Post-crisis masterplanning
A new approach to public spaces
Italy (2009–2021)
Quirino Crosta

In the aftermath of crisis, public space provides the opportunity to create new links, and to reinforce older ones, in order to help a community rebuild its future.

More than 10 years on from the 2009 earthquake, the city of L'Aquila still faces reconstruction of the urban, social and cultural fabric over a very wide area. L'Aquila is a medium-sized city with a polar role in the context of its territory and is surrounded by a network of villages, most of which are also damaged and facing depopulation. Within the theoretical framework of the tangible–intangible, material–immaterial duality, this chapter looks at local fragilities and analyses how urban fracture has provoked social fracture, overlaid with the collective trauma of disaster. In this context, public space has a central role in the life and management of a city, as well as in its suburban and rural surroundings. Obsolete planning tools based on limits and zoning,[1,2] have contributed to post-disaster social crises, which have themselves been compounded by the recent global pandemic. Indeed, there is a need to update the underlying technical and sociocultural objectives and, to this end, an alternative integrated toolkit is proposed for the planning and analysis of public space. Based on a much-needed multidisciplinary and transcalar approach, it is conceived to coordinate general needs with local peculiarities and by doing this, seek to patch up social fractures. A change in planning methods could stimulate a much-needed reinterpretation of contemporary public space and encourage a new pedagogical approach.

Public space and the public sphere

The concept of public space is closely linked to that of public sphere, as it provides a stage for the generation of collective thought and a place for the social interpretation[3] of common requirements and needs that can escape traditional methods of urban planning. Additionally, the fluidity of contemporary society[4] reveals novel issues, which require new reading methods and new points of reference.

According to Jurgen Habermas,[5] the concept of the public sphere – meant as an intangible space of democracy, where it is possible to communicate publicly and discuss issues and rules of collective interest – is linked to the social space generated by communicative action. In this space, citizens discuss matters related to everyday life and, through dialectic, construct the reality of the city. This is how located political action intercepts the technical action of the planning, management and realisation of public space and how public needs manifest themselves and take shape. And this is why it is thought that the public sphere somehow determines the transformation of public space.

Considering how public spaces have been used and occupied in the last decade, it can be seen that they have lost their traditional role and have become almost exclusively spaces of conflict and 'thematisation'. Occupy Wall Street thematised the abuses of financial capitalism through peaceful protest in 2011. The demonstrations that animated the Arab Spring stirred up the streets and squares of the main North African cities. Extinction Rebellion protests in the UK, North America, Australia, New Zealand and Germany have brought environmental and ecological protests into public space, physically connecting protest to the urban environment. Even in the depths of the COVID-19 emergency, public space has become the focus of anti-lockdown and anti-vaccine libertarian action. Beyond these phenomena, manifestations of gender rights and mobilisations for freedom of migration and protection of minorities have reclaimed urban spaces for vulnerable communities. More recently, spatial occupations by Black Lives Matter protesters have seen the reclaiming and renaming of the public realm and the removal of symbols of empire and slavery. These are emblematic cases in which revolutionary themes have broken into the domain of the contemporary public sphere through the corporeality of public space. These issues are linked to the great questions of fairness and freedom with respect to ecology, economics and solidarity. Public space has become for marches and demonstrations what the public sphere is for ideas and opinions – spaces for demonstration and elaboration.

In his work *The Rebel Cities,* David Harvey tells the story of the intertwining of class struggles, rights and cities, which are still today the most prolific breeding grounds for movements for the reappropriation of collective rights. Harvey interprets the right to the city not as an individual right of access to resources but rather the right of communities to 'change and reinvent the city more after our hearts' desire'. This is a collective right, not a personal, private or subjective one, since to change the city it is necessary to exercise collective power over the urbanisation process.[6]

The 'politics of the street' can be traced back to the plural and performative right of appearance of the body in the political field that is offered by public space.[7] Furthermore, the experience of collective gathering[8] is fundamental, because it gives substance to democratic political action and gives a physical dimension to the public sphere through the manifestation of public opinion, urban space and civil rights. The maxim of '*ubi societas, ibi ius*' can be interpreted literally as 'where there is society, there is law' – in other words, places of public gathering are the real birthplace of collective claim and political change.

All this happens in a space of interrelationship that can be referred to as the in-between, a circumstance that has two sets of dimensions, an intangible one that can be identified in the public sphere and a tangible one that can be recognised in traditional public space, such as the *agora.* Hannah Arendt visualised this circumstance as a table – a plane around which we sit, lean and converse. In this way, public space is the environment in which, together, we can build the network of relationships, proximity and solidarity that offers a possible solution to the crisis of the public sphere.

During the pandemic, the need for physical space has not disappeared, but our use of it has been radically altered. It has become both the means of measuring social distance and a pressure valve for the limitations of the private realm. But, as the state of affairs in post-earthquake L'Aquila exemplifies, public space has, too often, turned into a void or non-place.

Current debate seeks to make this void fertile and to give it purpose. In the suspended time of the pandemic, public space has rediscovered its role as an arena of mutual care. It has become a place where we can manifest ourselves to others in a unitary but distinct mass.[9] In public space we experience the interweaving of our individuality with the social and physical context in which we live,[10] and in it we rediscover the need for effective, equitable and sustainable social wellbeing. Thus, in order to overcome the contemporary crisis of the city as a whole, it is necessary to act on the specific crisis of public space.

Method

Traditional tools and methods alone do not seem to be sufficient to receive, interpret and translate the new social needs of the public sphere. Indeed, the technical limitations of traditional reference models for the formation of public spaces have led to an absence of clear terms for the creation and management of the public-space system. Failure to apply social science to planning and a lack of effective public engagement has compounded the problems. In Italy, the underlying applicable legislation dates from 1942, 1967 and 1968. It proscribes 'mandatory limits of building density, height, distance between buildings and maximum ratios between the spaces intended for residential and productive settlements and public spaces or those reserved for collective activities', both for the formation of new urban planning instruments and for the revision of existing ones.[11, 12]

A possible solution may emerge from the resources brought into play by urban communities[13] and by a return to the primary social actions that can reframe the requirements of underperforming, unsatisfactory public spaces and non-places. The creativity of the culture of 'being' provides the tools to reconnect individuals with spaces, to create meaningful places, and to promote inclusion in and accessibility to the processes of management and governance. This *partisan* action can be summarised as 'participation'.

In this vein, the authors have developed a toolkit for the analysis and design of public space, which integrates traditional reference models, standards and dimensions of public space with new components that respond to the needs emerging from the public sphere. The toolkit is adapted to new civic rights, sustainability and environmental performance, and to the new dimensions of public space that are required for accessibility and social distancing. And it is designed to work with new urban planning tools. This chain integrates not only the standard model[14] but also brings the urban plan together with urban design by creating a methodological space capable of incorporating requirements and performance at the appropriate scale of intervention. The toolkit embodies Richard Sennett's call for 'an open urbanism to build a flexible, non-overdetermined environment, so as to preserve the benefits of living together in cities, but avert their most dangerous threats'.[15]

110   INVISIBLE RECONSTRUCTION

Our research is closely connected to this theme of urban flexibility. And while this approach could be interpreted as a critique of traditional planning and standards-based models, it is possible to interpret 'standards' in their broader sense as 'banners' or symbols of what is known, obvious or unequivocal, and which flag or mark a norm or rule. Indeed, urban standards can be seen as being in constant evolutionary tension, denominating verifiable and measurable minimum requirements of recognisable value that must be renewed as circumstances change.[16],[17] Standards aim to guarantee every citizen equally the three fundamental rights: to public space, to safety, and to the healthiness of places and cities. Today we can say that these promises have only been partially fulfilled; standards provide an ideal model, not a real one and consequently on their own they are insufficient to guarantee real needs and demands are met.

In the context of L'Aquila, the superimposition of the COVID-19 emergency onto the pre-existing post-disaster scenario exemplifies the need for additional instruments with which to read or interpret public space. In this double state of emergency, as in states of conflict and inequality, there is a need to achieve a balance between urban spaces dedicated respectively to private use, to public use and to common enjoyment.[18] One consequence of the pandemic has been an acceleration in the securitisation of urban spaces from the institutional designation of distancing measures to changes in individual attitudes to proximity.[19] In L'Aquila, civic spaces are increasingly overwhelmed, particularly during the evening and night time, by uncontrolled and often underage drinking. Vandalism and the use of historic monuments and fountains as open-air latrines is provoking calls for increased surveillance and control, reinforced by concerns that these gatherings are breeding grounds for infection.

Our toolkit reinforces concepts of distribution, proximity, closeness and the relation of the city to its broader environment, territory and landscape. The relationship of a city to its surroundings is critical, with the pandemic placing ever-greater emphasis on the key role of landscape as a public resource.[20] Similarly, the ecological integrity of a city's spaces requires connectivity. Threats to this can be anticipated, and consequently reduced, through the use of an isolation index.[21]

L'Aquila and its surrounding villages have the potential to provide an exemplary quality of life, balancing the benefits of urban proximity with those of the surrounding landscape and its outstanding natural beauty.[22] This requires differentiated policies that can respond to the needs of different territorial contexts[23] while strengthening existing connections and the interrelationship of open and ecological spaces. At a national level, government policies need to be spatialised and territorialised in relation to their context.[24]

The layering of proximities requires multidimensional reflection on the organisation of places for living, learning, working, gathering and socialisation,[25] an approach exemplified by the ingeniously simple formula of the '15-minute city' popularised by Anne Hidalgo as Mayor of Paris.[26]

Additionally, urban space needs to be able both to adapt to change and to be resilient to natural, biological and man-made disaster.[27],[28] Indeed in cities at risk, urban space has a vital role in mitigating hazard and providing safety.

In response to these observations, our toolkit is based on five related principles:

1. The social model of the city must be fluid.[29]
2. Cities require flexible, adaptable organisation.[30]
3. Standards provide a quantitative method but cities are more than the sum of their parts.[31]
4. Qualitative methods are better suited to assess the needs and requirements of the city.[32]
5. Assessment should be by means of a broad set of qualitative performance indicators.[33]

To analyse public space for the purpose of conducting context-specific interventions on management and implementation, we adopted a method based on expanded categorisations.[34] Where traditional approaches recognise the form,[35] function[36] and type[37, 38] of urban space, together with its political and social role and how it is both perceived[39] and cared for, we proposed seven further taxonomies:[40] duality, multifunctionality, temporariness, safety, environment, inclusion, and scalarity. All of these classifications were derived via a methodological process illustrated in Figure 6.1. The process was based on analysis of the public sphere to derive the social needs which are inextricably interconnected to public space. These needs were translated into a lexicon of general concepts through the use of lemmas or keywords.[41] These lemmas were assessed and developed in response to the temporal and spatial context to derive a taxonomy of new rights to the city[42] to be integrated into and amalgamated with traditional standards.

This combined approach was enucleated to derive a domain of indicators from which a new system was created to complement the traditional toolset for the management and design of public space. In this way we

112   INVISIBLE RECONSTRUCTION

Figure 6.1 Evolutionary process from the public sphere to the integration of new standards.

developed a prototype toolkit with which to direct, verify and make participatory the project of urban space, and to guarantee its management and implementation[43] through the use of performance indicators and new urban planning tools.

Prototyping, testing and evolution of the toolkit

This methodology was tested and refined through its application to a number of different urban spaces and to scenarios of varying typologies and in different contexts. These case studies are listed below.

Analysis of these case studies allowed refinement of the new categorisations of urban space which could be encapsulated in a set of new citizen rights and provide the basis for new urban models. In light of the ongoing COVID-19 emergency, an eighth categorisation was included: social density.

Table 6.1 Urban case studies.

City	Public space	Reason for cases	Typology
Berlin	Potsdamer Platz	Stitching space	System
Berlin	PAC – common gardens	Cooperatives space	System
Bordeaux	New Jean-Jacques Bosc bridge – (Pont Simone Veil)	Contemporary space	Bridge
Liverpool	Docks	Spaces of an urban project	River front
Seville	Alameda	Historical space	Square
Alghero	Barcelona Promenade	Waterfront space	Sea front
L'Aquila	Castle Park	After shock space	Park
Gaza	Refugee camp	Conflict space	System

Table 6.1 con'd.

City	Public space	Reason for cases	Typology
Jerusalem	Holy city	Controlled space	System
Chattanooga	Miller Park	Tecnological space	Square
New Orleans	Pontchartrain Park	After shock space	Park
San Francisco	Market Street	After shock space	Street
Osasco	Nelson Park	Informal space	Park
Mexico City	Three Cultures Square	Plural space	Square
Kesennuma	Inner Port	After shock space	Sea front
Hagi	Oriuchi	Historic space	System
Paris	Parc de la Villette	Contemporary space	Park
NYC	High Line	Contemporary space	System
Christchurch	Liminer Square	After shock space	Square

Table 6.2 Dimensions, rights and urban patterns.

New Dimensions	New Rights	New Urban Models
ENVIRONMENT	*Ecology*	*Ecological or sustainable city*
SAFETY	*Freedom*	*Safe or aware city*
SCALARITY	*Landscape*	*Transcalar city or territory*
TECHNOLOGY	*Technology*	*Technological city or progress*
INCLUSION	*Inclusiveness*	*Inclusive or plural city*
PARTICIPATION	*Cooperation*	*Non-performing or non-competitive city*
TEMPORARY	*Relief*	*Temporary or emergency city*
MULTIFUNCTIONALITY	*Plurality*	*Multifunctional or complex city*
DUALITY	*Mediation*	*Dual city or balance*

Application of the toolkit to L'Aquila

The case study of L'Aquila was subjected to further and deeper analysis using the refined, comprehensive toolkit. The first step was the mapping of a spatial network in the city centre, identifying the principal open spaces to be examined. Within this, the axial system of the main central street was selected. Punctuated by a series of key nodal spaces, this axis runs for nearly two kilometres through the city from Piazza Battaglione Alpini (often referred to by the name of the mid-twentieth century sculptural fountain at its centre as La Fontana Luminosa) in the north to Porta Napoli at its south.

Analysis of this network of public spaces allowed the extrapolation of a prospectus which connected traditional tangible and intangible categorisations with new ones in the toolkit, and allowed comparison of innovations found among the approaches to recovery in L'Aquila with novel approaches that had been identified in international case studies.

Figure 6.2 The historic centre of L'Aquila indicating spaces under examination.

Table 6.3 New public space management tools, from the oldest rights to current urban planning instruments.

Traditional dimensions *TANGIBLE*	Traditional dimensions *INTANGIBLE*	*New dimensions*	*New instruments L'Aquila*	*New international instruments*
Type	Public	Inclusion	Register of facilitators	Participated plan
		Duality	Participation office	Urban commons
Shape	Social	Temporariness and multi-functionality	Participatory budgeting	Reconstruction shared and participated
		Technology	Territorial councils of participation	Street art
Function	Cure	Safety/security	Urban centre	Events in multifunctional spaces
			Festival of participation	Risk in dual spaces
Perception		Scale	Sites of the imaginary – event	Technological infrastructure
		Environment	Off-site art – event	Sustainability
			Cooperation agreements	Informal plans

The toolkit presents a matrix of choices which determine the set of instruments most applicable to effect design corrections and improve public space. Its ultimate aim is to allow the subjective evaluation of public space both pre and post implementation. In other words, it functions both as a design tool and as a means of analysis; this also means that it can be used iteratively. The toolkit is applied in five steps:

1. selection of whether the subject space is nodal or a network of spaces
2. selection of the categorisations that are recognisable in the public space
3. selection of the spatial typology of the subject space
4. parametric or qualitative evaluation of indices
5. determination of the appropriate urban planning and administrative tools.

The fourth step can be carried out either parametrically, by entering measurable values to obtain a percentage numerical index, or qualitatively by assigning one of five ratings: very bad, mediocre, sufficient, good or excellent.

Table 6.4 The toolkit applied to the central axis of L'Aquila.

SELECT contemporary dimensions of intervention	SELECT public spaces of intervention (Punct / Syst)	URBAN CONTINUITY OF PUBLIC SPACE	INDICATORS / Indexes	VALUE MIN/MAX (Colorimatric scale)	SELECT tools
MORPHOLOGY TYPOLOGY	SQUARE	INSTITUTIONAL ACTIONS	social communication efficiency $I = E/N$	yellow	New implementation procedures (equalisation, compensation for building rights) NPA
			institutional accessibility to governance $I = Mi/Mc$	magenta	
			efficiency of public space management $I = Mi/Mc$	yellow	
			effectiveness of planning in relation to public space $I = Mi/Mc$	magenta	
FUNCTION		QUALITY OF CULTURAL HERITAGE	efficiency regulatory plan tools $I = Mp/Mn$	magenta	Civic monitoring (Mon.Ci.Ci.)
			vehicular pressure $I = Sp/Sc * 100$; $I = Lp/Lc * 100$	magenta	
			degraded spaces $I = Af / At * 100$	yellow	
			safeguarding public space $I = (SPri + SPd) / (SPc + SPra) * 100$	yellow	
PERCEPTION	STREET		landscape value of the skyline $I = Si/Sc$ $I = Li/Lb$	green	Public–private partnership
			protection of personality places		
			protection places collective memory $I = Ec/Et * 100$	yellow	
			protection of heterotopic places		
DUALITY			protection of taste places		Administrative barter (Ba.Am.)
			viewpoint protection $I = Pd / (Pb + Pd) * 100$	green	
			protection of UNESCO sites		
			creation of cultural paths		
MULTIFUNCTION TEMPORARY			industrial archaeology protection		Design and participatory planning
			protection of architectural heritage $I = Sr/St * 100$	green	
			protection of archaeological heritage $I = Nr/Nt * 100$	green	
		URBAN QUALITY	technological accessibility $At = Ad/S * 100$	orange	
			degraded urban green $I = Sr/Sp * 100$	yellow	
SAFETY			urban green valorisation $I = (Sa + Sn)/Sa * 100$	green	Integrated designs (PrInt.)
			revitalisation of abandoned spaces $I = (SR + Sr)/St * 100$	orange	
			physical accessibility to space $A = Ae/S * 100$	yellow	
	GREEN		pedestrian spaces $I = Pe/S * 100$	orange	
TECHNOLOGY			acoustic well-being $I = Rs/Rt * 100$	orange	Collaboration agreements (Pa.Colla.)
		ENVIRONMENTAL QUALITY	fire risk $Rs = (PVE)e/(PVE)t * 100$	orange	
			hydrogeological risk $Ri = (PVE)e/(PVE)t * 100$	orange	
			seismic risk $Rs = (PVE)e/(PVE)t * 100$	magenta	Neighbourhood regulations (Re.Qua.)
ENVIRONMENT			quality of urban green $V = Vp/Vt * 100$	green	
			soil permeability $I = Sp/St * 100$	magenta	Neighbourhood agreements (A.Vic.)
			protection of constrained public spaces $I = SPep/SPet * 100$	magenta	
INCLUSION			air transparency $I = Rs/Rt * 100$	orange	Community cooperatives (Co.Co.)
	HYBRID	ORGANIC QUALITY	ecologically protected areas		
			protected species		
			endangered species		
			species richness $R = S/A$	orange	Urban contracts (Con.Ur.)
SCALARITY			biodiversity $I = (Sn - S1)/S1 * 100$	orange	
		URBAN CONTINUITY OF PUBLIC SPACE	Overall continuity index $I = T1*Ol1 + T2*Ol2 + T3*Ol3 / At$	yellow	

When applied to the system of spaces in L'Aquila as a pre-implementation instrument, the toolkit clarifies which planning actions and administrative choices would be useful to improve the quality of urban space. In the central axis, it particularly emphasises the need for participation at all stages, supported by integrated design and civic monitoring. From participatory design and planning and the negotiation of rights through neighbourhood consensus and administrative barter to the framing of neighbourhood regulations and collaboration agreements, public engagement is critical. Reassessment with the toolkit post-implementation would allow evaluation of the qualitative indices.

The COVID-19 emergency superimposes requirements for lower social density, which can be addressed and managed through these same processes. Indeed, it should be emphasised that through participatory institutions, methodological models and techniques of engagement, it is possible to leverage the power of community involvement to intervene on the social matrix. It can be argued that in this way, the conflicts and tensions, which might tend to break up social groups and reinforce the contradictions between community and society as a whole, can instead be used to strengthen responses. The toolkit provides the deconflictual methodology to achieve this:

1. Through the recovery or realisation of public spaces where they are lacking or have been abandoned. This type of intervention aims to regenerate meeting places that in turn can regenerate the relational network and networks of proximity and make up for deficiencies in the social model.
2. Through the participatory meeting of social groups for active listening and the exchange of – even conflicting – ideas. This type of intervention regenerates the relationships fundamental to the structuring of communities, allows the mediation of conflict and the tempering of individualistic tensions.

Conclusion

The toolkit presents a set of disciplinary innovations derived through research on public space. It promotes a model of integrated planning that combines traditional urban standards and new performance endowments, and introduces an evolutionary model that interprets contemporary issues of complexity and flexibility. Indicators and indices are used to translate the demands of the public sphere into civic rights and to orient the conception and management of public spaces. Through iterative application, the toolkit allows interpretation and refinement through the synchronous assessment both of proposals and their realisation. The research leaves some scope for further development by adopting interdisciplinary and transcalar points of view as illustrated in Figure 6.3. Future iterations of the toolkit itself could adopt these through open, permeable processes that are capable of dealing with differences of scale and approach.

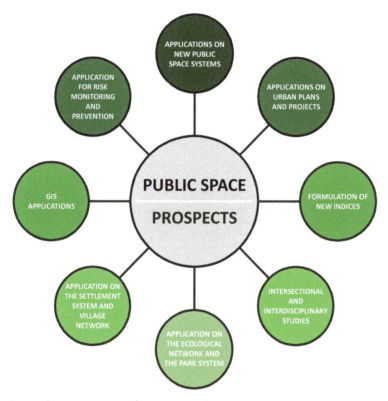

Figure 6.3 Summary of new research perspectives.

Notes

1 Falco, *Gli Standard urbanistici*.
2 Salzano, Fondamenti di Urbanistica.
3 Bianchetti, *Urbanistica e sfera pubblica*.
4 Bauman, *Modernità liquida*.
5 Habermas, *Teoria dell'agire comunicativo*.
6 Harvey, *Rebel Cities*.
7 Arendt, *Vita Activa*.
8 Butler, *L'alleanza dei corpi*.
9 Cavarero, *Democrazia sorgiva*.

10 Ammaniti, 'Jerome Bruner: "L'Ego ha fallito"'.
11 Gazzetta Ufficiale, Legge 6 August 1967.
12 Gazzetta Ufficiale, Decreto Ministeriale 2 April 1968.
13 Salvatore, *La reinvenzione della creatività.*
14 (DL 1444/68).
15 Battiston, 'Per Richard Sennett, dobbiamo immaginare strutture flessibili'.
16 Tutino, *Gli standard urbanistici nell'edilizia popolare.*
17 Falco, *Gli standard urbanistici.*
18 Flick, 'La pandemia e la pari dignità'.
19 Bianchetti et al., *Urbanistica e sfera pubblica.*
20 Zagari, 'Il paesaggio, opzione politica per il futuro'.
21 Esbah, *Isolation trends of urban open spaces.*
22 Properzi, 'La ripartenza passa dalle aree interne?'.
23 Coppola et al., 'Un'analisi dei territori per la fase 2'.
24 De Rossi et al., 'Sette punti per le aree interne'.
25 Bilò, 'A distanza di sicurezza, o della prossemica'.
26 Moreno et al., 'Introducing the "15-Minute City"'.
27 Pierro et al., 'Dalla città della resilienza alla città della resistenza'.
28 Adriani, 'Come abiteremo la città della distanza'.
29 Bauman, *Modernità liquida*, 2002.
30 Gabellini, *Tecniche urbanistiche,* 2018.
31 Salzano, *Fondamenti di urbanistica: la storia e la norma,* 1998.
32 Viviani, Silvia. 'Prefazione alla 1a edizione'.
33 Giaimo, *Dopo 50 anni di standard urbanistici in Italia.*
34 Crosta, 'Spazi pubblici', 2019.
35 Krier, *Urban Space*, describes a type-morphological approach.
36 Zucker, *Town and Square*, presents a typological-functional approach.
37 Sitte, *Der Städtebau nach seinen künstlerischen Grundsätzen* deals with the historical typological evolution of urban fabric.
38 Muratori, *Civiltà e territorio,* deals with historical typological evolution of urban fabric.
39 Allain, *Morphologieurbaine* presents an approach to perception of urban space.
40 Crosta, 'Spazi pubblici resilienti: L'Aquila' 2017.
41 Dubosc, *Lessico della crisi e del possibile.*
42 Lefefbvre, *Le Droit à la ville.*
43 Di Ludovico, *Il progetto urbanistico.*

Bibliography

Adriani, C. 'Come abiteremo la città della distanza'. *Il Giornale dell'Architettura*, 30 April 2020. Accessed 27 June 2020. https://inchieste.ilgiornaledellarchitettura.com/come-abiteremo-la-citta-della-distanza/
Allain R. *Morphologie urbaine. Géographie, aménagement et architecture de la ville*, 2004.
Ammaniti, M. 'Jerome Bruner: "L'Ego ha fallito, la psiche è ormai un Io collettivo"'. La Repubblica, 16 April 2015. Accessed 1 July 2021. https://www.repubblica.it/cultura/2015/04/16/news/jerome_bruner-112104846/
Arendt, H. *Vita Activa. La condizione umana.* Milano: Bompiani, 1964.
Battiston, G. 'Per Richard Sennett, dobbiamo immaginare strutture flessibili per un urbanesimo aperto', CheFare, 22 June 2020. Accessed 1 July 2021. https://www.che-fare.com/battiston-sennett-strututre-flessibili-urbanesimo-aperto/
Bauman, Z. *Modernità liquida*. Roma-Bari: Laterza, 2002.
Bianchetti, C. *Urbanistica e sfera pubblica*. Roma: Donzelli Editore, 2008.
Bilò, F. 'A distanza di sicurezza, o della prossemica', *Il Giornale dell'Architettura*, 30 April 2020. Accessed 27 June 2020. https://inchieste.ilgiornaledellarchitettura.com/a-distanza-di-sicurezza-o-della-prossemica/
Bruner, J. *La cultura dell'educazione*. Milano: Feltrinelli, 2000.
Butler, J. *L'alleanza dei corpi*. Milano: Nottetempo, 2017.

Cavavero, A. *Democrazia sorgiva, note sul pensiero politico di Hannah Arendt*. Raffaello Cortina Editore, 2019.

Coppola, A., Curci, F. and Lanzani, A. 'Un'analisi dei territori per la fase 2', *Forum disuguaglianze diversita*, 17 April 2020. Accessed 27 June 2020. https://www.forumdisuguaglianzediversita.org/covid-19-per-la-fase-due-si-parta-con-unanalisi-dei-territori/

Crosta, Q. and Di Ludovico, D. 'Spazi pubblici resilienti: L'Aquila'. *Urbanistica e Informazione*, 10th INU day Annual Event, Napoli, 2017.

Crosta, Q. and Di Ludovico, D. 'The reconstruction of L'Aquila: a new role of ancient walls'. *Putting Tradition into Practice: Heritage, Place, Design,* Proceedings of the 5th INTBAU International Annual Event, Vol 3 (2017): 105–113.

De Rossi, A. 'Aree interne e montane, gli atouts da giocare', *Il Mulino*, 21 April 2020. Accessed 27 June 2020. https://www.rivistailmulino.it/news/newsitem/index/Item/News:NEWS_ITEM:5169

De Rossi, A. and Mancino, L. 'Sette punti per le aree interne', *Il Giornale dell'Architettura*, 30 April 2020. Accessed 27 June 2020. https://inchieste.ilgiornaledellarchitettura.com/aree-interne-7-punti-per-un-autentico-rilancio/

Di Ludovico, D. *Il progetto urbanistico*. Roma: Aracne Editrice, 2018.

Dubosc, F.O. *Lessico della crisi e del possibile*. Torino: Edizioni SEB27, 2019.

Esbah. H., Deniz, B. and Cook, E.A. *Isolation trends of urban open spaces*. 5th International Symposium Remote Sensing of Urban Areas, 14–16 March 2005. Arizona State University, Tempe, Arizona.

Falco, L. *Gli Standard urbanistici*. Roma: Edizioni delle autonomie, 1978

Falco, L. *I 'nuovi' standard urbanistici*. Roma: Edizioni delle autonomie, 1987.

Flick, G.M. 'La pandemia e la pari dignità sociale nella città'. *Il Giornale dell'Architettura*, 30 April 2020. Accessed 27 June 2020. https://ilgiornaledellarchitettura.com/web/2020/04/17/flick-la-pandemia-e-la-pari-dignita-sociale-nella-citta/

Gabellini, P. *Tecniche urbanistiche*. Roma: Carocci editore, 2001.

Gazzetta Ufficiale, Legge 6 Agosto 1967, n. 765, Modifiche ed integrazioni alla legge urbanistica 17 agosto 1942, n. 1150. Accessed 1 July 2021. https://www.gazzettaufficiale.it/eli/id/1967/08/31/067U0765/sg

Gazzetta Ufficiale, Decreto Ministeriale 2 Aprile 1968. Accessed 1 July 2021. https://www.gazzettaufficiale.it/eli/id/1968/04/16/1288Q004/sg

Giaimo, C. *Dopo 50 anni di standard urbanistici in Italia*. Roma: INU Edizioni, 2018.

Habermas, J. *Teoria dell'agire comunicativo*. Bologna: Il Mulino, 2017.

Harvey, D. *Città ribelli*. Milano: Il Saggiatore, 2013.

Jacobs, J. *Vita e morte delle grandi città. Saggio sulle metropoli americane*. Milano: Piccola Biblioteca Einaudi, 1961.

Krier, R. *Urban Space*. London: Academy Editions, 1979.

Lefebvre, H. *Le Droit à la ville*. Paris: Anthropos, 1968.

Lynch, K. *The Image of the City*. Cambridge, London: MIT Press, 1960.

Moreno, C., Allam, Z., Chabaud, D., Gall, C. and Pratlong, F. 'Introducing the "15-Minute City": sustainability, resilience and place identity in future post-pandemic cities'. *Smart Cities* 4–1 (2021): 93–111. Accessed 6 June 2021 https://doi.org/10.3390/smartcities4010006

Muratori, S. *Civiltà e territorio*. Rome: 1967.

Norberg-Schultz, C. *Genius Loci*. Milano: Electa, 1999.

Pierro, L. and Scarpinato, M. 'Dalla città della resilienza alla città della resistenza'. *Il Giornale dell'Architettura*, 30 April 2020. Accessed 27 June 2020. https://inchieste.ilgiornaledellarchitettura.com/dalla-citta-della-resilienza-alla-citta-della-resistenza/

Properzi, P. 'La ripartenza passa dalle aree interne? Le opportunità per il post – epidemia', *INU Informa*, 30 April 2020. Accessed 27 June 2020. http://www.inu.it/news/la-ripartenza-passa-dalle-aree-interne-le-opportunita-per-il-post-ndash-epidemia/

Salvatore, R. *O.R.eS.T.E., Osservare, comprendere e progettare per ricostruire a partire dal terremoto dell'Aquila*. Faenza: Homelessbook, 2012.

Salvatore, R. 'La reinvenzione della creatività che non c'è...a partire dalla cultura dell'esserci', in *Creatività e crisi della comunità locale*, edited by Federici, Garzi, Moroni. Milano: FrancoAngeli, 2011.

Salvatore, R. and Chiodo, E. *Non più e non ancora. Le aree fragili tra conservazione ambientale, cambiamento sociale e sviluppo turistico*. Milano: FrancoAngeli edizioni, 2018.

Salzano, E. *Fondamenti di urbanistica: la storia e la norma*. Roma-Bari: Laterza, 1998.

Sitte, C. *Der Städtebau nach seinen künstlerischen Grundsätzen*. 1889.

Tonnies, F. *Comunità e società. Brani scelti*, curated by Avallone Gennaro. Roma: Edizioni04, 1963.

Tutino, A. *Gli standard urbanistici nell'edilizia popolare, La legge urbanistica e le cooperative di abitazione*. Firenze: La Nuova Italia, 1965.

Viviani, S. 'Prefazione alla la edizione' in *Dopo 50 anni di standard urbanistici in Italia*, edited by Giaimo, Carolina. Roma: INU Edizioni, 2018.

Zagari, F. 'Il paesaggio, opzione politica per il futuro'. *Il Giornale dell'Architettura*, 30 April 2020. Accessed 27 June 2020. https://partnership.ilgiornaledellarchitettura.com/2019/06/04/il-paesaggio-deve-essere-unopzione-politica-per-il-futuro/

Zucker, P. *Town and Square*. New York: Columbia University Press, 1970.

7
Rethinking inequality and the future
The pre-Hispanic past in post-disaster Lima, Peru

Rosabella Álvarez-Calderón Silva-Santisteban and Julio Sánchez García

The expansion of Lima in the twentieth century involved the partial destruction of its pre-Hispanic past and negotiations between different actors over what constitutes heritage. While some urban monuments have been carefully preserved, their protection has come at the expense of restricted access and use. This places them in the troubling position of either being open and accessible, yet neglected and vulnerable to illegal land traffickers, or well-cared for but mostly cut off from public life.

The COVID-19 pandemic brought into stark focus the city's inequalities, especially the privatisation, restriction of use and destruction of public spaces. This crisis highlighted the urgent need for open, safe and accessible 'third places' as described by Ray Oldenburg,[1] especially for the most vulnerable people. In a city where open public space is scarce and unevenly distributed, the large number of ancient sites are an extraordinary potential asset for resilience. How could we adapt these sites to serve as citizen space during periods of stress without compromising their integrity and heritage values? How can heritage also serve to promote 'third place' qualities like accessibility, equality, being a welcome place to regulars and newcomers, the right to roam responsibly and citizenship?

This chapter argues that for pre-Hispanic sites to be truly sustainable and reflective of diverse values and identities, it is necessary to go beyond material conservation and to foster greater citizen stewardship, while addressing structural barriers and inequalities in use and access. It presents Huaca Fest, a festival that addresses these challenges through research, urban placemaking and social engagement.

Lima, a city of (in)formality

Shortly after the World Health Organization declared that the novel disease known as COVID-19 had become a pandemic, on 11 March 2020, Peru imposed a nationwide state of emergency and lockdown. While measures were implemented to mitigate the economic, social and health crisis that followed, the outcome was devastating to people who rely on informal and often sporadic work, while living in overcrowded and poorly-ventilated homes, often without reliable access to basic services. The pandemic thus highlighted the deep inequalities in the city of Lima, founded by Spanish conquistadors in 1535 next to the Rímac river, which today is home to one third of the country's 30 million inhabitants.

For decades after Peru became an independent republic in 1821, Lima remained small, surrounded by towns, large agricultural estates (*haciendas*) and numerous sites of pre-Hispanic origin, locally known as *huacas* – the remains of settlements built over the last five thousand years in the valleys that now comprise the modern urban landscape. During the twentieth century, formal development by the state and private landowners urbanised rural areas. Most significant, however, was the development of the 'informal city', so called because it did not conform, at least initially, to legal requirements. This parallel city, which anthropologist Jose Matos Mar calls New Lima, was built mainly by disfranchised[2] migrants from different parts of Peru and their descendants in a mixed process that involved illegal, well-organised and highly symbolic takeovers of public and private land, as well as legal sales by *hacienda* owners. Over the past 70 years, New Lima has grown and consolidated to the point where it is almost undistinguishable from the 'formal' city.[3]

There are, though, some important differences between these two Limas. Building the formal city involved the destruction of many *huacas*, both to clear and flatten the land and to salvage their building materials – mostly unfired earth bricks known as *adobes*.[4] On the other hand, the creators of the informal city invested most of their time and resources in their communities, and in lobbying the government for land titles and basic services, so initially there was little benefit in demolishing *huacas*, especially since the informal city adapted to the topography of the land.

The second difference is that the formal city has more public open space, especially parks, but very few *huacas*. On the other hand, New Lima is home to most of the metropolitan area's surviving *huacas*, but contains significantly fewer public spaces considering its much larger area and population size. This difference affects how people use and relate to these spaces and what activities are possible. We propose here that for open space to become a resource for community recovery after a disaster, such space must feel like a 'third place'. It should not only have certain physical qualities such as scale, accessibility and openness, it must also be well-managed and people have to feel they have both a right to such space along with a sense of responsibility and knowledge on how to take care of it. We will explore these implications below.

Urban public space and social disasters

In the early twentieth century, when Lima had a population of less than 200,000 people, parks constituted 20 per cent of the city's area; a few decades later and with nearly eight million people, they made up less than 0.5 per cent.[5] Lima's first modern park, located just outside the historic centre and built as a setting for the Great Exhibition of 1872, was designed following Victorian-era ideals of promoting healthy, virtuous recreation to all people, especially working- and middle-class families.[6]

Peru has a long history of plazas and open spaces being used not only as civic spaces, but also as post-disaster safe spaces. Historian Charles Walker describes how after the 1746 earthquake that devastated Lima, 'with their homes destroyed or tottering and aftershocks continuing for months, most of Lima's population found refuge wherever they could: in plazas, courtyards, gardens'. In other cities, open space was similarly used, as happened to Cusco after a 1950 earthquake (Figures 7.1 and 7.2). This evidence implies that these spaces were considered safe due to their accessible and central location and openness, as places where people will gravitate to find friends, family and neighbours, as well as information, relief, supplies and guidance; and where community networks and efforts (bartering, the pooling of resources, the preparation and distribution of communal meals) will focus.

During the early months of the COVID-19 pandemic, the government closed many parks and severely restricted access to and use of those that remained open, in spite of the fact that the Inter-American Development Bank[7] has stressed the essential role that public space plays in the health and wellbeing of vulnerable communities, especially in informal

Figure 7.1 Survivors of the 1950 Cusco earthquake building temporary shelters in the main plaza. Source: Giesecke Collection, Riva Agüero Institute for Higher Studies, Pontificia Universidad Católica del Perú.

settlements. According to archaeologist Carlos Ausejo, former Director of Archaeological Built Heritage at Peru's Ministry of Culture (June 2017 November 2018), the layout and restrictions in many of Lima's parks can be explained in part by a belief that these are not spaces for recreation and 'commoning', but rather places to admire and pass through, where the benches are meant to be used for only brief periods, and the grass is often fenced off. The term 'commoning' here refers to the activities that take place in a shared, common space that everyone contributes to through direct investment and/or taxes, and also to 'the acts of mutual support, conflict, negotiation, communication and experimentation that are needed to create systems to manage shared resources'.[8] These scenarios illustrate the urgent need for more 'third places' for civic and

Figure 7.2 Survivors of the 1950 Cusco earthquake taking shelter in the main plaza. Source: Giesecke Collection, Riva Agüero Institute for Higher Studies, Pontificia Universidad Católica del Perú.

public life, and, in the context of a disaster, as 'homes away from home', safe spaces where people can meet as equals, to gather, shelter, distribute and obtain necessary supplies, and as the setting where community support networks can function effectively.

Public space and the practice of commoning at risk

Public spaces in Lima have become increasingly vulnerable to commodification, privatisation, size reduction and restriction of access. These processes have mobilised people to engage in acts of urban activism, protest and organisation of urban social movements.[9] This activism is based on the principle of a 'right to the city', described by Henri Lefebvre as a 'cry and demand'[10] and by David Harvey[11] as 'a common rather than an individual right, since this transformation inevitably depends upon the exercise of a collective power to reshape the processes of urbanization'. Two recent cases serve as examples of the increased importance of these movements. First, a community group called Defend Castilla Park, located in the middle-class neighbourhood of Lince, successfully lobbied against a municipal order banning active recreation.[12] Second, between 2016 and 2018, citizens of the working-class district of Comas fought to protect its Manhattan Park from an attempt to transfer a significant part of the land to a private developer.[13] According to the sociologist Abigail Gilmore, conflicts like these arise in part due to a crisis in the traditional funding models required for maintenance and can also be understood as the defiance of laws and regulations perceived as unjust. Despite the rising popularity of new funding streams like Friends groups,[14] partnerships with museums, and community ownership, there is a lingering expectation that the main responsibility for upkeep and funding of public space lies with local authorities.[15] Furthermore, in Peru a history of racism, inequality, political violence and terrorism has resulted in many people being unable or unwilling to exercise their human and cultural rights. People also do not have the right to roam in a responsible manner, similar to the legal right enjoyed in countries like Sweden and, to a lesser extent, the United Kingdom. Citizen activism is thus rooted in recognition of the social value of public space, the responsibilities of different stakeholders, and the capacity to identify when the right to engage in the practice of 'commoning' as equals is being breached. Public spaces can be understood as civic commons, a resource managed by a community by devising its own rules, traditions, and values,[16] and which serves the following purpose:

> They are community assets which serve localities and raise the overall quality of and satisfaction with local neighbourhoods. They are places where diverse groups can come together to practice civic participation, continue family life and make memories which carry long into adulthood. Everyday participation in parks requires negotiation of difference and distinction, however, and sometimes the rules of participation in common resources can be exclusionary and create segregation and segmentation of their users.[17]

Unfortunately, the same qualities that make a place a community asset may feel like over-regulation, surveillance, hostility and invisible limits designed to exclude people and activities deemed 'undesirable'. It can be argued that this is what happened in Castilla Park, where an order supposedly designed to protect the natural and heritage values of the park actually made it less accessible to many.

We propose here that Lima does not have sufficient high-quality, accessible public space, such as parks and plazas, to satisfy the needs of its citizens, and that sites of pre-Hispanic origin, especially those with large plazas, could serve as civic commons and 'third places', especially for disaster scenarios. The main question is how *huacas* could fulfil this role without affecting their integrity and authenticity, and what qualities they possess that make them suitable for this purpose. We shall explore potential answers to this challenge by evaluating some of the preliminary results of Huaca Fest: Roads Uniting Cities, an interdisciplinary project which was funded by a grant from Pontificia Universidad Católica del Peru's Office for Social Responsibility in 2019, and which focused on the relationship between the city and the pre-Hispanic sites located in and around the PUCP university campus. These sites are known as the Maranga Archaeological Complex, a cultural landscape that spanned three historical occupations known as the Lima society (200–750), the Ychsma society (750–1440) and the presence of the Inca empire in the central coast (1440–1532).[18]

The nature of pre-Hispanic sites in the city

Peru's General Law for National Cultural Heritage (law 28296) states that all sites of pre-Hispanic origin are the property of the state, not of the people, even if located in private property, and that only the state can manage them. The main institution responsible for this task is the Ministry of Culture[19] and its branch offices. This law also specifies that these sites cannot be privatised or sold, and are intangible assets, so the only physical interventions allowed are those related to academic research, conservation and adaptation for tourism and educational visits.[20] This interpretation of intangibility also determines that professional archaeologists hold the special privilege and responsibility of being the sole actors who can legitimately intervene in *huacas*. Historian Raul Asensio refers to this partnership between archaeologists and the state as the 'Peruvian heritage pact'.[21]

Unfortunately, this duty has proved to be almost impossible to realise, in part due to the many steps involved in protecting a site and the relatively meagre resources the ministry possesses for this purpose. According to the national culture policy (2020), there are over 25,000

Figure 7.3 The El Paraiso complex (3,500–1,800 BC) in northern Lima, with its blue marker. This well-known site has been mapped and documented, but is still vulnerable to land traffickers. Image: Rosabella Alvarez-Calderón, 2015.

sites in Peru and 538 in the Lima metropolitan area, all of which need to be mapped, documented, registered with the Office of Public Records, and clearly marked with signs and markers. This is a lengthy and complicated process that requires negotiating with multiple parties and to date only three per cent of sites nationwide have fully completed this process and only 10 per cent have been registered and have an approved map.[22] While there are many *huacas* that are well cared for, open to the public and where local communities are encouraged to participate as caretakers in partnership with the ministry, the Heritage Pact becomes a problem when *huacas* show signs of neglect and 'undesirable' users and activities. This implies that the ministry is failing in its duty, while preventing non-archaeologist citizens from taking on these responsibilities on their own initiative. This generates ambiguity in who can legitimately access, use and take care of these sites, negatively affecting their upkeep, protection and the way they are perceived by citizens.

Peru's national culture policy, designed to provide a vision for the 2020–30 time period, states that its main objective is to ensure that all people are able to exercise their right to culture in a sustainable manner as participants, creators and beneficiaries, while valuing diversity. State ownership of *huacas*, however, represents a conflict with this objective. We propose here that it is necessary to change the national heritage law so that sites of pre-Hispanic origin are property of the nation, with the state acting as the main, rather than the only, caretaker and protector, as well as the facilitator of partnerships and synergies for collaboration, including clearly defining the responsibilities and competencies of other state institutions. This would represent a positive step towards recognising and valuing the many different urban social movements as well as private actors and institutions, which advocate not just for the safeguarding of *huacas*, but also for the right to use them as civic commons, sacred spaces and as safe places for emergencies. We arrive thus at the possibilities of what this expanded role could be for all stakeholders, which was the objective of the Huaca Fest project. Having identified the structural barriers, we aimed to envision a more sustainable future for urban *huacas*, in which they become 'third places' with heritage value. For this, it was essential to identify opportunities for change in areas like urban/campus design, walkability and use of public/common spaces.

Huaca Fest: roads uniting cities

The bustling district of San Miguel in the city of Lima is home to the Maranga Archaeological Complex, which includes the remains of walls, plazas, a network of roads and canals, cemeteries and monumental buildings, now located within public parks, inside university campuses and within the zoo, also known as Parque de las Leyendas. Unfortunately, modern urban development has destroyed many buildings and enclosed most surviving structures behind walls and fences,[23] a notable example being the Mateo Salado complex, which is open to visitors (Figure 7.4).

Within the PUCP campus lie three sites: Huaca 20, a Lima period ceremonial mound, residential area and cemetery; Huaca 64, an Ychsma/Inca administrative building that was later sealed and used as a burial site; and a 400-metre section of a ceremonial road from the Ychsma/Inca period that originally linked Mateo Salado with the monumental buildings at the zoo, and is known as the Inca Road (Figure 7.5). Starting in the 1960s, the Riva Agüero Institute Archaeology Seminar, an interdisciplinary research group associated with PUCP, conducted extensive research at many of the Maranga sites. Today, the university's infrastructure office, and especially the campus archaeologist, are

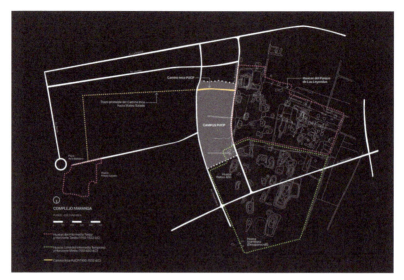

Figure 7.4 The Maranga Archaeological Complex, most of which is located inside the modern-day Parque de las Leyendas (right), PUCP campus (centre, in yellow) and the Mateo Salado complex (left, in red). The yellow line on the left shows the path that the Inca Road may have followed. Designed by Fabricio Torres, October 2018. Source: Office of Infrastructure, PUCP.

Figure 7.5 The Inca Road inside the campus of Pontificia Universidad Catolica del Peru (PUCP) is cut off from the pre-Hispanic sites inside Parque de las Leyendas (top) by a modern avenue. The large *huacas* at Parque de las Leyendas are surrounded by several pre-Hispanic and modern plazas and open spaces. Image: Julio Sanchez Garcia, 2019. Source: Office of Infrastructure, PUCP.

responsible for the conservation and protection of the pre-Hispanic remains in accordance with national and international heritage laws, as well as the university's institutional strategic plan. Although the university has proved itself to be a good caretaker, their isolated locations within campus, and the protective policies which ban people from visiting or even approaching them unless they are on an authorised visit, mean that for many people, the *huacas* are in a sense 'invisible', only to be admired from afar at best, and a nuisance at worst.

In view of these challenges, Huaca Fest: Roads uniting cities was developed in 2019 as a year-long venture in partnership with Parque de las Leyendas. Its objectives were to facilitate a more comprehensive understanding of the history of Maranga as a historic cultural landscape, as well as to promote conversations and actions on urbanism, citizenship, social responsibility and the different values associated with the pre-Hispanic past and heritage. Here we will briefly discuss the preliminary results for two of the activities: an archaeology workshop for campus security and an urban walkability workshop for the general public, which was done in partnership with Ocupa tu Calle[24], a Lima-based organisation that promotes urban placemaking activities to improve the quality of public space. These two workshops were complemented by information-gathering and cultural mapping activities during September and October 2019, where we documented patterns of behaviour in public spaces around the Inca Road, based on the methodology developed by urbanists like Jan Gehl, William Whyte and the non-profit organisation Project for Public Spaces.[25]

The archaeology workshop took place over two days in October 2019 and was designed to offer 60 members of the campus security staff a historic overview of the three *huacas*, give them recommendations on how to distinguish between negative, neutral and positive uses relating to how they affect the sites and encourage them to share information and guidance with interested visitors. The participants also shared their experiences and perceptions, as well as the many uses that they identified for the campus *huacas*, especially the Inca Road, among the university community: as a place for learning, for exploration, as a backdrop for pictures, as a stop on the way to visit the campus deer enclosure, and for activities requiring seclusion and solitude. They also communicated their frustration over being seen by students as mostly disciplinarians, and by policies that essentially dictate that all non-authorised intrusions to the *huacas* are considered trespassing. We also learned there is still much interest in these ancient sites, especially among freshmen and exchange students.

The second activity was the walkability workshop, which took place in November 2019 (Figure 7.6), where we aimed to evaluate the quality of the walk between Mateo Salado, PUCP and Parque de las Leyendas, considering comfort, safety and interest. Our methodology was based on those developed by Jeff Speck[26] and community organisations such as the Brazil-based SampaPé.[27] A group of eight participants documented the walk, remarking on the narrow sidewalks, often beset with obstacles that made navigating them difficult for wheelchairs and people with mobility problems (Figure 7.7); the lack of trees and other elements that offer shade and comfort; the long wait times at traffic lights and low number of pedestrian crossings; and especially the dull and dangerous walk between PUCP and Parque de las Leyendas, that offered pedestrians barely any protection from fast-moving traffic, noise and air pollution (Figure 7.8). They also identified several areas where the remains of *huacas* had prompted the creation of small parks and the fact that many monumental *huacas* had large plazas, both of pre-Hispanic and recent creation, the latter serving as buffer areas and recreation space for visitors. Participants indicated that several of the problems could be addressed through design, low-cost/high-impact interventions to test out new proposals, such as sidewalk widenings,

Figure 7.6 Walkability workshop in November 2019, designed to evaluate pedestrian connections between the complex of Mateo Salado, the PUCP campus and the Inca Road, and the Parque de las Leyendas. Organised by the Huaca Fest project and Lima-based *Ocupa tu Calle*. Images: the Estefani Delgado/Huaca Fest project.

Figure 7.7 Much of the walk between the pre-Hispanic sites in the Maranga area is along narrow sidewalks, with few trees for shade and high fences designed to protect pre-Hispanic sites. Image: Rosabella Alvarez-Calderon.

Figure 7.8 Pedestrian access between the PUCP campus and the nearby Parque de las Leyendas requires a long, uncomfortable walk along a very narrow sidewalk. Image: Rosabella Alvarez-Calderon.

pedestrian crossings and public art, and especially by collaborations between private institutions with the Ministry of Culture and district municipalities. The same qualities that improve walkability, access and participation, especially for the most vulnerable people, in ways that do not compromise the safety of *huacas* but rather encourage people to participate and share responsibility for their care, also contribute to transforming these sites and their plazas into safe spaces for disaster recovery.

Conclusions

Inequality in access to and use of urban public space negatively affects everyday quality of life, physical and mental health, as the still ongoing (early 2021) COVID-19 pandemic is proving. Lack of funding and maintenance, neglect, as well as policies and practices that prioritise profitable land uses, have resulted in many of these spaces being enclosed, diminished and privatised. These restrictions, however, have also bolstered citizen demands to improve and expand public spaces in order to promote public health, safety and a more sustainable and just city.

While Lima lacks sufficient places that function as civic commons, we propose that it is the urban *huacas* which could potentially serve this purpose and thus contribute to improving the city's resilience for disaster recovery, especially in places where there are few public parks and plazas. Most surviving *huacas* are located in Lima's most vulnerable districts, but many are also in close proximity to residential neighbourhoods, have large plazas and open spaces where people can gather and cannot be legally privatised or built on. However, making *huacas* more accessible involves implementing protective measures, as well as addressing the structural and legal barriers that discourage people from freely and responsibly using and improving these spaces, the most important being that these sites belong to the state rather than to the people. Restricting citizen initiatives in the name of protection and conservation has proved to be a significant weakness during the state of emergency, with an already overburdened ministry unable to fulfil many of its duties and needing to rely on others to monitor and protect sites from threats like vandalism and land traffickers. Therefore, a significant first step towards fulfilling the objectives of the National Culture Policy for the year 2030 involves sharing ownership and responsibility for this heritage with the public, developing trust and accepting that recognition of diversity involves respecting the different ways people value, perceive and use the past, as long as these do not go against the vision and duty to protect pre-Hispanic heritage and people's right to culture. The cases of activism in Comas and Lince have shown that people will stand up to protect the places that bring value and significance to their lives, but only if they have a shared right and ownership. Just as the 'right to roam' in the United Kingdom was the result of years of activism and lobbying[28] in Lima there are many urban social movements[29] interested in *huacas* as community heritage, as well as in issues such as sustainable mobility and protection of ecosystems.

From this, and from the response to and participation in Huaca Fest, we can claim that there is significant public interest in the pre-Hispanic past and in visiting, learning from and contributing to the improvement of *huacas,* even if the Ministry of Culture does not always fully approve of these actions. Finally, we should consider what protocols we need to design and implement to successfully adapt *huacas* into civic commons and 'third places' without compromising their integrity, authenticity and legibility. This would involve first rethinking the level of wear and maintenance that we are prepared to tolerate, the mitigation strategies we should adopt to make these sites more inclusive, accessible and suitable as shared social spaces where people can meet as equals, who should be responsible and how should funding be resolved. Second, we need to consider the potential that individuals and communities have for agency, especially for implementing low-cost/high-impact interventions and pilot projects where innovative ideas can be tested, while still lobbying for necessary legal and political changes. Third, it is important to foster collaborative relationships with different stakeholders and invest the necessary time and resources in order to develop mutual trust. This also involves actively seeking out opportunities for collaboration and synergies with different neighbourhood networks, private and especially public institutions, like the Health Ministry, the National Institute of Civil Defense, Municipalities and the Risk and Disaster Management Offices. These are all steps towards establishing a shared vision, ownership and responsibility for *huacas* as civic commons and 'third places' with heritage value – a shared space with many values that contributes to the resilience of the city and its people.

Acknowledgements

We wish to thank the Huaca Fest team: Luis Condori Aguilar, Daniel Huarcaya Flores, Estefani Delgado Chirinos, Alexandra Velasque Caballero and Katherine Albornoz Tamara. We are also grateful to Antonio Gamonal, Lucénida Carrion and the Archaeology team at Parque de las Leyendas, as well as everyone who contributed to the project.

Notes

1 Oldenburg, *The great good place.*
2 The 1933 Constitution of Peru, which was valid until 1979, stated in its fourth title that only able-bodied males aged 18 and over who could read and write had the right to vote, which resulted in most people being excluded from participating in political life, especially women, non-Spanish speaking, native and poor people in rural areas with little access to formal education.
3 Matos Mar, *Estado desbordado y sociedad nacional emergente.* Calderón Cockburn, *La ciudad ilegal.*
4 Museum of Archaeology and Anthropology, Universidad Nacional Mayor de San Marcos, *Cuadernos de Investigación del Archivo Tello No. 1.*
5 Ludeña, *Lima y Espacios Públicos*, 47.
6 Gilmore, *The park and the commons.*
7 Vera, Adler and Uribe ¿Qué podemos hacer para responder al COVID-19 en la ciudad informal?
8 Bollier, *Commoning as a Transformative Social Paradigm*, 5.
9 Domaradzka, *Urban Social Movements.*
10 Lefebvre, *Le Droit a ` la Ville.*
11 Harvey, *The right to the city.*
12 *Defend Castilla Park* is a citizen activist group who communicate their agenda and activities mainly through their Facebook page (https://www.facebook.com/defiendeelcastilla, accessed on 20 September 2020), especially their opposition to Ordinance 376, initially passed by the Municipality of Lince in 2016, which forbids activities related to active recreation in the name of preservation.
13 Taken from Indira Huilca's (Representative in Congress 2016–2019) blog http://www.indirahuilca.pe/parque-manhattan-comas/, accessed 20 September 2020.
14 Friends of Parks groups exist in many cities all over the world, usually dedicating themselves to fundraising and advocacy. New York City's park system works in partnership with many of these organisations, like Partnership for Parks, Prospect Park Alliance and the Central Park Conservancy. In Lima, Friends of Castilla Park can also be considered a Friends group, even though its main goal is advocacy rather than fundraising.
15 Gilmore, *The park and the commons.*
16 Bollier, *Commoning as a Transformative Social Paradigm*, 6.
17 Gilmore, *The park and the commons*, 10.
18 Carrión and Narváez, 'Descripcion general de Maranga' 34.
19 The Ministry of Culture was created in 2010 and one of its main legal competencies, as stated in article 8 of law 29565, is to promote the registry, research, preservation, conservation, communication of material and non-material, as well as adapting sites for visitors.
20 Casafranca Alvarez, 'Las áreas destinadas a la protección del Patrimonio Cultural en el Perú', 2.
21 Asensio, *Señores del Pasado.* While the Peruvian Heritage Pact grants professional archaeologists these privileges, the exercise of their profession is heavily regulated by the state, through the National Guidelines on Archaeological Interventions (2014), the Ministry of Culture and branch offices.
22 Ministry of Culture, *Política Nacional de Cultura al 2030*, 76.
23 Canziani, 'Territorio, monumentos pre-Hispanicos y paisajes', 81.
24 https://ocupatucalle.com/, accessed 25 May 2021.
25 Project for Public Spaces is a non-profit organisation founded in 1975 that aims to 'help communities transform their public spaces into vital places that highlight local assets, spur rejuvenation, and serve common needs' using an approach known as placemaking.
26 Speck, *Walkable City.*
27 https://sampape.org/?lang=en, accessed 25 May 2021.
28 *Right to Roam* is episode 313 of the podcast 99% Invisible, released on 26 June 2018. Accessed 1 October 2020. https://99percentinvisible.org/episode/right-to-roam/
29 The Ministry of Culture maintains a registry of associations known as *Puntos de Cultura* (Culture Dots) with the aim to identify, recognise, and enhance each dot into a network of community and social organisations. While most of these dots are related to arts and culture, there are now several that focus on the pre-Hispanic past as part of their agenda and vision, such as *Comunespacio* (Commonspace), the *Circulo Ciclista Protector de las Huacas* (*Huaca*

Protector Biker's Circle) and site-specific groups, such as Huaycán Cultural (based on the Huaycán de Pariachi site, Lima), the *Asociación Cultural Guardianes de la Huaca Bellavista* (Stewards of the Bellavista Huaca Cultural Association) and the *Comité de defensa y patrimonio cultural y natural de Mangomarca* – CODEPACMA (Committee for the defense and cultural and natural heritage of Mangomarca), all of them based in the city of Lima, Peru.

Bibliography

Alvarez-Calderón, R. and Sanchez Garcia, J. *Informe final de actividades en el Proyecto Huaca Fest Maranga 2019: Caminos uniendo ciudades.* Lima: Academic Office for Social Responsibility, Pontificia Universidad Catolica del Peru, 2019.

Asensio, R. *Señores del Pasado. Arqueólogos, museos y huaqueros en el Perú.* Lima: Instituto de Estudios Peruanos, 2018.

Bollier, D. *Commoning as a Transformative Social Paradigm,* 2015. Accessed on 1 October 2020. http://www.bollier.org/blog/commoning-transformative-social-paradigm.

Calderón Cockburn, J. *La ciudad ilegal: Lima en el siglo XX.* Lima: Fondo Editorial de la Facultad de Ciencias Sociales Universidad Nacional Mayor de San Marcos, 2005.

Canziani, J. 'Territorio, monumentos preHispanicos y paisajes'. In *Lima: Espacio Publico, Arte y Ciudad,* edited by Johanna Hamann Mazure, 73–89. Lima: Pontificia Universidad Catolica del Peru, 2013.

Carrión, L. and Narváez, J.L. 'Descripción general de Maranga'. In *Arqueología, catorce años de investigaciones en Maranga,* edited by Lucénida Carrión and Joaquín Narváez, 33–51. Lima: Patronato del Parque de las Leyendas y Municipalidad Metropolitana de Lima, 2014.

Casafranca Álvarez, A. 'Las áreas destinadas a la protección del Patrimonio Cultural en el Perú en torno a la regulación de las excepciones a la intangibilidad en las Áreas Restringidas a la actividad minera'. *Foro Juridico,* 16 (2017): 17–28.

Domaradzka, A. 'Urban social movements and the right to the city: an introduction to the special issue on urban mobilization'. *Voluntas,* 29 (2018): 607–620.

Gilmore, A. 'The park and the commons: vernacular spaces for everyday participation and cultural value' *Cultural Trends,* 26(1) (2017): 34–46. DOI: 10.1080/09548963.2017.1274358

Harvey, D. 'The right to the city'. *New Left Review,* 53 (2008): 23–40.

Lefebvre, H. *Le Droit à la Ville.* Paris: Anthropos, 1968.

Ludeña, W. *Lima y Espacios Públicos. Perfiles y estadística integrada 2010.* Lima: Pontificia Universidad Católica del Perú, 2013.

Matos Mar, J. *Estado desbordado y sociedad nacional emergente: Historia corta del proceso peruano, 1940–2010.* Lima: Universidad Ricardo Palma, Centro de Investigación, Lima, 2014.

Ministerio de Cultura. *Política Nacional de Cultura al 2030.* Lima: Ministry of Culture, 2020.

Museo de Arqueología y Antropología, Universidad Nacional Mayor de San Marcos. *Cuadernos de Investigación del Archivo Tello No. 1. Arqueología del Valle de Lima.* Lima: Museo de Arqueología y Antropología, Universidad Nacional Mayor de San Marcos, 1999.

Oldenburg, R. *The Great Good Place: Cafés, Coffee Shops, Community Centers, Beauty Parlors, General Stores, Bars, Hangouts, and How They Get You Through the Day.* New York: Paragon House, 1989.

Vera, F., Adler, V. and Uribe, M.C. (eds). ¿Qué podemos hacer para responder al *COVID-19 en la ciudad informal?* Inter-American Development Bank, 2020.

Walker, C. *Shaky Colonialism: The 1746 Earthquake-tsunami in Lima, Peru, and Its Long Aftermath.* Durham and London: Duke University Press, 2008.

8
(Re-) constructing the contemporary city in Latin America
María Andrea Tapia

This work has been conceived as a space for reflection on, and analysis of the (re-) construction of the contemporary city. Needless to say, no views on this issue can escape the state of current affairs worldwide and the emergence of COVID-19 – a challenging factor that questions the very principles that once structured the concept of 'city'.

Considering studies on urban recovery of favelas, such as Paraisópolis, or the cases of some cities in Brazil, Venezuela or Argentina, with a number of building construction projects carried out over the last 15 years, it can be stated that some of these have resulted in innovative developments. This has been possible thanks to the in-depth examination of existing social networks in informal neighbourhoods, and the need to make them visible and to organise them hierarchically through the materialisation of the public space, which serves as the cornerstone that ensures the development of civic values and the citizens' sense of belonging to the city they are part of. However, building construction projects led by the private sector – especially after the military coups in Latin America and during the early years of globalisation – were focused on housing as a whole, neglecting the process of creation of the city as a complex space that favours the formation of citizenship through its public spaces and public buildings. This approach can be identified not only in the construction projects of informal neighbourhoods, but also in their counter-proposals: private neighbourhoods or gated communities. In both of these models, the concept of public space, understood as a construction, is rejected and denied on the basis of the predominance of individual development and values in private neighbourhoods or due to unsatisfied basic needs in favelas or precarious neighbourhoods. Housing, then, affects public space, which becomes a type of 'residual space' for the construction of social networks and shared values. In other words, public space, which serves as the basic framework for the construction of citizenship, occurs in the urban interstices or the 'in-between' spaces of the cities.

With new policies of voluntary and mandatory isolation, social distancing and avoidance of close contact implemented in light of the COVID-19 pandemic, the debate around physical and material space has been highlighted, together with the subject of housing. It has revealed a number of issues which had not been considered essential until now, including the prolonged silencing and deprecation of discussions around public space. Such debate is now more than 30 years overdue. In order to reflect on concrete cases, three informal urban situations have been chosen in three different Latin American countries that have all suffered a structural housing problem since the middle of the twentieth century. Although the scales of the examples are different, Paraisopolis with 60,000 inhabitants and the neighbourhood 'Las 250 casas' with around 1000 inhabitants, they show the same deficiencies or absences and the same strengths: the public space as waste, the network of social links as support and engine for the improvement of the urban condition and policy as an instrument to build both the city and citizenship.

Invisible reconstructions

Today it is possible to provide a critical reading of Latin America's most vulnerable habitats and constructions, which have been explicitly exposed due to the impact of COVID-19. Both housing policies and policies for vulnerable urban sectors, which are usually informal, tend to respond to a single emergency with a sense of urgency: housing. By providing a quick solution, policies ignore the fact that, more often than not, households are sustained by an underlying invisible network of social links, mainly between women, who support one another to make their lives more enjoyable and tolerable as they try to manage the formal work and reproductive labour that take place in the domestic sphere and in the community.

In Latin America, the real catastrophe is that of the informal settlements, as they represent a serious emergency which requires urgent action, and calls for reconstruction. Originating in the twentieth century, they have been considered and treated as a contextual problem, initially triggered by the economic crisis of the 1930s. The considerable number of economic and political crises that followed were the main impediment to the proper management of these informal settlements, creating a tragedy in the making. It is hard to conceive that a catastrophe could last almost a century, yet it is true. Nowadays, 110 million Latin American people live in informal neighbourhoods, equivalent to 17 per cent of the population,[1] which means that almost a quarter of our cities have an informal origin.

This chapter presents stories, investigations and experiences from three different contexts: Caracas in Venezuela, Sao Paulo in Brazil and General Roca in Argentina, to provide the basis for the portrayal of the silent process of reconstruction of informal settlements.

Caracas, Venezuela

El Barrio Julián Blanco, Petare

Understanding the invisible reconstructions in our cities requires an understanding of the people and ideas that give birth to such reconstructions. For this purpose, we shall embark on an imaginary trip through the tales of some of the actors who have been silenced and made invisible. This trip begins with the initial premise in mind that:

> city life is a delicate and complex interwoven network of encounters and disagreements, and as such, it demands both sensitivity and sensibility so that its fragility is understood. We are talking about a balance sustained by the day-to-day and the subjective; a balance that should not be omitted in the processes of urban planning.[2]

In order to understand this complex network, one needs to pay attention to the women who live, or have lived, in vulnerable neighbourhoods which have been built autonomously, or self-built. These neighbourhoods provide the central spaces for urban reconstruction and are reminders that 'there are no disconnected or foreign worlds, and a mutual and attentive look, and a sympathetic listening, are necessary'[3] to promote understanding among individuals. This understanding paves the way for the construction of a common shared vision, a city-building, a network of neighbourhoods with public spaces where 'streets and their sidewalks, the main public places of a city, are its most vital organs. Think of a city and what comes to mind? Its streets. If a city's streets look interesting, the city looks interesting; if they look dull, the city looks dull.'[4]

With these beliefs as a starting point, we begin with the reconstruction of the Venezuelan chabolas through the history of their families. From a poetic perspective, 'the house was magical: it stretched and shrank according to need. Perched halfway up a hill, it offered a panoramic view of the bay; there were four rooms on the first floor, and an apartment below…'[5] This description is not entirely inaccurate, as the Venezuelan chabolas in the area of Caracas seem to hang, like pendants, from the surrounding hills. This vernacular architecture, which responds to the definition of opportunity, economy, availability of particular materials and local building techniques, is realised through land being occupied in an informal manner, with self-built houses distributed according to the topographic conditions and land availability. Such occupation is neither accidental nor casual. In fact, it is the result of the materialisation of invisible bonds built by families, through women, in pursuit of self-protection and mutual collaboration.

Figure 8.1 Exteriors of precarious homes, El Barrio Julián Blanco, Petare, Caracas, Venezuela, 2009.

Figure 8.2 Informal neighbourhoods, El Barrio Julián Blanco, Petare, Caracas, Venezuela, 2021. Source: Google maps.

If we describe these settlements by considering their public structure, we can say that the main public ways in the neighbourhoods are those which allow them to communicate with the formal city. They are generally plain, asphalted surfaces, where vehicles and people circulate freely. The main arterial road of the settlement is more lively, displaying the typical hustle and bustle of a city, so it could be seen as 'the neighbourhood's centre'.

The secondary public ways are commonly known as pavements and are generally built by the people who live in the neighbourhoods. These walkways are usually made of concrete and have a terraced or stepped design built on a steep slope. They hardly ever meet the minimum standards of usability, for instance, considerations of width are determined by the residual space available, and the tread and riser of a stair can vary depending on the slope of the land and available materials. Generally speaking, along these walkways you will not find a landing or a resting spot for long distances.

Privatised ways, better known as condominium staircases, are those which, according to the people in the neighbourhood, once offered public access but due to their location and insecurity issues were then locked with steel security doors. This permitted the emergence of a type of community space with shared household rules, agreed upon by the families living in the condominium. The size of the street and its centrality determine the activities that take place there. Similarly, each remaining interstitial space – the space resulting from the subdivision of a parcel of land – becomes a space full of life thanks to the people who live there. By means of recreational activities, such as basketball or football, or decision-making in community meetings or neighbourhood assemblies, the space is appropriated. In the case of secondary or less central streets or public ways, women do the laundry while little girls play with their dolls, and others gather in small groups for conversation. Doorways also provide a place for socialisation among female neighbours and a control centre for the neighbourhood's watch and protection.

The reading of the streets we have made, of the appropriation of space outside the scope of urban planning or projects in the city of Caracas, reveals that these so-called 'streets' are also the spaces that give people the possibility to access their housing. These houses become the central element of a new configuration. It is vital to understand this for action to be taken to reconstruct them and, in doing so, to restore a sense of dignity and visibility to their otherwise invisible support and containment networks. These groups are essential, especially in moments like the COVID-19 pandemic, since they are the pillars of the community and provide assistance to those in need – women, children and the elderly.

Through analysis of the houses, we will be able to grasp how much these housing units rely on one another: one single house may contain several houses or units and the groups that live in each unit may be correlated in different ways. Family bonds, business relations, landlord – tenant relations, friendship or cooperative relations, and even relations of 'invasion', in which individuals occupy a piece of land by force, all coexist here. Social and family relations, in particular those with blood bonds, are key to understanding these houses, since the social or family hierarchy, both within the group and within the neighbourhood, is closely connected with the hierarchical organisation of space. The society of this city presents such an extreme situation that, in order for people to survive, they need to forge close interpersonal links that allow mutual recognition and acceptance, cooperation and help.

In this neighbourhood, the reconstruction process was carried out on the basis of microcredits being granted, especially to women as heads of households, so that they could improve the living conditions of their households. The existing relationships and bonds were kept, but there was no clear attempt to make them visible, or to strengthen them. Thus, we observe that the responsibility for improvement lies solely with individuals (private), with no intervention or action on behalf of the state.

Sao Paulo, Brazil

Paraisópolis

Figure 8.3 Aerial image of the Paraisópolis favela, Sao Paulo, Brazil, 2009.

The second case we are concerned with is the reconstruction of one of the biggest favelas in Sao Paulo, Brazil. This project was implemented by the SEHAB (Secretaria de Habitação, or Housing Secretariat) whose director, architect Elisabete França, began the urbanisation and transformation process of Sao Paulo's favelas into new neighbourhoods. It was understood that public space had to be reconstructed and materialised into new configurations, which acknowledged that its underlying cooperative networks sustain, support and collaborate with it.

The favela can be read as a 'strange' configuration located in the city – partly due to its peculiar morphological traits, but also because of the lack of clear connecting elements between the favela and its surroundings, which result from the self-centredness of the favela's dwellers, and a marked feeling of rejection towards the favela by neighbours in the surrounding formal neighbourhoods.

The reurbanisation of Paraisópolis represents one of the most ambitious programmes of Sao Paulo's prefecture, which seeks to improve informal settlements in the city. Just as in the Venezuelan case, houses here are arranged in a disorderly and dense layout, occupying all the land available. Once more, public space is the remainder of private use of the space. Some of the houses are located in areas with dangerously steep slopes, prone to landslides and floods. Others are made with scavenged materials or waste, often built within the blocks themselves, putting the state of sanitation and safety at stake. Then, if one or more houses prove to be life-threatening to individuals or a group, they are removed or torn down.

Through observation of this and other favelas it became evident that the football field is the only public place respected by most, especially young and adult males. It is not occupied, whereas all the other spaces that could be considered public are residual spaces that surrender to the power and dominion of the strongest. This is why women occupy residual spaces within the private realm and the household, as these effectively represent an extension of their own houses. Identifying and making such residual spaces and the domestic realm visible can lead us to chart new maps that reveal the underlying invisible 'nets' necessary for the process of reconstruction of the public space, in order to make the favela a real neighbourhood where its residents' culture and idiosyncrasies are respected. Not only do these spaces alter our conception of the neighbourhood, they also help us to rethink housing standards. The focus here is not the material quality of houses in the favela, but the activities carried out by women, elderly people and children, as well as the roles they play in these spaces, which, although precariously built, provide support and life to the neighbourhood.

The reconstruction of Paraisóplois marked a turning point in urban reconstruction. Social workers played a key role in unveiling the existence of the complex social networks that enable women's self-support and personal development. Women can be seen as more than reproducers; they are active producers, working outside their households. It was then understood that a requalification and the reconstruction of these urban areas did not merely mean deciding whose house was to be torn down for being considered dangerous or in a deplorable state. It meant a complex process of relocating families, where each family's place within the long-established social network in the different sectors of the favela had to be carefully considered. One might say that a task resembling microsurgery was carried out, since it involved removing dangerous house units, relocating families to new houses, or exchanging their home for another unit located in the same original urban nucleus. Other improvements were the removal of houses which prevented other households from having proper lighting or ventilation. In turn, public spaces were built providing shared services to the nuclear unit of houses, since this could not be done within each house. This process of public space reconstruction has favoured the consolidation and strengthening of the social networks people are already part of.

Regenerating urban voids is a contemporary necessity in an area which lacks open spaces. When conditions permit it, removals are carried out in blocks' centres to create small squares or parks. New constructions are then built around their perimeter to resettle the local population. New buildings with three or four floors provide housing for families who have lost theirs, or have given it to others to sustain the existing social network. This type of operation is innovative, since it contemplates the intricate and delicate social networks – or the invisible strings – mentioned at the beginning of this discussion, thus foregrounding vulnerable groups and their social structure, and fostering their identity generation and sense of belonging.

General Roca, Argentina

Toma Las 250 casas

'Anthropology, as a discipline, has put great emphasis on the fact that social relations among individuals and/or groups are based on social obligations, which link and associate people within a community'.[6]

In 2007, the illegal taking and occupation of lands known as the '250 viviendas' (250 households) took place. The city council imposed

Figures 8.4 and 8.5 Public space in Paraisópolis, Sao Paulo, Brazil – before reconstruction (2009) and afterwards (2011).

measures including the withdrawal of lands owned by the Federal Penitentiary System (FPS) and their transfer to the new occupants in September 2011. The procedure involved the incorporation of these lands into the city council's land bank as social lots, so that the neighbours of the settlement could purchase and acquire them. Around 175 lots were distributed, with almost half the number to be granted once the occupants had been able to put their financial situation in order. This was the state proposal for legalising the tenancy of the lands, however there was no real reconstruction project. Nevertheless, there were cases in which social networks were created on the basis of a sense of belonging and an already existing collective identity. One example was Barrio las 250 viviendas,[7] a housing project from the Provincial Institute of Housing and Urban Planning (PIHUP).[8]

General Roca's case becomes emblematic as it is a project aimed at the materialisation of public space through the replication of social networks and the consolidation of the space. The Toma 250 casas[9] (take 250 houses) can be seen as an example of constructing a settlement based on recognition of and association with pre-existing social relations. This settlement originated with the second generation of residents of Barrio las 250 viviendas del IIPV – a neighbourhood that belongs to a formal social housing programme in the city. Located in the north of General Roca, this neighbourhood consists of small apartment units, built by the state to a standard design that does not permit horizontal expansion. For this reason, as families saw their numbers increase with the next generation, they occupied a piece of land right across the street, thus giving birth to informal settlements. As the sons and daughters of the neighbourhood started their own families, they also settled on the land opposite the neighbourhood. They received the help of relatives and neighbours in building their homes, focusing mainly on areas to rest and relax, since their basic needs of food and hygiene were still being provided by their parents in their own flats. In this way, the Toma 250 casas has a symbiotic relationship with the neighbourhood from which it stemmed, as it depends on the service infrastructure of the houses from that neighbourhood. The families settled in this 'occupied land' call themselves the 'sons and daughters of 250': their parents are part of the group of families able to access a housing programme from PIHUP. Currently, there are 240 such families – a second generation that decided to occupy a piece of land since their parents could not expand their own housing units to accommodate their children and grandchildren. The occupied land has been divided into lots with an area of 10 x 25 m, a configuration that bears a slight resemblance to formal land distribution.

Figure 8.6 Interdependent relationships between the formal neighbourhood and the Toma Las 250 casas. General Roca, Argentina. Image: Luciano Idda (2014).

This settlement has a special peculiarity in that the spaces which families lack in the formal house unit (the parents' house) are reconstructed in the Toma, with spaces for social events such as dining incorporated into the precarious house, which, even with few or no facilities, becomes a meaningful central space for family relations and other existing social networks.

These settlements are not part of state housing proposals or development programmes, yet they provide the space for social gatherings among neighbours, for social collaboration among women – who benefit from having a space for sharing and spending time together – for the potential creation of shared values, and in some ways, for the construction of citizenship. However, this is not enough, since the state should strive for a suitable construction of public space that guarantees the incorporation of these precarious, informal settlements into the urban structure and configuration of the city. These settlements constitute neighbourhoods in their own right, since they contribute to the creation of a new citizenship in a collaborative and horizontal way.

Figure 8.7 Toma Las 250 casas house distribution and classification. Images: Luciano Idda (2014).

Conclusions

These three cases have enabled us to reflect upon the issue of reconstruction of the city in the light of a catastrophe, whether of a natural or anthropic nature. The factors of emergency and urgency, for this particular study, have profound implications for rethinking and changing the paradigms of action in the context of traumatic events, such as losing one's home and social group of support and containment.

We are social beings and, as such, our development relies heavily on the collective aspect of belonging to social groups that share the same interests, values and desires – a right to which we are entitled as individuals. In spite of how banal this may sound, it is essential to resignify 'reconstructions', because simply providing a roof over someone's head is not enough. The experiences we have seen reveal that providing housing does not necessarily guarantee the construction of citizenship, neither does it facilitate social integration within communities, or a sense of belonging.

The current pandemic presents a new challenge: the construction of a social understanding with 'risk' as a predominant value. This in turn emphasises and strengthens individual rights and values over collective rights: the private realm over the public one. In the prologue of *The Death and Life of Great Cities*[10] is a quotation, which, although written some years ago, is relatable in the contemporary context of the COVID-19 pandemic:

Jane Jacobs is an advocate of a kind of urban lifestyle, which guarantees people certain faculties or choices. Among the elements Jacobs considers essential for life in the city, there are two we would like to stress; two aspects that seem both contradictory and mutually exclusive: security and privacy. The sense of freedom, granted by anonymity in big cities, is no longer a felt commodity in our cities, as now it is common to find surveillance cameras in public spaces and a strong police presence in neighbourhoods with a higher crime rate.[11]

The issue of security is a recurrent theme in discussions of reconstruction, especially for the most vulnerable social groups, including women, children and the elderly. When there is no vision for public space, house planning and material quality submit to the private sector and individual decision-making. This leads to residual spaces becoming part of the public sphere, since they generate and allow circulation of those who need to access the housing. Such residual space, now considered to be 'nobody's land', is an area that can potentially be transformed and materialised through the sociocultural development of its people.

Within the context of a pandemic, this challenge seems to be even greater. In Latin America, the lack of sanitation norms and preventive measures, as well as supplies to tackle COVID-19, has become clearly visible, especially in vulnerable settlements and neighbourhoods. This situation does nothing but add to the stigmatisation of this type of neighbourhood, since they have become the incubators and focus of infection. Moreover, the absence of civic regulations becomes evident as we fail to observe shared beliefs and the recognition of the other as one we can trust for our wellbeing. The other, understood as the neighbours who live in formal neighbourhoods, who meet the standards of a citizen: in those spaces, the state's presence and actions provide services that cater for basic needs, offer public spaces, institutions of representation and participation. Conversely, state regulation is nonexistent in informal neighbourhoods, since they are left out of the formal urban configuration.

Another consideration drawn from the analysis of the three Latin American examples is the meaning attributed to housing in each society. In Venezuelan chabolas, access to housing means ensuring a source of income. In the informal system, housing means being able to make a living, or renting a place. So, housing does not only mean having a place to live, but also, a place where survival is possible thanks to self-employment and jobs that provide an income.

In the case of Paraisópolis, housing and location represent possible access to formal work, as Paraisópolis originated with the construction of

Morumbi – one of the wealthiest neighbourhoods in Sao Paulo. Therefore, the men and women of Paraisópolis constitute a potential workforce for the different trades and domestic spheres of the residential Morumbi quarter. Living in this settlement allows people to reach their jobs in a short period of time and promotes the creation of flexible spaces where women work collaboratively with one another – for instance, to look after children or the elderly. In their masterplan, Ciro Pirondi, Analía Amorin and Rubén Otero materialise these small spaces which come in close contact with housing, and try to provide a new configuration of the space – one which takes into consideration the complex social networks of cooperation and dependency that are interwoven by the families living in the favela.

As for the Toma Las 250 casas, housing becomes an extension of the formal house, and family relations are central, with children choosing to live close to their parents. This situation can also be seen in the Venezuelan chabolas, where a single house may accommodate three or four generations within its walls. In General Roca, as the state's formal housing programme would not permit expansion, the younger generations occupied the lands nearby, opening up a symbiotic interaction between the two parts: formal houses and their informal growth and expansion no further than a hundred metres away.

In the three examples, public space, whatever its characteristics, is the resulting product of house occupation. These informal neighbourhoods have been constructed individually, with families building whatever house they can in the available land, with no collective project or vision behind the settlements. However, this has not prevented the emergence of social networks of help, support and collaboration – sustained and reinforced mainly by women. Still, it must be noted that the lack of planned and thought-out public space reveals the notable absence of the state: the entity that allows the development of citizenship and the creation of a sense of belonging and attachment to a bigger and complex system – the city.

Yet, when the state does take action and intervenes, whether it is with the granting of microcredits in Venezuela, or with reurbanisation projects elsewhere, the focus is primarily on solving housing issues without the generation of spaces that favour the development of social networks. Constructing public space should not only benefit the neighbourhood, but should also generate ways of connecting the neighbourhood with other surrounding areas, to construct the city. This aspect was only understood in Paraisópolis' ambitious masterplan, aided by a number of different professionals who worked to generate a more encompassing, inclusive and complex reconstruction project.

We are well aware that a serious and in-depth discussion about the construction of public spaces, understood as the aesthetic materialisation of socio-political ethics, has long been needed, and that for more than 60 years this discussion has been postponed in order to respond to the housing emergency. Needless to say, housing access needs to be guaranteed, yet it is of the utmost importance that the right to access the city should also be guaranteed, since the city is the epitome of public space – the space where our civic beings develop, and this can only be achieved when we become true members of society – individuals with full rights.

Notes

1 ONU-HABITAT. 'Estado de las Ciudades de America Latina y el Caribe', 12.
2 Colmenarejo, 'Más reflexiones sobre La Ciudad según Jean Jacobs' (translated quotation).
3 Colmenarejo, 'Más reflexiones sobre La Ciudad según Jean Jacobs'.
4 Jacobs, *Muerte y Vida de las Grandes Ciudades,* 55.
5 Allende, *La suma de los días*, 99.
6 Lekerman, 'Formas de habitar', 66–71.
7 'The 250 houses' neighbourhood.
8 In Spanish: Instituto Provincial de Planificación de la Vivienda (IIPV).
9 The word 'toma' refers to the illegal act of taking and occupying a piece of land. 'The TAKING of the land'.
10 *Muerte y Vida de las Grandes Ciudades*. Original name in English: *The Death and Life of Great American Cities*, first published in 1961. The Spanish reedition was released in 2011. The prologue corresponds to the Spanish edition.
11 Jacobs, *Muerte y Vida de las Grandes Ciudades*, 8 (translated quotation).

Bibliography

Allende, I. *La Suma De Los Días*. Barcelona: Arete, 2007.
Amorim, A., Otero, R. and Pirondi, C. 'Paraisópolis Plan de Desarrollo Urbano 2010–2025'. *DEARQ-Journal of Architecture*, 06 (2010):148–55. Accessed 16 June 2022 http://www.redalyc.org/articulo.oa?id=341630315015
Colmenarejo Fernández R. 'Más reflexiones sobre La Ciudad según Jean Jacobs', jardines en los que creo, 31 March 2018. Accessed 15 September 2020 http://rosacolmenarejo.blogspot.com/2008/02/ms-reflexiones.html.
Graterol Sardi, A. 'Sueños de Familia Casas sin límites'. Master Thesis, Fundación UPC, 2008.
Jacobs, J. *Muerte y Vida de las Grandes Ciudades*. Madrid: Capitán Swing, 2011.
Lekerman, V. 'Formas de habitar en una villa de emergencia: redes de relaciones y prácticas de urbanización'. *KULA Magazine*, 2 (2010): 65–75. http://www.revistakula.com.ar/numeros-anteriores/numero-2/kula-2-vanina-lekerman/
ONU-Hábitat, 'Estado de las Ciudades de America Latina y el Caribe', Programa de las Naciones Unidas para los Asentamientos Humanos. (August 2012) 11–12. Accessed 16 June 2022 www.senavitat.gov.py/pdf/deficit.pdf
Tapia, M.A. 'Construyendo indicios. Arquitectura, cultura y sociedad en la ciudad contemporánea'. *Corazonada Magazine*, 8 (2015): 17–27. Accessed 7 June 2022 https://revistacorazonada.files.wordpress.com/2015/09/corazonada-latido-82.pdf

9
Invisible regeneration
The communities of Shahjahanabad in times of pandemic
Abhishek Jain

Historic cities with an organic 'morphostructure' have always been considered as centres of public activity and strong sociocultural lifestyle. An example is the city of Shahjahanabad in India, whose neighbourhoods are renowned for their connected houses and rooftops, internal courtyards and narrow alleys, all providing a sense of connectivity that is both physical and social.

This chapter illustrates how the social fabric of these communities gives them the power to adapt to the different lifestyle that is necessary in times of pandemic. It looks at how societies based in the gated neighbourhoods of the historic city of Shahjahanabad provide model methodologies that could be helpful to other communities – and in turn to the city as a whole, considered as a network of such neighbourhoods. The city's close-knit social structure does, however, have a number of shortcomings that should be reassessed in the light of the current pandemic.

The COVID-19 epidemic in India

The first case of COVID-19 in India was reported on 27 January 2020 in Kerala.[1] By the beginning of March 2020, the number of cases had increased sharply and the impact of COVID-19 was significant both in the states and union territories of India.[2] The greatest number of total infections and the highest mortality rates across India have, at least apparently, been in metropolitan cities such as Mumbai, Delhi, Bangalore, Ahmedabad, Chennai and Kolkata.[3]

On 22 March 2020, the Indian government announced a nationwide lockdown called the 'Janta Curfew' to prevent the spread of the virus. This was later divided into four different phases. As cases decreased, the lockdown started to be lifted in India, although from 25 November 2020 the central government allowed the different state governments to impose local restrictions. A vaccination drive began on 26 February 2021.[4] Yet, from the middle of March 2021, the second wave of the pandemic proved to be even more catastrophic than the previous one. More than 400,000 cases were registered in India due to a new mutant strain of the virus, which the World Health Organization (WHO) identified as substantially more contagious than other variants.[5]

Due to a spiralling increase in cases, state governments have subsequently tried to generate new models to control the infections, while at the same time upgrading medical resources. Shortages of medicines, oxygen and medical facilities remain an additional and constant threat around the country. As infected cases rise and fall in different states in India, state governments remain responsible for policy and for imposing lockdowns based on the prevalence of cases. A variety of safety guidelines have been issued by different state governments and private authorised departments to reflect the recorded number of pandemic cases. On 19 April 2021 the city of Delhi announced another lockdown due to a surge in cases in the ongoing (May 2021) second wave of COVID-19.[6]

As the virus transmits very quickly, distance maintained between people plays a very important role in infection – and the number of people within a space can make a huge difference to levels of transmission. Looking at this issue in the context of the major Indian metropolises, all have an internal city that has grown organically over centuries. These compact settlements in inner cities have experienced major problems due to the spread of COVID-19 and lifestyles of the residents, directly related with the type of physical space in which they live or work, which are ill-suited to the social distancing required in times of pandemic. However, the organically grown morphostructures of compact settlements also provide multiple opportunities for maintaining distance, thanks to the availability of multiple access points to each neighbourhood and to the flexible uses of public spaces, which can be controlled in times of pandemic.

Case study – the city of Shahjahanabad

Delhi's inner city of Shahjahanabad was established by the Mughal king Shah Jahan in the seventeenth century and developed on principles of both Vastu Shastra[7] and traditional Islamic city planning.[8] Accordingly, the residential quarters of the city were intended to accommodate the organic growth of built fabric. However, the city has since seen many ups and downs, which have resulted in the superimposition of newer land-use and building-development rules. These have led to the abolition of the traditional development controls of the old Islamic city, with the urban structure being 'vandalised' by overpowering commercial activity merging with existing residential building use. From the time of East India Company rule in the nineteenth century, this led to an increase in the real-estate value of properties and a great deal of gentrification. To take advantage of the increasing commercial value of properties in residential areas, large old mansions were subdivided to create shops at ground level, and this led to the formation of compact houses without setbacks – spaces left around the buildings for light and ventilation. This was a gradual process which took years and continued, even after Indian independence from British rule, due to a lack of development controls for this special area and because of the city's dense organic urban fabric. Yet the traditional communities remain in these organically grown gated neighbourhoods, which are called *mahallas*. These characterful districts are governed around communal traits, based on the caste, religion and type of trade the community is involved in.

More recently, these neighbourhoods have become further divided into tiny plots with small shafts and narrow streets, occupying areas which previously had been the large courtyards of the mansions and the public space around them. This self-generated organic morphology can be compared to a human body with a dense mass of innumerable veins, cells and muscles. Uncontrolled vertical expansion and population growth has affected residential living space to a certain extent, as well as the light and ventilation of that space, but still the existing organic growth of physical built fabric in these settlements helps them to be more socially connected, retaining their original traits. This has led to many advantages: communities share physical and financial resources like an extended family and the sense of trust among community neighbours has made it natural for them to assist each other when health issues have arisen during the pandemic. Within their social groups, men, women and children take care of each other and support each other with food, household chores and even financial assistance.

Figure 9.1 Map of the city of Shahjahanabad.

Gated neighbourhood of Shahjahanabad: detailed study area

In the old city of Shahjahanabad, there are a number of these organically grown, gated *mahallas*. Usually, they begin with a connection to a bazaar street, with an entrance in a narrow alley marked by a huge arched gateway. Traditionally, the upper storeys of these gateways had rooms which were used by security guards, but today most of the upper storeys are no longer there, and the spaces have been taken over by small CCTV cameras. This main entrance alley then leads to a further secondary street with important community buildings such as temples, schools and dispensaries, which were earlier grouped around a public square called the *chowk*. These chowks have now been partially covered due to the expansion of large community buildings. This means that all of the public open spaces have been partially built over, leading to a shortage of external space for public interaction. Instead, in the absence of setbacks, neighbouring partitioned mansions are interconnected at their upper level where flat roofs – or terraces – act as major interaction zones for people of all age groups. There are, however, no other open spaces outside or inside the neighbourhood.

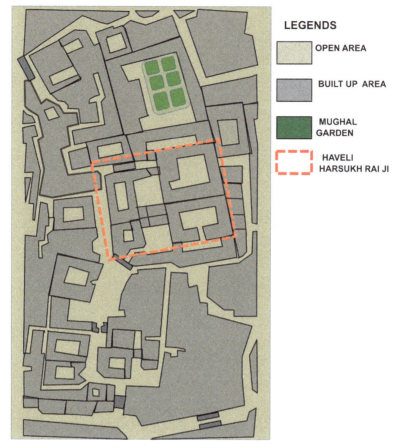

Figure 9.2 Map of nineteenth-century Roshanpura.

Within Shahjahanabad, the particular district at the centre of this study is known as Roshanpura. It was originally developed in the Mughal era and has been in a constant state of transformation since, with building uses changing, floor areas and plot ratios increasing, and incompatible mixes of land use emerging. The district has particularly narrow streets of only around two-metres width, and traditional mansions of three to four floors, with original facades below and extensions above. This compactness, which in normal times acts as a feature of social connection, has constituted a major problem during the pandemic when physical distancing has become necessary. Roshanpura is actually part of a series of neighbourhoods connected at one end with the major bazaar street known as *Nai Sarak* (New Road), which was built by the East India

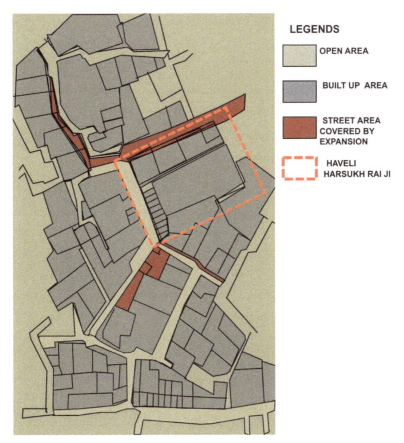

Figure 9.3 Existing map of Roshanpura showing detailed study area of divided Haveli in red box.

Company as part of its first renewal scheme in Shahjahanabad. This gradually led to the branching out of new neighbourhoods within the existing urban fabric, making the whole district even more compact. Dead-end alleys emerged as a byproduct of the land division of bigger mansions. These partitioned mansions now act as complexes of small residential buildings. Some are totally renovated, with old carved gateways still intact as symbols of the past, while some have new facades with uneven heights. This housing typology makes it more difficult for residents to maintain social distancing in times of pandemic.

Transformed housing and social distancing during the pandemic

Figure 9.4 shows the plan of one of the largest mansions of Roshanpura, known as Rai Ji Haveli. Over time, this mansion was subdivided and now acts as a shared housing block for lower-income groups. Where there was

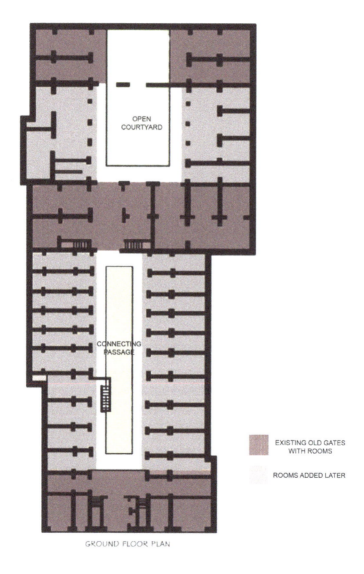

Figure 9.4 Plan of transformed grey part shown in Figure 9.3.

Figure 9.5 The courtyard of Haveli Rai Ji.

Figure 9.6 Cardboard file making activity has moved to the interior rooms in Haveli Rai Ji.

once a single extended family, 65 families are now accommodated, each occupying one room. It is clear that this housing typology makes it difficult to maintain social distancing. The difficulty is compounded by the fact that most of the people living there are employed as cardboard file makers and carry out their work in the shared courtyard, which is very narrow due to multiple and successive subdivisions. The overall width of the courtyard, including the walkways, is just three metres. This not only affects the lifestyle of the people residing there, but also their economic activity, since the restrictions implied by social distancing make it difficult for them to work in the courtyard. Compounding this, the connected market street, which is famous for handmade files and books, is suffering major economic losses due to the pandemic, a situation common in this part of the old city, where the roads are narrow and shops are very small and connected in such a way that it is impossible to maintain social distance.

Community collaboration: a resource for invisible regeneration

The social reaction of communities in Roshanpura to the pandemic has contrasted with that of nuclear families living in more elegant districts of New Delhi, for whom isolation in their bungalows has increased fear and stress for both young and old. Conversely, in the *mahallas,* where similar groups of people living together create small neighbourhoods inside larger neighbourhoods, this has resulted in the kinds of community collaboration that build resilience. This communal cohesion has given them the strength to get through the economic crisis, as a few families share whatever limited and sporadic work they can get with other households in the area, so that they all have income, while maintaining the social distancing needed to protect themselves from infection. This mutual support is a byproduct of the communities that have evolved along with the peculiar characteristics of these dense neighbourhoods. Somehow living together in small spaces next to each other has helped the populations of *mahallas* generate more visual and verbal interaction, even while following safety guidelines during lockdown. Indeed, the shared occupational traits of communities that grew historically around trade sectors appear to encourage resilient behaviour; despite the constraints of space, they have been able to share out work and provide each other with a livelihood.

This pattern of behaviour has also been apparent in wealthier neighbourhoods such as the Bania community involved in the paper trade who usually provide work to the workers in Rai Ji Haveli. Even though they already benefited from better living conditions due to their higher economic status, the absence of public space and the constraints of narrow lanes led to a resurgence of the use of roof terraces to transfer food and resources to the worker community, bridging social and ethnic divides.

Figure 9.7 Connecting terraces allow verbal and visual interaction between people in times of pandemic in Haveli Rai Ji.

Figure 9.8 Pictures showing residents working in self-created separate zones in Haveli Rai Ji.

Terrace networking as a resource for invisible regeneration

Connected roof terraces are another typology of dwelling that is common in Roshanpura. They also act as a resource for families living in the district, allowing them to interact without going out of their houses. Terraces act as controlled zones for children to play under their parents' watchful eyes, while allowing them to maintain an active lifestyle. This has helped distract children between and after the long hours of online learning imposed by the government, as schools are not able to afford the level of safety measures required in the current situation. Connected terraces have consequently played a very significant role in strengthening community living in these organically grown neighbourhoods, allowing people to develop mutual trust, which in turn has given them strength to

Figure 9.9 Left: a narrow tertiary street where controlled movement of people can be achieved. Right: a longitudinal section showing the benefits of terrace connections.

deal with the impact of the pandemic. Women and children have been able to maintain contact and exchange visits without exposing themselves to passers-by in mixed-use shared streets. This behaviour is the result of a close-knit community of varying incomes and from different ethnic groups and castes all coming together to help each other. The common factor in this process is trade occupation, with vertical connections emerging between merchants, artisans and craftspeople all engaged and interdependent in a trade ecosystem.

Organic morphostructures as a resource for invisible regeneration

The buildings of Roshanpura are not just connected longitudinally. Instead, the organically-grown branch-like street patterns generate clusters of houses for extended families within the tertiary streets, offering divided yet separate open spaces for households to interact while maintaining distance. These branches make it easier to control movement and reduce exposure to infection from outsiders, such as the mobile street vendors who move inside the neighbourhood to sell popular favourites such as *Nan Katai* (shortbread biscuits), *Kulfi* (ice lollies) and fruits and vegetables. Branching layouts also generate cul-de-sacs within these tertiary streets, further controlling movement around the dwellings themselves. While the gateways to such compact settlements cannot be closed during the day, they do provide checkpoints for taking peoples' temperatures, which helps to prevent the spread of infection. These safety measures are implemented and overseen by the residents themselves via *mahalla* resident welfare associations that bring together ethnic groups engaged in the same trade. Entering the series of neighbourhoods, visitors must pass through multiple checkpoints, where they are made aware of guidelines that apply to people from outside the neighbourhood, to community groups and to residents alike. These proactive preventive measures are not just helping people protect themselves, but also making it possible to keep using community buildings, such as temples and dispensaries, by controlling the influx of people. This contrasts with most of the primary streets, which are effectively shared spaces due to their connectivity into the city's main market streets.

Through their common trade, different ethnic groups share the same facilities and community buildings which have been used as vaccination centres with inoculation programmes organised in a free and safe way by the *mahalla* resident welfare associations.

Major issues: a barrier for invisible regeneration

While one advantage of the organic morphology of the gated neighbourhoods is the proximity of workplaces for residents, in the form of secondary bazaar streets, the infiltration of commercial activities into some of the *mahallas,* due to the lack of regulation on building use, has made it difficult to control the movement of workers into and out of the neighbourhood. This has become a major issue during the pandemic as activities such as loading and unloading at junctions, which are incompatible with social distancing, are inevitable and hinder control.

The lack of regulation and development control means that buildings in some areas also have very uneven heights. This prevents visual interaction in certain parts of the *mahalla* due to the different heights of adjacent terraces – and this, in turn, limits their utility as a resource. In some quarters of the neighbourhood this also creates a barrier in the visual interaction between different ethnic groups and limits social inclusion.

Finally, solid waste management constitutes a risk in these neighbourhoods. During the pandemic, *mahallas* have been unable to rely on community participation in waste collection. Exacerbated by the compactness of development and the lack of open space, uncontrolled waste disposal has placed the population in greater danger.

Conclusions

The organic development of the *mahallas* embodies their ability to adapt to change and the resilience of their society and architecture. Yet, while they possess unique characteristics that have helped their populations cope in the circumstances of the pandemic, the COVID-19 emergency has emphasised points of weakness.

A special disaster-management plan with specific controls for building use should be developed, taking account of the organic morphostructure of these particular neighbourhoods, and of their unique characteristics. This would reduce the negative impact of incompatible building uses and facilitate the regeneration and self-support of the communities. Similarly, planning regulation of building heights is required to help ensure positive future development and encourage visual connection of spaces at roof level. New rules should be sensitive to the particular needs of each neighbourhood according to its differing building typologies. Hygiene also needs to be addressed by developing a special morphostructure-specific solid waste management programme, educating and involving the community and encouraging residents to participate in its implementation.

These regulations would not only improve the day-to-day experiences of the neighbourhood, they would also help in maintaining controlled social integration through terrace networking, and prepare the gated communities to be even better protected and resilient in the future. These types of organic morphostructure should be treated as a resource for invisible regeneration in inner cities like Shahjahanabad, as their complexity and strong community structure have hidden advantages.

Notes

1 Andrews, Areekal, Rajesh, Krishnan, Suryakala, Krishnan, Muraly, Santhosh, First confirmed case of COVID-19 infection in India: A case report.
2 Siddiqui, Wiederkehr, Rozanova, Flahault, Situation of India in the COVID-19 Pandemic: India's Initial Pandemic Experience, 2020, 4.

3 Bhadra, Mukherjee, Sarkar, Impact of population density on Covid-19 infected and mortality rate in India.
4 The Economic Times, 'Janata curfew' to vaccination: India's year-long fight against COVID-19', 24 March 2021.
5 Choudhary, India reports over 400,000 daily cases for the third time in a week as second wave hammers country.
6 BBC News, Covid: Delhi announces lockdown as India's cases surge.
7 Sanskrit texts on the science of architecture.
8 Blake, *Shahjahanabad: The Sovereign City in Mughal India 1639–1739*, 15, 32.

Bibliography

Andrews, M.A., Areekal, B., Rajesh, K.R., Krishnan, J., Suryakala, R., Krishnan, B., Muraly, C.P., Santhosh, P.V. 'First confirmed case of COVID-19 infection in India: A case report'. Accessed 7 June 2022 https://www.ncbi.nlm.nih.gov/pmc/articles/PMC7530459/

BBC News. 'Covid: Delhi announces lockdown as India's cases surge', 19 April 2021. Accessed on 16 May 2021. https://www.google.com/amp/s/www.bbc.com/news/world-asia-india-56798248.amp

Bhadra, A., Mukherjee, A. and Sarkar, K. 'Impact of population density on Covid-19 infected and mortality rate in India', 14 October 2020. Accessed on 16 May 2021. https://www.ncbi.nlm.nih.gov/pmc/articles/PMC7553801/#__ffn_sectitle

Blake, S. *Shahjahanabad The Sovereign City in Mughal India 1639–1739*. Cambridge: Cambridge University Press, 1993.

Choudhary, S.R. 'India reports over 400,000 daily cases for the third time in a week as second wave hammers country', 7 May 2021. Accessed on 16 May 2021. https://www.google.com/amp/s/www.cnbc.com/amp/2021/05/07/india-covid-crisis-daily-cases-rise-above-400000-again.html

Ghosh, P., Ghosh, R. and Chakraborty, B. 'COVID-19 in India: Statewise Analysis and Prediction', 12 August 2020. Accessed on 16 May 2021. https://www.ncbi.nlm.nih.gov/pmc/articles/PMC7431238/#__ffn_sectitle

Siddiqui, A.F., Wiederkehr, M., Rozanova, L., Flahault, A. 'Situation of India in the COVID-19 pandemic: India's initial pandemic experience'. *International Journal of Environmental Research and Public Health*, 8994 (2020): 4. Accessed 7 June 2022. https://www.mdpi.com/1660-4601/17/23/8994

The Economic Times, '"Janata curfew" to vaccination: India's year-long fight against COVID-19', 24 March 2021. Accessed on 16 May 2021. https://economictimes.indiatimes.com/news/india/janata-curfew-to-vaccination-indias-year-long-fight-against-covid-19/articleshow/81669874.cms?from=mdr

Part III
Communication, prevention and protection

10
Rebuilding engagement with social media and consumer technologies

Barnaby Gunning and Lucia Patrizio Gunning

The psychological impact of a natural disaster can be compounded by the mechanisms of reconstruction and recovery that follow it, disenfranchising people who have been displaced, often at a moment when they are most psychologically vulnerable.

Following the 2009 L'Aquila earthquake, most of this central Italian city's inhabitants found themselves physically excluded and psychologically separated from a core part of their lives and disenfranchised from the processes of reconstruction and recovery. A 'red zone' established for safety censored visibility of the nature and extent of damage in the historic city and concealed the stalled reconstruction from scrutiny. In this context, the growth in use of social media in the post-earthquake period gave voice to the marginalised and dispersed populace of L'Aquila, providing platforms for protest and organisation. In parallel, emergent information technologies supplied free tools to map, photograph, film and 3D model the city's cultural heritage and to break the information curfew. The authors initiated and were closely involved with four projects that used web-based, mobile and consumer technologies to allow local people to engage with, record and share the state of the city. This chapter examines the strengths and limitations of these ground-up, citizen-driven initiatives and the long-term viability of independent, fast-response and crowd-sourced post-disaster projects. It looks at how similar techniques can be used to promote recovery and to create resilience to future disaster.

At 3.32 in the morning of 6 April 2009, the central Italian city of L'Aquila was struck by a 6.1–6.3 Mw magnitude earthquake. Three hundred and nine people lost their lives in the disaster. The swarm of tremors and aftershocks that followed the quake caused extensive damage to buildings throughout some 600 square kilometres of the surrounding seismic crater. The epicentre of the main tremor was located just 2 km southwest of the city walls at a depth of 8 km[1] and consequently a defining characteristic of the earthquake was its catastrophic impact on the extensive medieval city centre.

Within two days of the earthquake, an order[2] had been issued prohibiting access to all built structures in the communal territory of L'Aquila, and over the following months this was extended to create a number of no-entry red zones – the largest of which covered the entire medieval city centre. In practice this meant that with the exception of parts of the two principal axial streets, all access points into the city were closed-off with metal barriers. The primary motives behind this closure were to reduce the risk of personal injury and to limit opportunities for looting. Military checkpoints in several locations were established to act as a deterrent and to manage legitimate access.

In the immediate aftermath of the earthquake, the emphasis of activity was on managing the disaster, providing temporary accommodation to a displaced population of approximately 67,500 individuals, and shoring-up damaged structures. The only means of private access into the city was to individual property, following formal authorisation, with a fire-brigade escort and for a very limited amount of time. Citizens' individual perceptions of the impact of the earthquake were necessarily restricted to the sight of their own property and its immediate surroundings, with no overview of the true extent of the damage.

Prior to the 2009 earthquake, the city centre had been home to just 7,500 people, but it was an active urban area, home to most faculties of the University of L'Aquila, several primary and secondary schools, numerous public and private offices and a large number of shops, restaurants and bars. Since the early fourteenth century, the main cathedral square had hosted a daily food market and, at lunchtime and in the early evening, the main central streets became the social hub of the wider city, attracting a throng of people on their regular and highly social *passeggiata*. For residents of the *centro storico* as well as citizens of the broader metropolitan area of L'Aquila, the historic centre was the beating heart of their city.

Following the disaster, dispersed to temporary structures, into hotels along the Adriatic coast and to other cities around Italy, the citizens of L'Aquila were a fragmented diaspora, suddenly uprooted from their social territory and separated from their home city. In the consequent social vacuum, the emerging platforms of Facebook and Twitter provided partial respite and a means of aggregation and activism for a population that felt both physically excluded and disenfranchised from the decision-making processes of reconstruction. Facebook in particular was undergoing rapid growth in Italy in early 2009;[3] as one activist member put it at the time: '[In] L'Aquila the squares do not exist anymore, there are no physical spaces to meet … the virtual square became Facebook'.[4] Indeed in the absence of access to the physicality of their cities, internet access became increasingly important to the dispersed citizenry. Where previously most connectivity had been through landlines, the earthquake increased the use of mobile data connections either through smart phones or USB modem dongles.

Outside of the Abruzzo region, public perception was that the Berlusconi government had largely dealt with the problems of the disaster by the winter of 2009 through emergency-response measures and by the rapid construction of anti-seismic housing under the Progetto CASE.[5] For the people of L'Aquila, this view was in stark contrast to a silent, abandoned city centre, with the apparent absence of any reconstruction plan and with policies that required the buttressing of all of the buildings in the city centre, but that effectively prevented the commencement of any reconstruction work. The frustration created by the failure of the authorities even to commence clearing rubble was exemplified by wheelbarrow activists, *Il Popolo delle Carriole,* who began to force entry into key public spaces separating out recyclable building materials and physically reclaiming their city.[6]

A phrase commonly heard in conversation with L'Aquila citizens in this period was *'Come facciamo?'* – 'What can we do?' – both as a sign of despair and as a statement of determination, and this became the genesis of the first of four projects with which the authors of this paper were involved between 2009 and 2015.

Seeking a way to let citizens share their own photographs of the city and provide an overview of the actual extent of the damage to its historic fabric, the authors designed and developed a simple web application based on the Google Maps API.[7] The application presented a satellite view of the city, overlaid with map pins revealing photographs taken in L'Aquila before and after the earthquake. Users could upload digital images to the site and where photographs already contained location information, this was used to position them on the map. Alternatively, users could locate, label and date their pictures to indicate exactly when, where and by whom an image had been taken and in which direction the photographer was facing. All of this information was saved directly into the metadata of the digital file[8] and, if the image was located within 30 km of the centre of L'Aquila, a record was added into the database that furnished the contents of the map. The site was developed in the first two months of

2010 and initially contained just over two hundred photographs taken between September and December 2009. Shared among friends and family on Facebook, the website began to attract additional contributions and, when it came to the attention of national newspaper, *La Repubblica*[9] shortly before the first anniversary of the earthquake, this 'self-portrait' of the city provided a public glimpse beyond the barriers of what many feared at the time might be a new Pompeii. Images illustrated the broad spread of physical damage to private and public buildings, monuments and public spaces as well as the abandonment of the historic centre.[10]

Through architectural practice and commercial computer-modelling work, the authors had seen the utility of being able to view a city in its entirety in three dimensions, and were aware of how a publicly accessible model could encourage participation and improve the transparency of decision-making. This kind of model, accessible to anybody and from anywhere, could provide citizens with a compelling tool to illustrate the state of the city, as well as a means to plan its future. Reflecting on the lack of progress in L'Aquila and with a view to stimulating debate on reconstruction, Barnaby wrote an opinion piece for the Wall Street Journal,[11] explaining how, in the wake of natural disaster, photographic

Figure 10.1 Come Facciamo: Autoritratto web application, 2010.

documentation combined with aerial or satellite images and widely available 3D-modelling tools could empower citizens to regain some say in the process of reconstruction, as well as to get help from professional and amateur modellers elsewhere.

The Wall Street Journal article and subsequent coverage in the Italian national media came rapidly to the attention of the Google Earth team who were supportive of the initiative and indicated that they could provide training and technical support as part of their institutional outreach. Frequent communication and close collaboration developed with Laura Bononcini and Marco Pancini from the Google Policy team in Italy they oversaw all the institutional and practical aspects of the project and liaised with the American and British teams to make the collaboration happen. As the most widely used 3D platform, Google Earth appeared to provide the optimum way to publicly share the state of the centre of L'Aquila. At the time, the platform was primarily based on satellite photography overlaid on a three-dimensional mesh with about eight hundred points per square kilometre and almost all of the 3D building content had been produced by hobbyists. In L'Aquila the only structure to have been added was its distinctive fifteenth-century bastion castle, a model of which had been made post-earthquake by a Brazilian amateur, demonstrating the potential of the platform for international collaboration.

Over the course of the summer of 2010, a strategy was devised to undertake a photographic survey of the historic city centre. Permission to enter the red zone was negotiated with the council and the office for site safety in the city centre. In parallel with this, sponsorship was sought to cover the running expenses and the procurement of equipment.

A Facebook group, L'Aquila 3D, was set up to recruit volunteers to participate in Click Days and a L'Aquila 3D web application was created on the Come Facciamo domain. Facebook was the most effective platform to reach potential participants, reinforced by local media coverage both by *Il Centro* (the main local newspaper) and a newly-established news blog, *Il Capoluogo,* as well as local TV channel AQTV and the national third channel RAI 3, which broadcasts regional news. Local journalist Goffredo Palmerini, along with Google's own press team ensured that the initiatives were highly visible locally, nationally and among the wide community of Italians abroad.

In establishing the sequence of operations, Google Maps mark-ups were used to plan out a photographic campaign dividing the city into sectors and identifying every single urban block. Due to their architectural morphology some blocks were large and complex, others were simple, stand-alone villas and structures.

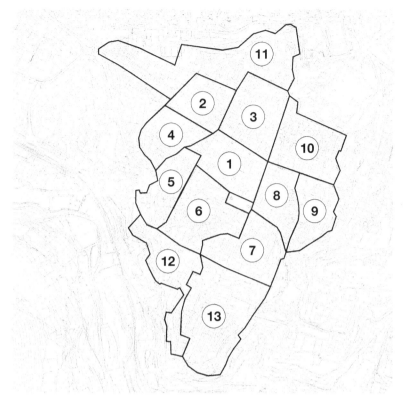

Figure 10.2 Click Days campaign map, 2010.

Click Days were carried out over the course of eight consecutive weekends from late September until early November. The initial Saturday was used to establish a health and safety procedure for working in what remained a hazardous environment, and to experiment with and develop a standardised and simple approach to comprehensively photographing all of the buildings.

In the autumn of 2010, the process of protecting and securing structures in the city centre was ongoing. A number of buildings already featured scaffolding buttresses which restricted visibility of their exteriors, but most were still either shored-up with temporary timber structures or in an ongoing state of collapse. As a consequence, each session began with a health and safety induction, the distribution of helmets and numbered lanyards and the sharing of mobile phone numbers.

Each Saturday and Sunday, groups of 20 people in the morning and a further 20 in the afternoon would assemble near the church of San Bernardino. Participants were instructed to work in pairs, alternating responsibility for assessing risk and directing photography or operating equipment and taking photographs. The first half-hour was spent carrying out trial photography with the whole team working together. From then on each couple was provided with a camera and tripod and assigned a memory card and record sheet for one urban block at a time. Photography of a block comprised firstly capturing wide-angle corner views and then taking multiple overlapping elevational pictures of all of the accessible and visible facades. On completion of the assigned block, the duo would return the memory card so that images could be saved, renamed to indicate which block they referred to and then copied to a removable hard drive. At the end of each day images were uploaded to the L'Aquila 3D server with paper records retained to record the map locations of each image set, to allow for error correction and to monitor progress.

Volunteers came from all walks of life, from teenagers to pensioners, from photographers, architects and engineers to students and professional clowns. Most were local citizens but a small number of people travelled from elsewhere in Italy, including Rome and Lombardy. For many local participants, these days spent photographing the city centre were their first opportunity since the earthquake to move freely within the red zone. Although there were early concerns that access into the city might be misused, all of the participants remained focused on capturing as much information as possible, working until the light failed each day and accumulating 38,211 photographs of 534 urban blocks and individual

Figure 10.3 Click Days work in progress, 2010.

buildings. It should be noted that despite the tacit support of the local council, permission to enter the city for the Click Days projects was in reality only informally granted, leading to awkward moments including an attempt by a single officer of the Carabinieri to arrest all 20 participants for being on the wrong side of the metal barriers.

Overlapping with the Click Days events, a series of training workshops was organised at the University of L'Aquila to teach volunteers how to model buildings for Google Earth. At the time, the preferred method of modelling was using the SketchUp software package which had been acquired by Google in 2006 and had gained geolocation tools in September 2010. Programme manager Nicole Drobeck and software engineer Simone Nicolò from the SketchUp team in Boulder, Colorado travelled to Italy to teach four one-day courses introducing participants to the principles of geomodelling. Satellite imagery and terrain data from Google Earth was used to position and plan out buildings. Photographs from the L'Aquila 3D website were then used to guide in extruding the height of each part of the structure, to determine the shape and pitch of roofs and to add in elevational and other details.

In early 2010, Google had additionally launched a web-based 3D-modelling platform called Building Maker. Using orthographic geometrically corrected aerial photographs, it allowed users to generate geographically-located building models. During the autumn of 2010, Google acquired aerial imagery of the centre of L'Aquila and in January 2011 a further two workshops were organised to teach the use of Building Maker. A further teaching workshop was also held in Palermo in June 2011 in association with ANFE,[12] a charitable foundation that looks after the interests of first- and second-generation Italian emigrants abroad.

Figure 10.4 L'Aquila 3D, web application, 2011.

In total, the courses provided training in 3D modelling to 206 participants in L'Aquila and a further 30 in Palermo. Most of the participants were aged between 18 and 30. Many had no previous modelling experience, though several prolific modellers had a background in engineering or architecture. In collaboration with hobbyists from across the globe, over the nine-month period from October 2010 to June 2011, participants modelled 618[13] urban blocks, stand-alone buildings and monuments covering approximately 60 per cent of the historic city centre.

The modelling process was somewhat hampered by differences between the low-resolution 3D terrain data downloadable from Google

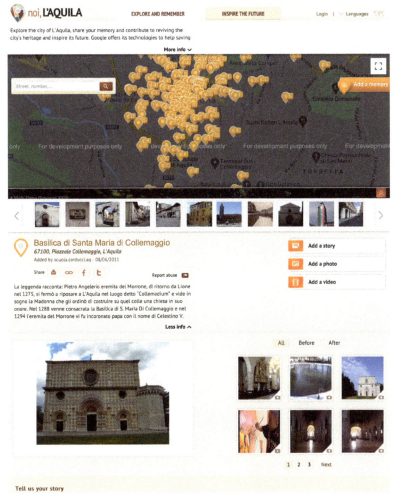

Figure 10.5 Noi L'Aquila web application, 2011.

Earth and the complex topology of L'Aquila. Furthermore, although much of the city centre was built on a gently sloping plateau and to a loose grid arrangement, the valleyed creases of parts of its underlying landscape created irregular street patterns, with steep streets and changes of level – none of which are perceptible in the terrain data. On top of this, SketchUp and Building Maker were tools best adapted to simple rectilinear constructions atypical of a medieval city.

While the 3D-modelling process was ongoing, Google launched its own platform to help the citizens of L'Aquila. Alice Repetto of Google's Italian office had proposed a platform that would combine a number of the company's different technologies to allow people to share memories, photographs and videos connected to physical places. The initiative was engineered by The Mad Pixel Factory in Madrid using Appspot, Google's cloud computing platform. Branded Noi L'Aquila or We L'Aquila, the platform was intended to be massively scalable and applicable to any location.

On the website, citizens could mark significant places and provide descriptions, comments and illustrative photographs, all of which could be accessed through a Google Maps interface and through Street View. Video interviews hosted on YouTube and linked to the site saw local experts describe the history of a number of key locations in the city, from the Basilica of Santa Maria di Collemaggio, to the theatre and the main market square. Additionally the website linked back to the L'Aquila 3D project and Google SketchUp and Building Maker.

The authors were closely involved with the creation of the Noi L'Aquila platform and insisted that the project be launched with a positive physical presence in the city centre. At the time, the paucity of mobile data coverage in the damaged city centre, and the absence of any free

Figure 10.6   Noi L'Aquila Infobox, 2011.

Wi-Fi connection were deterrents to readoption even of the only open parts of the city – its central axis. Barnaby Gunning Studio designed an 'Infobox' fitted out with a two-level accessible workbench, to be sited in the central location of Piazza Regina Margherita. Sponsored by Google, constructed from a converted shipping container and equipped with high-end laptops offering free wifi and internet access, the aim of the Infobox was to provide a place for young people to re-engage with the city and to encourage participation in the project.

Noi L'Aquila was launched in June 2011 with the opening of the Infobox. In a city centre still largely closed-off to the public and with limited data coverage, it proved to be a useful resource for the city and a handy base for several spin-off activities.

At the outset of the L'Aquila 3D project, modelling irregular structures such as the medieval and baroque architecture of the city required laser-scanning equipment, and while many restoration projects in the centre used 3D scans, the cost of the technology and equipment was prohibitive, and the surveying companies that produced the scans were unwilling to share even low-resolution output. However, during the course of 2012, new web-based software tools emerged that made it possible to automatically generate complex models from sets of overlapping photographs. The two key platforms were Hypr3D and Autodesk 123D Catch; both provided services that were free to the end user, and which allowed the download of open-source models that could be opened in a variety of different applications.

Using the Infobox as a base from which to upload images, in November 2012 experiments were carried out working with a small team of students from the Liceo Artistico Fulvio Muzi, a local secondary school specialising in the arts. Students used their own mobile phones and digital cameras to capture multiple views of buildings on Costa Masciarelli, and from these, highly detailed models were created. The process was relatively slow with approximately one hour elapsing between the upload of images and the availability of downloadable 3D models, however further experimentation showed that this technique was able to create realistic and accurate models of architectural detail and sculpted stone work.

In the same year, Google shifted the method of acquisition of 3D imagery for Google Earth from manual modelling to a computer-vision-based approach, selling SketchUp to Trimble Inc in June 2012. While the new method was initially limited to the centre of major cities, Google made a priority of covering the centre of L'Aquila carrying out aerial scanning in 2013 and finally creating a comprehensive model of the city post-earthquake.[14]

The second half of 2013 saw a further initiative that grew out of the original projects. Using just his mobile phone, Graziano di Crescenzo, a participant in both the Click Days and L'Aquila 3D projects, set about capturing the whole city centre of L'Aquila post-earthquake for Google Street View. Over a number of months he walked the empty streets accumulating several hundred panoramic views, which he then published to Google Maps, setting their position and orientation and providing connectivity metadata that allowed viewers to navigate between views. These panoramas created the first comprehensive street-level view of the city since the earthquake and provided a way to contrast the state of the city before and after the disaster.

Matteo Faraone, Barnaby Gunning and Massimo Prosperococco worked with Graziano to create a dedicated website for his project. Hello L'Aquila, as it was called, allowed visitors to enter this user-generated Street View to walk virtually through the city, including routes into some building interiors as well as providing bird's eye views from a tower crane.[15] The site was built with social media in mind and it allowed visitors to share specific views via Facebook and Twitter, as well as to generate shareable links and QR codes.

All of these projects were self-driven, ground-up initiatives that were only possible because of the dedication and effort of unpaid volunteers. Disenfranchised from an opaque reconstruction process, for many of them participation was a first opportunity to reconnect with the

Figure 10.7 Hello L'Aquila website, 2014.

city and to rebuild their affective links with its centre. In the course of these projects, we became acutely aware of how engagement is the key to creating or rekindling a sense of civic ownership. When the city of L'Aquila was sealed off in 2009, its buildings and its public spaces were essentially lost to the populace. In that context, the process of photographically cataloguing the historic centre was one of the first steps towards reconnecting citizens with their city and its rich architectural heritage. Using free software, ordinary citizens were able to create a vast database of images and publish models of their city for anyone to see, on a platform used by millions of people worldwide.

Over the 11 years since the earthquake, technological advances in mobile device hardware have made high-quality digital photography widely available and, combined with on-device 3D scanning and mobile broadband, the gap between professional software and consumer products has narrowed considerably. Prior to the L'Aquila earthquake there was little documentation of most of its rich cultural heritage; much fabric was lost permanently to the earthquake and there have been incidents where, through neglect or theft, other items have disappeared entirely. However low-cost or free-to-use consumer and mobile technologies now offer the unprecedented ability to document and record cultural heritage, both as a reference in the event of damage or as a visual record to prevent theft and resale.

With the exception of Noi L'Aquila, the projects were largely self-funded. In the summer of 2010 while organising the Click Days and L'Aquila 3D projects, the authors sought public support and commercial sponsorship from a number of sources to cover the cost of purchasing photographic equipment and the costs of transport. While the Commune of L'Aquila and the Abruzzo Region were prepared to offer unfunded patronage, it was evident that the timescales for raising public funding would make it impossible to commence the projects without very substantial delay. In addition to this, many potential sponsors were either suffering compassion fatigue or were still affected by the financial crisis of 2007–8. Support was eventually found from the charitable foundation of the local building society (Fondazione Carispaq) which provided €3,000 of sponsorship through the ANFE. Five sets of cameras and wide-angle lenses were sponsored through goodwill purchases of the cameras at the end of the project; purchasers included the Fondazione Carispaq, the Carispaq building society itself, the Computer Science Department of the University of L'Aquila, Nicole Drobeck of Google, and Suresh Bhudia, a small building contractor from London. Only the tripod manufacturer

Manfrotto was able to provide direct in-kind support by donating professional grade equipment and mounts.

The absence of formal support and public funding did allow the projects to be delivered quickly, efficiently and without external influence, but, although these ground-up initiatives were well received in the media and favourably viewed by local citizens and the incumbent mayor, they did not manage to gain traction with the public administration as a whole. One key aim of the initial projects had been to allow consultation on reconstruction and to increase the transparency of the decision-making processes. The 3D model of the city was intended to provoke debate and discussion, and ultimately to assist in the development and communication of a reconstruction plan. The office for reconstruction of the city of L'Aquila did eventually adopt a map-based interface to publish economic data and information about the state of progress, but post-disaster public information has largely remained obscure and hard to access.

The low-budget nature of the initiatives also brought with it issues in relation to data redundancy and the fleeting nature of internet technologies. Internet hosting and domain maintenance all incur ongoing running costs as well as the need for maintenance. In the period since the projects were concluded, several of the associated domain names have lapsed: comefacciamo.com fell victim to domain squatting in 2018 and neither the noilaquila.com nor welaquila.com domains were renewed by Google. The Noi L'Aquila web application remains accessible via its original Appspot server[16] but is hampered by changes to the underlying Google Maps APIs which make it impossible to see Street View content. Until 2013 the L'Aquila 3D project was the primary source of content for Google Earth's coverage of the area. This has now been superseded and there is no evidence that in future releases of Google Earth there will be any compatibility with pre-2013 formats. All of the models produced are currently retained on the 3D Warehouse, a vast resource of models for SketchUp, but it is likely that either the file format will become obsolete or that Trimble, the current owners of the platform, will retire the data. Conversion of the models to an open-source format such as COLLADA would prolong their useful life, but this is a time-consuming process. Recently, the extensive database of photographs taken during the Click Days has been moved by the authors to a new domain, AQ99.it.[17] In the 10 years since the projects were carried out, the database of photographs has allowed volunteers to pinpoint cultural heritage that had been thought lost to the earthquake.[18] Indeed the database remains the only comprehensive record of post-earthquake L'Aquila; as irreparably damaged buildings are demolished, it continues to provide a point of reference against which to assess the ongoing reconstruction. At the date of writing, the Hello L'Aquila website remains the only 'public' way to see inside the Cathedral of San Massimo.[19]

Despite the limitations imposed by a lack of funding and the absence of institutional adoption, these four projects illustrate several ways to re-engage disenfranchised citizens and, through participation, to give them back a sense of ownership. While they were responses to disaster, they showed how everyday technologies and low-cost equipment have the potential to increase knowledge about the cultural fabric of cities and to display that knowledge in a global, accessible manner. Indeed, these kinds of activities are a model for disaster preparedness. Noi L'Aquila and Come Facciamo were recognised by the UNESCO #unite4heritage campaign as positive examples of how to help communities protect cultural heritage at risk from destruction.

Engagement and participation are powerful tools in overcoming the shock provoked by disaster. Reconnecting people to their cultural heritage, their territory and their mental geography addresses problems of anxiety and separation while providing hope for the future.

As digital technologies improve and mobile phones become ever more powerful, photography, film making and 3D scanning become increasingly attractive activities for youth engagement and produce useful outputs to record cultural heritage and artefacts, strengthening the bond between people and places to create longer-term resilience.

Notes

1 I.N.G.V. event no. 1905389.
2 Comune Di L'Aquila, '*Ordinanza di Inagibilità*'.
3 Between September 2008 and July 2009, the number of Italian registered Facebook accounts rose from approximately one million to more than 10 million. Cosenza, 'I 10 anni di Facebook'.
4 Francesco Paolucci quoted in Farinosi et al., 'Inside the People of the Wheelbarrows'.
5 *Complessi Antisismici Sostenibili Ecocompatibili* literally Sustainable Environmentally-Friendly Anti-Seismic Settlements. Approximately 17,000 people were housed in 185 of these seismically isolated housing blocks.
   Commissario Delegato per la Ricostruzione, 'Planimetrie Progetto C.a.s.e.'
6 Nebbia et al., 'L'Aquila, Il Popolo delle Carriole'.
7 API Application Programming Interface. The Google Maps API allows third party web applications to use Google Maps with customised overlays for example graphic pins that identify the geographic location of specific items.
8 Files were saved in .jpg format with EXIF headers created using the PEL: PHP Exif Library Weberhofer, 'PEL: PHP Exif Library.'
9 La Repubblica 'L'Aquila ricostruita in 3d.'
10 Cartledge, 'L'Aquila Futura'.
11 Gunning 'How Google Can Help Rebuild L'Aquila'.
12 A.N.F.E. Associazione Nazionale Famiglie Emigrati.

13 A collection of the models is hosted in SketchUp 3d Warehouse.
    Di Crescenzo, Graziano 'ComeFacciamo.com L'Aquila 3D'.
14 At the date of writing, the 3D representation of L'Aquila on Google Earth is still the 2013 scan.
15 Di Crescenzo, 'Hello L'Aquila'.
    Di Crescenzo, 'Presentazione del progetto Hello L'Aquila'.
16 http://memoryofaplace.appspot.com
17 https://aq99.it Accessed 16 June 2022.
18 http://aq99.it/index.php?img=CD_08_03_004&blk=220 Accessed 16 June 2022
    https://www.facebook.com/groups/196408420393150/permalink/1258257017541613/
    Accessed 16 June 2022.
19 https://www.hellolaquila.it/?panoID=CAoSLEFGMVFpcFB0S2J5dGlpaFI4MGs0Rm
    VlWXhXUmhmckl5MFBvLWVuQWFOMGlF&lat=42.349222&lng=13.396857
    &heading=262.914998&pitch=39.836312 Accessed 16 June 2022.

Bibliography

Cartledge, R. 'L'Aquila Futura', 22 February 2010. Accessed 9 May 2021. https://www.youtube.com/watch?v=OY4HMe6zqcI

Il Commissario delegato per la Ricostruzione, Presidente della Regione Abruzzo. 'Planimetrie Progetto C.a.s.e.' Accessed 1 May 2021 http://www.commissarioperlaricostruzione.it/Informare/I-nuovi-insediamenti/Planimetrie-Progetto-C.a.s.e

Comune Di L'Aquila, 'Ordinanza di inagibilità del patrimonio edilizio in tutto il territorio comunale', 8 April 2009. Accessed 17 April 2021 https://www.comune.laquila.it/moduli/downloadFile.php?file=oggetto_atti_pubblici/111211448450O__Oordinana%20sindaco%20inagibilit%E0%20intero%20patrimonio.pdf

Cosenza, V. 'I 10 anni di Facebook visti dall'Italia: statistiche e trend', Vincos Blog. Accessed 9 May 2021 https://vincos.it/2014/01/27/i-10-anni-di-facebook-visti-italia-statistiche-social-network/

Di Crescenzo, G. 'Presentazione del progetto Hello L'Aquila' 29 March 2014. Accessed 9 March 2021 https://youtu.be/1bp3Gwnu5Io?t=314

Di Crescenzo, G. 'ComeFacciamo.com L'Aquila 3D' Collection on SketchUp 3d Warehouse. Accessed 9 May 2021 https://3dwarehouse.sketchup.com/collection/2bdcf89751407b29c9af2c9b25c272f1/ComeFacciamocom-LAquila-3D

Di Crescenzo, G., Faraone, M., Gunning, B., Prosperococco, M. 'Hello L'Aquila', March 2014. Accessed 4 April 2014. https://hellolaquila.it/

Farinosi, M., Treré, E. 'Inside the "People of the Wheelbarrows": participation between online and offline dimension in the post-quake social movement'. *The Journal of Community Informatics*, 6(3) (2010) Special Issue: Prato Community Informatics Conference: 2010.

Gunning, B. 'How Google can help rebuild L'Aquila'. *Wall Street Journal*, 5 April 2010. Accessed 16 June 2022 https://www.wsj.com/articles/SB100014240527023043730045751515936896095912

Istituto Nazionale di Geofisica e Vulcanologia [I.N.G.V.] event no. 1905389. Accessed 17 April 2021 http://cnt.rm.ingv.it/event/1895389

La Repubblica Rep TV. 'L'Aquila ricostruita in 3d', 18 March 2010. Accessed 9 May 2021 https://video.repubblica.it/dossier/terremoto-in-abruzzo/l-aquila-ricostruita-in-3d/44099

Nebbia, F. and Puliafito, A. 'L'Aquila - Il Popolo delle Carriole', 1 March 2010. Accessed 9 May 2021 https://www.youtube.com/watch?v=psRRX5jI_Yo

Weberhofer, J. 'PEL: PHP Exif Library. A library with support for reading and writing Exif headers in JPEG and TIFF images using PHP'. Accessed 9 May 2021 https://github.com/pel/pel/blob/master/README.markdown

11
The Great East Japan Earthquake and COVID-19
Through the lenses of gender and age

Miwako Kitamura

As in L'Aquila, crucial problems emerged during post-disaster management in the town of Otsuchi in Iwate prefecture, damaged by the Great East Japan Earthquake of 2011. Recognition of these problems offered a perspective that allowed the town to protect its most vulnerable citizens during the COVID-19 pandemic of 2019.

This study examines how people in Otsuchi, who experienced severe damage during the Great East Japan Earthquake of 2011, responded to COVID-19 from early 2020, and significantly mitigated infection in the first wave of the pandemic. A retrospective analysis of survivor testimony from the earthquake and of life stories from the period before the tsunami exposes how vulnerable facilities were for the elderly at the time of the disaster. Since the Great East Japan Earthquake, Otsuchi has encountered various problems in the process of managing evacuation centres and reconstruction planning. Currently, the government and community are cooperating to provide reconstruction support. Considering the situation through the lens of gender, the study measures efforts undertaken developing facilities for the elderly in Otsuchi and compares community policies adopted to prevent COVID-19 infection with approaches implemented at the time of the Great East Japan Earthquake.

Introduction

Iwate prefecture has a markedly low birth rate and an ageing population. According to data from the Ministry of Health, Labour and Welfare, Iwate prefecture had no cases of COVID-19 infection from 16 January 2020 until 29 July 2020, when the first case of infection occurred.[1] The town of Otsuchi is located in Iwate prefecture in a coastal area and has been repeatedly hit by tsunamis; two of the most devastating tsunamis in the region were the 1933 Sanriku tsunami and the 1960 Chilean tsunami. Due to Japan's modernisation and economic development, seawalls were constructed in the area after the Chilean tsunami in 1960. Evacuation drills have also been conducted in schools and workplaces to ensure residents' safety. However, during the Great East Japan Earthquake, despite these preparations for evacuation and the time lag between the earthquake and arrival of the tsunami, Otsuchi suffered colossal human losses.

After the devastation of the Great East Japan Earthquakes, people who lost their homes took refuge in shelters. As the affected area lies in northeast Japan, where the temperature was low, hygiene and other factors were considered because influenza and other illnesses were prevalent in the densely populated shelters. In the disaster's immediate aftermath, people in the affected areas witnessed the harm done to their families and friends. Consequently, they cherish the lives of their community's survivors. Therefore, studying how the people of Otsuchi town coped with COVID-19 will help us develop better awareness of disaster preparedness by drawing on local people's wisdom and knowledge. We hypothesise that the lessons learned from the devastating disaster of the Great East Japan Earthquake may have helped devise strategies to keep the pandemic in check, although COVID-19 is a new disease that is still developing. We conducted several interviews in Otsuchi about the relationship between disaster experiences and pandemic awareness, as the people here have lived through several challenges.

Japan experiences diverse natural disasters, including earthquakes, tsunamis, typhoons and landslides. Earthquakes and tsunamis repeatedly damaged the Sanriku coastline of Iwate prefecture in the Meiji, Taisho, Showa and Heisei eras (covering the years 1868–2019). The town of Otsuchi is located in the northern part of Japan and has a harsh climate even in midsummer, due to local geographical conditions. Before the Great East Japan Earthquake, the population of Otsuchi was about 16,000, but this number has fallen to 12,000; about 1200 people died or went missing during the Great East Japan Earthquake and the town has a declining and ageing population.[2] The region has experienced several famines due to a diminished harvest of rice, an important staple in Japan. Inlets and cliffs unique to the region surround the ria coast and its complex, picturesque topography attracts many tourists. Furthermore, along the coast, the Oyashio and Kuroshio currents intersect, thereby providing plenty of fishing grounds and rich fishery resources. However, this ria coast has many inlets vulnerable to tsunamis because their topography increases the height at which tsunamis reach the coast. In addition, despite the scenic beauty of the mountains and the sea, residents struggle to find flat, habitable land to build their houses,[3] while they also have to live with the threat of tsunamis. The historic residents of Otsuchi, who experienced repeated tsunamis, left behind documents and stone monuments to warn people of the necessity for immediate evacuation and the dangers of living near the sea.[4]

The town of Otsuchi has experienced several tsunamis. The damage caused by the 1933 Showa Sanriku tsunami and the subsequent reconstruction of the town have both been well documented. Historically, people repeatedly moved to higher ground after each tsunami, but then returned to the coast. However, after the Showa Sanriku tsunami, relocation to higher ground included negotiations with landowners and installation of wells.

The population of Otsuchi grew as a result of the influx of many people to the area. To provide housing, residential localities in the tsunami inundation area expanded rapidly. Many seawalls were also developed around Otsuchi due to rapid economic development during the 1970s. Otsuchi has increasingly invested in tsunami preparedness, but much of the disaster management was developed through a top-down structure, which ignored social vulnerabilities and risks. The tsunami disaster management plans were not updated by local bodies or the national government.[5]

Living Testimony

The Great East Japan Earthquake: Otsuchi's victims remember

In this study, we analysed the memoirs of victims of the Great East Japan Earthquake in Otsuchi, collected as *Living Testimony*. There are two editions of *Living Testimony*, 2016 and 2017, which describe 620 residents of Otsuchi who lost their lives in the earthquake. The testimonies also illustrate the daily lives and activities of survivors in the days before the tsunami hit. These kinds of community-based archives are essential to understanding local community life.[6]

In the aftermath of the Great East Japan Earthquake, the loss of numerous lives cast such a dark shadow over Japanese people's hearts that it became taboo to talk about the deaths to survivors. Because they believe that grieving endlessly keeps the victims' souls in this world, many survivors still feel intense regret about being unable to help those who died. Hence, the post-earthquake archive was primarily positive, focusing on those who survived. A significant factor in being able to publish *Living Testimony* was the presence of the temple in Otsuchi, and this victims' retrospective is a living record of the 620 people who died in the Great East Japan Earthquake. It is oral history, told by surviving families, of events that led from each person's birth to his or her death in the tsunami. According to Buddhist funeral rites, in Japan, when a person dies, the priest with whom he or she is associated gives him/her a new 'precept' name. After the Great East Japan Earthquake, the temple priests collected the histories of the many people who died, so they could give them new names. Thus, most of the testimony analysed here was collected through the efforts of the temple priests. This valuable community testimony has been published based on the wishes of priests, who are trusted by most community members, and who believe that local knowledge of community members' true stories will mitigate the effects of future disasters.[7]

The historical background of tsunami evacuation

Tsunamis frequently hit the Sanriku coastline. The residents of the coastal area hold regular disaster drills in the community and have invested large sums of money in building a tsunami breakwater to protect the town. Despite such drills, people lost their lives in the Great East Japan Earthquake, as they did not evacuate quickly enough, although they had enough time to leave before the arrival of the tsunami. A study of evacuation behaviour undertaken in Japan has focused on the contradictory behaviour of people who think they are still safe even when they are in a dangerous situation. Hirose called this 'bias behaviour' and noted that it prevents people from reacting to current danger on the spur of the moment.[8] This kind of behaviour was common in Otsuchi, where local people knew of the tsunami danger, but did not evacuate during the Great East Japan Earthquake. A study that focused on the fact that women are more likely to die in tsunamis revealed that, for example, most local women believed that the tsunami would not be able to reach their current location.[9] Enarson investigated how gender differences can lead to death, while emphasising that women are at greater risk than men during natural disasters because they lack free time due to their household responsibilities and because, occupying a low rank in the social hierarchy, they lack decision-making power for evacuation.[10]

In the Great East Japan Earthquake, individualised disaster management was not only needed for women but also for vulnerable populations, especially those in need of assistance and the elderly.[11] However, the implementation of formal evacuation drills and top-down disaster management plans overlooked the need for such detailed disaster preparedness for many of these vulnerable populations.[12]

With Japan's ongoing risk of earthquakes and tsunamis, the Japanese government conducted a questionnaire survey to understand the reasons for the hesitation to evacuate. Results revealed that disaster management was mishandled at the time of the Great East Japan Earthquake. After the earthquake, digital data was recorded not only in the form of written testimonies but also video, audio and satellite photographs of the damage. Big data from these disasters was used to study and analyse a simulation of the evacuation behaviour during the tsunami, with particular attention paid to the behaviour of those who died in Otsuchi.[13] Along with data used for studying evacuation routes from the tsunami, the spontaneous keeping of records of local survivor narratives is also important in understanding the social risk of the community. There are still few studies that have considered *Living Testimony* in detail. Furthermore, few studies have been conducted on the relationship between pandemic preparedness and experiences of major natural disasters.

Analysing *Living Testimony*

Descriptions of the situation at the time of the earthquake were coded and categorised from 620 memoirs. Consequently, 30 categories in Table 11.1 were created applying the KJ method, introduced in 1967 by the cultural anthropologist Jiro Kawakita in *Idea Method* as an effective way to organise information and analyse data. The method involves grouping sentences in the same category, and when they cannot be grouped further, revealing essential parts by connecting the contents collected in each group. The following process was adopted:

a) Extract the situation at the time of the earthquake from *Living Testimony*.
b) Prepare a summary based on (a).

c) To increase reliability, repeat step (b) three times.
d) Code the results of step (c), and determine categories using the KJ method.
e) To increase the reliability of the categories obtained in step (d), a multi-person category workshop was held to review the categories.
f) Classify the categories of evacuation behaviour with special attention to the diverse patterns of evacuation behaviour.
g) Conduct another review of the categories according to the KJ method.
h) Refine the content of the analysis, recheck the descriptions of each of the 620 people against the data created.
i) Create Table 11.1 as a coding result containing a list of the resulting 30 categories.

Table 11.1 Coding results.

01. Evacuated or tried to evacuate without stopping at other place	11. Prompted others to evacuate, but did not evacuate themselves	21. Believed that home was safe
02. Returned home or tried to return	12. Relatives have a disability or are unable to evacuate for a physical reason	22. Checked around after the earthquake
03. Stopped or tried to stop	13. Disabled	23. Experienced previous earthquake and tsunami
04. Stayed put	14. Using car	24. Prompted someone to evacuate
05. Earthquake-related death	15. At home or at office	25. Rescued someone
06. In hospital and other medical facilities at the time of the disaster	16. Home has already been set as a disaster shelter	26. Tsunami will be 3 metres, early warning, which was later increased
07. Picking up or waiting for relatives	17. At home	27. Caring for pet
08. Highly evacuation conscious	18. Tidying at home	28. Continued to city office work, went back to city office
09. Husband absent/did not know how to act	19. Picking something up	29. Fire-fighter, trying to close the water gate
10. Having tea at a neighbour's	20. Took time to prepare for evacuation	30. No information

Results of the analysis of *Living Testimony*

Discovering age-related differences in evacuation behaviour

In addition to the gender-based analysis, testimonies were classified into two groups based on age: those aged 65 years and older and those younger than 65 years. Figure 11.3 lists the categories wherein a significant difference in evacuation behaviour was observed between the elderly and the young. Many elderly victims had disabling conditions involving, for example, their legs and backs, or were in care (13). It was cold and snowing on 11 March, the day of the disaster, which also contributed to older adults not being able to evacuate and preferring to stay indoors. Most people over 65 had experienced the Showa Sanriku tsunami and Chilean tsunami, either personally or as reported by relatives. According to their recollection, the tsunami did not come at that time, or it came only slowly and gradually flooded the area. Older residents were therefore more likely to think their houses were safe (21). The frail health and experience of previous tsunamis, in addition to the cold weather on the day of the earthquake, may have contributed to the reluctance of the elderly to evacuate (04). For example, another woman, C, was over 65 years of age. She was at home at the time of the earthquake (17) while her husband checked on her relatives. A neighbour advised her to evacuate (11), but she waited for her husband to return. They were then trapped by the disaster (04). Some older adults did not evacuate immediately because they had left the management of daily activities to their husbands, who were not home at that moment.

Table 11.2 Categories characteristic of the 65+ age group.

04. Stayed put	13. Disabled	22. Checked around after the earthquake
05. Earthquake-related death	17. At home	23. Experienced previous earthquake and tsunami
11. Prompted others to evacuate, but did not evacuate themselves	21. Believed that home was safe	

A broader view

Up to this point, we have examined the distinct categories for gender, the elderly and young. Figure 11.3 shows whether the 30 categories were significantly different (or distinctive) for each group. When there was a significant difference between the two rates, we labelled the higher one 'above', and the lower one, 'below'. In this study, statistical analyses (tests of independence) were conducted separately for gender, age and district-specific conditions.

Gender	Male		Female	Apply	Male	Female	Overall applicability	Rate of male respondents	Percentage of female respondents
Total	47%		53%	620	290	330			
07. Someone to pick up or wait for someone	33%		67%	127	42	85	20.5%	14.5%	25.8%
09. Husband absent	0%		100%	30	0	30	4.8%	0.0%	9.1%
10. Having a tea with nighbougher	20%		80%	15	3	12	2.4%	1.0%	3.6%
11. Prompted others to evacuate but did not	40%		60%	164	66	98	26.5%	22.8%	29.7%
13. Disabled	36%		64%	145	52	93	23.4%	17.9%	28.2%
15. Evacuated to main house /parents house	14%		86%	7	1	6	1.1%	0.3%	1.8%
17. At home	44%		56%	388	170	218	62.6%	58.6%	66.1%
19. Picked up something	66%		34%	41	27	14	6.6%	9.3%	4.2%
24. Rescued someone	57%		43%	65	37	28	10.5%	12.8%	8.5%
25. Promped evacuation to someone	72%		28%	53	38	15	8.5%	13.1%	4.5%
27. Picked up pet	8%		92%	12	1	11	1.9%	0.3%	3.3%
28. Continued govermental office work, back to govermental office	78%		22%	18	14	4	2.9%	4.8%	1.2%
29. Firefighter / closed to water gate	100%		0%	9	9	0	1.5%	3.1%	0.0%

Figure 11.1 Gender differences.

By old age and youth	Under the age of 65 years		Over the age if 65 years old	Apply	Under the age of 65years	Over the age of 65 years old	The percentage of apply	Applicable rate under 65	Applicable rate over 65 years old
Total	60%		40%	620	369	251			
02. Retured to home or tried to return	44%		56%	159	70	89	25.6%	19.0%	35.5%
03. Stopped or tried to stop on the way to evacuate	28%		72%	88	25	63	14.2%	6.8%	25.1%
04. Staying put	67%		33%	371	250	121	59.8%	67.8%	48.2%
05. Earthquake related death	93%		7%	14	13	1	2.3%	3.5%	0.4%
07. To picked up relatives or wait for someone	50%		50%	127	64	63	20.5%	17.3%	25.1%
09. Husband absent /did not know how to act	37%		63%	30	11	19	4.8%	3.0%	7.6%
11. Prompted others to evacuate but did not	74%		26%	164	122	42	26.5%	33.1%	16.7%
13. Disabled	81%		19%	145	117	28	23.4%	31.7%	11.2%
14. Evacuated by car	29%		71%	72	21	51	11.6%	5.7%	20.3%
17. At home the time of earthquake	69%		31%	388	269	119	62.6%	72.9%	47.4%
21. Belived that home was safe	77%		23%	131	101	30	21.1%	27.4%	12.0%
22. After the earthquake check tsunami status	69%		31%	99	68	31	16.0%	18.4%	12.4%
23. Experienced previous earthquake and tsunami/but no damage or small damage	78%		22%	68	53	15	11.0%	14.4%	6.0%
24. Rescued someone	26%		74%	65	17	48	10.5%	4.6%	19.1%
28. Continued govermental office work ,back to govermental office	6%		94%	18	1	17	2.9%	0.3%	6.8%
29. Firefighter /Closed to water gate	0%		100%	9	0	9	1.5%	0.0%	3.6%

Figure 11.2 Age differences.

Table 11.3 Categories characteristic of men aged 65+.

11. Prompted others to evacuate, but did not evacuate themselves	13. Disabled	17. At home

Table 11.4 Categories characteristic of men under age 65.

25. Rescued someone	28. Continued to city office work, went back to city office	29. Fire-fighter, trying to close the water gate

Figure 11.2 illustrates the categories in which there was a significant difference in evacuation behaviour between the elderly and the young. Tables 11.3 and 11.4 show the categories, namely, characteristics of men aged 65 years and older and men under 65 years, respectively. Factors characteristic of males aged 65 years and older include being at home at the time of the disaster (17), having physical disabilities (13) and not evacuating when prompted to do so (11).

Testimonies reveal truths about the tsunami's arrival

Figure 11.3 illustrates the ways in which the 30 categories were significantly different (or distinctive) in each category. As mentioned above, when there was a significant difference between the two rates, the higher one was labelled as 'above' and the lower one as 'below'. As the figure shows, various types of conditions affected the reasons why each person was overcome by the tsunami. Because *Living Testimony* is a record of the victims of the Great East Japan Earthquake, it is necessary to prevent the types of behaviour revealed in this study. These analyses also provide insight into the vulnerabilities that existed in Otsuchi, which can better inform the disaster management planning team in reducing tsunami disaster risk directly. A key finding is that towns such as Otsuchi should consider gender and age when managing evacuation behaviour and local emergency response.

COVID-19 response in Iwate Prefecture

In 2020, nine years after the Great East Japan Earthquake, the COVID-19 pandemic began its worldwide spread.

In Japan, where the population is significantly older, the rate of infection among the elderly was low. A noteworthy example of this was in Iwate prefecture where there were no reported cases of COVID-19 in the first wave of infections. Comparatively, in neighbouring Aomori prefecture which has a population density similar to that of Iwate prefecture, a cluster of COVID-19 infections occurred in elderly care facilities. To date (April 2021), however, Iwate prefecture, which has an ageing population, has had no clusters of COVID-19 infections in elderly facilities.

Interviews were conducted in the study area to understand the response to COVID-19 in Iwate prefecture. These interviews revealed that local people felt a drive to maintain a zero-incidence situation and lived

Data Summary	women	over 65 years	Applicable rate as a whole area	
01. Evacuated or tried to evacuate without stopping at other place	-	-		15.6%
02. Retured to home or tried to return	-	under ↓		25.6%
03. Stopped or tried to stop	-	under ↓		14.2%
04. Staying put	-	above ↑		59.8%
05. Earthquake related death	-	above ↑		2.3%
06. At hospital and other medical facilities at the time of the disaster	-	-		2.6%
07. Someone to pick up or wait for someone	above ↑	under ↓		20.5%
08. Highly evacuation conscious	-	-		11.1%
09. Husband absent	above ↑	under ↓		4.8%
10. Having a tea with nighbougher	above ↑	-		2.4%
11. Prompted others to evacuate but did not	above ↑	above ↑		26.5%
12. Realtives has disable or unable to ecvacuate physical reason	-	-		16.3%
13. Disable	above ↑	above ↑		23.4%
14. Evacuate by car	-	under ↓		11.6%
15. Evacuated to main house /parents house	above ↑	-		1.1%
16. Didn't move because I decided to leave my home as an evacuation destination	-	-		1.0%
17. At home at the time of the disaster	above ↑	above ↑		62.6%
18. Tidied up after the disaster	-	-		15.6%
19. Picked up somethig	under ↓	-		6.6%
20. Took time for evacuate preparation	-	-		10.0%
21. Belived that home was safe	-	above ↑		21.1%
22. Checked tsunami status	-	above ↑		16.0%
23. Experienced previous earthquake and tsunami	-	above ↑		11.0%
24. Evacuated others to safe place	under ↓	under ↓		10.5%
25. Urging neighbours to evacuated	under ↓	-		8.5%
26. Heared tsunami early warning it said tsunami will be 3meters	-	-		1.6%
27. Cared to pet	above ↑	-		1.9%
28. Contuinueted own jod /backed work	under ↓	under ↓		2.9%

Figure 11.3 Summary of Living Testimony.

under restrictions in their daily lives. For those living outside Iwate prefecture, it was not easy to find people willing to be interviewed under pandemic conditions. However, a woman from Otsuchi, with whom I had built a trusting relationship for several years in researching *Living Testimony*, was available to be interviewed. In total, we interviewed four women living in Otsuchi using an open-ended questionnaire. Each interview lasted about two hours. The characteristics of the participants are shown in Table 11.5.

Table 11.5 Characteristics of interviewees

	Gender	Age	Occupation	Place of residence at the time of the earthquake	Period of residence
A	Female	30s	NGO representative	USA	9 years
B	Female	30s	Food bank	Hokkaido	Over 70 years
C	Female	70s	Storyteller guide	Otsuchi town	Over 70 years
D	Female	70s	Owner of a guesthouse	Otsuchi town	Over 70 years

Preparing for future disasters through lived experiences

The analysis of *Living Testimony* revealed that the experience of the tsunami became important in COVID-19 countermeasures. In Otsuchi, about 8 per cent of the population, 1200 people, lost their lives in the Great East Japan Earthquake. As the testimonies reveal, several factors led to delays in evacuation. Survivors of the disaster well know the importance of protecting lives saved from the tsunami, and although they cannot evacuate from COVID-19, they can act in ways that show they understand the value of life. In Otsuchi, for example, local people are undertaking decisive action to save lives by wearing masks, washing their hands and patrolling the area to make sure that no one from outside the community visits the region. It was observed that there were many community activities such as tea ceremonies, which hindered the evacuation as they occurred in an area where people could not live without being part of the community. There was a strong desire not to let infected people leave their homes. Women, in particular, valued harmony among community members because they are more involved in the community.[14] Because of this characteristic behaviour, they cancelled their business trips and did not interact with relatives outside of Otsuchi town. There was also a connection between the temple and people's lives, similar to that evident in *Living Testimony*.

Comparing interviews with *Living Testimony* analysis

I analysed *Living Testimony* to clarify the risk from the tsunami in Otsuchi, and then interviewed residents of Otsuchi about COVID-19 infection. Based on these interviews, it appears that the experience of the Great East Japan Earthquake strengthened the local ties. Because residents have a greater appreciation for the importance of life, they believe they should wear masks and never go out. These communities appeared to work together to undertake measures against COVID-19 infections. In particular, the elderly, who are the most susceptible to COVID-19, said that they would not leave their home to avoid the risk of infection.

Finally, people interviewed in the COVID-19 survey are currently living in the Machikata area, where the damage caused by the Great East Japan Earthquake was significant. According to four interviews with townspeople, the main findings concerning tsunami countermeasures, nine years after the earthquake are as follows:

- Residents have to escape immediately after an earthquake, even if living at a higher altitude.
- The route from one's house to the shelter on the hill should be checked.
- Lessons learned from the Great East Japan Earthquake should be remembered.

Conclusion

Thirty categories of negative behaviours related to tsunami evacuation were identified from the 620 living testimonies. This information contains key lessons for future natural disasters, and some of the items seemed valuable for civil protection in response to COVID-19. The strong community ties that appeared both before and after the tsunami were the reason the community took measures against infectious diseases this time: they did not want to disturb the harmony of the community. One example of these community measures was that community members monitor each other, patrolling the parking lots at each house to see if there were any cars with non-community plates parked there.

As can be observed, there is no single right answer to disaster response. In the case of tsunami evacuation, a split-second decision can make the difference between life and death, but the countermeasures against infectious diseases require patience, such as not being able to see relatives and friends on an ongoing basis. After the tragic experience of the Great East Japan Earthquake, the survivors helped each other in the community, which has made the community ties even more substantial. Perhaps as a result of this, during the COVID-19 pandemic, the people of Otsuchi have been monitoring each other for infection. We can assume that these actions were motivated by the importance of life and the importance of community, which they learned through witnessing people forced to flee from the tsunami. Further disaster reconstruction management should therefore consider community participation and using local knowledge.[15]

The number of COVID-19 cases in Otsuchi town was still zero as of 28 April 2021. The tsunami risk in Otsuchi understood from *Living Testimonies,* and our analysis of those testimonies, revealed that there is a vulnerable population in Otsuchi, mainly elderly people and women. In the town, the priority is to value the lives saved from the tsunami. Furthermore, local people wear masks and patrol the town to prevent people from entering the city, where there are many infected people and the elderly. In this way, the people of Otsuchi help prevent the spread of COVID-19 by local people. These activities seem to help prevent COVID-19 infection.[16] The town's successful response to the pandemic is attributed to the community's self-help efforts, public support and lessons learned during tsunamis.

As of February 2021, a vaccine for COVID-19 has developed, and vaccination is now available worldwide. However, the process of developing this vaccine has been fraught with cost and political agendas, and it is difficult to say that vaccine uptake has been equitable worldwide.

This research may help in the ongoing management of natural disasters, which are becoming increasingly common.

Notes

1 Takahashi, 'How Iwate Prefecture in Japan maintained a low COVID-19 infection rate'.
2 Statistics Bureau of Japan, 'Statistical Handbook of Japan 2020'. Accessed 15 May 2021 https://www.stat.go.jp/english/data/handbook/c0117.html
3 Wisner, Ilan and Jean-Christophe, 'Hazard, vulnerability, capacity, risk and participation', 244–245.
4 Tierney, *The Social Roots of Risk*, 6–10.
5 Alexander, *Principles of Emergency Planning and Management*, 5–7.

6   Ketelaar, *A Living Archives, Shared by Community Records*, 112–115.
7   Alexander, *How to Write an Emergency Plan*, 99–103.
8   Hirose, *Why Do We Fail to Escape*, 87–115.
9   Issar, 'Managing local level risks for sustainable development'.
10   Enarson and Dhar, *Women, Gender and Disaster*, 5–10.
11   Nonoguchi and Tanaka, 'How can promoting women's participation (and agency) and responding to their needs improve disaster risk reduction?'
12   Watanabe, 'We shall never forget: recording the last movements of tsunami disaster victims'.
13   Mika, *Disasters, Vulnerability, and Narratives*, 7–13.
14   Fordham and Meyreles, 'Gender aspects of disaster management', 29–33.
15   Mosse, *Cultivating Development*, 240–243.
16   The author researched the areas affected since the Great East Japan Earthquake and Tsunami in 2011. The author has worked in the study area for more than five years. Furthermore, the author has developed a relationship of trust with the women in the area. Although only two official surveys were conducted, the author has a long history of rapport with the participants. Each interview lasted around two hours.

Bibliography

Alexander, D.E. *Principles of Emergency Planning and Management*. Oxford University Press on Demand, 2002.
Alexander, D.E. *How to Write an Emergency Plan*. Edinburgh: Dunedin Academic Press, 2016.
Enarson, E. and Dhar Chakrabarti, P.G. *Women, Gender and Disaster*. SAGE Publications India, 2009.
Fordham, M. and Meyreles, L. 'Gender aspects of disaster management'. In *Disaster Management: International Lessons in Risk Reduction, Response and Recovery*, edited by Alejandro Lopez-Carresi, Maureen Fordham, Ben Wisner, Ilan Kelman and Jean-Christophe Gaillard, 24–42. New York: Routledge, 2013.
Hiratada, H. *Why Do We Fail to Escape*. Tokyo: Shueisha, 2004.
Issar, R. 2015. 'Managing local level risks for sustainable development: Policy specialist, disaster, and climate risk governance', https://www.undp.org/content/undp/en/home/b.
Ketelaar, E. *A Living Archives, Shared by Community Records*. Cambridge: Facet Publishing, 2009.
Mika, K. *Disasters, Vulnerability, and Narratives*. New York: Routledge, 2018.
Mosse, D. *Cultivating Development*. London: Pluto Press, 2005.
Nonoguchi, A. and Tanaka, Y. 'How can promoting women's participation (and agency) and responding to their needs improve disaster risk reduction? Case from post-disaster reconstruction (operations and measures) in the Philippines and Sri Lanka', 2016. Accessed 16 June 2022 https://www.jica.go.jp/jica-ri/publication/other/20170529_01.html
Tierney, K. *The Social Roots of Risk*. Stanford University Press, 2014.
Takahashi, S. and Kawachi, I. 'How Iwate Prefecture in Japan maintained a low COVID-19 infection rate.' *World Health Organisation Western Pacific Surveillance and Response Journal (WPSAR)*, 2(4) (2021).
Watanabe, H. 'We shall never forget: Recording the last movements of tsunami disaster victims'. Accessed 20 February 2021. http://en.wasurenai.mapping.jp.2018.
Wisner, B., Kelman, I. and Gaillard, J.C. 'Hazard, vulnerability, capacity, risk and participation'. In *Disaster Management: International Llessons in Risk Reduction, Response and Recovery*, edited by Alejandro López-Carresi, Maureen Fordham, Ben Wisner, Ilan Kelman, and Jean-Christophe Gaillard, 13–5. New York: Routledge, 2013.

12
Disaster risk management, social participation and geoethics
An Italian answer to earthquakes and pandemic

Piero Farabollini, Francesca Romana Lugeri and Francesco De Pascale

Introduction

How to clearly understand and make understandable what risk is and identify the best and most effective ways of communicating and managing it are among the most delicate questions for the Anthropocene society. The recent dramatic disasters related to pandemic and extreme natural events, in Italy and the rest of the world, demonstrate the urgency of this dilemma. The concept of risk has long been subject to interpretation and lacked a rigorous definition. More recently, thanks to the Probabilistic Risk Assessment approach, the process of risk assessment (or the determination of the extent of damage) is based on the assumption that the real risk results from the product of the probability of occurrence of a certain event and the extent (magnitude) of its consequences.[1] Risk, therefore, expresses the consequences of a particular harmful event: the expected number of lives lost, material damages to buildings and infrastructure, destruction of economic activities or natural resources. In other words, risk is the product of the probability of an event occurring and the expected value of the outcome due to the size of the damage.[2] A dialectical definition of risk integrates and clarifies the earlier analytical expressions: 'risk is the possibility that human actions or events lead to consequences that have an impact on what men consider relevant'.[3] It is clear that we cannot escape from the disturbing awareness that human action is often the basis of those events with disastrous effects.

Referring to the current situation in Italy, it is clear that risk management strategies must be aligned with social practices and the pre-existing social fabric. This constitutes an effective risk management approach, which should be determined by at least four factors: objective characteristics of the risk; risk perception by society; credibility of the guarantor of the potential source of risk and involvement and decision-making tools.[4] In parallel, the basic elements identified as useful for risk management can be summarised as follows: the identification of the nature and extent of the public concerns; the structuring of the public debate; new strategies for conflict resolution; advanced knowledge of public reactions to the introduction of new safety regulations; public education and information; and finally, planning and implementation of systems and policies related to public health and safe environment. In a context of overlapping risks, it is all the more necessary to analyse and formulate, as we do in the following sections, strategies useful for managing multiple disasters such as the pandemic and an earthquake, which could, together, subject a vulnerable territory to a difficult challenge. In addition, we begin to deal with some critical issues that emerged from the management of disasters linked to the earthquakes in Central Italy in 2016, in order to then discuss the educational, social, cultural and geoethic implications of risk management, also in relation to the recent pandemic experience.

A case study

The 2016–2017 Central Italy earthquakes

The last big earthquake in Italy has been characterised by spatial/temporal properties that make it a significant case for study. On 24 August 2016, a first seismic event of magnitude 6.0 Mw hit Lazio, Marche, Abruzzo and Umbria in Central Italy, causing numerous deaths and injuries, destroying towns, infrastructure and historical sites (Figure 12.1). The epicentre was located near the little town of Accumoli (Rieti, Lazio), at the juncture of the above-mentioned four regions. Multiple tremors came in succession, until four major seismic events occurred, between October 2016 and January 2017 (respectively of 5.7, 5.9, 6.5 and 5.7 in magnitude), extending the affected area to about 2000 km². In total, the experts counted over 20,000 events of a magnitude equal to or greater than three. The origin of the 2016 earthquake is due to the Monte

Vettore–Monte Bove fault system, which consists of several segments of normal and/or transtensive faults, and extends for about 30 km along a north/west–south/east axis.[5] After the first event, the Italian Council of Ministers announced a state of emergency, and the Civil Protection Department started the first emergency phase by establishing the so-called Di.Coma.C – Directorate for command and control, a special structure aimed at immediately supporting the population, as well as productive activities.

Subsequently, the management of the reconstruction phase was entrusted to a special government commissioner, whose role it was to organise the implementation of the post-earthquake reconstruction phase.[6] Such an assignment is related solely to reconstruction after the emergency phase, since the commissioner does not have the competencies necessary to guide or make decisions on the emergency phase, something that is completely managed by the National Civil Protection. A decree of the President of the Italian Republic appointed the politician Vasco Errani (the former extraordinary commissioner for the Emilia earthquake in 2012) as the government's extraordinary commissioner for the reconstruction of the areas destroyed by the 2016–17 earthquakes. Three

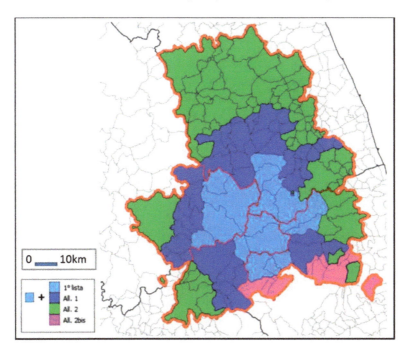

Figure 12.1 Area and municipalities in the so-called seismic crater. Source: https://sisma2016.gov.it.

further commissioners were appointed; the Hon. Paola De Micheli, a politician; Professor Piero Farabollini, a geologist; and the commissioner in charge, Giovanni Legnini, a politician. Professor Piero Farabollini is one of the authors of this paper. His experience as one of the government's extraordinary commissioners for the reconstruction of the areas destroyed by the 2016–17 earthquake was the only case of assignment to a geoscientist from October 2018 to February 2020. The insights gained through his assignment and field experience directly inform the key points raised here in relation to disaster reconstruction and recovery.

The above-mentioned series of seismic events revealed once again the endemic difficulties in managing the effects of earthquakes in a country as fragile as Italy. One of the most significant problems is the social consciousness of what risk is: the related consequences involve all the aspects inherent in disaster management. A comprehensive analysis of the various components contributing to the cost of catastrophes is thus mandatory, regardless of their origin. Different types of natural hazards, if affecting a vulnerable territory, inevitably cause disasters, as happened with the pandemic and the earthquakes of Central Italy, quantifiable in terms of expected magnitude and hazard zoning.[7] Regulative tools that have been available up until now in the field of risk prevention must be strengthened by integrating scientific knowledge, technical modelling, information and communication, with the aim of enhancing social/environmental resilience against risks. In relation to seismic risk specifically, there is an urgent need to focus on 'coordinated emergency and post-emergency interventions and on the re-establishment of the economic structure and the cultural impact of the territory, in order to guarantee the quality of the reconstruction'.[8]

Post-earthquake recovery and reconstruction

Cultural heritage and rubble removal

One of the most sensitive points in managing the consequences of a destructive earthquake is the removal of the rubble. It is the first step towards reconstruction and, at the same time, represents the disappearance of the tangible location where people have shared their lives. In a country like Italy, cultural heritage is widespread, representing the roots of social settlements. In some remote areas, the destruction of buildings that may be simple, yet are full of local significance, causes further injury to local communities, breaking links based on the common, lived experiences of such places (Figures 12.2 and 12.3).

Figure 12.2 Abbey of Sant'Eutizio, Preci (PG) Italy. Source: authors.

Figure 12.3 San Salvatore, Castelluccio, Norcia (PG) Italy. Source: authors.

At a different scale, the ruins of big and famous monuments involve the emotions of the whole society, even crossing the national borders (Figure 12.4).

Especially in the case of religious sites, the rubble removal process is extraordinarily delicate, both for institutional and cultural reasons. The common denominator is society: it lives and operates in a way that is akin to a human body, through a range of systems and interactions, with culture being one of them. Seen in this light, the 2016 seismic sequence has destroyed settlements, cultures, lives and habits – resulting in a profound fracture of the regional and national social fabric.

One of the most significant consequences has been the displacement of entire communities from the most affected territories towards the adjacent coastal areas. A 'forced exodus' (following emergency orders aimed at avoiding further risk) caused a gradual depopulation of mountain areas. At the same time, older people proved their strong loyalty to their own native places by refusing to leave them, exposing themselves, in effect, to further risks. This reaction was based on the affective identification of inhabitants with the place where they live.[9] In some ways, this constitutes a negative factor for territorial resilience because emotive, affective ties with a place of birth contribute to an increase of exposed value and vulnerability through the presence of people and buildings in areas of high seismic hazard. In other ways, ties to the territory constitute a positive factor, in that they act as an important driver to continue and survive in one's native community.[10]

In order to better understand the complexity of local reconstruction processes, it is helpful to highlight that emergency and reconstruction are

Figure 12.4   San Benedetto Abbey, Norcia (PG) Italy. Source: authors.

two different processes, for which authority is separated, although both are directly managed by the Italian government. A particularly sensitive issue, both for its objective and symbolic value, is reconstruction related to churches and places of worship. Religious artistic sites are widespread in the areas hit by the Italian earthquakes of 2016–17, and a special programme has been dedicated to the management of this specific problem. For the central Apennines, all places of worship – from the *porziuncole* (old and small country churches) to the cathedrals, from the road icons to the abbeys – represent not only the area's cultural roots, but also a driving force for economic recovery, for tourism and the enhancement of cultural heritage.

As a result, MiBACT (Italy's Ministry of Cultural Heritage and Activities and Tourism), has taken steps to restore the usability of such priceless heritage, drawing up the so-called Church Programme. This programme provides technical support to find rapid and easy ways for reconstructing churches where renovation works will cost less than €600,000. Dioceses can currently play the role of implementing bodies. Overall, the balance of the actions taken by the commissioner is certainly positive: the great majority of envisaged interventions have been implemented, thanks to special ordinances. The removal of rubble is also an extremely delicate aspect in the management of post-seismic damage. Regions have been given special powers so that they 'can make use of the help of the municipalities, for the collection, transport in temporary deposits, recovery or disposal of materials deriving from collapses and demolitions of dangerous buildings' (ordinance DPC n. 391/2016). With reference to toxic and harmful materials, such as asbestos, there is a special procedure set out by the ordinance. Particular attention is paid to the artistic and cultural heritage damaged by the earthquake; a special procedure involves supervision by MiBACT.

In the context of the high local and cultural significance of rubble removal and reconstruction efforts, the Commission structure performs an important cultural mediation function, with special reference to the stakeholders and the affected population. The difficulties in collecting data, in analysing the necessary situations and interventions, and in disclosing clear communications both to the relevant institutions and to citizens, require that the Commission structure nurtures a less media-based and more operational management of relations with the various participants in the reconstruction, favouring the creation of a dense network of meetings and contacts.[11] The experience of a disaster lived across a vast and differentiated territory, and between populations with different history and cultures and different needs, has demonstrated the need to meet frequently with the representatives of all the committees of earthquake victims, and give them the opportunity to express their requests. It is also essential to strengthen the relationship between different parties coordinating the reconstruction effort and its stakeholders, primarily mayors and representatives of the institutions in the territories, professional networks, production activities and universities.[12] Unfortunately, in some cases, there was a strong political relationship between the choices of the managers of the Commission structure and the type of the activities of the structure itself, often oriented towards financial and media performances, which are not particularly useful for an effective reconstruction process for the most affected communities.

Instead, in the face of public calamities that involve (obviously to varying degrees) everyone, the only right attitude should be that of collaboration, discipline and mutual aid. That is, that fundamental anthropological form should be activated, based on long-term relationship building, trust and a sense of mutual support in the face of a shared experience of disaster. Therefore, if we want to introduce a different sense of bonding and collaboration in communities (life-saving in situations of calamity), it is necessary to resort to specific forms of narration, risk education and collaboration between all parties involved in the reconstruction process, including stakeholders and citizens.

A participatory and inclusive approach

Pandemic and earthquake: risk communication and education

Before 2020, few communities seriously considered the need to deal with a pandemic on top of a natural hazard. COVID-19 shows we need to be prepared for all eventualities[13] which might happen simultaneously. The set of Italian regulations for responding to an earthquake, landslide or flood does not include, for example, the need to consider social distancing in emergency shelters, or how to get help from other states when a widespread health crisis is underway.

It seems superfluous to recall the importance of risk communication, whatever risk it is. Yet the facts show that something is not working, and this is – in different ways – a worldwide issue. Communication is the prerequisite for informing, and both actions have the purpose of contributing to the reduction of disaster risk. However, nowadays, communication perhaps suffers from an impoverishment of meaning caused by the multiplication of means and contents, which – as effectively defined by the paradigm of postmodernity – reflects a superficial and fragmented reality, like an image on a broken mirror. The fact that social media make it possible for anyone to become an author, distributor or multiplier of information presents both an increase in communication potential and a series of risks, in terms of assuring the correctness of the information and its purpose and relevance for a given target audience. Such problems become particularly acute in emergency periods and are linked to the prevalent absence of a culture of prevention. Whatever the hazard to be faced, social media exploit the mechanisms of confusion, misunderstandings and partiality, which are superimposed – and often impose themselves – on the official communication disseminated by the competent authorities.

The issue is, of course, linked to the complex question of freedom of information, plurality, the nature of democracy itself, and participatory democracy in particular. However, it should be noted that, in a democratic environment, in emergency conditions, it is necessary and sufficient to use accredited sources of information, and these should be disclosed by the offices in charge through the public media, for example. This flow of information must reach the whole population, and be understandable. But this essential goal cannot be achieved without adequate preparation of the public.

The school system, the educational programmes that concern issues related to prevention and civil self-protection, and the battle against educational poverty are all fundamental to decreasing the social vulnerability of a community, as well as to increasing its ability to analyse information on risks and hazards, and respond to it appropriately. However, an emphasis on more tangible 'academic' gains and immediate pressures facing the school systems, the 'here and now', conflicts with the long-term perspective and preparation.

Even in the COVID-19 era, as in post-earthquake periods, the school represents a focal point, both concrete and symbolic. The material reconstruction of a destroyed school building, or the reconstruction of school spaces, real and ideal, are significant for a social reconstruction, because they centre on young people and on the passage of knowledge and consciousness between the various social components. In both emergency situations (COVID-19 and an earthquake) the problems to be addressed are: how to restart, how to mitigate and how to prevent risks. The same questions become common teaching and research themes. Given the experiences lived so far, in any catastrophic event there are phases in which anger, bewilderment and despair alternate. These are then followed by progressive disinterest and a move to focus on regrowth goals, based on the usual methodologies, oriented to rapid profit and not supported by adequate programming based on effective prevention measures.

Citizen action in requesting appropriate approaches, through participatory democracy processes, should contribute to navigating these changing phases of disaster response and reconstruction. Therefore, citizens must be ready to demand prudent and effective policies with a view to the sustainability and resilience of their territory, without settling for short-term solutions. So, the weapon to combat institutional, managerial and social myopia is education based on scientific knowledge, communicated with new, unconventional methods and transmitted through innovative vectors. The intergenerational nature of the educational process is fundamental. In the context of disaster risk reduction and prevention, educating should mean inducing people to adopt appropriate behaviours in relation to situations and in interaction, and adapt their modalities independently and conscientiously. Paradoxically, in the aftermath of the earthquakes and in the times of COVID-19, our country, so beautiful yet fragile, offers us a favourable field of action: the possibility of promoting, in direct contact with the environment, personal growth, community evolution and social development. It sounds like a paradox, but COVID-19 requires us to adopt some new behavioural rules that actually direct us to the re-evaluation of open spaces, which can at the same time become places of meeting and community exercise (school, assembly, worship and so forth) and open spaces for direct observation and study. It is hoped that this renewed sense of urgency of citizen response in times of crisis, which the current pandemic makes clear, will feed into and translate into long-term, grassroots-driven and locally-sensitive risk awareness and risk mitigation policies and practices.

Decreasing territorial vulnerabilities

The need for a geoethic vision

The serious pandemic that we are still in the midst of highlights once more how necessary it is to push for the synthesis of the know-how of social sciences and human and natural sciences in order to understand global processes. In the current phase of crisis management in Europe, various factors of social, institutional and cultural vulnerability are emerging. As for earthquakes, landslides and floods, or even epidemics, if they impact on a vulnerable territory they can turn into disasters. In fact, epidemics, if accompanied by a mismanagement of institutional communication, uninformed behaviour and inadequate education of citizens, and an insufficient number of health structures and medical personnel, may cause disasters. In Italy it is also necessary to take into account the high number of elderly people, as well as citizens in difficult socio-economic conditions, both of which contribute to increasing the social vulnerability of the country.[14]

The crisis of the last months due to the pandemic caused by COVID-19 makes us reflect on the need for a 'geoethic look' at human behaviour towards the environment. Degrading and disrupting the ecosystems, and especially the primary forests, allows the so-called 'species jump' by viruses present in wild animals to other mammals – such as human beings. COVID-19, in fact, is an object (hybrid) belonging to both nature and culture,[15] a 'product' of the Anthropocene.[16] From this perspective, the relatively recent geoethic approach consists of research and reflection on the values that underpin appropriate behaviours and practices wherever human activities interact with the Earth system. Geoethics deals with the ethical, social and cultural implications of geoscience education, research and practice, and with the social role and responsibility of geoscientists in conducting their activities.[17] Moreover, geoethics also aims to create a framework for meaningful cooperation between governments, industries (representing geo-resource developers), civil society (geo-resource users), non-governmental organisations (NGOs) and geoscientists, with the aim of an eco-sustainable development of geo-resources.

Placet natura regi terram ('It is a shared opinion that the Earth is supported by nature') – this sentence has been chosen by the International Association for Promoting Geoethics for a comparison between our own body and the planet we live on.[18] The phrase, based on the philosophic work of the most important Roman Stoic philosopher, Lucio Anneo Seneca, is taken up further in a later poetic formulation. In *The Prophet*, Kahlil Gibran writes: 'Your home is your largest body'.[19] Both poetic formulations echo a possible Aristotelic syllogism: the deep interrelation between individual/community/society and environment is a cultural consciousness, clearly rooted in time – a forgotten cultural heritage, especially in postmodernity. Anchored by such a commitment to relationality, geoethics can provide the correct categories to ensure that policymakers, local communities and stakeholders are oriented towards adequate behaviours to mitigate both earthquake and pandemic risk, helping to reduce the social vulnerability of a territory.

Conclusion

According to Marone and Bohle, the 'geoethic rationale' may provide guidance for adequate decision-making and actions against the COVID-19 pandemic.[20] In short, the geoethic rationale is actor-centric, virtue-ethics-focused, responsibility-focused, knowledge-based, all-actor inclusive, and universal-rights based. This rationale description is informed by and relevant to everyone from Earth scientists to epidemiologists, from healthcare personnel to law-enforcement units, and to all of society.[21]

In the last 50 years, various currents of thought have rejected the trivialisation of disasters as the exclusive result of uncontrollable natural forces, considering them rather as a consequence of the human and social vulnerability created, developed and reproduced in the complexity of the social and economic structures that govern the planet[22] as a consequence of power and inequalities.[23] In the Italian case study, inadequate governance, the absence and 'invisibility' of a risk awareness and prevention culture, a confused risk-communication strategy and the absence of civil-protection plans for the pandemic and for the management of multiple disasters in real time, contribute to making a territory that is already compromised and subject to various natural extreme events even more vulnerable.

As research in disaster studies makes clear, marginalised people and groups that suffer the most discrimination on an ethnic, religious, gender, skill, income or citizenship basis are those most vulnerable to disasters.[24] In the time of COVID-19, it is inevitable that analogies are drawn between disasters related to epidemic events and those related to extreme natural hazards, such as earthquakes. An extreme natural event, such as an earthquake or a flood, therefore converges more on these people and these groups than those with greater powers and resources. So it is the interaction between the environmental hazard and these vulnerabilities that creates a disaster. Not an 'exceptional' phenomenon with respect to the context in which we live and its conjunctures, but a social and political construction, rooted in the everyday of this context and normalised in its foundations.[25]

The COVID-19 pandemic is the first pandemic in the post-Second World War globalised world. It may be a test-ground for assumptions that relate the societal level of moral adequacy to the modus operandi of governance, as well as the successes and failures in handling the pandemic in a multidisciplinary way.[26] It is, therefore, necessary to adopt an inclusive, multidisciplinary and integrated approach, one that takes an ethical look at our actions, in order to prevent future disasters and crises that have in common the vulnerability of the territories in which extreme events occur.

Acknowledgements

The authors thank Dr Kasia Mika and Georgina Phillips for the language revision.

Notes

1 Franklin, *The Science of Conjecture: Evidence and Probability Before Pascal*; Di Bucci, *Elementi di scienze comportamentali nella comprensione (e comunicazione) dei rischi di protezione civile*.
2 Luhmann, *Modern Society Shocked by its Risks*; Lugeri et al., *Unconventional Approach for Prevention of Environmental and Related Social Risks: A Geoethic Mission*.
3 Renn, *'Three decades of risk research: accomplishments and new challenges'*, 51.
4 Farabollini, *'The 2016 Earthquake in Central Italy. The Alphabet of Reconstruction'*; Farabollini et al., *'The role of Earth Science and Landscape approach in the ethic geology: communication and divulgation for the prevention and rediction of geological hazard'*.
5 Aringoli et al., *'The August 24th 2016 Accumoli earthquake: surface faulting and DeepSeated Gravitational Slope Deformation (DSGSD) in the Monte Vettore area'*.
6 Valeriani and Bertelli, *'L'attività del Commissario Straordinario ed il futuro della ricostruzione del Centro Italia: una strategia sostenibile'*.
7 Farabollini, *'The 2016 Earthquake in Central Italy. The Alphabet of Reconstruction'*.
8 Farabollini, *'The 2016 Earthquake in Central Italy. The Alphabet of Reconstruction'*.
9 Mazzoleni, *'Identità ambientale e terremoto del 1980 nella ricerca universitaria: il lavoro del Comitato Interdisciplinare Universitario (1980–81)'*.
10 De Pascale et al., *'Hazardscape, Territorial and Individual Resilience in an interdisciplinary study: the Case of Pollino, Southern Italy'*; Antronico et al., *'Climate Change and Social Perception: A Case Study in Southern Italy'*.
11 Farabollini, *'The 2016 Earthquake in Central Italy. The Alphabet of Reconstruction'*.
12 Farabollini, *'The 2016 Earthquake in Central Italy. The Alphabet of Reconstruction'*.
13 Abkowitz, *'Can your community handle a disaster and coronavirus at the same time?'*.
14 De Pascale and Roger, *'Coronavirus: An Anthropocene's hybrid? The need for a geoethic perspective for the future of the Earth'*.
15 Latour, *Nous n'avons jamais été modernes. Essai d'anthropologie symétrique*.
16 Crutzen and Stoermer, *'The "Anthropocene"'*, Crutzen, 'Geology of mankind'.
17 IAPG, *'The meaning of the IAPG logo'*.
18 IAPG, *'The meaning of the IAPG logo'*.
19 Gibran, *The Prophet*.
20 Marone and Bohle, *'Geoethics for Nudging Human Practices in Times of Pandemics'*.
21 Marone and Bohle, *'Geoethics for Nudging Human Practices in Times of Pandemics'*.
22 O'Keefe et al., *'Taking the "naturalness" out of natural disasters'*.
23 Gaillard and Peek, *'Disaster-zone research needs a code of conduct*; Peek, *The Vulnerability Bearers'*.
24 Kelman et al., *The Routledge Handbook of Disaster Risk Reduction Including Climate Change Adaptation*.
25 Forino and Carnelli, *'Di cosa si parla quando si parla di rischio in Italia?'*; Gaillard, *'Preface'*; García-Acosta, *'Unnatural Disasters and the Anthropocene: lessons learnt from anthropological and historical perspectives in Latin America'*; Mika, Disasters, *Vulnerability, and Narratives: Writing Haiti's Futures*; Forino, *'Il Coronavirus e le altre catastrofi, ovvero la disastrosa normalità della pandemia'*.
26 Marone and Bohle, *'Geoethics for Nudging Human Practices in Times of Pandemics'*.

Bibliography

Abkowitz, M. 'Can your community handle a disaster and coronavirus at the same time?', *Prevention Web*, 30 April 2020. Accessed 31 August 2020, https://www.preventionweb.net/news/view/71578

Antronico, L., Coscarelli, R., De Pascale, F. and Di Matteo, D. 'Climate Change and Social Perception: A Case Study in Southern Italy'. *Sustainability*, 12(17) (2020): 1–24.

Aringoli, D., Farabollini, P., Giacopetti, M., Materazzi, M., Paggi, S., Pambianchi, G., Pierantoni, P.P., Pistolesi, E., Pitts, A. and Tondi, E. 'The August 24th 2016 Accumoli earthquake: surface faulting and DeepSeated Gravitational Slope Deformation (DSGSD) in the Monte Vettore area'. *Annals of Geophysics*, 59 (2016) 1–8.

Crutzen, P.J. and Stoermer, E.F. 'The Anthropocene'. *Global Change Newsletter*, 41 (2000): 17.

Crutzen, P.J. 'Geology of mankind'. *Nature*, 415 (2002).

De Pascale, F., Bernardo, M. and Muto, F. 'Hazardscape, territorial and individual resilience in an interdisciplinary study: the Case of Pollino, Southern Italy'. *Engineering Geology for Society and Territory*, 7 (2014): 109–113.

De Pascale, F. and Roger, J-C. 'Coronavirus: An Anthropocene's hybrid? The need for a geoethic perspective for the future of the Earth', *AIMS Geosciences*, 6(1). (2020) 131–134. DOI: 10.3934/geosci.2020008

Di Bucci, D. 'Elementi di scienze comportamentali nella comprensione (e comunicazione) dei rischi di protezione civile'. *PRISMA Economia - Società – Lavoro*, 3 (2018): 46–58. DOI: 10.3280/PRI2018-003004

Farabollini, P. 'The 2016 Earthquake in Central Italy. The alphabet of reconstruction'. In *Earthquake risk perception, communication and mitigation strategies across Europe*, edited by Piero Farabollini, Francesca Romana Lugeri and Silvia Mugnano, 145–171. Lago, Italy: Geographies of the Anthropocene book series, Il Sileno Edizioni, 2019.

Farabollini, P., Lugeri, F.R., Aldighieri, B. and Amadio, V. 'The role of Earth Science and landscape approach in the ethic geology: communication and divulgation for the prevention and rediction of geological hazard'. *Engineering Geology for Society and Territory*, 7 (2014): 115–120.

Forino, G. 'Il Coronavirus e le altre catastrofi, ovvero la disastrosa normalità della pandemia', *Lo Stato delle Cose. Geografie e storie del doposisma*, 7 July 2020. Accessed 01 September 2020, http://www.lostatodellecose.com/scritture/disastrosa-normalita-della-pandemia-giuseppe-forino/

Forino, G. and Carnelli, F. 'Di cosa si parla quando si parla di rischio in Italia?', *Lavoro Culturale*, 5 December 2017, Accessed 5 September 2020, https://www.lavoroculturale.org/cosa-si-parla-si-parla-rischio-italia/

Franklin, J. *The Science of Conjecture: Evidence and Probability Before Pascal*. Baltimore: Johns Hopkins University Press, 2001.

Gaillard, J-C. 'Preface'. In *Natural Hazards and Disaster Risk Reduction Policies*, edited by Loredana Antronico, Fausto Marincioni, 8–10. Lago, Italy: Geographies of the Anthropocene book series, Il Sileno Edizioni, 2018.

Gaillard, J-C. and Peek, L. 'Disaster-zone research needs a code of conduct'. *Nature*, 575 (2019) 440–442.

García-Acosta, V. 'Unnatural Disasters and the Anthropocene: lessons learnt from anthropological and historical perspectives in Latin America'. In *Disasters in Popular Cultures*, edited by Giovanni Gugg, Elisabetta Dall'O', Domenica Borriello, 237–248. Lago, Italy: Geographies of the Anthropocene book series, Il Sileno Edizioni, 2019.

Gibran, K. *The Prophet*. New York: Knopf, 1923.

International Association for Promoting Geoethics, 'The meaning of the IAPG logo'. Accessed 10 December 2020, www.geoethics.org

Kelman, I., Mercer, J., Gaillard, J-C., Eds. *The Routledge Handbook of Disaster Risk Reduction Including Climate Change Adaptation*. London: Routledge, 2020.

Latour, B. *Nous n'avons jamais été modernes. Essai d'anthropologie symétrique*. Paris, La Découverte, L'armillaire, 1991.

Lugeri, F.R., Farabollini, P., Amadio, V. and Greco, R. 'Unconventional approach for prevention of environmental and related social risks: a geoethic mission'. *MDPI Geosciences,* 8(54) (2018): 1–19.

Luhmann, N. *Modern Society Shocked by its Risks*. Social Sciences Research Centre in association with the Dept. of Sociology, University of Hong Kong, 1996. Accessed 12 June 2022 http://hub.hku.hk/handle/10722/42552

Marone, E. and Bohle, M. 'Geoethics for nudging human practices in times of pandemics'. *Sustainability*, 12(7271) (2020). DOI:10.3390/su12187271

Mazzoleni, D. 'Identità ambientale e terremoto del 1980 nella ricerca universitaria: il lavoro del Comitato Interdisciplinare Universitario (1980–81)'. In *Rischio sismico, paesaggio, architettura: l'Irpinia, contributi per un progetto*, edited by Donatella Mazzoleni, Marichela Sepe, 119–129. Napoli: CRdC, AMRA, 2005.

Mika, K. *Disasters, Vulnerability, and Narratives: Writing Haiti's Futures*. London: Routledge, 2019.

O'Keefe, P., Westgate, K. and Wisner, B. 'Taking the "naturalness" out of natural disasters'. *Nature*, 260 (1976): 566–567.

Peek, L. 'The Vulnerability Bearers'. *Natural Hazards Center*, 12 December 2019. Accessed 6 September 2020. https://hazards.colorado.edu/news/director/the-vulnerability-bearers

Renn, O. 'Three decades of risk research: accomplishments and new challenges'. *Journal of Risk Research*, 1(1) (1998): 49–71.

Valeriani, E. and Bertelli, A. *L'attività del Commissario Straordinario ed il futuro della ricostruzione del Centro Italia: una strategia sostenibile*. Rome: Presidenza del Consiglio dei Ministri, 8 September 2017. Accessed 15 March 2021 https://sisma2016.gov.it/2017/09/13/il-futuro-della-ricostruzione-una-strategia-sostenibile/

13
Soundscapes of non-reality
Alternative approach to post-disaster reconstruction
Paola Rizzi, Nora Sanna and Anna Porębska

Extending the theme of community engagement, this chapter looks at how sound, a powerful part of the urban experience, can be used to shape public space, promote awareness, mitigate risk and, in the wake of disaster, encourage healing.

One of the most distinctive urban elements is noise. Across time, the changing sources of noise, whether the wheels of wagons, horses' hooves, people, or later cars and motorbikes, produce a variety of noisy landscapes that characterise the life of the town. Soundscape design, sound studies and acoustic engineering are not new, yet they can be considered innovative when it comes to disaster mitigation, risk awareness and risk reduction. Since the earthquake of 2009 and during its ongoing reconstruction, L'Aquila has been characterised by a fragmented and non-cohesive urbanity, in which the concept of community is no longer present. The current non-reality of its historic city centre is defined by a state of transition, uncertainty, constant change and, at the same time, stagnation. In this context, the authors reflect on how sound can shape public spaces in the wide context of risk – be that warning, healing or mitigation – with the aim of incorporating sound design into the proposals to turn the evacuation points of L'Aquila's emergency management plan into dual spaces, suitable for emergency as well as everyday life.

Introduction

Cities are multitudes of properties, characters and signs that are perceived with all the senses, through various stimuli mixed with memories of other places. Hence, a semantic identity of a place is built with more than its image, as being in a place is much more than seeing it. It is more, as Pallasmaa[1] put it, 'one single continuous existential experience'. And yet, urban spaces, in all their complexities, are still being reduced to their visual aspects. Among the consequences of such an approach is the potential for what Welsch saw as aesthetics of a reality reduced to its image[2] that has been bothering theorists for the last three decades. In this reality, the individual, filled with images and deprived of any sort of windows that are open to the deeper sense of reality, turns into a 'televisionary monolith' and becomes the perfect monad, lonely and manipulable. At the same time, most of the inhabitants of a city possess the technology to separate and isolate themselves, to privatise their micro-space, reducing their contact with the surroundings to a minimum. People attempt to escape the endless onslaught of audiovisual messages into a reality that is individually created. A reaction to the virtualisation of reality is constituted by playing by the very rules of the phenomenon. It is among the most telling reasons why, prior to the 2020 pandemic, the crowded scenes of modern cities were devoid of spectators fully embracing their spaces. It goes beyond aesthetics as it erodes social relationships; people and places become merely acquaintances. In this context, soundscape – even considered simply as a set of sounds typical of a place – is a component of the identity of a place, to be studied carefully with utmost attention, as much as it is a tool for reading, understanding, addressing and eventually rebuilding a territory.

Soundscape is a term popularised by Schafer in the 1970s and its application varies from ecology, through urban ecology and urban design, to aesthetics. It is a more detailed and complex category than acoustic environment, which is the combination of all the acoustic resources, natural and artificial, within a given area as modified by the environment. Soundscape is considered an immersive environment, which has a significant impact on tools and methods for its analysis. As defined by Schafer, it consists of three main elements: keynote sounds, sound signals (foreground sounds) and soundmarks, which together define the unique character of a given place.[3] Like a landmark, a soundmark is considered an environmental and cultural value that should be protected.

One of the most distinctive urban elements is noise. Over time, the nature of urban noise has moved from the natural to the mechanical, and is increasingly seen in the fields of urban ecology and sound studies as noise pollution. However, the extents of how subjective definitions of noise and silence can be were shown by John Cage in one of his last interviews, recorded in 1991 in New York, when he said: 'The sound experience which I prefer to all others is the experience of silence, and the silence almost everywhere in the world now is traffic. If you listen to Beethoven or Mozart, you will see they are always the same. But if you listen to the traffic, you will see it is always different.'[4]

The power of soundscapes is rooted deeply in our bodies. Homo sapiens are considered primates strongly dependent on the sense of sight, but the very first sense that starts to receive and interpret information is hearing. The noises and murmurs of the prenatal life are the first stimuli that shape our brains. Later on, we learn how to depend on what we see, but it is our ears, as opposed to our eyes, that keep updating us on our surroundings, in the full range of 360 degrees. Ours are not the best ears in the world of mammals, but they have adapted to how we move in space: slowly and horizontally. Not only do we not know how to close them, they are, in a way, the last to be closed, as hearing is the last sense in life to be deactivated, just as it was the first one to be turned on.

How to explain the healing aspects of an urban soundscape? McCullough[5] depicts a perfect urban space he refers to as ambient commons: 'An ambient commons, if there were such a thing, would be quiet enough but seldom silent. In this alone it could change what it means to be here and now. Like a quiet evening on the square, it might help recall how the noisy clamour of the morning market was a means, not an end in itself.' It is worth emphasising how, by simply adding the description of the soundscape, the overview becomes a multisensory experience, a space filled with smells and textures as much as images and sounds. A space that one can almost taste.

And yet, a centuries-old heritage of visual aesthetics, fuelled by the rampant image production and consumption of our times, is strong enough to keep reducing urban spaces to their visual aspects. Traces of such an approach can be found even in cases that consider themselves progressive, with research on Perceived Sensory Dimensions (PSD) in the context of stress recovery being among the most recent and prominent examples.[6],[7] The weakness of such a narrow understanding of the complex phenomenon of urban space reveals itself as particularly critical in vulnerable areas if, regardless of the regeneration process aiming to address or increase the social dimension of a space, all actions are focused on improving its appearance. As mentioned, while extending the theme of community engagement, this chapter offers an insight into how sound as a powerful part of urban experience can be used to shape public space, promote awareness and mitigate risk, as well as contributing to the process of post-disaster healing and recovery.

The reason soundwalks and sonographies are such effective tools for evaluating urban space is that observations and experiences, as Brambilla[8] emphasised, do not depend exclusively on the sound environment and its acoustic descriptors, but on numerous other non-acoustic factors, including the visual aspect. Hence the need for a holistic approach that also takes into account the user's individual characteristics, as indicated in some theoretical models recently proposed in the literature.

Method

Diver S City LAB is an international research and education network that is active in the field of urban design and planning, with particular focus on issues related to risk, disasters and community preparedness. In 2004 it launched specific research on soundscape and its potential to engage with the complexities of urban places, as well as to open up different urban contexts and scenarios to experimentation. Among the first activities was a workshop held as part of a course at the Department of Architecture, Design and Urban Planning (DADU) of the University of Sassari at Alghero, a medieval coastal city in Sardinia, Italy. The aim of the workshop was to analyse the soundscape of Piazza Civica, one of the city's squares, along with its adjacent spaces. Piazza Civica is one of the main squares in Alghero. It sits within the original urban plan of the town and is surrounded by fifteenth- and sixteenth-century buildings of particular architectural importance. The square is a connecting node between three of the main axes of the historic centre and a space of flux between differing activities and occupants, both residents and tourists. In the summer, as well as beyond the end of the tourist season into the start of winter, this square is a point of reference in the city as well as a meeting point.

The students carried out an empirical study of space through the design of sound mappings – spatial patterns that identify certain sounds and vibrations at different moments in time. From the drawings a clear differentiation emerged between the space of the square, characterised by anthropic sounds of conviviality and commerce, and that of the passage leading to the port. Within the same research context, the Acoustical Society of Italy (AIA), active since 1972 to facilitate the exchange of information regarding the results of research and news concerning the various themes of acoustics, has analysed the space of Piazza Civica from a technical–acoustic point of view.[9]

The studies described above confirmed the hypothesis of the coexistence of at least two – if not more, for participants in soundscape surveys usually have some difficulties with describing the way they perceive sounds – distinct soundscapes within a seemingly singular space conventionally considered a rectangular and well-defined whole. The study proved that landscape and soundscape are disjunct and separable; while one sees a single square, one hears several squares. In other words, the number of urban interiors distinguishable and definable with eyes and ears may differ. This leads to further research questions of utmost importance, especially if we are trying to manipulate both tangible and intangible elements of urban space.

Research on soundscape was soon to be aligned with other themes, including the contemporary urban phenomenon of urban solitude,[10] and in particular those related to disaster risk reduction and disaster mitigation in urban areas. In an urban context such as the post-disaster one, quality of life is based above all on a multidimensional experience of the space. If the relation between an individual and a space is broken, its restoration and reconstruction goes beyond what can be described by quantitative parameters.

L'Aquila: a case study

Destroyed in 2009 and in a constant process of reconstruction ever since, the Italian city of L'Aquila was a theme of the 2017 International School on Awareness and Responsibility of Environmental Risk, originally launched in Alghero in 2005. Its tenth edition was dedicated to tangible and intangible aspects of loss resulting from the 2009 event. To date, the city's soundscape has undergone profound changes caused by the delayed, slow and ongoing reconstruction.

The aim of the workshop was to understand the nature of soundscapes that characterised the city eight years after the disaster. In a preliminary analysis of the urban context, the axes of the city's *cardo* and *decumanus* (Via Roma, Corso Principe Umberto, Via San Bernardino) were identified as representative, for these were the parts where the reconstruction was most active (Figure 13.1). Lined by monumental buildings, which were the active part of the city pre-earthquake, these main axes of the town are still the principal connectors of all the spaces and streets in a large historic centre that is enclosed within the medieval walls. As in the case of Piazza Civica in Alghero, described above, there was a decision to conduct two different types of experiments within the same spatial scheme, both implemented with a continuous soundwalk through the spaces. One was focused on empirical data of both hi-fi and lo-fi components and was conducted by the AIA experts. The other one was an experiment in sonographies. Participants – students of the school, of both local and international origin – were asked to describe graphically the sound they perceived during the walk, in the manner they found most convenient. No rules or suggestions were given on how their experience should be represented. The result was a collection of sonographs that highlighted different sounds, some not immediately recognisable, but still present on a sublevel of the city's sound plane (Figure 13.2).

AIA experts described the soundscape of L'Aquila as a lo-fi environment with construction sites, cranes and heavy vehicles being the sources of predominant sound signals. Conversely, the sounds of humans and nature were either completely lost, imperceivable or simply absent.

On the basis of these results, a decision was made to propose a more empirical approach. A hypothesis was formulated that the acoustic environment of a city, or more generally a society, can be a starting point for a study on its social conditions, and for creating lines of development

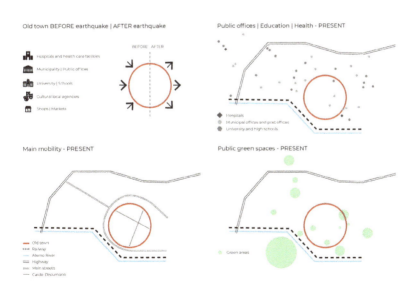

Figure 13.1 Urban analysis diagrams regarding main services and points of interest outlined by the citizens of L'Aquila during the survey held in 2017. © Nora Sanna.

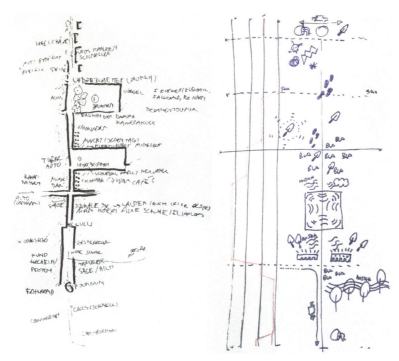

Figure 13.2 Examples of freehand sonographies resulting from soundwalks along Corso Vittorio Emanuele II in L'Aquila that took place during the 2017 International Summer School on Awareness and Responsibility of Environmental Risk. © Federico Puggioni. © Francesco Cherchi.

and redevelopment of the spaces that compose it.[11] The aim was to define which strategies could be applied, and which processes launched, to engage the community and enable it to establish a new relationship with its spaces. First, however, it was necessary to understand the reasons why the community had become detached, and why this detachment had lasted for so many years.

The research sought to address, among other aspects, the social dimension of individual perception of urban spaces. To this end, participatory processes were chosen as a reference for planning, as their reliability is proven in the context of risk, risk mitigation and community preparedness.[12] Indeed the constant exchange of experiences with local people, and their involvement in each phase of the project, brought added value to the final results. By definition, participation is a process that introduces the points of view of people who inhabit a territory, and allows

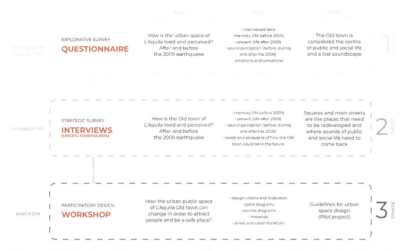

Figure 13.3 Participatory process flowchart as applied in the L'Aquila case study. © Nora Sanna.

definition of the real needs of a community by placing greater importance on elements that they find relevant. It also creates a bond between the local community and the outcome of the project, which may have a significant impact on its maintenance in the future.

Participation in the field study took place between September 2017 and March 2018, and was divided into three phases: questionnaire-based surveys, interviews with the key members of the community, and workshops with selected teams (Figure 13.3).[13]

Phase one, the surveys, took place between October 2017 and February 2018. Respondents were mostly young, from 18 to 40 years of age, studying, working at the university or unemployed. Most were residents of L'Aquila, and more than half had lived in the historic city centre prior to the earthquake. The mixed structure of the questionnaires aimed to give people the chance to express their individual views without the rigidity of closed questions. They were divided into sections with questions about:

- profiling – recollections of the city before the 2009 earthquake, focusing on everyday spaces and habits
- the city's current state

- sounds of the city before the earthquake, during the shocks, and in the present day.

Participants were encouraged to express their emotions regarding sound memories of those events. Open-ended questions were limited to three keywords describing the sound and emotions related to it. This approach allowed participants to paint a more nuanced picture on how their perceptions of the city had changed over time (Figure 13.4).

The record of a living city – neither 'vision' nor 'image' seem applicable terms in this context, which also proves the very limits of language we use to describe spaces – which emerged from the answers collected was as much one of busy spaces as it was of spaces of leisure and social life. The contrast between these memories and the new state of the city was striking. The keywords used to describe its present state were 'work' and 'home', but not 'bars', 'restaurants' or 'people'. The sounds of everyday life were those that had faded or fallen silent. The sounds of construction sites that characterise the new soundscapes of the city centre were perceived as disturbing by most of the respondents. However, just as John Cage found silence in the sound of traffic, for some respondents these sounds represented hope, change and the rebirth of the city.

This phase of the study provided a general context in which to operate, revealing many interesting, sometimes contradictory, perceptual nuances. A very strong attachment to the historic centre was particularly

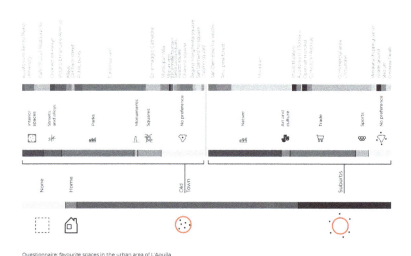

Figure 13.4 Results of the survey regarding favourite urban spaces in L'Aquila, 2017. © Nora Sanna.

evident, with respondents referring to the sequence of squares and alleys as well as glimpses of the past city. In fact, many citizens reported that they returned to the centre to walk without a precise reason, waiting for the reconstruction to end. These responses showed how, even if abandoned, the city centre is intrinsic to local identity, for this is the place with which the local community identifies itself (Figure 13.5).

The aim of the second phase, the interviews, was to enrich individual perspectives. Interviews were semi-structured, with every participant given 10 basic open-ended questions. These ranged from how they compared everyday life in the city before the earthquake with the present, to their individual needs or opinions on reconstruction. Uninterrupted narratives were allowed, even welcomed. The participants for phase two were chosen from among local stakeholders. Traditionally, these fall into four categories: the decision-makers, those who own the resources, those who are well informed about territory and/or community, and the people with expert or deep knowledge. In the case of L'Aquila, it seemed appropriate to distinguish young people who had only known the city after the earthquake from those who had lived there long enough to witness consciously the different phases of its transformation.

What emerged from the interviews was that, even in the case of a city in a state of recovery, its fulcrums of conviviality and everyday activities are intrinsically linked to public space, more specifically to squares and main streets. The social dimensions of urban space, which start in the streets and squares and reach deeper behind the facades and into the buildings, are difficult to reconstruct after an earthquake. The ideal preliminary strategy is to secure and revive the interstitial spaces as

Figure 13.5 L'Aquila Old Town's Sonography, 2018. © Francesco Cherchi, Nora Sanna.

soon as possible, to allow new memories to be collected and new bonds to be established.

Currently, while the city centre of L'Aquila is at the very core of its local identity, it is perceived as an unsafe space. The reconstruction process is perceived both positively and negatively, but the absence of people, other than construction site workers, in the city centre cements a negative impression, since people tend to perceive inhabited or frequented spaces as safer. Ghost towns and ruins, holiday destinations out of season, peripheries and suburbs during the day, and deserted office districts at night and over the weekend are all manifestations of this same absence. As Porębska[14] has pointed out, the comfort of tranquillity and the dull silence of a permanently or temporarily abandoned city may have similar properties expressed in decibels, but evoke different types of solitudes and correspond with different levels of vulnerability.

The solution would be to bring people back to the city centre. However, while its rebuilt and redeveloped spaces are restored in their visual aspects, perception of them is still dominated by the rumbles and vibrations of construction sites. The lo-fi soundscape of the centre continues to convey sensations related to the chaos and abandonment of the period immediately following the earthquake.

Comparison of the results of the survey with the emergency and evacuation plan for the historic centre of L'Aquila revealed that many of the places defined as important for the local community are also assembly points. These spaces consequently already meet two basic requirements: familiarity and safety. The challenge to be addressed during the third phase of the study was to define how they can also be perceived as pleasant and attractive prior to the – still distant – end of the reconstruction process.

The aim was to create a new soundscape, or network of soundscapes that would coexist with a sound environment currently dominated by construction during working days and by dull silence after hours and over the weekends. Among proposals that emerged from the questionnaires and interviews was one that used the sounds of water: in a city renowned for its 99 fountains, water and its movement could convey both life and calm. Unfortunately, due to damage to the water and sewer system, most of the existing fountains were shut off.

A low-cost, low-power and reversible alternative was needed, and a solution was proposed with a sound frame for the new soundscapes based on the system of rain chains (*kusari-doi*) typical of Japanese gardens. Passing through a sequence of rings and small concavities, rainwater makes sound similar to that of natural waterfalls. Such a soundscape is characterised by rhythm and constancy as the signal spreads throughout the course. Visual continuity is obtained by selecting porphyry flooring of local provenance. These paths, apart from brightening the environment both aurally and visually, would connect assembly points and waiting areas as identified in the emergency plan, allowing their adoption by the local community.

The third phase of the study was the workshop. It was organised to scrutinise the initial concept described above and to work jointly, collaboratively and voluntarily on a final version of the project. A specific area, namely the stairs leading to the Basilica of San Bernardino and the square in front of it (Figure 13.6), was proposed as the site for the case study, as it met the criteria of being both safe and familiar. The Basilica di San Bernardino with its particular staircase, combines monumentality with connections to nature. A space of public aggregation that forms a stepped seating arrangement for events, the stairs are flanked by wide green escarpments and provide views beyond the city to its surrounding territory and mountain landscape. Variants of configurations, including materials and street furniture, were presented to seven jurors, each of whom brought not only experience and skill to the workshop, but also, and most importantly, their concern about the city. Various options were presented, including the water-based proposals described above. Four spatial layouts, each with four different configurations, created a range of different spaces, all focused on the attenuation of noise generated by the surrounding construction sites.

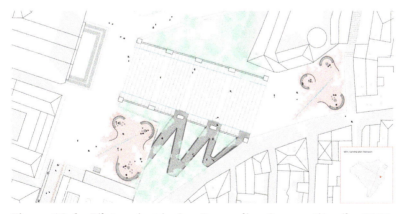

Figure 13.6 Pilot project in San Bernardino Square, L'Aquila, 2018, resulting from the workshop held in March 2018. It consists of two meeting points of light wooden structures with sound-absorbing properties and a walkway inside the park. © Nora Sanna.

Working with sound is intrinsically linked to working with materials: how they absorb or reflect sound, how they age, whether they are resistant to sun and water – be it rain, or snow, or ice, and whether they are light enough to be moved around or strong enough to carry weight. Ultimately, the palette of materials was reduced to three: wood (solid or structural, natural or clad), polycarbonate (used mostly as finishing surface for sound-absorbing materials), and urban greenery (considered an acoustic barrier, with elements diminishing the local heat-island effect). Technical drawings were avoided in favour of mood boards because many participants had nontechnical backgrounds. Each participant had to express their opinion on the solution they presented. The final step of the workshop was to encourage participants to imagine two alternative futures for the space in question: one with the project carried out and one without it. Participants were asked to write down their vision and then present it to others. Although the workshop was intended to critique the design proposal and to discuss individual opinions and perceptions, rather than obtain fixed and firm results, it is worth emphasising that the solution eventually identified by the group was the one that used water as a constituent element of space and provided structures that enclosed meandering spaces from their surroundings. A conclusion can be drawn that – within the limits of the experiment – there is a strong need for more cohesive and compact soundscapes, detached from the acoustic congestion of a city under reconstruction. However, the fragile and unstable equilibrium of the city must be taken into consideration to avoid further confusion, distortion and lack of security. People need spaces they know and can easily become familiar with. Preferably, new elements should enhance positive properties of spaces without changing their connotations. Properly designed systems of micro-architecture, based on paths and elements of street furniture that are flexible and accessible to all would allow this goal to be achieved at a tiny fraction of the general cost of the reconstruction.

Summary

The methodology described works on the unconscious perception of visual and acoustic spaces and the signals, indications and implicit meanings they can provide in the absence of danger as well as during emergency. Subsequently, the COVID-19 pandemic has shed new light on the consequences of disconnecting people from their surroundings, as well as on the very definition of trauma, silence and solitude.

The aim of our research was to define the theoretical and practical guidelines of a process to reconstitute the lost relationship between the city and its citizens. We presented how considering sound as a tool for urban analysis and an element of urban composition can contribute to increasing the social performance of public spaces. This research develops an applicable method that could be part of a more extensive general plan, in which many more participants are involved, bringing to bear different needs and critical points of view. The research, therefore, does not aim to solve the problem in its entirety, but to study and provide tools and strategies for how an architect or an urban planner could operate within a similar situation, empathising with a population that has lost its city.

In addition to hypothesizing a solution applicable to the entire territory of the historic centre of L'Aquila, we investigated a universal method that implements paradigms of both soundscape and participatory planning of a territory. None of this would have been possible without the contribution of the citizens of the city of L'Aquila, and a collaboration based on trust, with the joint aim of working together for the future of the city: if not ideal, liveable and, above all, alive again.

Notes

1   Pallasmaa, *The Eyes of the Skin: Architecture and the Senses*, 2005, 40.
2   Welsch, *Ästhetisches Denken*, 1990, 18.
3   Schafer, *The Soundscape: Our Sonic Environment and the Tuning of the World*, 1977, 22.
4   Interview recorded on 4 February 1991. Accessed 12 June 2022 https://thearchivecollective.com/2015/03/silence/.
5   McCullough, *Ambient Commons: Attention in the Age of Embodied Information*, 293.
6   Grahn and Stigsdotter, 'The relation between perceived sensory dimensions of urban green space and stress restoration', 2010, 264–275.
7   Hamzah et al., 'Perceived Sensory Dimension for Mental Health and Well-Being: A Review', 2020, 179–189.
8   Brambilla et al., 'The Soundwalk at Alghero', 2016, 52–62.
9   Brambilla et al., 'The Soundwalk at Alghero', 2016, 52–62.
10 Porębska, *Spaces of Solitude: People and Spaces in Deadened Cities*, 2016, 16–44.
11 Sanna, *La partecipazione come strumento di progettazione: paesaggio sonoro e rigenerazione urbana. Il caso studio di l'Aquila*, 2018, 90.
12 Rizzi and Porębska, 'Towards a Revised Framework for Participatory Planning in the Context of Risk', 2020, 1–23.
13 The first, participative, phase of the questionnaire, was undertaken between September 2017 and January 2018. It involved 102 people, of whom 78 responded via online platforms and 24 in person. The online platforms allowed wide reach but did not screen or gather data on the participants. In relation to direct contact participants, 40 people were invited but only 24 replied and completed the questionnaire.
    The second phase was carried out in November 2017, at that time we had only partially undertaken the first stage questionnaires. This phase involved six people, each with different characteristics and interests in the urban and sound space of the city. The technique used was that of a was semi-structured interview, which allowed the free flow of thoughts and emotions. The final participatory phase, the workshop, involved the same people as the interviews and were mediated by the researchers themselves.
14 Porębska, *Spaces of Solitude: People and Spaces in Deadened Cities*, 2016, 131.

Bibliography

Beard, D. *Musicology: The Key Concepts*. Abingdon: Routledge, 2006.

Blesser, B. and Salter, L-R. *Spaces Speak, Are You Listening?* Cambridge (MA): MIT Press, 2007.

Botteldooren, D., Andringa, T., Aspuru, I., Brown, A.L., Dubois, D., Guastavino, C., Kang, J., Lavandier, C., Nilsson, M., Preis, A. and Schulte-Fortkamp, B. 'From Sonic Environment to Soundscape'. In *Soundscape and the Built Environment*, edited by Jian Kang and Brigitte Schulte-Fortkamp, 17–41. Boca Raton: CRC Press, 2017.

Brambilla, G., Masullo, M., Pascale, A. and Sorrentino, F. 'The Soundwalk at Alghero'. *Rivista Italiana di Acustica*, 40(3) (2016): 52–62.

Bull, M. *Sound Moves: iPod Culture and Urban Experience*. Abingdon: Routledge, 2007.

Farina, A. *Soundscape Ecology: Principles, Patterns, Methods and Applications*. Berlin: Springer, 2013.

Gehl, J. *Cities for People*. Washington: Island Press, 2010.

Grahn, P. and Stigsdotter, U.K. 'The relation between perceived sensory dimensions of urban green space and stress restoration'. *Landscape and Urban Planning*, 94 (2010): 264–275.

Holl, S., Pallasmaa, J. and Perez-Gomez, A. *Questions of Perception: Phenomenology of Architecture*. San Francisco: William Stout, 2006.

La Belle, B. *Site of Sound: Architecture and the Ear*. Berlin: Errant Bodies Press, 2011.

McCullough, M. *Ambient Commons: Attention in the Age of Embodied Information*. Cambridge, MA: MIT Press, 2013.

Merleau-Ponty, M. *Phénoménologie de la perception*. Paris: Librairie Gallimard, 1945. First English edition: *Phenomenology of Perception*, translated by Colin Smith. Abingdon: Routledge & Kegan Paul, 1962.

Pallasmaa, J. *The Eyes of the Skin: Architecture and the Senses*. Chichester: Willey, 2005. First edition: 1996.

Nor Hamzah, A.I., Kuang, L.C., Kamaruzzaman, Z.A. and Wahab, N.A. Perceived sensory dimension for mental health and well-being: a review'. In *Charting a Sustainable Future of ASEAN in Business and Social Sciences*, edited by Naginder Kaur and Mahyudin Ahmad. Berlin: Springer, 2020. https://doi.org/10.1007/978-981-15-3859-9_17

Porębska, A. *Spaces of Solitude: People and Spaces in Deadened Cities*. Doctoral Thesis supervised by Paola Rizzi. Alghero: University of Sassari, 2016.

Rizzi, P. and Porębska, A. 'Towards a Revised Framework for Participatory Planning in the Context of Risk'. *Sustainability* 12(14) (2020): 1–23. https://doi.org/10.3390/su12145539

Ross, A. *The Rest Is Noise: Listening to the 20th Century*. New York: Farrar, Straus i Giroux/MacMillan, 2007.

Sanna, N. *La partecipazione come strumento di progettazione: paesaggio sonoro e rigenerazione urbana. Il caso studio di l'Aquila*. Master Thesis supervised by Paola Rizzi. Alghero: University of Sassari, 2018.

Schafer, R.M. *The Soundscape: Our Sonic Environment and the Tuning of the World*. New York: Random House Inc, 1977.

Stern, J. *The Audible Past: Cultural Origins of Sound Reproduction*. Durham (NC): Duke University Press, 2003.

Welsch, W. *Ästhetisches Denken*. Ditzingen: Reclams Universal-Bibliothek, 1990.

Part IV
Tourism, culture and economy

14
Atmospheric images
Photographic encounters in L'Aquila's historic centre
Federico De Matteis and Fatima Marchini

In many cases of post-disaster reconstruction, the primary rationale driving the process is grounded on technical aspects and functional considerations related to the urge of reinstating disrupted activities. Such reliance on the quantifiable dimensions of the complexity of urban systems, uncritically espoused by most political decision-makers and administrators, is often unresponsive towards the affective sphere of citizens and visitors alike, who sense that the reconstructed city feels cold, unreal, or distant from what it was before the catastrophic event.

While data provide tools to visualise key indicators of urban mechanisms, the non-representational sphere of emotion eludes quantification. Yet, these aspects are crucial in supporting a reconstruction capable of addressing the deeper layers of human experience, which assume even greater importance when a city is recovering from trauma. This chapter addresses a strain of creative and descriptive practices connected to photography, both as a medium for public art and as a tool to create affective descriptions of lived space.

Invisible reconstruction?

L'Aquila, 2020: as a multitude of building sites occupies the city's historic centre, the reconstruction proceeds. Eleven years after the fatal night of 6 April 2009, a significant number of the damaged or destroyed buildings now stand again, facades newly painted in bright colours. The Corso and many other streets are open for business, and summer nights bring a crowd of people to revel in town, much to the dismay of the few who have chosen to return to live in the historic area.[1] Most residential buildings lie empty, deprived of their once-thriving student population, which has migrated to newer parts of town. If – and when – a more consistent number of people return to inhabit the centre largely depends on future local policies, but also on economies and demographics that hover above the administrations' heads.

Yet despite the gradual return to urban life, the impression that a stroll through the centre affords to either a citizen of L'Aquila or to a casual visitor is that something is not entirely right. And we are not speaking of the fact that branching off from the reconstructed areas one stumbles upon quarters that lie entirely in ruins; a strange atmosphere pervades the city's core.[2] It is as if the newly reconstructed buildings were incapable of harbouring an affective bond between citizens and city, one that has been dramatically severed by the catastrophe. The overly pragmatic character of the reconstruction's architecture, which has failed to adopt a critical position towards the process of restoration and rebuilding, has been widely criticised,[3] but the feeling is not only a consequence of the neat removal of any trace of the earthquake. What one senses is that the trauma has not been negotiated, no 'grief' elaborated, and denial has set in, pretending that everything can return to normal, as if nothing had happened.[4] This results in what we could term a 'lack of trust' towards the city's space. Ineffable as this sensation might be, it could be compared to the awkward feeling a couple experiences after a distressing argument that leaves both parts angry and unsatisfied. And if we are to credit the hypothesis that we, as humans, interact with our environment as if it were a living being, then we can imagine that in L'Aquila this relationship is constantly on the verge of a break-up, after a disastrous fight that has not yet been settled.

Undeniably, there is also a question concerning the timeframe of the reconstruction. Besides a handful of 'pioneers' who never abandoned the historic centre, life started creeping back to the old streets several years after the event had displaced the entire population elsewhere, to new parts of town or temporary housing in the suburbs. Through this translation, the bond of habit towards the urban space and human life that once populated it were severed, in many cases for ever. Over a decade, different habits, practices and forms of life developed, as citizens grew accustomed to their new environments. Inevitably, such a timeframe leads people to evolve into new stages of life, developing habits that find their spatial setting elsewhere. Returning to the centre, thus, may bring back memories of a felicitous past, but no longer strikes an affective chord tied to people's existential conditions, one made of a sense of belonging and rootedness, the essential characteristics of 'dwelling'.

The process of reconstruction, in its political ambition, has opted for the 'easy' way out of the crisis: rebuild what was destroyed, reinstate collapsed facades, bring activities back to the centre and create opportunities for jobs. All of this can be accounted for by measurable indices: how many buildings have reopened? How many shops are open for business? But everything that concerns affect – the emotional sphere bonding human subjects among themselves and to their habitat – defies quantification. To bring it to light, we need more sophisticated tools that make the invisible visible, addressing a deeper layer of experience. One possible way is to work through images, in this case photography: a medium capable of articulating reality in a non-representational way, bringing to the foreground the stirrings of affect.

In what follows, we will attempt a two-sided approach to the issue of photographic images as catalysers of affect. First, we will recount and discuss an unfortunate public art installation organised to commemorate the earthquake's decennial, an exhibition entitled 'L'Aquila, 6 aprile 2019. Ricordo. Memoria. Futuro'. Secondly, we will present a photographic project on the historic centre – an attempt to describe the conditions of lived space encountered in L'Aquila's reconstructed streets, alleys and squares.

On the power of images

We live, as some say, in the age of the image. What once was the 'Gutenberg Galaxy', theorised by McLuhan[5] as the cultural evolution shaped by the book, has been superseded by a far-reaching 'iconic turn'. It is a rather recent cultural shift, with highlights in the mass diffusion of illustrated printed matter during the industrial revolution, the invention and popularisation of still and moving photographic images, the advent of television and, finally, the arrival of the internet. Well before this last event placed an image-producing-viewing-and-sharing device in the pocket of every second human being on the planet, Mitchell recognised the onset of a 'pictorial' turn in various cultural symptoms, questioning the centrality of verbal language in communication and sense-making: 'a postlinguistic, postsemiotic rediscovery of the picture as a complex interplay between visuality, apparatus, institutions, discourse, bodies, and figurality'.[6]

Among the implications of this cultural transformation is a deep change in the ontological statute of the image. Pictures are no longer conceived – as per the classical Platonic understanding – as a mere mimesis of reality,[7] or, in the Western hermeneutic tradition, as bearers of hidden meanings and signs. In this latter sense, images conceal their meaning deep beneath the appearing surface, and only an informed observer can disentangle the web of references to reach the underlying message. They are thus distancing mechanisms, as Panofsky wrote:

> Man is indeed ... the only animal whose products 'recall to mind' an idea distinct from their material existence. Other animals use signs and contrive structures, but they use signs without 'perceiving the relation of signification,' and they contrive structures without perceiving the relation of construction. To perceive the relation of signification is to separate the idea of the concept to be expressed from the means of expression.[8]

Increasingly, however, later authors recognised that images are more than imitations of nature or sophisticated riddles, where meaning is separated from expression: Gombrich, for one, states that 'the visual image is supreme in its capacity for arousal'.[9] A full revision of this paradigm sets in with Freedberg's 1989 *The Power of Images*, where the author retraces the history of art not from the perspective of the author, rather from that of the beholder's response. Our relationship to pictures, in this sense, is anything but a frigidly analytical one: we can love or loathe them, be sexually aroused or offended; images can spark emotions and modulate moods. If in classical thought figurations were considered either representations of reality, or technical devices separated from it, Freedberg claims that 'the time has come to acknowledge the possibility that our responses to images may be of the same order as our responses to reality'.[10]

Recognising the survival of some form of premodern thought that attributed to images 'magical powers',[11] Mitchell goes further and argues that 'images are like living organisms ... best described as things that have desires ... therefore, the question of what pictures want is inevitable'.[12] In fact, these drives animate the beholder, prompting an emotional response.[13] Bredekamp argues that, as 'living' presences, pictures possess an *energeia*, or acting quality:[14] they can perform acts such as gazing, alluring, seducing, menacing. And, as Warburg had keenly observed, a figure's gestures are not only bearers of meaning, but also of emotions the observer empathically responds to.[15] This 'animated' ontology of images is relevant, as we shall see, for the first photographic project discussed in the following pages.

The power of images is primarily unleashed by anthropomorphic figures: the portrait of a face, for example, can 'freeze' us by means of its gaze, which we may return in antagonistic confrontation.[16] Portrayals of humans have historically been the object of both iconoclastic crusades and vandalistic acts,[17] attesting to the stirrings they are capable of triggering. Images lacking human figures are far less often victims of these impulses, yet this does not imply that they are incapable of being themselves active generators of feeling. A landscape painting can afford the observer a cheerful or sombre mood, an emotional intonation to which we corporeally respond.[18] By means of expressive features such as colours, shadows and highlights, grain and texture, weather effects, a painting can become atmospheric, in the sense that it stages a 'spatialised emotion'.[19]

Again, a figureless landscape painting is not a simple reproduction of reality. A natural scene is not a landscape: in order to become one, it needs a conceptual unity, a perspective and a frame. But once this technical endeavour is achieved, an image becomes more than reality, acting as its increment,[20] bringing to appearance things that may otherwise remain latent, presenting them to the viewer.[21] In the post-hermeneutic age wherein the iconic turn unfolds, the concept of 'presence' becomes crucial to understanding the mode of being of images. In a key text, Gumbrecht stresses that 'any form of communication implies such a production of presence, that any form of communication, through its material elements, will "touch" the bodies of the persons who are communicating in specific and varying ways'.[22] An artistic object or performance – image, theatre, music and so on – can elicit 'effects of presence' that, in their being spatially extended and corporeally sensed, create a productive tension with the 'effects of meaning' that emerge from the 'hermeneutic field'.[23]

Endowed with these powers, images become formidable descriptors of the qualities of lived space, capable of making present that exceedance otherwise remaining opaque to purely objective, analytical methods. In contemporary urban and architectural studies, a wide range of practices leverage on what we could term 'atmospheric techniques', relying – among others – on images that strive to pin down phenomena as they unfold in the built environment. Sourcing from first-person experience, 'phenomenographical' methods engage with the affective dimension of spatial settings, as encountered by means of an extended sensorial sphere and an enriched corporeality.[24]

There are thus at least two fields where images deploy their power and allure: as 'living' presences – that, as we will see, can invade the public realm and elicit strong affective responses, in a fully political interplay – and as tools to describe the lived dimension of the city, its urban atmosphere. In this latter sense, we refer to the transdisciplinary outlook on the city that in recent years has focused on the collective affects, vaguely indeterminate agencies that are transversally experienced in their spatial unfolding.[25]

Remembering, memory, future

Photography and public space

Among the celebrations organised in L'Aquila for the 2019 decennial of the earthquake, one public art event struck a particular chord. Just days before 6 April, the cultural association Il Segno installed an exhibition in the arcades of a building on the historic centre's main Corso, with artwork by Roberto Grillo, a well-known local photographer (Figure 14.1). The exhibition consisted of 13 large-scale photographs of faces of people who had been affected by the earthquake: ordinary residents and local authorities, a child born two days after the catastrophe, a mother who had lost her children ... Faces were depicted in desaturated colours in very narrow frames, and retouched to enhance contrast, showing in exaggerated detail the skin's imperfections, wrinkles and marks, making the faces appear somewhat older and uglier (Figure 14.2). Most notably, all subjects wore serious expressions and had their eyes closed, as if they were sleeping. The portraits, once printed, were handed to the depicted subjects, who were asked to annotate them with their thoughts on the concept of 'L'Aquila 2009–2019'. The final result was thus a collaborative effort between photograph and models.

Installed on the street, the impact of the images was extremely powerful. Despite the fact that several of the subjects were public figures known to be alive, one could not avoid associating the portraits to images from autopsies. The rhythmic arrangement along the arcades further provided a solemn tone, as if the goal of the exhibition were a commemoration of victims – albeit in a metaphoric, mediated way. The project, in fact, was the third part of a series started by Grillo in 2012, when he first devised the idea of working on the earthquake's aftermath – not by photographing the city in ruins or under reconstruction, but rather metaphorically through the faces of affected people.[26] By asking

Figure 14.1 The exhibition 'L'Aquila, 6 aprile 2019. Ricordo. Memoria. Futuro' installed on the Corso. Photo: Roberto Grillo.

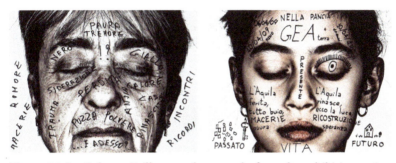

Figure 14.2 Roberto Grillo, two photographs from the exhibition series.

the subjects to recollect specific moments of their personal history, the photographer's goal was to recapture gestures and expressions related to the emotional stirrings they had experienced, and that would be empathically felt by viewers through the portraits.

Immediately after the opening, harsh criticism erupted. On social media, Grillo was attacked primarily because the 'dead faces' exhibited in the street were conveying a negative image of L'Aquila: the supposedly necrological message was considered a setback after a decade of painful and tiresome reconstruction. Citizens and visitors, the critics claimed, had to be welcomed by positive images rather than by a gallery of 'corpses'.[27] The case reached L'Aquila's City Council, where some

ATMOSPHERIC IMAGES   241

requested that the exhibition be removed – almost a form of public censorship. The space where the images were located, however, was of regional property, and the owners never withdrew their support to the event. Furthermore, the entire operation was self-financed by the cultural association, since the City Council had rejected the application for financial support, so it had no authority to request the removal. Nevertheless, the exhibition also received ample support and appreciation, and was covered by national and local media.

Due to the animated debate, in September 2019 Grillo eventually decided to replace the exhibition with a second one, quickly launching an amateur photo contest and displaying the winning pictures. The new installation, showing much more 'comforting' views of the city, quite predictably sparked no criticism at all.

Needless to say, the story of this exhibition is an archetypal demonstration of the power of images. The visages, 'invading' public space, had become potent activators of emotions, from which it was impossible to distance oneself. Reconstructing the events and the debate in retrospect, Grillo offers an interpretation of the split opinions of the public, referring to the psychotherapeutic sphere. A part of the town's population has suppressed the events of the earthquake in a form of denial: for them, seeing the faces proved an overwhelming emotional experience. On the other side, a different sample of public – which had more efficiently negotiated the grief – was equally struck by the portraits, but bridged the gap between their being representations of 'real' dead people and the installation's artistic dimension.[28] This form of art is obviously not redemptive, at least not in a conventional way, and to recognise this quality requires a structured feedback on the public's side.

Beyond the evidence that different subjects responded to the images according to their personal history and disposition, what is equally relevant is that the installation produced an atmosphere that, for the time of the exhibition, 'tuned' the spatial setting of L'Aquila's centre. The pictures, by no means neutral, collectively struck residents and visitors, and despite the fact that the event ended in conflict, one could claim that this 'political' dimension initiated a debate. If the photographs had been on display in some indoor art gallery, perhaps there would have been little talk and certainly much less animated discussion. On the other hand, since we are arguing that L'Aquila has not collectively engaged in the mourning and in the renegotiation of its urban space, it was perhaps the first event to open a discussion, potentially facilitating such a process as a political 'therapeutic' form. Images, thus, can be considered catalysers of collective affective transformations.

Silence is an answer, too

Stepping behind the lens, we have ourselves attempted to use photography as a tool for the observation of the 'state of affairs' in L'Aquila's centre. The photographer, one of this essay's authors, is a longtime resident (but not native) of the city, who witnessed the 2009 earthquake and its aftermath, leaving for several years to then return.

The photographic record, including around 150[29] shots taken on several separate occasions between October 2019 and June 2020, was conceptualised as an exercise in the observation of L'Aquila in terms of its lived space and urban ambiance. It is, in this sense, a 'phenomenography', intending to map a felt atmosphere, bringing it to presence through photographs taken within the precinct of the city's historic walls.

Although the project of producing a photographic record was deliberate and intentional, the subjects and framings of the individual images were not. The shots were categorised and grouped observing the recurrence of some salient subjects. These sets of images, however, were only labelled for practical purposes, since the overall effect of the work is meant to emerge from the pictures' mood rather than by their typological classification or thematisation.

A bias must be declared in advance: the photographs are not – nor were intended to be – an 'objective' restitution of the city's urban space. On the contrary, they were collected as a form of visual support capable of articulating an otherwise indefinable atmosphere that the shots' author had been experiencing ever since the gradual reopening of the centre. In other words, the process was not intended as an investigation aiming to uncover some hidden knowledge; the knowledge was already tacitly there, as a form of affective cognition accumulated over time, but needed the images in order to be recorded and made present for other viewers to share.

As we have discussed in the introduction, the atmosphere pervading L'Aquila's centre today is one of emptiness. This emptiness does not relate to a physical condition of abandonment, at least not in the parts of town where life has restarted – during daytime and into the evening, an abundant flow of people occupies and makes use of urban space. In various parts of the centre, the large number of building sites produces a bustling activity, starting in the early morning and extending into the afternoon. The emptiness experienced thus refers to something else – for example, to the expressive character of the reconstructed buildings, where human life does not seem to penetrate the interior and upper floors. It merely grazes the ground floors, where shops have been reopened and attract customers, while the upper windows lie almost invariably dark and empty, attesting to a condition of hollowness (Figure 14.3).

The black-and-white photographs present this atmosphere by the fact that many were taken at night. Even those shot in daylight display dark hues and little contrast. Rather than portraying the places where people gather, they insist on those that are avoided or only used as thoroughfare from one location to another. In the few instances where people do appear, they are always walking, depicted sideways or from behind, never looking at the photographer's lens, as if they were hurrying to leave the place.

The countless building sites also produce a distinctive atmospheric feeling. For several years now, the topography of the city's centre has experienced a continuous shift in accessibility, as construction areas are opened and closed, temporarily disrupting pedestrian movement. The well-organised sequence of the reconstruction process de facto produces a labyrinthine condition, reducing the possibility of a linear use of the urban fabric, based on the adoption of habitual routes that allow the subject to hodologically 'carve' a familiar space.[30] Yet beyond this indirect effect, which prevents people from 'furrowing' the streets with their habitual paths, a more direct expressive fact derives from the abundance of provisional structures set up by the building sites. Scaffoldings, enclosures, cranes, warning signs, aerial cables, ducts and pipes, all speak of a temporary condition that discourages any form of further use (Figure 14.4). And while the life of the reconstructed areas extends into the evening and sometimes into the night, here any movement comes to a halt in the afternoon, as the workers leave. Walking here at night provides a suspended feeling – perhaps only a temporary atmosphere – which however promises to evolve into a stable condition of hollowness.

Figure 14.3 Deserted streetscapes in L'Aquila's historic centre. Photo: Fatima Marchini.

Figure 14.4 Building site at night. Photo: Fatima Marchini.

Finally, what the photographs suggest is that the atmosphere of emptiness is oftentimes expressed as a form of haunting. The earthquake interrupted countless forms of human life, and parts of L'Aquila's inner core – not to speak of the multitude of smaller villages within its suburban area – lie abandoned, crystallised in the precise moment of the shake. 'Any spirit of place,' writes Heholt, 'is also indelibly linked to the past. Places are always marked by what has gone before, by the people who populated and shaped the environment in many different ways, by the weather of millennia'.[31] What haunts L'Aquila are the traces of past human life, spectrally surfacing with tantalising frequency (Figure 14.5). Again, the images express the absence of a bond between built space and human life: in this case, we are witnessing signs of a life now extinct and bound not to rise again, regardless of the final outcomes of the reconstruction.

Our photographic mapping may ultimately appear as a ruthless chronicle of all that has gone 'wrong' in the reconstruction – a portrayal of the failures that deliberately ignores the colossal efforts made. Yet there is no polemic or critical intent in this work; it is rather the presentation of a current condition, produced from the point of view of a specific subject who witnessed the earthquake and remains sceptical of the direction the reconstruction has taken. Observing these photographs conveys this sensation and sparks a reflection on possible alternatives for the future of the city's historic centre.

Figure 14.5 Ruined building. Photo: Fatima Marchini.

Conclusion: images of the future

Images are indeed powerful and complex devices and, as we have seen, their relation to urban space – either as presences, or as descriptors – can be both fruitful and controversial. In the case of L'Aquila, they appear as a litmus test of the assumption set forth in the opening of this paper: that beneath the surface of the immaculate reconstruction, the affective sphere animated by the city's space is still fractured, the bonds severed.

The two photographic projects we have illustrated bring to the surface several questions. Would the visages exhibited in the Corso have sparked a different kind of reaction, had they been installed in some other city that had not suffered the trauma of the earthquake? Or would it have been rather considered as a purely 'artistic' installation, thus devoid of deeper affective implications? Secondly, is the particular atmosphere that we recorded in the city's streets through our own photographic mapping specific to L'Aquila – considering its recent history, from 2009 onwards – or is it a type of feeling that can be more broadly encountered, for example in other historic centres in Italy or abroad?

Needless to say, these are not questions that can have an exact answer, nor do they prompt one. As we have stated in the introduction, we are not seeking a quantifiable response to our queries, rather trying to bring to the surface and make present an existential sphere that is otherwise difficult to access. In our opinion, the 'all-will-be-well' rhetoric of the reconstruction has implicit limits, since the earthquake has severed bonds that have not yet been negotiated, causing spatial conflict. An event such as the photographic exhibition is symptomatic of the fact that these latent frictions are ready to burst into political life whenever affects are stirred.

A different outlook on what the reconstruction could have been leads to the idea that the wounds and scars may have remained visible, at least to a certain degree; rather than hiding them, they could have become manifestos of a city's ability to change, transform and resist, even in the face of the most catastrophic events. What's more, pursuing the reconstruction in the way it has been done is obviously futile, since there is by now a wide awareness that the human dimension of the city's urban space is no longer what it was before, nor will it return to that condition – at least not while the generation that has witnessed the earthquake is alive. Perhaps, the opening of new forms of public discourse focusing precisely on the centre's precious urban space could help reorient the inhabitants' feeling *of* and *for* the city. For example, the inauguration of new urban rituals anchored to the political dimension – the opening up to arts, temporary uses, social and bottom-up initiatives, all that, in other words, does not strictly refer to the ordinary uses of space – could soften the otherwise dominant backward-cast gaze of all other extant practices, orienting a glance towards a potentially different future. This transformation might sustain a gradual elaboration of the grief, and the birth of new affective ties to the city's space.

Notes

1   Exact data on the number of permanent residents within the precinct of the city's historic walls is not available. Nevertheless, recent estimates show that around 3,350 citizens have returned, around half of the pre-earthquake population. See: Comune di L'Aquila, Deliberazione di Giunta comunale n. 334 del 13.08.2019: *Approvazione del 'Piano parcheggi provvisorio del centro storico'*, Accessed 14 July 2020 http://www.albo-pretorio.it/albo/archivio4_atto_0_335776_0_3.html.
2   This phenomenon often emerges in cities reconstructed after catastrophic events such as wars. One poignant description is given in Steiner, 1971, p. 60.
3   See among others Varagnoli, 2019. Indeed, both among scholars and in the common discourse, the feeling is that the 'à l'identique' reconstruction which has been carried out in most cases in fact conceals the inability to critically interpret the aesthetic and affective impact of the earthquake on the buildings and urban fabric.
4   De Matteis, 2019, 80–85.
5   McLuhan, 1962.
6   Mitchell, 1994, 16.
7   Böhme, 1999, 17.
8   Panofsky, 1955, 5.
9   Gombrich, 1982, 138.
10 Freedberg, 1989, 438.

11 Examples of images endowed with actual magical powers – if not altogether witchcraft – also abound in modern fiction, from Gogol's *The Portrait* to Wilde's *Dorian Gray*.
12 Mitchell, 2005, 11.
13 Bredekamp, 2018, 8.
14 Bredekamp, 2018, 7.
15 Freedberg and Gallese, 2007.
16 Schmitz, 2011, 31; Griffero, 2017, 94.
17 Freedberg, 1989, 395–408.
18 Gumbrecht, 2012, 66–67.
19 Schmitz, Müllan and Slaby, 2011, 47.
20 Böhme, 1999, 92.
21 Brandt, 1999, 10.
22 Gumbrecht, 2004, 17.
23 Gumbrecht, 2004, 19, 28.
24 De Matteis, Bille, Griffero and Jelić, 2019.
25 Anderson, 2009, 78.
26 From a personal interview with Roberto Grillo, 21 July 2020. Parts of the exhibition and of the previous work in the series can be viewed on the photographer's website, https://www.robertogrillo.it/arte/album/rughe/ accessed 7 July 2020.
27 Further criticism was elicited by the selection of subjects, due to the presence of several local politicians and the Head of the Civil Protection Department at the time of the earthquake. In the weeks following the opening, two portraits of politicians were tampered with, and one eventually stolen. This was most probably an act of vandalism carried out on political rather than 'affective' grounds. During the entire duration of the installation, however, no one criticised on artistic grounds.
28 Freedberg, 1989, 42–43.
29 View the entire gallery at https://photos.app.goo.gl/bpbjAEbgcXmXWe636. Accessed 13 June 2022.
30 Bollnow, 2011, 186–187.
31 Heholt, 2016, 2.

Bibliography

Anderson, B. 'Affective atmospheres', *Emotion, Space and Society*, 2 (2009): 77–81. https://doi.org/10.1016/j.emospa.2009.08.005
Böhme, G. *Theorie des Bildes*. Munich: Wilhelm Fink, 1999.
Bollnow, O.F. *Human Space*. London: Hyphen Press, 2011.
Brandt, R. *Die Wirklichkeit des Bildes*. Munich: Hanser, 1999.
Bredekamp, H. *Image Acts*. Boston: De Gruyter, 2018.
De Matteis, F. 'On the natural history of reconstruction. The affective space of post-earthquake landscapes'. *Studi di Estetica*, 47(14) (2019): 65–87. https://doi.org/10.7413/18258646083
De Matteis, F., Bille, M., Griffero, T. and Jelić, A. 'Phenomenographies: describing the plurality of atmospheric worlds'. *Ambiances*, 5 (2019): 1–22. https://doi.org/10.4000/ambiances.2526
Freedberg, D. *The Power of Images*. Chicago: University of Chicago Press, 1989.
Freedberg, D. and Gallese, V. 'Motion, emotion and empathy in esthetic experience'. *Trends in Cognitive Sciences*, 11(5) (2007): 197–203. https://doi.org/10.1016/j.tics.2007.02.003
Gombrich, E.H. *The Image and the Eye*. Ithaca: Cornell University Press, 1982.
Griffero, T. *Quasi-things*. Albany: SUNY Press, 2017.
Gumbrecht, H.U. *Production of Presence*. Stanford: Stanford University Press, 2004.
Gumbrecht, H.U. *Atmosphere, Mood, Stimmung*. Stanford: Stanford University Press, 2012.
Heholt, R. 'Unstable landscapes: affect, representation and a multiplicity of hauntings'. In *Haunted Landscapes*, edited by Ruth Heholt and Niamh Downing, 1–20. London and New York: Rowman & Littlefield International, 2016.
McLuhan, M. *The Gutenberg Galaxy*. London: Routledge and Kegan Paul, 1962.
Mitchell, W.J.T. *Picture Theory*. Chicago: University of Chicago Press, 1994.
Mitchell, W.J.T. *What Do Pictures Want?* Chicago: University of Chicago Press, 2005.

Panofsky, E. *Meaning in the Visual Arts*. Garden City, Doubleday, 1955.
Schmitz, H. *Der Leib*. Berlin and Boston: De Gruyter, 2011.
Schmitz, H., Müllan, R.O. and Slaby, J. 'Emotions outside the box–the new phenomenology of feeling and corporeality'. *Phenomenology and the Cognitive Sciences*, 10(2) (2011): 241–259. https://doi.org/10.1007/s11097-011-9195-1
Steiner, G. (1971). *In Bluebeard's Castle*. New Haven: Yale University Press, 1971.
Varagnoli, C. 'L'Aquila, dieci anni di ricostruzione'. *Opus*, 3 (2019): 3–4.

15
Providing disaster information to inbound tourists
Case study for the historical city of Kyoto, Japan

Kohei Sakai and Hidehiko Kanegae

Tourism is one of the most promising industries in Japan, and with the number of foreign tourists increasing, how to protect them in a disaster is an important issue – not least to allow the industry to recover quickly afterwards. In this sense, the provision of disaster-prevention information is essential.

Introduction

There has been a steady increase in the number of tourists travelling to Japan in recent years. For example, in the city of Kyoto, the number of foreign visitors rose from approximately 520,000 in 2011, to over 4.5 million in 2018.[1] It is expected that increasing numbers of foreign tourists will come to Japan in the future, drawn by events such as the Tokyo Olympics and Expo 2025 in Osaka. However, there are reports that foreign tourists were confused and unsure of what was happening during the 2018 Osaka earthquake and the 2018 Hokkaido Eastern Iburi earthquake.[2] From now on, the number of foreign tourists impacted by natural disasters is expected to rise, so protecting these visitors from disasters is an important issue.

The importance of self-help in independent disaster-risk-reduction behaviours and mutual aid performed in tandem with local people has been identified in the discussion on disaster risk reduction for local residents. For this reason, one must first be aware of the risk. Various initiatives and studies have been carried out to develop people's ability to engage in self-help and mutual aid. However, there are limiting factors when it comes to improving tourists' capacity for self-help and their performance of independent disaster-risk-reduction behaviours – especially for inbound tourists. It is impractical for tourists to carry around the required three days' worth of water, or a helmet to protect the head during earthquakes, as local residents might be expected to. The disaster-risk-reduction measures that tourists are most likely to be able to take are checking disaster-risk-reduction information and preparing the means of acquiring that information when a disaster occurs. Establishing an environment that enables foreign tourists to acquire information for themselves has an added advantage in that resources for mutual aid, and assistance in sightseeing areas can be allocated for other, more urgent, cases.

In light of this background, this chapter seeks to ascertain the level of awareness with regard to disaster risk reduction and recognition of risks among foreign tourists, with the aim of proposing effective methods for providing disaster-risk-reduction information to foreign tourists.

Research on disaster risk reduction for foreign tourists

There is a well established body of research that avers that risk awareness is essential for promoting the capacity for self-help and independent disaster-risk-reduction behaviours among local residents. In the context of floods, research has shown the impact that recognising flooding risks and having a geographical risk awareness can have on decision-making during evacuations.[3] With regard to tsunamis, tsunami risk-recognition before and during disasters reduces the amount of time needed to start an evacuation, based on data from a survey of residents of Kesennuma City in Miyagi prefecture.[4] Research has also shown that, with regard to earthquakes, risk recognition is a highly significant factor in recognising the importance of independent disaster-risk-reduction behaviours.[5]

As noted above, there are many studies that focus on risk recognition during disasters – earthquakes, floods, tsunamis – by local residents, though it cannot be said that the research in this area has been adequate in regard to tourists. There have, however, been several studies of risk awareness and disaster-risk-reduction behaviours among tourists. One such study investigated how certain factors affect tourists' decision-making processes during evacuations from hurricanes. It found that tourists travelling in large groups and with children, as well as tourists who are travelling to the destination for the first time, are more likely to evacuate.[6] Another study found that knowledge of tsunami disaster-risk-reduction behaviours increases evacuation awareness, which is associated with an early start to evacuations.[7] Another study showed that, in making the decision to evacuate, it is more effective to increase apprehension about tsunamis than to increase knowledge of disaster risk reduction.[8] With the increase in inbound demand, studies that focus on inbound tourists are being conducted. Based on interviews and surveys of foreign tourists in the city of Kamakura in Japan, a study identified the issues around supporting provision. The study found that, while foreign tourists have relatively high risk-recognition and motivation to evacuate during tsunamis, there are misunderstandings about the direction of evacuation and the location of evacuation areas.[9] Based on a survey of foreign tourists and sightseeing facilities in the city of Kamakura, a further study noted the importance of providing evacuation guidance through individuals who are aware of disaster-risk-reduction activities, and of maintaining proper signage. It proposed the release of a smartphone app as a means of sharing information.[10]

As stated earlier, there are reports that some foreign tourists got lost because they were unaware of what was happening and what to do during the 2018 Osaka earthquake and the 2018 Hokkaido Eastern Iburi earthquake. Studies on how foreign tourists acquire disaster-risk-reduction information have only started in recent years. The novel aspects of this study can be summarised in the following two points: it focuses on inbound tourists, who have received little attention until now, and it proposes a means of information sharing based on a risk-recognition survey targeting foreigners in Japan.

Study method

The study area was the city of Kyoto in Kyoto prefecture. Kyoto was the capital city of Japan for 1,000 years after the movement of the capital in 794 by Emperor Kanmu, and before the capital was relocated to Tokyo. For this reason, Kyoto has a wealth of cultural heritage, including the Historic Monuments of Ancient Kyoto,[11] which are registered World Heritage sites. Today, it is Japan's foremost tourist site, with more than 50 million tourists visiting Kyoto in 2018.[12] However, it has been confirmed that there are several geological fault lines, including the Hanaori fault, in the vicinity of the city of Kyoto, and as such, an increased risk of an earthquake occurring,[13] making support for tourists during disasters a pressing issue for the city of Kyoto.

Survey overview

A survey of foreign tourists who visited a kimono rental shop in Shimogyo-ku, Kyoto was conducted with the cooperation of its owners. The survey was carried out between 28 December 2018 and 10 January 2019 and all the questions were in English. The survey included 151 people and there were 150 valid responses (Table 15.1). All the respondents were informed that their answers would only be used for the purpose of the study after their consent had been sought and received. The shop itself was selected because it is within a 3 km radius of sightseeing areas such as Kyoto station, which serves as a starting point for visitors to Kyoto; the Shijo-Kawaramachi area, which includes the Teramachi shopping district and the Shinkyogoku shopping district; as well as the World Heritage sites of Kiyomizudera Temple, Nijo Castle and the Kyoto Imperial Palace (Table 15.2).

Table 15.1   Summary of questionnaire survey of inbound tourists.

	Details
Scope	Foreign tourists visiting a kimono rental shop in Shimogyo-ku, Kyoto
Method	Self-administered questionnaire (English)
Period	28 December 2018 to 10 January 2019
Questionnaire content	• Natural disasters that may occur in the city of Kyoto • Probability of a major earthquake in the city of Kyoto in the next 30 years • Ratio of those who have seen Japanese evacuation pictogram while sightseeing in Japan • Impression of Japanese evacuation pictogram • Impression of going to the locations shown on the Japanese evacuation pictogram after a disaster • Information obtained regarding disasters in Japan when arriving and while staying in Japan • Sources of information about disasters in Japan (when arriving in Japan) • Sources of information about disasters in Japan (while staying in Japan) • Knowledge of websites and apps that provide information during disasters • Motivation to install apps that provide information during disasters • Sources of information that are important to follow during disasters
Valid response rate	99.3 per cent(150/151)

Table 15.2 Distance between survey area and sightseeing areas.

Destination near study area	Distance from study area (direct distance)	Foreign tourist destination ranking (Kyoto City Industry and Tourism Bureau, MICE Promotion Office, 2019b) Figures in parentheses show the ratio of foreign tourists who had visited the destination
Kiyomizudera Temple	Approx. 2.0 km	1st (66.6%)
Nijo Castle	Approx. 2.1 km	2nd (57.3%)
Fushimi Inari Shrine	Approx. 3.3 km	3rd (52.1%)
Gion	Approx. 1.3 km	7th (29.2%)
Kyoto station	Approx. 1.3 km	13th (14.8%)

Figures 15.1 to 15.4 compare a summary of the respondents to this survey with the factual investigation of foreign tourists conducted as part of the 2018 Kyoto City Tourism Comprehensive Survey. In the latter, survey participants were selected randomly and the survey was conducted using methods such as interviews at a total of six major tourist facilities in Kyoto (Table 15.3). With regard to the point of origin of the respondents in the present study, as depicted in Figure 15.1, there were many respondents from Southeast Asia and only a small number from Europe, while the majority of the respondents were women, as shown in Figure 15.3. Nonetheless, it was confirmed that the extraction of the sample had no bias toward a particular attribute.

Table 15.3 Summary of the factual investigation with regard to foreign tourists in the 2018 Kyoto City Tourism Comprehensive Survey.

Study period	Winter (February), spring (May), summer (August), autumn (November)
Study items	Accommodation, transportation used, number of days, gender, age, travel arrangements, areas visited in the city, tourism costs, satisfaction, etc.
Sample size	1,740 people

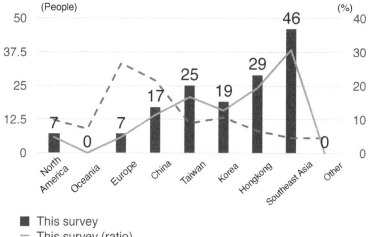

Figure 15.1 Point of origin of respondents.

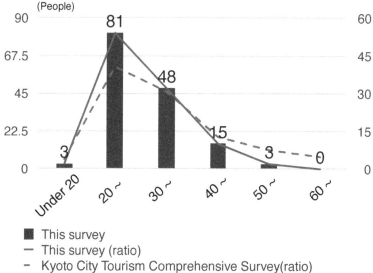

Figure 15.2 Age of respondents.

PROVIDING DISASTER INFORMATION TO INBOUND TOURISTS

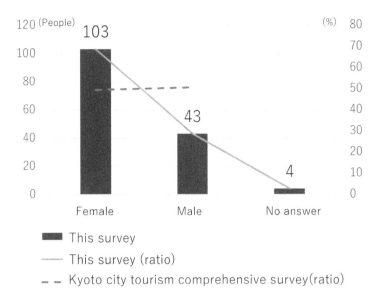

Figure 15.3 Gender of respondents.

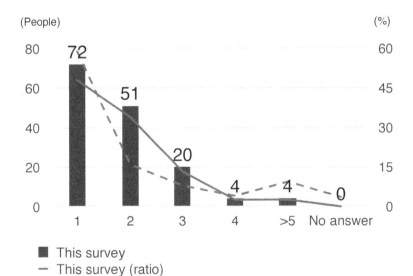

Figure 15.4 Number of times respondent has visited Japan.

Survey results

Awareness of disasters and evacuation procedures in Japan

Figure 15.5 shows the results of the questions about natural disasters that may occur in Kyoto. The most common answer was earthquakes (97) followed by storms/typhoons (72) and floods (27). These disasters are likely to occur in Kyoto. However, some of the respondents (15) picked tsunamis, which are unlikely to occur in Kyoto.

Figure 15.6 shows the replies to the possibility of a large-scale earthquake in the city of Kyoto in the next 30 years. Eighty-two per cent of the respondents said the possibility of a large-scale earthquake in the city of Kyoto in the next 30 years is likely (78), very likely (41) or virtually certain (5), indicating that foreign tourists think that Kyoto will suffer from a large-scale earthquake in the near future.

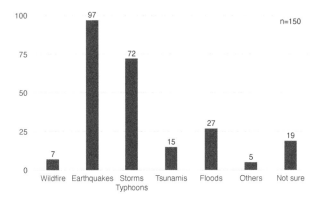

Figure 15.5 Natural disasters that the respondents think may occur in Kyoto.

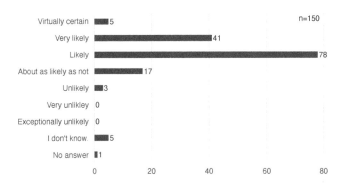

Figure 15.6 Likelihood of a large-scale earthquake occurring in Kyoto in the next 30 years.

Evacuations are required to ensure safety in situations other than earthquakes and tsunamis. Therefore, in this survey, respondents were asked about their impression of the pictogram (Figure 15.7) used to highlight major evacuation sites in Japan. Figure 15.8 shows the percentage of respondents that have seen the pictograms of evacuation sites while sightseeing in Japan. While 20 respondents said they have seen them, the remaining 130 said they had not. Figure 15.9 shows the results of asking for respondents' impressions of the corresponding pictogram: 128 (more than 85 per cent) said the pictograms did not convey an impression of safety, even though the pictogram showed safe locations, that is, evacuation sites. Figure 15.10 shows the results of asking whether it is correct to go to the evacuation sites shown on the pictograms during disasters (Figure 15.7). Most respondents (119) said that they think 'It is not correct'.

Figure 15.7 Pictogram used in Japan to indicate an evacuation site.

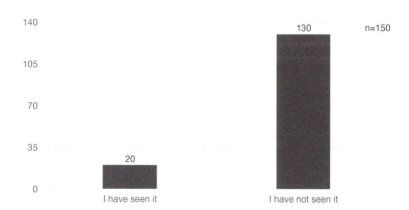

Figure 15.8 Ratio of those who had seen Figure 15.7 while sightseeing in Japan.

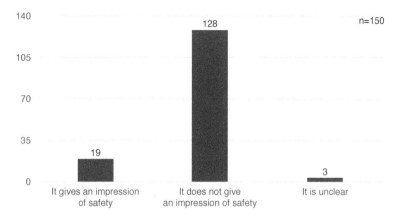

Figure 15.9 Impressions of Figure 15.7.

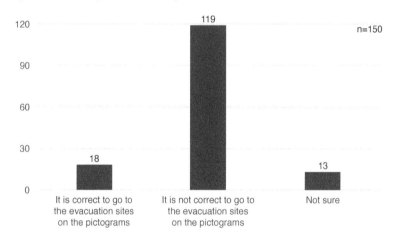

Figure 15.10 Impression about going to the location indicated by Figure 15.7 after a disaster occurs.

How to acquire information in advance

Figure 15.11 shows the results of asking whether respondents had obtained information about disasters in Japan prior to visiting, or while in Japan. While many respondents (117) had seen and heard information about disasters in Japan prior to visiting, a few (58) acquired such information while staying in Japan. Figure 15.12 shows the sources of information regarding disasters in Japan that participants acquired prior to coming to Japan, while Figure 15.13 shows the sources of such information when they arrived in Japan. The majority of the respondents acquired the information from television or the internet.

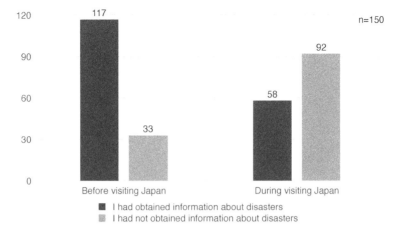

Figure 15.11 Obtaining information about disasters in Japan before coming to Japan/while in Japan.

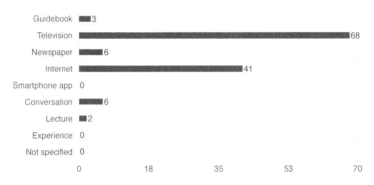

Figure 15.12 Sources of information about disasters in Japan (before arriving in Japan).

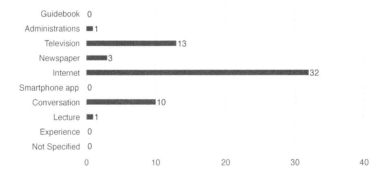

Figure 15.13 Sources of information about disasters in Japan (while in Japan).

Websites and smartphone apps are expected to play a role in the provision of information during disasters. Therefore, the respondents were asked if they have any knowledge of websites and apps for sharing information in an emergency. The results are shown in Figure 15.14. Figure 15.15 shows the result of asking the respondents if they would install an app that provides information during disasters. Most of the respondents (74.6 per cent) picked 'I would not install it' or 'I would never install it', which indicates that most respondents had no motivation to install such an app. However, the respondents think that broadcasts via public-address systems and signs are important sources of information that can be relied on if an earthquake occurs (Figure 15.16).

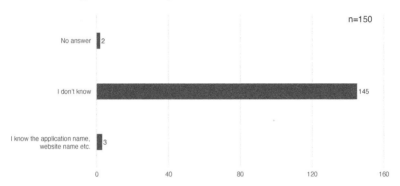

Figure 15.14 Knowledge of websites and apps that provide information during disasters.

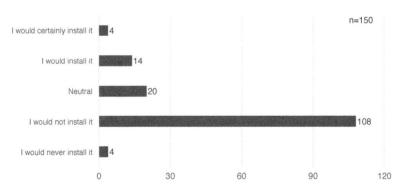

Figure 15.15 Intention to install apps that provide information during disasters.

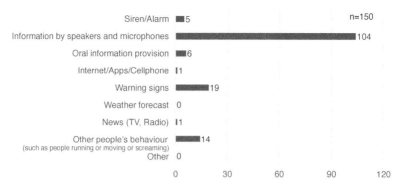

Figure 15.16 Important sources of information to be relied upon during disasters.

Tourists' risk recognition – lack of knowledge and misunderstandings

The survey results showed that the respondents have a relatively high awareness of the risk of natural disasters occurring in Kyoto. The top three disasters named by respondents – earthquakes, typhoons and floods – are natural disasters that are highly likely to occur in Kyoto. Kyoto City has produced earthquake-hazard maps that show the damage from earthquakes, flood-hazard maps that show the Kamo-gawa and Katsura-gawa rivers flooding and landslide disasters caused by heavy rain in typhoons and landslide-hazard maps that deal with landslide disasters. However, there were respondents who said tsunamis are a possible natural disaster, but this is not true for the city of Kyoto. This shows that, although local residents and Japanese tourists are aware that tsunamis cannot reach Kyoto because it is far from the sea and is surrounded by the Kyoto Basin, foreign tourists may not have information about the local terrain or area. This lack of knowledge/information among inbound tourists was also identified in a study by Arce.[9] One of the causes of this lack of knowledge and misunderstanding seems to be that different countries have different cultures when it comes to disasters. For example, different typology or a different frequency of disasters affects their citizens' perception and understanding of the risk. Most of the respondents thought it likely that a major earthquake would occur in the city of Kyoto in the next 30 years. This shows that despite lacking the requisite knowledge and information, foreign tourists do have a certain degree of risk recognition.

Yet do foreign tourists have the knowledge to protect themselves during earthquakes? Responses to the questions focusing on the pictogram showing evacuation sites indicate that most respondents did not see the pictogram while sightseeing. Searching for something during an emergency that has never been seen before presents many difficulties, so it is likely that foreign tourists would find it impossible to escape to an evacuation site. Another problem is that the meaning of this pictogram is likely being misunderstood. The impression of many foreign tourists regarding the pictogram showing evacuation sites was: 'It's not safe'. Many said, 'I do not think it is correct' to go to that location during a disaster. This misunderstanding means that evacuation is unlikely, even in the case of having seen the pictogram. Further, there is almost no likelihood that a foreign tourist would know the location of the nearest evacuation site relative to a tourist site that they are visiting for only a few hours. Based on these results, it is clear that tourists lack knowledge of, and misunderstand risk-recognition and disaster-risk-reduction behaviours.

Issues and proposals for sharing information with foreign tourists

For tourists who lack knowledge and have some misunderstandings, providing appropriate information prior to and during disasters can facilitate smooth support. That being so, what is the best way to provide information about topics such as evacuations to foreign tourists? During the 2018 Osaka earthquake and the 2018 Hokkaido Eastern Iburi earthquake, foreign tourists were found to lack important information. Although this may be due to language and culture barriers, there are disaster-risk-reduction apps for foreigners in Japan. However, the study results show that only a small number of foreign tourists know about such apps and websites, and it was clear that there is little motivation to install the apps. These issues are similar in structure to those of the use and distribution of hazard maps. Enomura lists two issues in the distribution of hazard maps: public awareness and accessibility of the maps.[15] The challenge with public awareness refers to the idea that local residents are not aware of the existence of hazard maps, or have never seen them. The challenge of accessibility refers to issues such as not having or not knowing where the hazard map is, for a range of reasons – for example the size being unsuitable for display on a wall or a refrigerator, despite having seen the map before. With regard to disaster-risk-reduction apps, the survey results show a public-awareness challenge, which is that foreign tourists do not know of the existence of such apps. In a study by

Nagai, reference is made to the lack of awareness and the challenge of widely distributing 'Safety Tips',[16] an app for sharing disaster information with foreign tourists, which is supervised by the Japan Tourism Agency. So how can these issues be solved? The challenge of accessibility in relation to hazard maps can be mitigated if they are displayed in everyday locations such as toilets and refrigerators. Apps such as Safety Tips have the potential to make a real difference in a disaster scenario. However the information they provide is needed immediately after a disaster occurs, and because of the time needed to install and establish settings, this will not happen unless the app has already been downloaded. Yet, it seems unlikely that tourists will download the apps in anticipation of a disaster. This shows that multilingual apps on disaster risk reduction in Japan have the same issues in regard to accessibility as many hazard maps.

What kind of app is needed to solve this challenge? Two proposals are made below. First, rather than an app that is used only during disasters, there is a need for an app that is used in daily life. For example, in Kyoto prefecture, KYOTO Trip+, in addition to sharing information for disaster risk-reduction, is a multilingual app with the objective of providing sightseeing information for all of Kyoto prefecture during daily life.[17] Also, the difficulty of installing and establishing settings is reduced with disaster-risk-reduction apps that are connected to existing apps in wide use, and this will also likely promote widespread use. The second proposal is to establish an environment where disaster-risk-reduction information can be accessed during disasters. For example, by posting QR codes containing URL information of websites that publish disaster-risk-reduction information in highly visible places, foreign tourists will be able to access this information during disasters simply by scanning the QR code with a smartphone (Figure 15.17).

Figure 15.17 Post box displaying a QR code for information access. Source: author.

Morever, respondents' low motivation to install an app may be connected to the emphasis they placed on direct communication via public-address systems. For this reason, initial disaster-response manuals that feature model phrases for the purpose of evacuating foreign tourists to calm and safe areas are being produced,[18, 19] and evacuation training is taking place for those who struggle to return home – including foreign tourists – using speakers and placards with multilingual translation devices.[20, 21] In this way, the importance of direct communication is addressed.

Conclusion

This study employed a questionnaire conducted among foreign tourists visiting the city of Kyoto to identify issues they face and make proposals based on respondents' disaster-risk awareness, knowledge of evacuation measures, and access to information. The findings indicated that foreign tourists have a high risk-awareness of disasters, but lack knowledge of and misunderstand evacuation measures. Despite the expectation that apps and smartphones can be a means of providing information, respondents had almost no knowledge of how to access them, and had little motivation to install apps that could provide information during disasters. Therefore, solutions were proposed to provide apps that are useful in daily life and to prepare an environment to facilitate access to disaster-risk-reduction information during disasters.

This study shows the continued importance of sharing information by direct communication and the need to clarify discrepancies between the preparations made by those who provide support or information to foreign tourists and the issues faced by foreign tourists themselves.

Notes

1 Kyoto City Industry and Tourism Bureau, Tourism and MICE Promotion Office, 'Kyoto Tourism Comprehensive Survey 2018'.
2 Mainichi Shimbun. 'Editorial: Dealing with Foreign Tourists in Japan During Disasters – A Major Issue for Japan as a Tourist Destination'.
3 Isagawa and Ohno. 'Influence of Residents' Cognition of their Local Environment on Evacuation Behavior from Tsunami', 2412.
4 Sato et al., 'Did Disaster Tradition Activities Promote Tsunami Evacuation Behavioir?: Case Study Using Questionaire Survey in Rikuzentakada City, Iwate Prefecture', 73.
5 Hashiue et al., 'The Analysis of People's Importance Believes about Administrative and Self-Help Measures for Disaster Prevention', 343.
6 Cahyanto et al., 'An Empirical Evaluation of the Determinants of Tourist's Hurricane Evacuation Decision Making', 256.
7 Masumoto et al., 'Decision-making and Evacuation of Beachgoer against Tsunami Disaster'.

8   Sugimoto et al., 'The Tohoku-Pacific Ocean Earthquake Make Change for Beachgoer's Evacuation Decision', 1320.
9   Arce et al., 'Risk Awareness And Intended Tsunami Evacuation Behaviour Of International Tourists In Kamakura City, Japan , 191.
10 Nagai et al., 'Study on Refuge Instruction to the Foreign Tourists such as the Tourist Facilities at the Time of the Tsunami Disaster', 198.
11 Kyoto Prefecture. 'World Cultural Heritage: Historic Monuments of Ancient Kyoto (Kyoto, Uji and Otsu Cities)'.
12 Kyoto City Industry and Tourism Bureau, Tourism and MICE Promotion Office. 'Kyoto Tourism Comprehensive Survey 2018 (Summary Version)'.
13 Kyoto City Disaster Prevention and Crisis Management Office. 'If A Big Earthquake Occurs, How Much Damage Will It Cause To Kyoto City ?'.
14 Ministry of Land, Infrastructure, Transport and Tourism. 'Safety(PDF): Barrier-free: Guidance symbol (JIS Z8210)'.
15 Enomura. 'Study on Measures to Enhance Residents' Recognition and Understanding of Flood Hazard Map', I_105.
16 RC Solution Co. 'Safety tips (Japanese)'.
17 Kyoto Prefecture Department of Policy Planning, Information Policy Division. 'About "KYOTO Trip +", An App That Provides Information On Tourism Disaster Prevention In Kyoto In Multiple Languages'.
18 Kyoto City Fire and Disaster Management Bureau General Affairs Department. 'Initial Response Manual In The Event of a Disaster'.
19 Tokyo Metropolitan Government Bureau of Industry and Labor. 'Revised the disaster manual to ensure the safety of foreign travelers'.
20 Asahi Shimbun Digital. 'If an Earthquake Occurs While Sightseeing in Kyoto… 5000 people participate in disaster risk reduction training'.
21 Kobe Shimbun NEXT. 'Practice to Guide Inbound Tourists During Evacuations From Disasters, Use of Translation Devices and Smartphones; Kobe City'.

Bibliography

Arce, R.S.C. Onuki, M., Esteban, M., and Shibayama, T. 'Risk awareness and intended tsunami evacuation behaviour of international tourists in Kamakura City, Japan'. *International Journal of Disaster Risk Reduction*, 23 (2017): 178–192. Accessed 15 September 2020. https://doi.org/10.1016/J.IJDRR.2017.04.005

Asahi Shimbun Digital. 'If an Earthquake Occurs While Sightseeing in Kyoto… 5000 people participate in disaster risk reduction training'. https://www.asahi.com/articles/ASG8Y5H54G8YPLZB015.html

Cahyanto, I., Pennington-Gray, L., Thapa, B., Srinivasan, S., Villegas, J., Matyas, C., and Kiousis, S. 'An empirical evaluation of the determinants of tourist's hurricane evacuation decision making'. *Journal of Destination Marketing & Management*, 2(4) (2014): 253–265. Accessed 15 September 2020. https://doi.org/10.1016/J.JDMM.2013.10.003

Enomura, Y. 'Study on measures to enhance residents' recognition and understanding of flood hazard map'. *Journal of Japan Society of Civil Engineers, Ser. D3* (*Infrastructure Planning and Management*), 68(5) (2012): I_103–I_110. Accessed 15 September 2020. https://doi.org/10.2208/jscejipm.68.I_103

Hashiue, K., Kikuchi, A., Fujii, S., and Kitamura, R. 'The analysis of people's importance believes about administrative and self-help measures for disaster prevention'. *Infrastructure Planning Review*, 20 (2003): 337–344. Accessed 15 September 2020. https://doi.org/10.2208/journalip.20.337

Isagawa, T., and Ohno, R. 'Influence of residents' cognition of their local environment on evacuation behavior from tsunami'. *Journal of Architecture and Planning* (*Transactions of AIJ*), 79(705) (2014): 2405–2413. Accessed 15 September 2020. https://doi.org/10.3130/aija.79.2405

Kobe Shimbun NEXT. 'Practice To Guide Inbound Tourists During Evacuations From Disasters, Use Of Translation Devices and Smartphones; Kobe City'. Accessed 15 September 2020. https://www.kobe-np.co.jp/news/sougou/201907/0012545530.shtml

Kyoto City Disaster Prevention and Crisis Management Office. 'If A Big Earthquake Occurs, How Much Damage Will It Cause To Kyoto City ?', Kyoto City Official Website, May 2013. Accessed 18 July 2020. https://www.city.kyoto.lg.jp/gyozai/page/0000015489.html

Kyoto City Fire and Disaster Management Bureau General Affairs Department. 'Initial Response Manual In The Event of a Disaster', Kyoto City Official Website, n.d. Accessed 10 August 2019 https://www.city.kyoto.lg.jp/shobo/page/0000179727.html

Kyoto City Industry and Tourism Bureau, Tourism and MICE Promotion Office. 'Kyoto Tourism Comprehensive Survey 2018 (Summary Version)'. Kyoto City Official Website, 3 July 2019. Accessed 15 September 2020. https://www.city.kyoto.lg.jp/sankan/cmsfiles/contents/0000254/254268/gaiyo.pdf

Kyoto City Industry and Tourism Bureau, Tourism and MICE Promotion Office. 'Kyoto Tourism Comprehensive Survey 2018'. Kyoto City Official Website, 3 July 2019. Accessed 15 September 2020. https://www.city.kyoto.lg.jp/sankan/cmsfiles/contents/0000254/254268/30tyosa.pdf

Kyoto Prefecture. 'World Cultural Heritage: Historic Monuments of Ancient Kyoto (Kyoto, Uji and Otsu Cities)'. Accessed 18 July 2020. http://www.pref.kyoto.jp/isan/

Kyoto Prefecture Department of Policy Planning, Information Policy Division. 'About "KYOTO Trip +", An App That Provides Information On Tourism Disaster Prevention In Kyoto In Multiple Languages'. Accessed 18 July 2020. https://www.pref.kyoto.jp/gyomusuishin/kyototripplus.html

Mainich Shimbun. 'Editorial: Dealing with Foreign Tourists in Japan During Disasters – A Major Issue for Japan as a Tourist Destination'. Accessed 15 September 2020. https://mainichi.jp/articles/20181007/ddm/005/070/146000c

Masumoto, K., Kawanaka, R., Ishigaki, T., and Shimada, H. 'Decision-making and evacuation of beachgoer against tsunami disaster'. *Journal of Japan Society of Civil Engineers, Ser. B2 (Coastal Engineering)*, 66(1) (2010): 1316–1320. Accessed 15 September 2020. https://doi.org/10.2208/kaigan.66.1316

Ministry of Land, Infrastructure, Transport and Tourism. 'Safety(PDF): Barrier-free: Guidance symbol (JIS Z8210)', 20 July 2019. Accessed 10 August 10 2019. https://www.mlit.go.jp/common/001245708.pdf

Nagai, Y., Yamamoto, K., Miyazaki, W., Suzuki, K., Tomoeda, M., and Akutsu, K. 'Study on refuge instruction to the foreign tourists such as the tourist facilities at the time of the tsunami disaster'. *Papers on Environmental Information Science*, ceis33 (2019): 193–198. Accessed 10 August 10 2019. https://doi.org/10.11492/ceispapers.ceis33.0_193

RC Solution Co. 'Safety tips (Japanese)'. Accessed 18 July 2020. https://www.rcsc.co.jp/safety

Sato, S., Hirakawa, Y., Shinka, A., and Imamura, F. 'Did disaster tradition activities promote tsunami evacuation behaviour ? : Case study using questionaire survey in Rikuzentakada City, Iwate Prefecture'. *Journal of Social Safety Science*, 32 (2018): 69–76. Accessed 20 May 2021. https://doi.org/10.11314/jisss.31.69

Sugimoto, A., Ishigaki, T., Muto, Y., Baba, Y., and Shimada, H. 'The Tohoku-Pacific Ocean Earthquake make change for beachgoer's evacuation decision'. *Journal of Japan Society of Civil Engineers, Ser. B3 (Ocean Engineering)*, 68(2) (2012): I_132–I_137. Accessed 18 July 2020. https://doi.org/10.2208/jscejoe.68.I_132

Tokyo Metropolitan Government Bureau of Industry and Labor. 'Revised the disaster manual to ensure the safety of foreign travelers', 30 March 2018. Accessed 10 August 2019. http://www.metro.tokyo.jp/tosei/hodohappyo/press/2018/03/30/21.html

16

Landscape as a post-earthquake driver of resilience
The intangible multiple values of territory

Paola Branduini and Fabio Carnelli

Although after an earthquake territory appears less damaged than the built environment, the focus on reconstructing buildings fails to address the essential role of the broader landscape. Following the 2016 and 2017 earthquakes in Central Italy, taking the small Umbrian town of Norcia as a case study, this chapter looks at institutional and personal perceptions of the material and immaterial, and at the close links between urban and rural heritage. Interviews with local people and associations reveal the vast intangible repertoire of heritage, comprising local food production practices, local knowledge, traditions, religious practices and a way of life connected to the surrounding territory.

Introduction

According to UNESCO, intangible heritage includes traditions or living expressions that are inherited, created, manipulated and passed through generations – oral traditions, performing arts, social practices, rituals, festive events, knowledge and practices relating to nature and the universe, as well as knowledge and skills for traditional crafts.[1] Among these, the agricultural intangible heritage includes techniques and skills that enable the creation of landscapes, the construction of houses and furniture, and the production of local products; it also includes local dialects, music and oral literature that have emerged from non-written traditions.[2] The landscape itself is not the sum of tangible and intangible elements, but a system of relationships evolved over time[3] and 'constantly recreated by communities and groups in response to their environment, their interaction with nature and their history'.[4]

In academic literature, the consequences of earthquakes on the cultural heritage are usually analysed 'in terms of physical destruction of … select monuments'[5] both on the recovery side and on the disaster-risk-reduction side.[6] Yet, rural heritage can contribute to enhancing resilience in facing disastrous or potentially disastrous events,[7] where resilience is understood as the capacity to tackle disturbances without altering the main characteristics of social-ecological systems.[8] This was the main aim of our research as part of a bigger project, called Reach Culture H2020. The pilot of the project's Italian case studies was led by the Italian Ministry of Economic Development, in collaboration with the Department of Architecture, Built Environment and Construction Engineering of the Polytechnic University of Milan. One of the communities featured in that study and analysed in this chapter was in the Norcia area in Central Italy, hit by five earthquakes between 2016 and 2017.[9]

When faced with a loss of tangible heritage due to traumatic events such as an earthquake, the presence of intangible heritage can foster cohesion and strengthen the sense of identity. Moreover, landscape and rural heritage can be key factors in recreating local identity during the recovery phase of a disaster, since 'the emotional sphere has an even greater value and people's expressed desires to return to everyday life can indicate which environments individuals feel the strongest relationship with'.[10] Therefore, in 2019 we chose to undertake our focused field research mainly in Norcia, a small town of five thousand inhabitants, containing the most important cultural heritage affected by the earthquakes, where all the churches had collapsed, and in Castelluccio, Norcia's biggest mountainous hamlet, located on one of the broadest and highest (1,452 m) plateaus in Central Italy which was almost entirely destroyed after the 6.5 Mw shock of 30 October 2016. Norcia and Castellucio are both located in the rural area of the Sibillini National Park, where agro-sylvan pastoral activities have turned the mountainous environment into a living body where 'every ridge, stream, spring, pasture or glade had its own name, representing stories and experiences, destinations or senses of belonging'.[11]

Objectives and methodology

Our aim was to understand how the intangible aspects of the rural landscape, which can be framed as cultural heritage, can help the social reconstruction of a town, even where the tangible – religious and historical – elements of its heritage have completely collapsed and houses are severely damaged. We adopted a qualitative method:[12] first we collected initiatives promoted by institutions, stakeholders and the public through a document analysis (using policy documents, reports, local newspapers, websites and social media); then we undertook 14 semi-structured classic and walking interviews with institutional actors, stakeholders and local people[13] (Figure 16.1). Geographers and sociologists[14] have shown the power of 'walking interviews' in highlighting how relationships between human actors and the surrounding environment can emerge strongly. This helped us with the interpretation of the perception of tangible and intangible, urban and rural heritage by the local population and institutions.

We transcribed the interviews[15] and carried out a thematic analysis of all our collected data. The results were organised under three topics:

1) what the different actors consider to be heritage
2) how they perceive their landscape
3) their view on the impact of earthquakes on their heritage and rural landscape.

Finally, we discuss below how the rural landscape can enhance resilience.

Figure 16.1 Our actors' map of the study area.

Urban and rural heritage: the 'official' representation

Urban heritage

According to the official representation of the Norcia Proloco Association, rural and urban heritage can be conceived of as strictly interlinked, due to a vast intangible heritage whose origin is commonly acknowledged as being in ancient times. Cultural heritage is usually closely linked to the urban history of Norcia, especially through local knowledge, folklore and local products:

> On one side, there is the Basilica of San Benedetto, there are numerous churches, the Castellina [local civic and church museum], the Palazzo Comunale. On the other side there is a rural, peasant culture, deep and alive, nourished by ancient wisdom and closely linked to nature and its cycles. Two souls that merge and complete each other, creating a town with a multifaceted and seductive personality, where everything is 'knowledge': nature and good food, art and work.[16]

The town centre with its historical buildings and churches is officially identified as urban heritage; its origins are closely connected with the personal history of San Benedetto da Norcia, Europe's patron saint and founder of the Benedictine order.

Rural heritage

Norcia's rural heritage is known for its food and wine products, which fuel tourism and include its famous ham, sausages, black truffle and Castelluccio lentils. The link between Norcia and pork processing is so ancient that it gave the name to a profession, the *norcino* (traditional local butcher), clearly and historically derived from Norcia's inhabitants. Castelluccio lentils, renowned for their small size and strong taste, are grown in Pian Grande on the slopes of Mount Vettore (Figure 16.2). The colourful spectacle of their flowering in June attracts hundreds of tourists from all over Italy and abroad. There are different kinds of cheese, especially ricotta, fresh or salted, and caciotta, as well as different types of legumes and cereals, from chickpeas to spelt and *cicerchia* (chickling peas).

The beauty and charm of the local landscape are the dominant features communicated by tourist websites and the Proloco Association:

... the blue of the summer sky, the green of the gentle hills, the multi-coloured spectacle of the cultivated and flowered fields. In Norcia, nature is the real protagonist, seductive and delicate. Around our village unfurls a sweet relaxing landscape, which conquers at first sight ... Dominating everything, powerful and uncontested, there is Monte Vettore, with its strong and massive appearance, at the foot of which lies the spectacular plateau of Castelluccio, with its lentil fields and its lunar profile. [17]

Downstream, the Santa Scolastica plain is the area devoted to the *marcita* (Figure 16.3) – a historical agriculture technique developed by Benedictine monks – which is now in ruins. It is described as 'an area of great naturalistic interest, because it is characterised by the abundant presence of groundwater, which makes it extremely fertile'.[18] It is crossed by the Torbidone stream that reappeared after the 2016 earthquake, after almost 40 years of absence.

Figure 16.2   The Castelluccio plain.

Figure 16.3 The landscape of *marcita* meadows surrounding Norcia.

Main folklore initiatives

In Norcia and Castelluccio there are a number of different initiatives linked to preserving and promoting rural heritage. In Norcia, *Nero Norcia* (the festival of black truffle) and the Benedictine religious celebrations; the August feasts in Castelluccio and the summer feasts in Norcia; the flowering of legumes and lentils and their threshing on the Castelluccio plain, as well as the *faoni* (bonfires made of broom branches stacked around a pole and arranged in the squares around the town), also Santa Lucia and the nativity scene in every neighbourhood; *l'Addolorata* feast (*questua* and fireworks); *il feston in Campi* (a questua with conviviality); the Holy Friday procession; the St Antonio feast with bonfires and benedictions; the *Epifania*, (a rural questua) and finally the *Pasquarelle* both in Norcia and Castelluccio, another rural *questua* with traditional songs sung while walking from household to household.

Community perception of urban and rural heritage

The close mutual link between urban and rural heritage emerged strongly among most interviewees, who consider both the landscape with its surrounding mountains and the historical buildings in the city centre as cultural heritage. Almost all of what was acknowledged locally as heritage collapsed after the earthquake, including many churches. The sudden loss of physical religious heritage made local inhabitants reflect on the origins of their sense of belonging.[19] Their attachment to the place created by the historical buildings was palplable, as emphasised by one of the farmers interviewed:

> cultural heritage is everything that concerns the [collapsed] village ... all the houses inside the village, every house has its own history, they were all made in different periods, including the reconstructions that were carried out.[20]

Here cultural heritage turns into collective history, which can be experienced in individual habits and ways of life. Half of the interviewees acknowledge the presence of a vast intangible heritage repertoire made up of local food production practices, knowledge and traditions, religious practices and a lifestyle closely linked with being a small town: 'the heritage is the environment, the food and wine, especially the pork butchery'.[21] Indeed, according to the farmers and local associations, cultural heritage is the productive agricultural landscape, 'the product of the alternation between the cultivation of legumes and sheep and cattle pasture',[22] which also produces remarkable visual effects, in particular, the flowering on the Castelluccio plain. Rural heritage also comprises the repertoire of local traditions explained above: food processing, legends and folklore practices, all acting as an expression of this vast heritage

The rural landscape and marcita meadows

Although generally presented as part of the cultural heritage, for some institutions (such as Norcia's local government and Proloco) the rural landscape is considered to be the frame surrounding the historical city: 'the landscape is the cake and Norcia is its icing', according to an aesthetic outlook:

We had a city that is practically similar to a wedding favour, before the earthquake [of] 2016, but the beautiful thing was also all these green areas that we have around us.[23]

But it is the productive landscape characterised by lentils that makes the territory aesthetically valuable and recognisable: 'The lentil has always been here also since ancient times, there is a particular one, it is all coloured, the soil makes it so, thanks to our climate, too'.[24] Together with the lentils' flowering, black truffle and pork processing are often presented as symbols of Norcia. A progressive, slow and evolutionary change of the landscape has also been acknowledged:

… the landscape is not a fixed element that we put there and so we look at it and so it remains over time; it evolves over time, it is very dynamic, so it depends on the presence of man-made agricultural activities.[25]

The same agriculture that is fundamental in shaping the landscape responds to market logic: the landscape was strongly characterised by vineyards until the 1960s, but now the vines are hardly present. In the past decade there have been various initiatives to rediscover a more traditional kind of agriculture, but many were interrupted by the seismic event and had to reorganise and find new energy. *Marcita* are generally known by the population: 'everyone in Norcia knows more or less what they are … every elder knows them. Keep in mind that there were seven mills, they produced flour, cereals, rye, corn, all local varieties'[26]. The area was frequented by locals and reported in travel guides; it was considered an 'extraordinary place but left abandoned'. They are part of the local landscape's memory, because 'they are a link with what we had before, which in thirty/forty years has disappeared'.[27] Numerous interventions have been carried out over the years on the *marcita* meadows, including restoration of mills, canals and ditches, but they were only temporary, linked to singular project funding, without lasting maintenance and a long-term vision and for that reason all the restored mills, except one, collapsed after the earthquakes.

The earthquakes and their impact on rural landscape

The impact of the earthquakes on the rural landscape is fourfold, according to different actors. At first some, including local institutions, didn't mention any direct impact from the earthquakes on the rural landscape, since what collapsed were the main historical buildings rather than residential ones. The Consortium of Agricultural Commons reported how 'almost nothing has happened to us'.[28] Yet others stressed how severe the impact of earthquake management had been on the rural landscape:

> [The impact] was noteworthy for the installation of prefabricated modules[29] on unbuilt areas: 50 hectares of land consumption. The problem is the impact on the landscape, starting from Norcia, towards Preci; already from there – especially at night – you see large illuminated areas of SAE [recovery housing modules], very invasive interventions of medium-term duration, if not longer. [30]

Among local associations there is no common idea of the earthquake's impact on rural landscape, because this is not intuitively associated with possible damage caused by the earthquakes. A typical view was: 'the rural landscape is there, it didn't suffer'.[31] However, although not directly affected immediately, the landscape has since been devastated by contested urban planning choices and emergency and recovery initiatives: 'They are not considering the landscape at all, because they made a mess in placing all these houses and all the restaurants in a modern structure close to the historical walls of Norcia'.[32] Planning choices designed to help local businesses recover are criticised for their impact on the landscape. This is another point of view largely shared in Castelluccio:

> Castelluccio was not reachable for almost two years, roads were closed, but open only for buses that came for the flowering; therefore a different use of the same [landscape], has repercussion on the activities of farmers and the economy of farmers themselves; flowering has been saved but/yet encouraged for tourism.[33]

Farmers and farmers' associations have complained a great deal about negligence at all levels during the emergency, recovery and reconstruction phases, reporting what a devastating impact the earthquake had on their activities. According to some of our interviewees[34] it was severe for various reasons: inaction or excessive bureaucracy in recovery and reconstruction, bad choices in terms of land use and excessive touristification of local food production. Local associations, farmers and research group Emidio di Treviri also highlighted that the earthquake and its management have accelerated already ongoing processes, such as depopulation and the loss of public spaces to promote the local collective intangible heritage. In Castelluccio, this issue is very problematic, as only two inhabitants still live there today, while many activities were happening before the earthquake:

> [Do you think are they considering the landscape?] Not much! Because last year in Castelluccio they made some temporary structures, but before the earthquake there were 53 activities, let's say ... back then the people who came up here to go trekking, walking, in summer, winter, let's say all year round, also had a place to sleep ...[35]

The impression is now that local inhabitants are leaving Norcia, while Castelluccio is already almost abandoned:

> ... the young are leaving ... people don't notice the others are leaving. We know that next year will be like 2019 (that is, without jobs); now it's a drifting community, it attracts no one any more.[36]

Discussion

The interviews highlighted a conflict between rural heritage and local economy: as Scazzosi and the ICOMOS-IFLA principles state,[37] heritage is clearly recognised as a system of tangible elements (agricultural landscape with urban and rural buildings) linked by intangible relationships (farmers' knowledge and community's traditions)[38] – but the landscape's qualities are threatened by exploitation of this natural wealth for profit. The research group Emidio di Treviri made this point clearly, also mentioning the construction of a new commercial building, the Deltaplano – a big new dining venue opened in 2018 and located between the plain and the collapsed village:

> I have [really seen] the conflict between nature, value and work: the landscape, from the aesthetic point of view, is very much linked to the territory, to Mount Vettore, to the Castelluccio plain; but when it comes to protecting it, the rural landscape is suddenly subject to the logic of economic exploitation. Therefore, not to abandon the plain, we accept what they proposed us ... the construction of the Deltaplano.[39]

On one side, this is normal in an inland area in the Apennines, but here there is a clear conflict between touristification of the heritage and local needs, partly due to the acceleration of processes triggered by the earthquakes. The rural landscape can be a vehicle for promoting the territory as long as it is 'usable by the people who actually live there'.[40] The risk of this commodification is the loss of perceived authenticity, which can be avoided if cultural commercialisation is managed by the local population.[41] Many points of view converge, especially from the commercial world, in the agri-food industry as it was before the earthquake: 'the rural landscape is an opportunity [to attract tourists] if seen together with the agri-food industry and psychophysical well-being'.[42] The *marcita* meadows are mentioned as an opportunity for wellness tourism by local associations, with one commenting that now that the Torbidone is a river, it would be 'beautiful as a water route'.[43]

When the tangible religious heritage collapsed after the earthquakes, the huge repertoire of intangible heritage made up of local agricultural food processing techniques, folklore traditions and religious feasts helped to ease the sense of discouragement caused by the collapsed buildings. This intangible heritage could be the glue of a post-seismic community,[44] whose 'being together' is highly threatened by recovery and reconstruction management. Indeed, in the absence of people living there, the risk is the consequent loss of such heritage, as the IGP Lentil Farmers Association clearly stated:

> … if we don't cultivate, in a short time everything ends. As long as there are few farmers who still manage to go on, it will go on; then afterwards, once we are no longer able, everything will end here.[45]

The earthquakes clearly had a direct and indirect influence on the landscape. There was a direct consequence, as in the *marcita* meadows with the re-emergence of the Torbidone and the collapse of the mills. If on one hand, this was seen as an interruption of the ongoing enhancement activities, on the other, it was considered a fatal blow that invites reflection on the reappropriation by nature of its spaces.[46] The man-made impact was evident on the landscape, in the choice of location for the emergency housing units which, due to the current lack of an effective reconstruction plan and negligence in evaluating the negative effects on the landscape, are becoming long-term new accommodation.[47] These semi-temporary units have been much criticised by farmers, because they have permanently damaged the scenic quality of Norcia's visual basin and its productive farmland, the two factors that most contributed to its tourist appeal. It follows that the reconstruction management has threatened both the quality of the rural landscape and its survival, because a community is required to take care of it and keep tradition and knowledge transmission alive, as it 'is constantly recreated by people'.[48] Therefore the reconstruction management should take into account both tangible and intangible values of landscape as opportunities to drive resilience.

Conclusions

The main threats acknowledged by the different actors interviewed were: the loss of urban heritage, depopulation, the ongoing abandonment of Norcia and Castelluccio di Norcia, the need for socialisation, negligence in recovery and reconstruction management, and the removal of business activities. The rural landscape is acknowledged by local inhabitants as a multifaceted resource of identity. They feel it to be damaged more by the aftermath than by the earthquakes themselves. The recovery and reconstruction policies implemented by local, regional and national authorities further influenced the depopulation. In these, the rural landscape was directly threatened by the location of temporary housing under emergency law, and by new commercial buildings and shopping centres.

The touristification of the local landscape is nowadays the greatest threat to both tangible and intangible heritage, as tourism is evicting local communities and violating their rural landscapes. The landscape could have been acknowledged as a vector of resilience, especially in the first phase of recovery; it is usually less affected in terms of damage and can function with its intangible elements as an element of continuity and reassurance. Taking a more visionary approach, a rethinking of the economic model could trigger new circular models of sustainable economy based on the richness of this specific landscape, but this can only happen if combined with local knowledge and traditional practices. In this way, rural heritage can have a strong role in shaping the community's sense of belonging and aiding its recovery.

Notes

1 UNESCO, 'Convention for the Safeguarding of the intangible Cultural Heritage', 2003.
2 Conference of the European Ministry of Territory (CEMAT), 'European rural heritage observation guide', 2003.

3 Scazzosi, 'Lombardy', 2013; Scazzosi, 'Landscapes as systems of tangible and intangible relationships. Small theoretical and methodological introduction to read and evaluate Rural Landscape as Heritage', 2018.

4 UNESCO, 'Convention for the Safeguarding of the intangible Cultural Heritage', art. 1.

5 Jigyasu, 'From Natural to Cultural Disaster: Consequences of the Post-earthquake Rehabilitation Process on the Cultural Heritage in Marathwada Region, India' 237, 2001.

6 O'Brien, Geoff., O'Keefe, Phil, Jayawickrama, Janaka and Jigyasu, Rohit, 'Developing a model for building resilience to climate risks for cultural heritage', 2015.

7 Branduini and Carnelli, 'The preservation of rural landscapes for building resilience in the context of small towns: insights from North Italy', 2021.

8 Plieninger and Bieling, Resilience and the Cultural Landscape Understanding and Managing Change in Human-Shaped Environments, 2012; Berkes et al. 'Rediscovery of traditional ecological knowledge as adaptive management', 2000.

9 This area was hit by five major shocks (6 Mw, 5.4 Mw, 5.9 Mw, 6.5 Mw, 5.5 Mw), which from the 14 August 2016 to the 18 January 2017 struck the central Apennines area including four regions: Marche, Umbria, Lazio and Abruzzo.

10 Marincioni, Casareale and Byrne, 'Beautiful and Safe Landscapes for Sustainable Disaster Risk Reduction', 111.

11 Strampelli and Carnelli, 'Ricostruire i sensi del luogo per comprenderne le trame dell'abbandono. Un'etnografia del paesaggio a Montegallo, nei Monti Sibillini colpiti dai terremoti del 2016–2017', 2021.

12 Creswell and Poth, Qualitative inquiry and research design: Choosing among five approaches, 2018.

13 Among local institutional actors, interviewed are: the head of the technical department of Norcia local government; the chair of the Norcia Proloco, the official agency for cultural, heritage and tourism promotion in Norcia; the head of Comunanza Agraria di Norcia (Consortium of Agricultural Commons of Norcia), a collective rural land management; the Valnerina and Umbrian Apennines Ethnographic Research Centre, a rich archive of local cultural and ethnographic heritage founded in 1990. At the regional level: a member of the Monti Sibillini National Park management board and the manager of the Regional Forest Agency in charge for Valnerina. Among stakeholders: the local committee that was established in 2018 for the reconstruction of the town after the 2016/2017 earthquakes, the interdisciplinary research group Emidio di Treviri, created in 2017 to study from different perspectives the impact of emergency and recovery management on local communities. At a local level, we collected the opinions of two local associations established after the earthquakes. 'I love Norcia' focused on productive and cultural aspects, Montanari Testoni, which helps locals to tackle the recovery process in a collective way, existing associations supporting the rural landscape, one involved in preserving the traditional cultivation of lentils on the Castelluccio plan, the other in promoting the marcita. Among the public, we interviewed a farmer and cattle owner who were hardly affected by the earthquake, and an expert on local culture, a retired full professor of cultural anthropology at the University of Perugia.

14 Kusenbach. 'Street Phenomenology. The go-along as ethnographic tool', 2003; Evans and Jones, 'The walking interview: methodology, mobility and place', 2011.

15 Except for one actor, who refused to be recorded, we used our notes and we didn't obviously report any quotations.

16 Proloco Norcia, 'Proloco official website', 2021.

17 Proloco Norcia, 'Proloco official website', 2021.

18 Proloco Norcia, 'Proloco official website', 2021.

19 Carnelli, 'La festa di San Giovanni a Paganica: riti e Santi fra le macerie del post-sisma aquilano', 2015.

20 IGP Lentil Farmers Association, 19 November 2019.

21 Proloco and I love Norcia associations, 19 November 2019.

22 Consortium for Agricultural Commons Norcia and Castelluccio, 19 November 2019.

23 Norcia local government, 19 November 2019.

24 IGP Lentil Farmers Association, 19 November 2019.

25 Regional Forest Agency, 19 November 2019.

26 Montanari Testoni, 20 November 2019

27 Montanari Testoni, 20 November 2019.

28 Consortium for Agricultural Commons, 20 November 2019.

29 As emergency housing units during the recovery process [NoAs].
30 Norcia local government, 19 November 2019
31 Montanari Testoni, 20 November 2019.
32 Farmer, 18 November 2019.
33 Emidio di Treviri, 14 January 2020.
34 The farmer/cattle owner, Emidio di Treviri and the local expert we interviewed.
35 IGP Lentil Farmers Association, 19 November 2019.
36 I love Norcia committee representative 2019.
37 Scazzosi, 'Landscapes as systems of tangible and intangible relationships. Small theoretical and methodological introduction to read and evaluate Rural Landscape as Heritage', 2018.
38 Scazzosi, 'Landscapes as systems of tangible and intangible relationships. Small theoretical and methodological introduction to read and evaluate Rural Landscape as Heritage', 2018.
39 Emidio di Treviri, 14 January 2020.
40 Regional Forest Agency.
41 Chang, 'Heritage as a Tourism Commodity: Traversing the Tourist–Local Divide', 2002.
42 I love Norcia committee representative. 2019.
43 Norcia Reconstruction Committee, 18 November, 2019.
44 Carnelli, 'La festa di San Giovanni a Paganica: riti e Santi fra le macerie del post-sisma aquilano', 2015.
45 IGP Lentil Farmers Association, 19 November 2019.
46 Montanari Testoni and Norcia Reconstruction Committee.
47 Sisti, 'Paesaggio ed emergenza sisma', 2017.
48 UNESCO, 'Convention for the Safeguarding of the intangible Cultural Heritage', 2003.

Bibliography

Berkes, F., Colding, J. and Folke, C. 'Rediscovery of traditional ecological knowledge as adaptive management'. *Ecological Application* 10(5) (2000): 1251–1262.

Branduini, P. and Carnelli, F. 'The preservation of rural landscapes for building resilience in the context of small towns: insights from North Italy'. In *Historic Cities in the Face of Disasters*, edited by Fatemeh Farnaz Arefian. Berlin: Springer, 2021.

Carnelli, F. 'La festa di San Giovanni a Paganica: riti e Santi fra le macerie del post-sisma aquilano'. In *Fukushima, Concordia e altre macerie: vita quotidiana, resistenza e gestione del disastro*, edited by Pietro Saitta, 135–148. Firenze: Editpress, 2015.

Chang, T.C. 'Heritage as a tourism commodity: traversing the tourist–local divide'. *Singapore Journal of Tropical Geography*, 18(1) (2002): 46–68. DOI: 10.1111/1467-9493.00004.

Conference of the European Ministry of Territory (CEMAT). 'European rural heritage observation guide', 2003. Accessed 28 February 2021. https://rm.coe.int/16806f7cc2%20/

Creswell, J.W. and Poth, C.N. *Qualitative Inquiry and Research Design: Choosing Among Five Approaches*. London: Sage publications, 2018.

D'Angelo, A. 'Prima il *food* e poi le case? Gastroturismo e strategie di sviluppo nelle aree colpite dai sismi 2016–2017 (il caso di Amatrice e di Castelluccio di Norcia)'. Masters Thesis, University of Siena, A.Y. 2017/2018, 2018.

Emidio di Treviri. *Sul fronte del sisma. Un'inchiesta militante sul post-terremoto dell'Appennino centrale (2016–2017)*. Roma: DeriveApprodi, 2018.

Evans, J. and Jones, P. 'The walking interview: methodology, mobility and place' *Applied Geography*, 31 (2011): 849–858.

Jigyasu, R. 'From natural to cultural disaster: consequences of the post-earthquake rehabilitation process on the cultural heritage in marathwada region, India'. *Bulletin Of The New Zealand Society For Earthquake Engineering*, 34(3) (2001): 237–242.

Jigyasu, R. 'The intangible dimension of urban heritage'. In *Reconnecting the City: The Historic Urban Landscape Approach and the Future of Urban Heritage*, edited by F. Bandarin and R. Van Oers. London/New York: Wiley, 2015.

Kusenbach, Margarethe. 'Street Phenomenology. The go-along as ethnographic tool'. *Ethnography,* 4 (2003): 455–485.

ICOMOS. 'ICOMOS-IFLA Principles Concerning Rural Landscapes As Heritage'. Adopted by the 19th ICOMOS General Assembly, New Delhi, India, 15th December, 2017.

Marincioni, F., Casareale, C. and Byrne, K. 'Beautiful and safe landscapes for sustainable disaster risk reduction'. In *Disaster Research and the Second Environmental Crisis, Environmental Hazards*, edited by James Kendra et al., 105–116, 2019. Accessed 25 February 2021. https://doi.org/10.1007/978-3-030-04691-0_5

O'Brien, G., O'Keefe, P., Jayawickrama, J. and Jigyasu, R. 'Developing a model for building resilience to climate risks for cultural heritage'. *Journal of Cultural Heritage Management and Sustainable Development*, 5 (2) (2015): 99–114.

Pitzalis, S. 'A che punto siamo a tre anni dal terremoto del Centro Italia?', *Le Nius*, 2019. Accessed 24 July 2020. https://www.lenius.it/terremoto-in-centro-italia/

Plieninger, T. and Bieling, C. *Resilience and the Cultural Landscape Understanding and Managing Change in Human-Shaped Environments*. Cambridge: Cambridge University Press, 2012.

Proloco Norcia. 2021. Official website. Accessed 25 February 2021. https://www.proloconorcia.it/

Scazzosi, L. 'Lombardy'. In *Italian Historical Rural Landscapes, Environmental History* 1, edited by M. Agnoletti, 221–245. Dordrecht: Springer, 2013.

Scazzosi, L. 'Landscapes as systems of tangible and intangible relationships. Small theoretical and methodological introduction to read and evaluate Rural Landscape as Heritage'. In *The Conservation and Enhancement of Built and Landscape Heritage. A New Life for the Ghost Village of Mondonico on Lake Como*, edited by E. Rosina and L. Scazzosi, 19–40. Milano: Poliprint, 2018.

Sisti, A. 'Paesaggio ed emergenza sisma'. In, *Rapporto sullo stato delle politiche per il paesaggio*, edited by R. Banchini, L. Scazzosi, 260–286. Roma: Mibact, 2017.

Smith, L. and Akagawa, N. 'Introduction'. In *Intangible Heritage. Key Issues in Cultural Heritage*, edited by Laurajane Smith and Natsuko Akagawa. London: Routledge, 2018.

Strampelli, I. and Carnelli, F. 'Ricostruire i sensi del luogo per comprendere le trame dell'abbandono. Un'etnografia del paesaggio a Montegallo (AP), nei Monti Sibillini colpiti dai terremoti del 2016–2017'. In *Sulle tracce dell'Appennino che cambia*, edited by Emidio di Treviri, Campobasso: Il Bene Comune, 2021.

Teti, V. 'Abbandoni, ritorni. Nuove feste nei paesi abbandonati della Calabria'. In *Festa viva. Tradizione, territorio, Turismo*, edited by Laura Bonato. Torino: Omega edizioni, 2006.

UNESCO, 'Convention for the Safeguarding of the intangible Cultural Heritage', *UNESCO*, 17 October 2003. Accessed 6 May 2021. https://ich.unesco.org/doc/src/01852-EN.pdf

17
Heritage assets, fairs and museums
Places of encounter and presence in times of pandemic

Alessandra De Nicola, Piero Magri and Franca Zuccoli[1]

Since February 2020, our everyday habits have undergone a process of radical change. Initial news stories from China about the COVID-19 outbreak seemed far removed, and this perception of distance made us feel safe. However, as time went on, the situation evolved into an unstoppable crescendo that has ultimately impacted all aspects of billions of lives. Everything came to a halt: work, school, culture ... to be progressively restored via the only viable strategy available: the deployment of distance modes of delivery. As the emergency escalated, governments around the world identified different levels of response. Social isolation arrangements meant that people would be confined to their homes for an unquantifiable length of time. Many parts of the cultural sector were particularly and severely affected by the lockdown, given that they are usually perceived as the places of encounter and exchange par excellence. Some workers were offered temporary unemployment relief, while others had their contracts put on hold. Cultural institutions began to redefine themselves and reprogramme the immediate future, choosing between suspending their activities while waiting, and working to identify the most appropriate means by which they could remain active at a distance. They set out to invisibly heal a breach perceived as irreparable, via a process that saw each individual cultural operator seeking to establish new expressions of the notion of sustainability, as evoked in *Agenda 2030*.[2] This document, produced by the United Nations in 2015,[3] called for all actors, collective and individual, to pursue change in the form of 17 sustainable development goals. It offered a guide to determining what was truly sustainable, necessary and meaningful at this time of uncertainty, as well as to revisiting existing prospects and plans – *Agenda 2030* suddenly took on new relevance. Cultural institutions were now faced with a novel challenge to their priority status as public services. The extraordinary time of the pandemic forced us to pause and consider the importance of such places as open spaces of exchange that are part of, and facilitate the construction of, our collective identity. Here, in the dual role of organisers and citizens who missed the cultural interaction with museums, we examine the case of Fa' la cosa giusta! (Do the right thing!)[4] – an event on the themes of critical consumption and fair trade. This example is compared to other international initiatives, to reveal how, in a moment when it became impossible for people to visit museums, museums took themselves to the people.

In recent years, Fa' la cosa giusta! has encouraged the participation of museums and cultural heritage sites with a view to jointly exploring an alternative approach to the cultural experience, as well as slow, sustainable forms of tourism, and rendering culture more participatory. Here we present a chronological account of the steps that led to this event being cancelled and reprogrammed on an entirely different basis as a result of the COVID emergency. Its example provides a starting point for examining the strategies adopted by some of the participating museums to engage their communities during the lockdown and the early phases of recovery in 2021. International examples of cultural initiatives launched during the public health emergency are also analysed, to understand the different strategies adopted and their longer-term implications.

Fa' la cosa giusta!

A fair as a place for a live encounter

On Saturday 22 February 2020, almost all the preparations were in place for a fair that was to host 700 exhibitors and 518 events, including conferences, debates and workshops; 3,600 students, from kindergarten through secondary school, were ready to take part in tours guided by a hundred students on work experience; and 300 volunteers were ready to assist the expected 70,000 visitors. The 17th edition of Fa' la cosa giusta! – Italy's leading fair on critical consumption and sustainable lifestyles – was scheduled to take place in the 32,000 m² of Milan's exhibition centre, Fieramilanocity, from 6–8 March 2020.

Fa' la cosa giusta! was launched in 2004 by the publishing house Terre di mezzo, itself founded to tell the story of the 'in-between lands where all people meet,[5] where the social, beautiful, and ugly dimensions of our world all come together, where fragility has become, and goes on becoming, a resource'. With the aim of disseminating 'good practices' and showcasing examples of ethical and sustainable consumption and production, the fair is organised in collaboration with the local government, associations and businesses. A place of encounter and dialogue between exponents of organic farming, critical fashion, responsible tourism, cooperation, sustainable mobility and circular economies, it promotes a contemporary lifestyle that lays the ground for a sustainable future. It represents a responsible way of doing business: organising our purchases, conceptualising work and using our planet's resources, while generating new connections and opportunities and thereby creating a new culture.

It is a melting-pot of encounters and initiatives, a breeding ground of ideas: La Grande Fabbrica delle Parole (the great word factory), a creative writing laboratory for primary and middle school children, has seen over 10,000 children participate over the course of 10 fairs; FuoriCastello (outside the castle) has brought the suburbs into Milan's Castello Sforzesco; Scuola delle buone pratiche (school of good practice) offers local administrators a place to learn and share innovative administrative practices. SFIDE – La scuola di tutti (challenges – a school for everybody) helps schools to become more inclusive, play a leadership role in their communities and participate actively in disseminating culture. In 2019, SFIDE addressed the theme of museum heritage. Schools visiting the exhibition had the opportunity to learn about recent research and innovation projects in museums.

The themes of the 2020 event were the environment, justice and sustainability. A special space had been reserved for museums to narrate their projects. The seminar 'What does sustainability mean for museums? Past experience, ideas and future prospects', had been jointly organised by the Lombardy regional government, Milano-Bicocca University and ICOM-International Council of Museums Italy.

On Sunday 23 February, due to the COVID-19 emergency, the regional government issued an order mandating the cancellation of exhibitions. The fair was rescheduled for November. The emergency began to be seen as an opportunity to 'reconceptualise' the event, in case nothing could ever go back to being exactly as it was before COVID-19.

The starting point was the fair's objectives: 'narrating ethical consumption and production practices, offering knowledge about sustainable lifestyles, creating a space of encounter to give life to new projects'. In parallel, we wanted to apply what had been learnt from a three-month period of home confinement, especially the need to build alliances to overcome the effect of the virus. We concluded that it would be possible to deploy an alternative set of means of narration, all of which remain intricately connected and interdependent:

- A cultural programme beginning well in advance of the dates of the fair and continuing long after, in spaces other than the exhibition centre and involving the exhibition's partners, including museums, in different districts around the city. This would have the advantage of spreading the narrative of the fair over a longer timeframe, and of bringing additional visitors to the museums. The museums would have the opportunity to run the activities they had originally planned, albeit with the additional health and safety measures required because of COVID-19. These encounters could be held in part or entirely online, making it possible to participate from anywhere in the world, and enabling far larger audiences to be reached.
- A live fair hosting a limited number of preregistered visitors, offering thematic tours based on visitors' interests – including the environment, critical fashion, ethical tourism and 'resistant communities' (such as small villages and small enterprises in inland areas) – with the opportunity to meet exhibitors in person and purchase products already presented.

The museums involved in the fair's cultural programme

In the months leading up to the fair, the organisers, along with a team from the Department of Human Sciences and Education at Milano-Bicocca University and representatives of the cultural department of the Lombardy Region had issued an official call to museums to apply to take part in the fair. The purpose was not just to make museums known to a wider audience, but to showcase projects that were in keeping with the fair's theme for 2020: 'Museum projects promoting slow, participatory, sustainable, and inclusive tourism'. In other words, a 'slow' time was to be dedicated to museum heritage, which would contrast with the frenetic pace that has become the everyday norm, offering an opportunity to consume heritage in a way that is participatory, sustainable and truly inclusive. Different types of museum applied to take part, ranging from the Museum of Contemporary Photography in Cinisello Balsamo[6] to museum networks such as the Museums of the Diocese of Como;[7] from museums linked to landscape heritage, such as the Lombard side of Lake Maggiore, designated as a MAB (Man and the Biosphere) reserve by UNESCO,[8] to museums about the lives of artists and/or craftsmen and other traditional occupations that are now close to extinction, such as the Casa Museo Pietro Malossi;[9] museums that are the homes of famous collectors, such as the Museo Poldi Pezzoli[10] and Museo Bagatti Valsecchi;[11] and even natural science museums such as Civico Museo di Scienze Naturali 'G. Orlandi'.[12] The institutions involved were invited to participate in three preparatory meetings that were characterised by a high level of combined expertise, with the goal of involving and including all segments of the population. Each of the museums asked themselves how they could continue to actively contribute to the social and cultural life of their community. With all regular activity suspended, all those with a professional role in the cultural heritage sector were faced with the question of what they could do instead, with what purpose and meaning, and by what means. The museum closures were so generalised that the only parallel in recent history is the Second World War period. Nevertheless, soon after the initial lockdown, the first signs of an invisible 'reconstruction' of this sector began to appear, and the production of digital materials of various kinds grew steadily day after day. In the words of Claudio Rosati:

> Museums had never been closed down like this since the Second World War and never had they projected their contents outwards on such a vast scale … They say that museums are more oriented towards broadcasting than towards exploring the potential for authentic interaction with their audiences. But the most important thing, right now, is the sense of public service that they are displaying in this way. They are in any case offering a useful starting point for a future that will certainly be challenging for museums. The highest quality offerings have mainly come from institutions that historically, in their everyday practice, from their reception area to their exhibition rooms, concretely prioritized the relationship between people [visitors] and collection.[13]

Interestingly, the key themes originally chosen for the event in 2020 re-emerged as predominant. Museums that had already prioritised the needs of their audiences in presenting their heritage assets and collections, in designing their offerings and deciding what to do and how to do it, continued their efforts to keep their relationship with the public alive and value the voices of their audiences. As an example, GAMeC, the Gallery of Modern and Contemporary Art in Bergamo, one of the Italian cities most seriously affected by COVID-19, implemented a bold strategy designed to make its presence visible despite the lockdown, deploying innovative techniques[14] to remain in contact with its audience and to reach segments of the population who had never visited the museum prior to the public health emergency. The 'DNA' of these museums, in terms of their determination to be in touch with their audiences despite the emergency, was remarkable. In contrast, when the desire to remain active and visible was essentially a marketing strategy, museums tended to produce products that were not designed to invite audiences' reactions and interpretations, rather to be consumed via a single click.

From presence to distance

A brief overview of museum offerings during the first waves of the pandemic (2019–20)

Through an exploration of how museums can be a social resource, a node in a network of relationships, engage in activism and function as educational agencies,[15] this chapter aims to show how the #quarantineculture phenomenon has accelerated a process that was already underway.[16]

Museums deployed diverse strategies to remain in touch with communities, leading to the development of new forms of mediation. In the uncertainty surrounding the pandemic, they sought to keep culture alive by producing new content or offering safe means for audiences to discover or rediscover, in digital form, cultural heritage assets that are geographically both close and distant. This mirrored a pattern already observed during emergencies such as environmental disasters or brutal acts of terrorism, where heritage assets serve as key identity markers for communities actively seeking to re-establish their identities. It is at times of crisis such as these that the public perceives assets held in museums as a key resource, with the power to reinforce the local community.[17]

Given the unprecedented scale and diversity of the digital cultural content produced during the emergency, this section attempts an analysis of the aspects that are most salient to our purposes. The rich variety of output was facilitated by the fact that the cultural sector was more prepared than others, as it had been engaging for some time with the themes that came to the fore during the social isolation phase of the emergency. Digital technologies, physical versus virtual, the educational value of digital surrogates,[18] fixed versus mobile locations, open versus closed systems[19] and the space in which cultural products are consumed had long been the object of reflection and study.

We have been witnessing what Nancy Proctor, in different times and with different aims, defined as the transition from the 'distributed museum'[20] to the 'museum of everywhere'.[21] To keep their communities alive, museums have used formal channels of communication and social media to become creative platforms designed to inspire and encourage critical and participatory dialogue. Many institutions have published videos on their YouTube channels offering walk-throughs of their museums and explanations of the most important works in their collections. In parallel, museums have made their presence felt in other ways, albeit mainly in offline mode. For some, it has been challenging to produce livestreamed events due to a lack of expertise in managing live broadcasts and a lack of funding. Offering workshops is costly and a number of organisations, such as GAMeC in Bergamo, Italy, and looking afar, the Detroit Institute of Arts (DIA), Kalamazoo Institute of Arts (KIA) and others in the US, partly covered this expense by charging a participation fee.

Some galleries have made their most unique pieces available for consumption. The Broad in Los Angeles put together a series of YouTube videos offering a close-up look at the material masterpieces in its *Infinity Mirror Rooms* by Yayoi Kusama, coupled with music to provide a more deeply immersive, multisensory experience.[22]

The Los Angeles County Museum of Art (LACMA) rebranded its website to include a virtual tour, soundtracks and live recordings, and online teaching resources. Its gaming initiative entailed working with Minecraft, the Microsoft video game, to develop the theme of the museum's spaces and exhibits. M9 Museo, an Italian multimedia museum, leveraged its experience in the field of distance learning by offering its partner schools access to educational video games taking advantage of free licences offered by Microsoft for teachers during the emergency. At LACMA, the virtual reconstruction of the museum's spaces had already been developed, making it possible to quickly provide educational games set in the various sections of the museum on the themes of landscape, travel, identity and robotics.

Art in the age of new normal was the title of a webinar, jointly organised by three Michigan museums – DIA, KIA and Grand Rapids Art Museum (GRAM) – which had each identified different means and methods of accompanying their audiences throughout the pandemic. The DIA offered a programme called Access to art online,[23] a music programme via SoundCloud and a catalogue of educational offerings divided into units, lesson plans and self-guided materials for families, teachers and young learners (as did other major museums, such as the National Gallery of Art in Washington, the Met in New York, and the Tate in London). Another key project launched by the DIA targeted older adults,[24] with the aim of keeping senior citizens learning, exploring and connecting with the institute.

The National Gallery Singapore is a case that invites reflection on the different timescales observed during the lockdown. Invited by the government to support educators, this museum introduced an experimental blended learning programme that combined online resources with on-site visits and targeted the families of 4- to 12-year-old children with a view to fostering more creative approaches to everyday life. Virtual tours replaced on-site visits with ready-to-use teaching packs – discussion guides were sent to schools so that children could continue to benefit from the museum's educational offerings via distance-learning modes. The museum became a platform for diverse and accessible education in which artists became a resource and art a means of coping with mixed emotions. Putting itself forward as a place with a responsible, care-oriented ethos, the museum has been hosting a biweekly online interview with an artist on the themes of wellbeing and creativity as tools for coping with the emergency.[25]

Institutions with limited resources have tried to take advantage of their accumulated learning experience by digitalising it. The Botanic Gardens Network in the Italian Lombardy region used its tried-and-tested educational materials to design online encounters to be offered to schools to support their regular teaching–learning activities. A similar strategy was pursued by the MUVE Fondazione Musei Civici di Venezia network of museums in Venice, through a newsletter offering both educational and play activities to regular visitors and the Chinati Foundation in Marfa, Texas, created a set of stories about the works in its collection.[26]

This has been a period rich in events that have had a significant impact on communities around the world. The global movement in support of Black Lives Matter also found its expression online, through posting a black square on Instagram or publishing messages of solidarity on social media platforms. Also in this case, museums have played an activist role, as seen at the Brooklyn Museum of New York, whose bonds with the local community and African-American culture go back to its founding and are part of its mission.[27] The museum interviewed its audience to explore their needs and found that the hunger some community members were experiencing was more physical than intellectual. In response, it became a hub mobilising its sponsors and organising a system for serving healthy meals in the open spaces adjacent the building. Museums have also taken an activist stand for minority rights and acted in support of local communities. New York's Cooper Hewitt Smithsonian Design Museum intercepted the voices of audiences via its website.[28] The section entitled 'A message to our community' offers a rich range of resources and tools for teachers, families and the general public that are both specific to the pandemic and in addressing perceived social and racial intolerance. Finally, it is worth citing one of the initiatives launched by GAMeC in Bergamo. The project[29] 'Non recidere, forbice, quel volto' ('O scissors, do not cut that face') embodies the significance of education based on art, beginning with the project title, which is a verse by the Italian poet Eugenio Montale. GAMeC launched a cycle of free workshops on creating memory and narrating identity as a means of processing the city's collective experience of the COVID-19 crisis. With the input of mediators from the charitable organisation Caritas,[30] creative and artistic work became a secular rite with cathartic value. This had necessarily to be performed in the museum, the place par excellence where action transcends use and becomes a memory with the capacity to survive into the future.

Conclusions

The article: 'People trust museums more than newspapers. Here is why that matters right now'[31] published in 2017 by Colleen Dilenschneider, referred to the role of museums vis-à-vis the abundance of fake news found on the internet. The statistics it reported help us to understand the role of museums during the #quarantineculture. They show that the public health crisis has forced the acceleration of a process that was already underway and resulted in the even speedier adoption of new paradigms. Dilenschneider set out to show that people trust museums as custodians of culture because of their scientific credibility, research activity, mediation of collections, educational outreach and provision of entertainment, as well as their engagement with audiences in promoting active citizenship and social cohesion, and thereby reinforcing the identity of their local communities. The Guide edited by the Organization for Economic Co-operation and Development (OECD) and the International Council of Museums (ICOM)[32] supports our view that the organisations, whose mandate it is to conserve cultural heritage, have extraordinary potential to function as invisible (re)builders of communities, thanks to their emphasis on sustainable and integrated development. In such an uncertain time, the leading sustainable priority has become seeking to minimise new forms of social exclusion, which are almost always a function of economic factors, with a focus on the environment. For museums, one of the greatest challenges in this regard is clearly identifying ways to support the communities around them, and to further reinforce their cultural role as constructors and facilitators of awareness and knowledge in relation to the current emergency. Access to a computer and a good internet connection alone are enough to support a wide range of formats, including webinars, performances, meetings, posts, podcasts and radio art. Museums have used formal channels of communication, but more frequently social media, to become creative platforms that are designed to inspire and encourage critical and participatory dialogue, and most importantly, to keep their communities alive. From the examples given, it is possible to say that during the lockdown museums showed that they are prepared to take up a role as changemakers with respect to individual behaviours and collective decision-making from an independent position that is neutral vis-à-vis political factionalism. In short, we have witnessed the realisation of what, in 2015, Elizabeth Crooke identified as a challenge: the realisation of the 'active museum'. The museum that, in close relationship with its community, understands its needs and produces actions and content collaboratively. In this new context, the audience is no longer the end user, but has become part of the process.[33]

Against this backdrop, our fair on sustainable consumption, facilitating a new mode of community building, appears to be a particularly farsighted initiative. Hence, looking back today at the major debate surrounding ICOM's efforts to come up with a new definition of what a museum actually is, we can see that initiatives made by museums to 'operate within a system of relations at the service of society and its sustainable development', are merely first steps toward a new interpretation of their role. The changes imposed by the pandemic have made this fundamental role much more evident.

Notes

1　This paper was jointly planned by all the authors but the writing up of the various sections was divided between them as follows: Alessandra De Nicola: Abstract, section *From presence to distance,* Conclusion; Piero Magri: Abstract, section *Fa' la cosa giusta!*; Franca Zuccoli: Abstract, Introduction, section *The museums involved in the cultural programme.*

2　This Agenda is a United Nation plan of action for people, planet and prosperity. It also seeks to strengthen universal peace in larger freedom. Accessed 14 June 2022. https://sdgs.un.org/publications/transforming-our-world-2030-agenda-sustainable-development-17981

3　United Nations, ' Transforming our world: the 2030 Agenda for Sustainable Development', 2015.

4　Fa'la cosa giusta! Accessed 14 June 2022 https://www.falacosagiusta.org

5　Terre di mezzo. Accessed 14 June 2022 https://www.terre.it/en/

6　It is the first public museum of photography in Italy. The mission is the conservation, cataloguing, study and promotion of photography, with a particular focus on the relationship between photography and other arts and the current technological transformations.

7　Accessed 14 June 2022 http://cultura.diocesidicomo.it

8　'The MAB is an intergovernmental scientific programme that aims to establish a scientific basis for enhancing the relationship between people and their environments.'

9　The museum hosts the collections left by the Brescian antiquarian Pietro Malossi.

10　The house-museum, opened in 1881 in Milano from the collection of Gian Giacomo Poldi Pezzoli.

11　A historic house museum that is the fruit of the collection of Barons Bagatti Valsecchi at the end of the nineteenth century.

12　The exhibits are dedicated to naturalistic and archaeological aspects of the Voghera and Oltrepadano (North of Italy) area.

13　Rosati, 'Musei dopo il corona virus', 2020, 4.

14　Colombo, *Musei e cultura digitale. Fra narrativa, pratiche e testimonianze,* 2020.

15　On this widely researched topic, we propose the recent reading Delgado, Cuenca, *Handbook of Research on Citizenship and Heritage Education*, 2020.

16　Copeland, *European democratic citizenship, heritage education and identity,* 2006.

17　De Nicola, 'Scommettere sul pubblico. Arte e Scienza. Quando non è bello ciò che è bello, ma è bello ciò che capisco', 2016.

18　Rhee, 'Mediation between digital surrogates and viewers based on the technology acceptance model, 2018.

19　Bautista & Balsamo, 'Understanding the distributed museum: Mapping the spaces of museology in contemporary culture', 2011.

20　Dewdeney et al., *Post critical museology. Theory and practice in the art museum*, 2013.

21　Proctor 'Mobile in Museums: From Interpretation to Conversation', 2015.

22　This project is no longer available online: https://www.youtube.com/playlist?list=PLmql00Mj9v8XNKKBKsVlnMmn7DG-iVjQM

23　Accessed 14 June 2022 https://www.dia.org/art/collection

24　DIA project targeted older adults. Accessed 14 June 2022 https://www.dia.org/thursdaysathome

25　Webinar "Musei, Famiglie e Bambini verso un Futuro Insieme: accessed 14 June 2022 https://bit.ly/lilliputyoutube

26　At the beginning of the pandemic, Chinati education initiated a series of online learning programmes, producing four distinct virtual curriculums.

27　'Our Mission: To create inspiring encounters with art that expand the ways we see ourselves, the world and its possibilities. Our Vision: Where great art and courageous conversations are catalysts for a more connected, civic, and empathetic world.'

28　'A   message   to   our   community'   https://www.cooperhewitt.org/2020/06/04/a-message-to-our-community/

29　The project *Non recidere, forbice, quel volto* https://www.gamec.it/non-recidere-forbice-quel-volto/

30　Caritas is the pastoral body of the Italian Episcopal Conference for the promotion of charity; Caritas Bergamo operates in the field of education and promotion of culture, charity, protection of civil rights and social and sociomedical assistance.

31 Dilenschneider, 'People Trust Museums More Than Newspapers. Here Is Why That Matters Right Now (DATA)', 2017.

32 OECD/ ICOM,'Culture and local development: maximising the impact: A guide for local governments, communities and museums', 2019

33 Crooke,'The 'Active Museum': How Concern with Community Transformed the Museum', 2015.

Bibliography

Bautista, S. and Balsamo, A. 'Understanding the distributed museum: mapping the spaces of museology in contemporary culture'. In *Museums and the Web* 2011: *Proceedings,* edited by Jennifer Trant and David Bearman, 55–70. Toronto: Archives & Museum Informatics, 2011.

Brooklyn Museum of New York (USA). Accessed 21 May 2021. https://www.brooklynmuseum.org

Chinati Foundation in Marfa, Texas (USA). Accessed 21 May 2021. https://chinati.org

Civico Museo di Scienze Naturali 'G. Orlandi' (ITA). Accessed 21 May 2021. http://www.museoscienzevog.it

Colombo, M.E. *Musei e cultura digitale. Fra narrativa, pratiche e testimonianze.* Milan: Editrice Bibliografica, 2020.

Copeland, T. *European democratic citizenship, heritage education and identity.* Council of Europe, 2006.

Cooper Hewitt. 'A message to our community'. Accessed June 2020. https://www.cooperhewitt.org/2020/06/04/a-message-to-our-community/

Crooke, E. 'The 'Active Museum': How concern with community transformed the museum'. In *The International Handbooks of Museum Studies: Museum Practice,* edited by Conal McCarthy, 481–500. Chichester: John Wiley & Sons, Ltd., 2015.

Delgado-Algarra, E.J. and Cuenca-López, J.M., eds. *Handbook of Research on Citizenship and Heritage Education.* IGI Global, 2020.

De Nicola, A., 'Scommettere sul pubblico. Arte e Scienza. Quando non è bello ciò che è bello, ma è bello ciò che capisco'. In *Paesaggi Culturali [...]* Edited by Alessandra De Nicola, Franca Zuccoli, 63–78. Santarcangelo di Romagna (RN): Maggioli, 2016.

Dewdeney, A., Dibosa, D. and Walsh, V. *Post Critical Museology. Theory and Practice in the Art Museum.* London: Routledge, 2013.

Dilenschneider, C. 'People Trust Museums More Than Newspapers. Here Is Why That Matters Right Now (DATA)' (2017) Accessed 17 June 2020. https://www.colleendilen.com/2017/04/26/people-trust-museums-more-than-newspapers-here-is-why-that-matters-right-now-data/

Dziekan, V. and Proctor, N. 'From elsewhere to everywhere'. In *The Routledge Handbook of Museums, Media and Communication,* edited by Kirsten Drotner, Vince Dziekan, Ross Parry, & Kim Christian Schroder, 177–192. London: Routledge, 2019.

GAMEC. 'The project *Non recidere, forbice, quel volto*'. Accessed June 2020. https://www.gamec.it/non-recidere-forbice-quel-volto/

Grand Rapids Art Museum (USA). Accessed 21 May 2021. https://www.artmuseumgr.org

The Los Angeles County Museum of Art. Accessed 21 May 2021. https://www.lacma.org

Kalamazoo Institute of Arts (USA). Accessed 21 May 2021. https://www.kiarts.org

Museo Bagatti Valsecchi (ITA). Accessed 21 May 2021. https://museobagattivalsecchi.org/en/

Museo di Fotografia Contemporanea (Museum of Contemporary Photography) di Cinisello Balsamo, Milano (ITA). Accessed 21 May 2021. http://www.mufoco.org/en/info/the-museum/

Museo Pietro Malossi, Ome, Brescia (ITA) Accessed 21 May 2021https://www.fondazionemalossi.org

Museo Poldi Pezzoli (ITA). Accessed 21 May 2021. https://museopoldipezzoli.it/en/

MUVE- Fondazione Musei Civici di Venezia network of museums in Venice (ITA). Accessed 21 May 2021. https://www.visitmuve.it

The National Gallery of Singapore. Accessed 21 May 2021. https://www.nationalgallery.sg

OECD/ICOM (2019), 'Culture and local development: maximising the impact: A guide for local governments, communities and museums', *OECD Local Economic and Employment Development (LEED) Papers*, No. 2019/07, OECD Publishing.

Proctor, N. 'Mobile in Museums: From Interpretation to Conversation'. In *The International Handbooks of Museum Studies VOLUME 3: MUSEUM MEDIA. Part IV Extending the Museum*, edited by Andrea Witcomb, 499–527. Chichester, West Sussex: Wiley/Blackwell, 2015.

Rhee, B. and Kim, J. 'Mediation between digital surrogates and viewers based on the technology acceptance model'. *Journal of Theoretical and Applied Information Technology,* 96(6) (2018): 1668–1679.

Rosati, C., 'Musei dopo il corona virus', *Cultura Commestibile* (25 aprile 2020): 4–5.

Part V
Schools, social integration and rights

18
Dimensions of educational poverty and emergencies
What are the protective factors for wellbeing?

Nicoletta Di Genova

Emergencies and their management tend to overlook the factor of educational risk or the increased chances of educational poverty. Catastrophes, including the recent pandemic, affect a multitude of aspects that influence and modify the educational functions of territories and cities, impacting on issues of equality, or rather equity, in the access of citizens to quality educational experiences. This chapter examines research carried out in the 11 years following the 2009 earthquake in L'Aquila, linking it to data that emerged from studies carried out in the city between 2018 and 2020, close to the tenth anniversary of the event. It highlights the factors that contribute to educational poverty and that are related to emergency situations, and places them in the perspective of their long-term consequences. Reflecting on the safety of school buildings, the need for fair accessibility to cultural meeting places and on protective measures for the wellbeing of children involved in emergencies, this chapter focuses on resilience as an educational goal.

Introduction

The earthquake that hit the city of L'Aquila in 2009 represented an important scenario to define, through numerous research studies, some areas of educational wellbeing vulnerability that represent, at the same time, risk factors of educational poverty closely related to emergency situations. In general, the trauma of the earthquake, the housing policies adopted, the absence of measures to support the economy, employment and income, have all led to a deterioration in the quality of economic and social life. From this point of view, the scenario has been characterised by various political and economic choices that are clearly in line with what Naomi Klein calls the 'shock economy'.[1] These have led, with both immediate and long-term consequences, to 'the impoverishment of the territory, a growth in unemployment and a sharp increase in discomfort and social marginality'.[2]

There have also been direct repercussions for the inhabitants with regard to their 'territory'. The city itself has acquired a new territorial structure with the indiscriminate construction of temporary and permanent houses, and shopping centres, throughout its surrounding areas. This has caused a number of problems for the citizens of L'Aquila, related to the logistics and management of the 'urban' spaces and habits experienced in everyday life, such as the lack of transport services and the extension of distances between parts of the city. In turn, this has led to a widespread sense of bewilderment accentuated by the ongoing lack of services and the only very partial reopening of the historic city centre, a particularly important gathering place where all services were concentrated and which served as a meeting point for the entire population. This is the context in which the educational intervention and pedagogical research have concentrated their efforts, through different forms of research and action aimed at investigating the relationship between children and the city. In particular, we report here on a project coordinated by Alessandro Vaccarelli and supported by an international collaboration with the Grupo de Innovacìon Educativa 'Aretè' of the Polytechnic University of Madrid.[3] Narration and outdoor education were the main tools used for these investigations.

The researchers asked the children to write and draw freely in response to the theme: 'My City' and collected over a hundred texts in 2012. The results offer different interpretations of their experiences as citizens and their perception of the city of L'Aquila post-emergency. We report a few brief excerpts of these interpretative categories in Table 18.1. The earthquake certainly emerges as a a powerful theme among the children, who often identify themselves as being citizens of the disaster. The ruins, destruction, temporary structures, heavy vehicles, cranes of work in progress and the changing landscape of the city have all been constant features throughout these children's lives. A present characterised by negative elements emerges, as opposed to a past described with nostalgia, as something beautiful and unlikely to return. At the same time, their words point to aspects worth highlighting and keeping in mind in order to develop methods and contents

Table 18.1   Research project 'My City'. Brief excerpts of the texts written by the children of L'Aquila in 2012.

- L'Aquila, my city has changed after the earthquake of 6 April 2009.
- L'Aquila before the earthquake of 6 April 2009 was beautiful, everything was there, nothing was missing.
- My city is called L'Aquila and before the earthquake it was beautiful with churches, buildings and shops, then the centre full of people. You could walk under the arcades, but now it is not as beautiful as it used to be because they are barricaded.
- But before L'Aquila was a beautiful city adorned with castles, fountains, churches and squares that are now under renovation. Boys and girls went out in the evening and went under the arcades to laugh and joke and people always walked with an ice cream in their hands illuminated by the streetlights, the moon and the stars.
- Now L'Aquila is being restored, with propped buildings, streets with few people that live either at M.A.P.* or at Progetto C.A.S.E. According to me, the only desire they have is to return to their homes.
- Piazza Duomo instead is perfect for eating an ice cream or enjoying a concert or playing outdoors.
- I like my city and I would never want to leave it.

* Translator's note: M.A.P. = Moduli Abitativi Provvisori (Temporary Housing Modules).

for an education oriented towards active and participatory citizenship. A desire to stay, to trace out the beauty and the potential of the space in which they live, emerges from their writings, alongside the pleasure of using common spaces, to share playful, cultural and educational experiences – the dimension of encounter. Their sense of belonging and community emerges as a protective factor of resilience and resistance, helping them to leverage resources, bonds and solidarity, to exercise a conscious citizenship and take care of that common space together.[4]

Vaccarelli writes:[5]

> The city educates, and therefore, through its symbolic, architectural, historical, social, and we would also say institutional spaces, continuously shows its members the necessary knowledge, values and behaviours to live together, building that sense of belonging and identity that accompanies, as the first imprinting, individuals in the paths of their social life, even when they move home. The city is 'educated', therefore the city and the citizens together, intended as 'citizenship' (the community of individuals, and with that the sense of social living and the set of rights and duties associated with it), are the result of a pedagogical work of construction and research of links, selection of values, time and space management, in order to give the city back to the citizens and the citizens back to the city.

It is clear here that the idea of an 'educating city'[6] has failed, compounded by the shortages and holes left by the disaster. This has had direct consequences. For children born in L'Aquila straight after the earthquake, it has affected the possibility of building their own individual and collective identity around the community experience, intended in terms of living, experimenting and exercising democracy as an educational practice, in line with Dewey's thinking.[7] Vaccarelli explains[8] that this is the 'generation without a city', which has great difficulties in identifying its roots and in living and growing up 'in' and 'with' its own city, since it has been deprived of its historical memory. This has direct consequences for the development of the children's sense of belonging, built and identified, in this case, in the emergency context.

The reopening of schools and the resumption of teaching activities in the MUSPs (Modules for Provisional School Use) represented a first significant moment to develop resilience, guaranteed by the commitment, in L'Aquila, of the Higher Education Institution in welcoming back the school community within a common space. This common space, as precarious as its name suggests, offers characteristics of structural security – and in some cases innovation in teaching, logistics and furniture – moreover, it is configured as a base from which people can finally meet and relate to each other. To initiate these processes, it was necessary and beneficial to identify new educational and teaching methodologies that could delve into the theme of citizenship education in emergency and post-emergency situations related to natural and environmental disasters, and to social and economic crisis. The 'Outdoor Training and Citizenship' project was carried out with the general aim of supporting teachers and operators through training pathways, workshops and research activities. With the sole aim of explaining and reporting some of the results of this research, those relating to the ability of children to respond to environmental stress seem significant, telling us that between 2014 and 2015:

> 66.7 per cent of children in L'Aquila don't respond adequately to environmental stress, as opposed to 50 per cent of children in the control group, with a percentage difference of 16.7 … This suggests that children living in a post-emergency situation are subjected, even after five years, to environmental pressures and thus they suffer the consequences of weak parental support, which is in turn affected by the general psychosocial stress.[9]

This scenario, which has been described here very briefly considering the complexity of all the factors involved, also reveals possible educational risk situations that can be observed from a pedagogical point of view. Educational poverty can be amplified and exacerbated by emergencies in which imbalances affecting the psycho-educational, social and economic area significantly enhance forms of educational disadvantage and risk. To better explain the specific risk elements that affect educational poverty, it is possible to refer to the definition provided by Save the Children:

> educational poverty is the impossibility for children and teenagers to learn, experiment, develop and freely foster their capacities, talents and aspirations. For a child, educational poverty means being excluded from the acquisition of the skills needed to live in a world characterized by the knowledge economy, speed and innovation. At the same time, educational poverty implies limitations on the opportunity of emotional growth, relationships with other people and discovery of oneself and the world.[10]

These words underline and confirm the multidimensional aspect of this phenomenon, comprised of economic, social and cultural elements linked to various forms of disadvantage, inequality and social exclusion. The same multiple problems that generate educational poverty are in turn interconnected, further limiting healthy development. In order to select the factors that influence levels of educational poverty in L'Aquila, it is necessary to take a holistic view encompassing children's schools, families and environment as areas of production and enjoyment of interdependent educational experiences. It is then possible, among the components of educational poverty, to isolate factors that concern the socio-economic and sociocultural status of the family,[11] as well as the characteristics of the territory, the benefits of formal, informal and non-formal education,[12] academic performance[13] and the phenomenon of early school leaving.[14] In addition, one must factor in prejudices, gender stereotypes or previous migratory experiences and the obstacles and difficulties they caused.[15] In an emergency, these factors are subject to great vulnerability and, as we have seen in L'Aquila, they represent significant educational risks. In the state of crisis or in an unexpected circumstance requiring immediate intervention such as a change of perspective or practices adopted (including those related to education), these elements involve the individual, the community and the territory. Emergencies therefore, generate conditions in which educational poverty is produced and reproduces. Where it already exists, it risks being amplified and becoming a characteristic and structural feature of a territory and its social context.

Twelve years later

Twelve years after the earthquake, in L'Aquila there is still much to do to guarantee children, adolescents, families and its wider population an authentic and tangible everyday 're-appropriation' of the city. The urban spaces in the historic city centre are mostly the setting for evening and nightlife, of which young people and university students are the main beneficiaries. Due to the very scarce cultural and commercial offer, the city centre remains unattractive for families. In 2021 parents and their children use and enjoy the city centre for initiatives or moments of gathering created by the council or local associations. Although these are important, they are not spontaneous. Walks are limited to the few public parks, yet in this historical moment, with the exception of one playground, there are no child-friendly public spaces that favour sociality and creativity in the centre of L'Aquila. All this in a scenario in which social interaction becomes a fundamental tool for the community to rebuild a shared reality. In this context, the provision of a meeting and interaction place, where the community as a whole can focus on disaster recovery, is of crucial importance. The extreme social fragility of this situation highlights the lack of an overall strategy to merge the efforts of institutional and civil society. A strategy to pull together the initiatives would allow families and citizens to be part of the destiny of their city and finally have a place for meeting and confrontation. The project 'Solo posti in piedi. Educare oltre i banchi' (standing places only – educating beyond desks) financed by the social enterprise Con i Bambini (With the Children), was born precisely with the intention of responding to this need. The project, conceived to fight educational poverty, was launched in December 2018 and ended in May 2021. Its specific objective was to bring children, families and the entire 'educational community' back to the centre of L'Aquila thanks to the co-management of a municipal toy library. It offers an accessible place to bring people together, promote culture and develop new forms of citizenship. The role of the University of L'Aquila as an active partner of the project is to give theoretical structure and scientific supervision to the project actions, enhancing their educational role from the perspective of social pedagogy. The crucial monitoring activity is under the direction of the Chair of General and Social Pedagogy, which has been supporting the project in its biennial development. In order to achieve the objectives, differentiated questionnaires were prepared for children, parents and teachers involved in the project. The target population was made up of parents, teachers and pupils from 30 target classes. The total number of pupils participating in the first year was 631, with 631 parents (one respondent per household) and 30 teachers (one for each class considered) – with a total of 1,292 subjects. More specifically, in the first year (from January to May 2019), the project activity related to laboratories in schools, while the survey was interrupted in its second year due to the COVID-19 emergency and is currently being reprogrammed.

According to the data produced by these studies, although more than 10 years have now passed, the issue of the earthquake remains central and keeps resurfacing in conversations about its consequences and effects. In fact, the point of view of the teachers participating in the project is quite clear on this topic. To the question: 'In your opinion, are the social, economic and urban problems caused by the 2009 earthquake still weighing on the wellbeing of the population?' 58.62 per cent of the teachers answered 'moderately' and 41.38 per cent answered 'very'; while none answered 'not at all' or 'slightly' (Figure 18.1).

Looking to the future, from the point of view of the parents surveyed, it is possible to detect perplexity about the opportunities provided by the territory of L'Aquila for minors while they recognise its resources with regard to quality of life and livability (Figure 18.2).

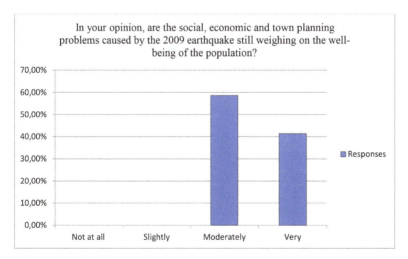

Figure 18.1 Teachers' survey question: 'In your opinion, are the social, economic and urban problems caused by the 2009 earthquake still weighing on the wellbeing of the population?'

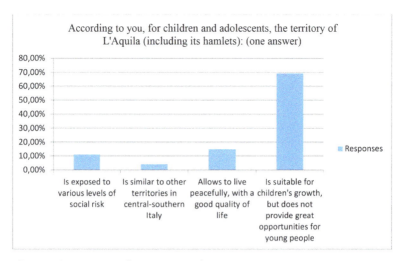

Figure 18.2 Parents' survey question.

The qualitative data resulting from the questionnaire addressed to children, in particular in relation to the question: 'When you think of your city, what are the first three words that come to mind?' are of great interest. Analysing the frequency of recurrent words in the children's choices and grouping them with similar terms referable to the same category of interpretation, we created a word cloud (Figure 18.3). The bigger and bolder the word, the more often it is mentioned. 'Beautiful' is the most mentioned word followed by 'ancient', which underlines the sense of belonging to a city that draws its beauty from its historical, cultural and artistic roots. L'Aquila, with its many monuments and buildings of artistic and architectural interest, has one of the largest historic centres in Italy. Children recognise these elements and use them as keywords to describe their city. The third most mentioned word is 'earthquake', followed by other earthquake-related terms. Taking into account that the age of the children surveyed ranges from 8 to 11 years old, it must be explained that none of them can have any memory of the event experienced at first-hand. Yet, observing the word cloud, the acquisition of a terminology that closely describes the emergency and post-emergency situation is evident. Continuous reference is made to the destruction and sadness that can be traced back to this specific disaster. Other significant terms are 'reconstructed,' 'rebirth' and 'crane', which have now become the symbol of the ongoing reconstruction. The sense of city and citizenship of these children, whom we could define as 'children of the earthquake', is still expressed through a strong identity link with the earthquake and its consequences, underlining how the critical issues related to the emergency are constantly present and perceivable. They maintain a substratum that risks chronifying some of the aspects of the emergency and thus marking generations, communities and territories. This outcome is also due to specific political, social, economic or urban choices that continue to significantly affect the dimensions of educational poverty or inhibit actions to counteract it. Alongside this topic, it is interesting to observe the children's sensitivity towards ecological and environmental issues. Among their most mentioned words are 'nature' and 'mountain', identified as fundamental elements of this territory. These are followed by 'pollution' and 'smog', while the adjective 'dirty' is mentioned frequently. The children show awareness of these themes and demonstrate an interest in collective issues, with positive and collaborative energy aimed at reconstructing a participatory and active social fabric.

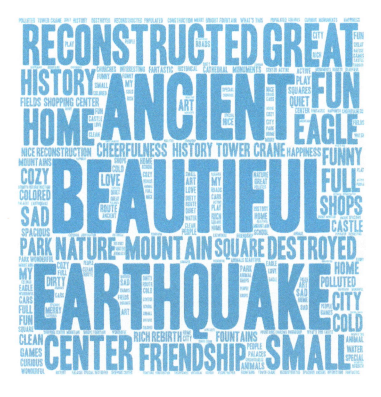

Figure 18.3 Word cloud: 'When you think of your city, what are the first three words that come to mind?'

To conclude the passage on the key words related to the city, it might be useful to note that the recurrent use of the word 'home' makes it a starting point for dealing with the theme of the role of the city as a 'safe base'. Approaching Bowlby's concept of attachment,[16] the city is seen as a place to have experiences, learn, have fun, stop, rest, build solid relationships, feel safe. The concept of the city as an educational space and community should imply greater awareness of and responsibility for all these dimensions, for developing all those elements that constitute and strengthen individual and social wellbeing. It should promote actions to actively combat educational poverty and also to prevent it. The nature of the bond with the city must be solid and stable, but never closed and rigid. In fact, the 'safe base' feature refers to a place from which to start, and to which to return, during the process of exploration of and openness to the world. The city, both through the design of its places and through the activity of its educating community, must act as an imprinter and incubator of solidary values that find their highest expression and application 'outside' the city. The city forms its citizens just as a family inculcates values in its members. These concepts assume greater significance if we broaden our gaze from this specific emergency to all those emergencies experienced by individuals, families or other groups, generated by inequality and marginality.

Conclusions

What we have said so far leads us to stress the principles of equity that imply social inclusion as a value that territories should promote. Martha Nussbaum[17] places the issue of inclusion – in terms of extended education, healthcare, political rights, freedom and equal citizenship rights – among the major problems of social injustice still unsolved today. The philosopher identifies the need for a reformulation of the theoretical approaches linked to the concepts of citizenship, social cooperation and care as a primary social good. She defines the dimension of care as a framework in which to insert an educational relationship oriented towards justice. There is therefore the need for the construction (and reconstruction) of a global educational environment characterised by equity, able to identify itself with individual identity narratives. This would enhance resources and support for those resilient[18] and resistant processes necessary to achieve the wellbeing of children, their families and their community of reference, with an integrated and participatory perspective.[19] In Dewey's melioristic perspective, all this is embodied in a view that places the school at the centre of this process, not only as the product of a substantially democratic system, but also as an active promoter of democracy. The school should in fact be capable of relaunching democracy in its best forms, becoming a social and political 'laboratory'. A school that dialogues with the territory and creates a 'whole' with the educational community, sharing responsibilities and actions in full continuity and educational integration.

These themes are still strongly debated today in L'Aquila, where the connections between visible and invisible reconstruction should find synthesis in a pedagogical work that aims to follow and support the reconstruction of a city seen as an educational context. It is important to take into account all those transversal aspects that can guarantee the quality of the educational experiences concerning sociality, sharing and the construction of both individual and collective ideas of citizenship and democracy. We are talking about a 'quality educational environment' that offers its users a positive perception of its 'total social order'[20] made up of relationships with other actors, the feeling of full involvement in experiences, the emotions it arouses and the resulting sense of self-efficacy. In essence, an environment that contains a set of positive interactions capable of satisfying the wide range of needs of an individual. The level of perceived wellbeing will therefore be closely related to education opportunities, which interdependently involve the school, the family and the territory as areas of production and enjoyment of educational experiences.

The issues dealt with in this chapter are deeply intertwined with the global health emergency that is affecting societies and causing a dramatic widening of social and health inequalities. The close link between emergencies and educational poverty is underlined by worrying economic data showing a significant increase in households in absolute poverty. This goes hand in hand with alarming data related to the digital divide[21] and the progressive reduction of egalitarian and democratic processes at the basis of access to education, knowledge and culture.[22] Amartya Sen,[23] describing the measures taken by the British government during the Second World War (in terms of fair distribution of food, healthcare and policies to address the material difficulties faced by the entire society), concludes that disasters can either increase social inequalities, or provide an opportunity to remove imbalances, improving fairness in the distribution of resources and strengthening the sense of social cohesion of the population. Following Sen's line of reasoning, it might not be utopian to think about the possibility of supporting resilience through political choices that structurally modify – in response to specific needs – the realities of micro and macro contexts. All this would support the aim of breaking the vicious circle of the social reproduction of inequality by enhancing individual potentialities in a context of educational equality.

Notes

1 Klein, *Shock Economy. L'ascesa Del Capitalismo Dei Disastri*, 185.
2 Puglielli, 'L'Aquila 2009. Shock Economy e Rischi Di Marginalità Sociale Tra La Popolazione Adulta', 239.
3 Calandra, Gonzàlez, Vaccarelli, *L'educazione Outdoor: Territorio, Cittadinanza, Identità Plurali Fuori Dalle Aule Scolastiche.*
4 Di Genova, Ferretti, Puglielli, 'Educare per ricostruire: i bambini nel post-sisma aquilano', 493.
5 Vaccarelli, 'La Generazione Dei Senza-Città. I Bambini All'Aquila Dopo Il Terremoto', 729.
6 Frabboni, Guerra, *La Città Educativa: Verso Un Sistema Formativo Integrato,* 51.
7 Dewey, *The school and society*, 59.
8 Vaccarelli 'Emotions and Representations of "the City" after the 2009 Earthquake in L'Aquila: Children, Education and Social Re-Construction in a Post-Catastrophe Context', 2015, 83.
9 Vaccarelli, Ciccozzi, Fiorenza, 'Resilienza, Socialità e Intervento Pedagogico a Cinque Anni Dal Sisma Dell'Aquila Del 2009: Una Ricerca-Azione Nelle Scuole Primarie', 2016, 101.
10 Save the Children, 'La Lampada Di Aladino. L'indice Di Save the Children per Misurare Le Povertà Educative e Illuminare Il Futuro Dei Bambini in Italia', 2014, 4.
11 Franzini, Raitano, 'L'istruzione Dei Genitori e Dei Figli. Disuguaglianze Che Persistono', 2007, 258.
12 Nuzzaci, *Patrimoni Culturali, Educazioni, Territori: Verso Un'idea Di Multiliteracy*, 35.
13 Alivernini, Manganelli, Lucidi, 'Dalla Povertà Educativa Alla Valutazione Del Successo Scolastico: Concetti, Indicatori e Strumenti Validati a Livello Nazionale', 2017, 35.
14 Benvenuto, *La scuola diseguale. Dispersione ed equità nel sistema di istruzione e formazione*, 54.
15 Di Genova, 'Uno Studio Sulla Povertà Educativa All'Aquila. Scuola Ed Extrascuola Nella Percezione Dei Genitori Italiani e Di Altra Cittadinanza', 185.
16 Bowlby, *Una Base Sicura*, 25.
17 Nussbaum, *Le Nuove Frontiere Della Giustizia. Disabilità, Nazionalità, Appartenenza Di Specie*, 425.
18 Malaguti, *Educarsi Alla Resilienza: Come Affrontare Crisi e Difficoltà e Migliorarsi,* 12.
19 Vaccarelli, *Le prove della vita*, 94.
20 Dewey, *Esperienza e Educazione*, 32.
21 ISTAT, 'Spazi in Casa e Disponibilità Di Computer per Bambini e Ragazzi per Gli Anni 2018–2019', 3.
22 Save the Children, 'Secondo Rapporto «Non Da Soli» Cosa Dicono Le Famiglie', 2.
23 Sen, *Lo sviluppo è libertà,* 55.

Bibliography

Alivernini, F., Manganelli, S. and Lucidi, F. 'Dalla Povertà educativa alla valutazione del successo scolastico: concetti, indicatori e strumenti validati a livello nazionale'. *Journal of Educational, Cultural and Psychological Studies (ECPS Journal),* 1(15) (2017): 21–52.
Benvenuto, G., ed. *La Scuola Diseguale*. Dispersione ed equità nel sistema di istruzione e formazione. Roma: Anicia, 2011.
Benvenuto, G. (ed.) *Stili e Metodi Della Ricerca Educativa*. Roma: Carocci, 2015.
Bowlby, J. *Una Base Sicura*. Milano: Raffaello Cortina, 1989.
Calandra, L.M. 2012. *Territorio e Democrazia. Un Laboratorio Di Geografia Sociale Nel Dopossisma Aquilano*. L'Aquila: L'Una, 2012.
Calandra, L.M., Aja, T.G. and Vaccarelli, G. *L'educazione Outdoor: Territorio, Cittadinanza, Identità Plurali Fuori Dalle Aule Scolastiche*. Lecce: Pensa Multimendia, 2016.
Crocetti, G. *Il bambino nella pioggia. Il significato del disegno infantile nel dialogo terapeutico*, Armando Editori, 1991.
Cyrulnik, B. 'Abbandono e Tutori Di Resilienza'. In *Costruire La Resilienza. La Riorganizzazione Positiva Della Vita e La Creazione Di Legami Positivi*, edited by Boris Cyrulnik and Elena Malaguti. Trento: Erickson, 2005.

Cyrulnik, B. and Malaguti, E. (eds) *Costruire La Resilienza. La Riorganizzazione Positiva Della Vita e La Creazione Di Legami Significativi*. Edizioni Erickson, 2005.

Dewey, J. *The school and society*. 1899. Roma: Newton Compton, 1976.

Dewey, J. *Esperienza e Educazione*. 1938. Milano: Raffaello Cortina, 2014.

Di Genova, N. 'Uno Studio Sulla Povertà Educativa All'Aquila. Scuola Ed Extrascuola Nella Percezione Dei Genitori Italiani e Di Altra Cittadinanza'. In *Intercultura e Scuola. Scenari, Ricerche, Percorsi Pedagogici*, edited by Silvia Nanni and Alessandro Vaccarelli. Milano: FrancoAngeli, n.d.

Di Genova, N., Ferretti, M.G. and Puglielli, E. 'Educare per ricostruire: i bambini nel post-sisma aquilano'. In *Pedagogia, didattica e ricerca educativa: approcci, problemi e strumenti*, edited by Antonella Nuzzaci, 487–98. Lecce: Pensa MultiMedia, 2019.

Frabboni, F. and Guerra, L. *La Città Educativa: Verso Un Sistema Formativo Integrato*. Bologna: Cappelli, 1991.

Franzini, M. and Raitano, M. 'L'istruzione Dei Genitori e Dei Figli. Disuguaglianze Che Persistono'. *Meridiana* (2007): 2007, 257–291.

Iorio, C., Vaccarelli, A. and Mariantoni, S. 'La Relazione d'aiuto in Emergenza'. In *Individui, Comunità e Istituzioni in Emergenza. Intervento Psico-Socio-Pedagogico e Lavoro Di Rete Nelle Situazioni Di Catastrofe*. Milano: FrancoAngeli, 2018.

Isidori, M.V. and Vaccarelli, A. *Pedagogia Dell'emergenza/Didattica Nell'emergenza*. Milano: FrancoAngeli, 2013.

ISTAT. 'Spazi in Casa e Disponibilità Di Computer per Bambini e Ragazzi per Gli Anni 2018–2019'. ISTAT, 6 April 2020. Accessed 14 June 2022 https://www.istat.it/it/files//2020/04/Spazi-casa-disponibilita-computer-ragazzi.pdf.

Klein, N. *Shock Economy. L'ascesa Del Capitalismo Dei Disastri*. Milano: Rizzoli, 2007.

Lichtenberg, E.F. 'Draw-A-Person-in-the-Rain-Test'. In *Drawings in Assessment and Psychotherapy: Research and Application*, 164–83. New York, NY, US: Routledge/Taylor & Francis Group, 2014.

Malaguti, E. *Educarsi Alla Resilienza: Come Affrontare Crisi e Difficoltà e Migliorarsi*. Trento: Edizioni Erickson, 2005.

Mariantoni, S. and Vaccarelli, A. *Individui, Comunità e Istituzioni in Emergenza*. Milano: FrancoAngeli, 2018.

MIUR. 'Gli Alunni Con Cittadinanza Non Italiana. Anno Scolastico 2017/2018'. 2019. Page no longer available https://miur.gov.it/documents/20182/250189/Notiziario+Stranieri+1718.pdf/78ab5 3c4-dd30-0c0f-7f40-bf22bbcedfa6?version=1.1&t=1562782116429

Nussbaum, M.C. *Creare Capacità: Liberarsi Dalla Dittatura Del Pil*. Bologna: Il mulino, 2012.

Nussbaum, Martha Craven. *Le Nuove Frontiere Della Giustizia. Disabilità, Nazionalità, Appartenenza Di Specie*. Bologna: Il Mulino, 2007.

Nuzzaci, A. (ed.) *Patrimoni Culturali, Educazioni, Territori: Verso Un'idea Di Multiliteracy*. Lecce-Brescia: Pensa Multimedia, 2011.

Nuzzaci, A. (ed.) *Progettare, Pianificare e Valutare Gli Interventi Educativi*. Lecce-Brescia: Pensa MultiMedia, 2012.

Nuzzaci, A. (ed.) *Valutare La Qualità Dei Servizi Extrascolastici*. Roma: Kappa, 2006.

Puglielli, E. 'L'Aquila 2009. Shock Economy e Rischi Di Marginalità Sociale Tra La Popolazione Adulta'. In *Individui, Comunità e Istituzioni in Emergenza. Intervento Psico-Socio-Pedagogico e Lavoro Di Rete Nelle Situazioni Di Catastrofe*, edited by Alessandro Vaccarelli and Stefania Mariantoni. Milano: FrancoAngeli, 2018.

Save the Children. 'La Lampada Di Aladino. L'indice di Save the Children per Misurare Le Povertà Educative e Illuminare Il Futuro Dei Bambini in Italia.' Save the Children Italia Onlus, 2014. Accessed 14 June 2022 www.savethechildren.it/sites/default/files/files/uploads/pubblicazioni/la-lampada-di-aladino.pdf

Save the Children. 'Nuotare Contro Corrente Povertà Educativa e Resilienza in Italia'. Save the Children Italia Onlus, 2018. Accessed 14 June 2022 https://s3.savethechildren.it/public/files/uploads/pubblicazioni/nuotare-contro-corrente-poverta-educativa-e-resilienza-italia.pdf.

Save the Children. 'Secondo Rapporto «Non Da Soli» Cosa Dicono Le Famiglie'. Save the Children Italia Onlus, 2020. Accessed 14 June 2022 https://s3.savethechildren.it/public/files/uploads/pubblicazioni/secondo-rapporto-non-da-soli-cosa-dicono-le-famiglie.pdf

Sen, A. *L'idea di giustizia*. Milano: Mondadori, 2010.

Sen, A. *Lo Sviluppo è Libertà*. Milano: Mondadori, 2014.

Sen, A. *The Standard of Living*. New York: Cambridge University Press, 1988.

Vaccarelli, A. "Emotions and representations of "the city" after the 2009 earthquake in L'Aquila: children, education and social re-construction in a post-catastrophe context'. *Ricerche Di Pedagogia e Didattica. Journal of Theories and Research in Education*, 10(3) (2015): 81–118.

Vaccarelli, A. 'La Generazione Dei Senza-Città. I Bambini All'Aquila Dopo Il Terremoto'. In *Progetto Generazioni: Bambini e Anziani: Due Stagioni Della Vita a Confronto*, edited by Michele Corsi and Simonetta Ulivieri. Pisa: ETS, 2012.

Vaccarelli, A. *Le Prove Della Vita: Promuovere La Resilienza Nella Relazione Educativa*. Milano: F. Angeli, 2016.

Vaccarelli, A., Ciccozzi, C. and Fiorenza, A. 'Resilienza, Socialità e Intervento Pedagogico a Cinque Anni Dal Sisma Dell'Aquila Del 2009: Una Ricerca-Azione Nelle Scuole Primarie'. *Epidemiologia e Prevenzione*, 40(2) (2016): 98–103.

19
Existential and identity displacement in catastrophic events
Teacher training: skills and strategies for coping
Antonella Nuzzaci

Catastrophic events and literacy risk

Earthquakes, tsunamis, COVID-19: these are moments of great disorientation that force us to define new conditions for continuous learning, if we do not want to risk being swamped by events. In the presence of a pandemic or catastrophic event, the personal and social world of an individual is overwhelmed by a form of existential displacement that leads them to completely rethink the meanings of their actions and life. In the educational field, such situations constitute existential challenges. Teachers are called upon to redesign their professionalism through precise forms of reflection. They also have to develop interventions aimed at strengthening students' learning processes at different levels, helping them to connect the 'before', 'during' and 'after' of the catastrophic or pandemic event. One wonders, therefore, how it is possible for a teacher to continue to create authentic learning opportunities for all students at all school levels, primary and secondary, from the moment an event such as the COVID-19 pandemic event occurs, helping them in their progressive recovery related to the existential displacement that encompasses them.

After the first moments of uncertainty related to a crisis, there is always an attempt to support the condition of 'relational and social loss' with a lively preparation of 'lifelines', but this is not effective enough to

Figure 19.1 *San Francesco Solano indicates an earthquake next to Saints John the Evangelist and John the Baptist.* Giovanni Battista Tinti, *c. 1570*. Source: Wikimedia Commons.

keep alive an experiential, cultural and social fabric that often appears lost or altered in the perception of the individual.

Among the various 'lifelines' in the period of the COVID-19 pandemic, for example, technologies have been and continue to be a valid support for learning. However, if not used effectively from an educational point of view, they will end up widening the pre-existing gaps, extending the forms of exclusion borne by the weakest and increasing the divide between populations that can benefit from a certain economic wellbeing and *popolazioni di riserva* (reserve populations) who lack the means of subsistence and culture to be able to live adequately.

In the school environment, for teachers, the main question at this time continues to be how to restore forms of meaningful education that best support students in their process of overcoming difficulties following a critical event that lasts for a long time and makes them more vulnerable, often radically changing their thoughts, behaviours and attitudes.

Reflecting on the status of teaching and learning in such contexts recalls the issue of the skill-set that a teacher needs in their professional background in order to be able to promote – and continue to do so over time – the skills and psycho-physical wellbeing of all students. Not least of these is the family of competencies that revolve around the construct of resilience. This is because, in a time of crisis such as a disaster or pandemic, literacy processes are put to the test and the school population is exposed to literacy-risk conditions. Literacy is understood here as 'living literacy', which tends to include how people write and read their lives.[1] Underlying this concept is a form of knowledge that allows students to integrate literacy processes at deep levels of their personalities, as well as helping teachers to meaningfully structure their professionalism by also teaching students 'who they are and what they are'.[2] But literacy is also an essential human right and a 'treasure',[3] consisting of a repertoire of basic knowledge and skills that individuals need to live in a rapidly changing world and an indispensable condition for their ongoing participation in social, cultural, political and economic activities. Over time, it has become an essential tool for eliminating educational inequalities, through the development of policies and virtuous practices aimed at shaping the educational system. The relationship between literacy processes and emergencies calls for a distinction between natural disasters and pandemics, as well as clarification of the multifactorial nature of the literacy construct. The complexity of the concept of emergency varies in relation to the different situations of vulnerability involved.

However, vulnerability implies an idea of 'risk education', which sees individuals and communities able to perceive and interpret the difficulties to which they are exposed in the vulnerable environment, and to make appropriate decisions generated by this awareness.

Activating quality literacy processes during and after a catastrophic or pandemic event is an arduous but indispensable task if education is to succeed in helping people to cope with the difficulties, crises and challenges that societies, communities and the environment present to them on a day-to-day basis. It is very difficult for a teacher to activate quality teaching processes in a situation of crisis, looking for the meanings of what is happening, has happened, or will happen – when it is in fact only possible to give an account of everything that is happening and its implications. This is particularly true when you are trying to make students understand how important it is for them to continue learning by helping them to manage thoughts and emotions.

Pandemic or catastrophe experiences leave indelible marks in people's lives and in the cultural and social context in which they live, opening internal and external cracks that make them more vulnerable from that moment on, in the face of subsequent events. In education, they challenge the entire repertoire of teachers' skills, and confront them, both during and after the pandemic or disaster, with a series of problems related to the ability to manage uncertainty in everyday life. These problems concern how to:

a)   use their own knowledge to solve problems concerning the sense of belonging and identity of themselves and their students, undermined by the emptiness that is created
b)   resist the temptation to give in to fatalism
c)   not feel useless with respect to the cultural proposals to be implemented
d)   activate appropriate decision-making processes
e)   explain phenomena with a series of hypotheses, and so on.

By compromising the emotional–relational and social dimension, which continually interferes with the cognitive one, pandemic or catastrophic events can lead individuals to have perceptions of low efficacy, thoughts of immobility in action, paralysis, inactivity, stasis, anger and so on, which prevent them from interacting correctly and pertinently in everyday contexts.

Let's think about what has happened in schools during the COVID-19 emergency period, when technologies have become all-embracing and it is understood that, if not well governed, they can end up worsening the state of disorientation of teachers and students, and their families, putting teachers in the condition of feeling unable to support the cultural, emotional and social needs of their students. Teachers are in fact required, above all, to be reliable and able to govern teaching by adopting appropriate strategies and forms of modelling to give students the ability to analyse what has happened and objectify it.

Recognition and taking charge of students' difficulties and early educational intervention are central, especially in the first moments following the occurrence of the pandemic or catastrophic event. This requires the identification of information that comes from multiple sources and demands critical analysis of its veracity. The first problem concerns the area of 'desirable learning', within which to redirect students' engagement with what they do and who they are. The main concerns of teachers then are: how best to support students' learning when much of their confidence has been undermined by uncertainty; how to continue to foster in them a desire to learn and to make good use of knowledge and literacy processes now and in the future; and most importantly how to encourage them to rediscover and maintain a focus on life.

In the face of catastrophic events, it becomes essential to develop well-structured training interventions directed at supporting teachers' efforts to reduce, mitigate and manage post-traumatic stress in positive ways. These training interventions help teachers to speed-up recovery, maintain relationships with others, develop coping skills, recover from adversity, prepare for possible future experiences and adapt effectively. At the same time, they can provide them with meaningful opportunities for recovery and improvement of their practices through professional learning pathways to help address further problematic situations. Although the literature does not always agree as to which modes of intervention are most effective in emergencies, there is consensus that one of the most effective ways to improve educational assistance during or after disasters is precisely to support those who work directly with children and youth,[4] who often report themselves as unprepared to cope.[5]

In the analysis conducted by Mundy and Dryden-Peterson[6] on education in contexts of environmental fragility, it emerges how, in the moments following a disaster, the general focus is mainly on daily needs – provision of housing, security and food – but not on the support of parents or teachers. Parents, who are caught up in other pressing problems, on one hand would like their children to continue going to school, even amidst fears and uncertainties, and on the other are unable to fully accept this because of their personal concerns about safety (as evident in the COVID-19 pandemic).

For teachers and school leaders, risk education is sometimes even considered unnecessary. Instead, Moorosi and Bush[7] believe it is essential to increase knowledge and interventions in this area at all levels and for all, especially in leadership processes,[8] while recognising the complexity of the various interacting factors – political, social, and economic – that influence the overall situation. Similarly, Brooks and Normore[9] make the case for leadership based on local problems and global risks, requiring teachers and leaders to expand their understanding of catastrophic and pandemic phenomena in order to intervene at the local level in increasingly precise ways.[10] This highlights the importance of supporting these figures in local contexts, even where resources are scarce. School communities facing crisis situations require various stakeholders to have rapid responses involving decision-making, planning and foresight skills that, if not present, could expose them and others to serious risk.[11] Possessing appropriate skills to deal with 'a crisis'[12] becomes, therefore, the best defence for understanding the consequences it could have for the school and its population if not adequately addressed.[13] Schools can prevent individuals from constructing beliefs and misconceptions and assuming incorrect attitudes and behaviours in situations, thus ensuring that harm can be minimised.[14]

The unpredictability of pandemic or catastrophic events leads to the question of how to prepare for each possible event, anticipating the crisis without being overwhelmed by it.[15] However, while planning plays a very important role, the way leadership skills are managed during and immediately after a 'critical' event plays a significant role in its outcome.[16] The same applies to the way in which educational communities support individuals in an attempt to increase their responsiveness,[17] triggering the action of various stakeholders to overcome specific difficulties. In fact, communities that are successful in networking also increase their ability to be responsive to aid operations and to be resilient.[18] With the occurrence of a critical event, strong relational responses between people, organisations and local emergency management groups can be produced, before and during the event. Crises – as evidenced by COVID-19 – cause people to increase their zest for life and support for the community to which they belong. However, crises do not always succeed in developing identity processes that push the community to participate in an 'identity refounding'.

How to train teachers to become resilient?

Traditionally, studies of catastrophic events have focused on the analysis of post-traumatic stress disorder (PTSD),[19] in which the role of resilience is recognised as a protective factor for an individual's mental health and quality of life. Resilience is generally defined as a dynamic process of positive adaptation in the face of exposure to adversity,[20] trauma or tragedy, threats, or other significant sources of stress,[21] as well as resilience or coping with experiences of crisis or environmental risk. It asserts itself in an experiential continuum that can occur to different degrees and in different domains of life. Resilient behaviour is traced to skills that enable an individual to effectively withstand adversity based on the ability to make and implement realistic plans, manage their feelings and impulses in a healthy manner, have good communication skills,[22] have confidence in their strengths and abilities, and be capable of problem solving. In essence, resilience appears to be a continuously developing multidimensional construct[23] that involves positive responses to significant adversity and is characterised as a dynamic process within a system of interrelationships influenced by the interaction between the individual and the environment and that means it can be fostered, nurtured, and improved.[24] It differs from traditional concepts of risk and protection in its focus on individual variation in response to comparable experiences. Consequently, training leaders and teachers in resilience could be understood as building resilience to hazards that may result from controlled exposure to risk, rather than avoidance of risk, as well as acquisition of concrete coping strategies rather than assessment of external risks or protective factors.

Risk and protective factors influencing resilience interact with other components that influence them. In major disasters (such as earthquakes), individual developmental pressures and problems are considered more severe risk factors the lower the age.[25] In fact, school-age children appear to be more likely than adults to experience severe problems after a disaster (62 per cent and 39 per cent, respectively), with negative cognitive effects in some areas such as memory, learning and school performance and increased risk for later development.[26] This is also evident in the COVID-19 pandemic regime, where children and young people have been shown to be overwhelmed by such large-scale disruption to their daily lives. However, it is important to note the differences between disaster and pandemic: while in the former, following the traumatic event, teachers should be prepared to facilitate a rapid return to normal routine and school functioning, possibly maintaining some form of pre-disaster order within their interventions, in the latter this is not always possible. Identifying urgent solutions seems critical, as in both disaster and pandemic cases, physical, economic and social losses affect individuals and communities, disrupting their daily lives and human activities.

For this reason, the structures and resources of the school community must be used to support children and young people who may present difficulties of a different order (such as concentration or behavioural problems),[27] which end up emerging at school.[28] Facilitating peer interactions and activating the social support network within and outside of school and family allows all intervening professionals, particularly in the post-disaster phase, to help children and young people restore a fabric of rules and routines within the family that reinforce perceptions of normality.[29] The support that teachers can give students to strengthen the bond with their peers becomes central – and not to be underestimated – to prevent them from perceiving themselves as 'survivors' of a crisis. Thus, for a teacher, talking with students and having them talk with others who have gone or are going through similar experiences helps to reassure them in responding and reacting to the event,[30] in terms of any inappropriate attitudes and behaviours they might have assumed.[31] The effectiveness of teachers, therefore, depends on the quality of the interventions they are able to activate during and after the emergency, and this ability is obviously linked to their preparation to deal with problems of this kind.

With this in mind, at the height of the pandemic in the 2020 lockdown in Italy, at the regional and national levels, a series of training days were carried out by a group of academics, led by the author of this paper, which focused on supporting teachers 'in a stressful situation' while delivering only online teaching and where decision-making was related to a high degree of accountability and a number of systemic factors (heavy use of technology, redesign of teaching, lack of social support, integration of children with special needs, effective management of learning environments, etc.). This was training in the use of coping strategies as a form of situated learning in 'real teaching life' and in teachers' interaction with students. The training was preceded by a preliminary phase of preparation and knowledge of such strategies in an effort to conceptualise the stressful to learn how to be proactive in situations. This has produced significant results in terms of the acquisition of techniques and tools for coping with difficulties, implementing a 'generative social practice' through which the teacher gradually learns to rationalise and assess the risk in the situation, but above all to control their 'doing teaching' while teaching in new environments and contexts through technologies. The survey on teachers' perception of the pandemic emergency prior to the training had revealed the strong pressure that teachers were under at that time and the appreciation for the training space that supported them in such a difficult time for them in which they felt abandoned, by institutions. A group of teachers, about 30 per cent of the total number of participants (554), considered teaching such a stressful job in that situation, that they would have wanted to abandon it or were tempted to do so. Eighty-five per cent raised questions about the stability of the school and its resources to provide an education that could be called such, questioning the integrity of the education system as a whole and its functionality in delivering quality training.

To broaden the comparison, the training was concluded with a self-examination of pandemic-period lifestyle, which helped to alleviate the general malaise felt by teachers at work with the aim of making them feel less alone. This approach stood in continuity with all those studies and scientific orientations that look at supporting teachers 'in action' through interventions aimed at preventing, decreasing, eliminating or managing stress in situations, and those training programmes that may be able to influence the way in which stress is managed through the use of a series of techniques and tools[32] capable of reducing the phenomenon.

Studies clearly show how all those programmes that have been directed at broadening the participation in schools – even with different perspectives and strategies – have shown a significant correlation with reductions in PTSD, depression and pain. Teachers, in fact, can guide students toward understanding more painful experiences, using their efforts to achieve positive outcomes under adverse conditions. Within this interpretive framework, strengthening the teachers' skills in facilitating the development and implementation of positive daily behaviours must be integrated within a developmental vision, which leverages active coping, mutually supportive actions, trust in existing resources and resilience.

The family of competencies related to the ability to 'withstand work adversity', which are connected to the individual responses that take place in context with the goal of preserving the quality of teaching under conditions of instability and trauma, concern what Palmer[33] calls the 'courage to teach'. This perspective of broadening the cultural horizon of teachers in terms of 'educational risk management' could equip them with the ability to build decision-making and planning processes to transform the culture of teaching into a form of 'preventive action' based on the acquisition of techniques for coping with difficulties. However, in Italy this has not been taken into account, even in highly vulnerable territories and even after the enactment of Law No. 249 of 2010, which regulated the official recognition of teaching as a profession in society.

The methodologically resilient teacher

In an emergency, the system of social[34] and cultural support that a school community implements for children and young people before a crisis – in a preventive dimension – is as important as post-emergency interventions. We need only look at the experience of L'Aquila in 2009 and its follow-up studies on the interventions implemented – among which the most incisive concerns the training of teachers and the ability to integrate their efforts by reactivating the function of mediation with children and young people – in an attempt to provide children with relief and wellbeing. Here, it is a matter of pursuing resilience training. This sees in the positive correlation between trauma and resilience[35] the possibility that the former may cause an individual to change their assessment of the latter, making that individual stronger when facing adversity[36] and not subject to burnout.[37] Protective factors related to resilience include optimism, finding purpose in life, internal control skills, self-efficacy, sociability, goal achievement, personal contributions (as well as awareness of these situations, one's emotions, and behaviours), family support skills, school experiences, community–parent–child relationships,[38] relationships with colleagues or alumni, ability to implement intervention projects in schools[39] and teacher support.[40]

The nature of teacher resilience is crucial in situations where children and young people have experienced trauma and conflict, thus it is necessary to understand what kinds of skills they need to act professionally in the right way, starting with the fact that a teacher's resilient qualities are associated with, and shaped by, the professional context in which they operate. Although studies are still in their infancy, evidence confirms that resilience is not only associated with personal attributes,[41] but can be understood as 'a social construction'[42] that is influenced by several factors.

It is well known, for example, that managerial support of learning within the school, training, confidence in leadership, and positive feedback from parents and students act positively on motivation and resilience,[43] just as it is equally well known that judgement and recognition from 'significant others' helps to increase teachers' individual and collective resilience,[44] allowing them to maintain their commitment to teaching practices even under difficult conditions.[45] Teachers' resilience is, therefore, not simply associated with their ability to recover from traumatic events, but rather with their ability to manage and maintain their balance and ethical commitment in everyday life. It shows a close link to self-efficacy, which appears to be the factor that, more than any other, influences teachers' beliefs related to their ability to help their students find their way to goals effectively. Furthermore, research findings suggest how early teacher-mediated instructional intervention at school actually facilitates the activation of an overall improvement process of reducing trauma associated with the emergency. This would lead to the assumption of more adaptive attitudes and behaviours in learners, allowing them to achieve positive psychosocial and educational goals (coping area).

Educational action, aimed at expanding coping strategies and releasing the greatest amount of cognitive and affective resources in students, succeeds in promoting positive adaptation in students when it is activated early and in a meaningful way through the use of proactive measures that leverage cross-system collaboration (psychological, medical, educational) with the help of culturally adapted, empirically validated and ready-to-use intervention protocols.

Conclusions

At times when pandemics or catastrophes threaten individuals, claiming large numbers of human victims and leaving indelible traces on people, environments and territories, education appears to be the most responsible and viable preventive solution, where teachers become stable and reliable references for both children and parents, providing them with a sense of security.[46] Making psycho-pedagogical support available to teachers who experience the same difficulties as their students[47] would allow them to choose the best teaching and relational strategies to promote self-management and individual and social awareness in their students, the very building blocks of resilience. This confirms schools as ideal places to understand what a disaster or pandemic is, how it occurs, how it affects the environment and people, what kind of actions should be implemented to protect oneself from it, and what material and human resources should be employed to carry out appropriate interventions that help rebuild the personal and social identity of individuals within the community to which they belong.[48]

Notes

1 Neilsen, *Literacy and living: the literate lives of three adults*.
2 Nuzzaci, *Competenze riflessive tra professionalità educative e insegnamento*.
3 Delors, *Learning: the treasure within. Report to UNESCO of the International Commission on Education for the Twenty-first Century*.
4 Gordon, Farberow and Maida, *Children and disasters*.
5 Gainey, 'Crisis management's new role in educational settings', 2009, 267–274.
6 Mundy and Dryden-Peterson, *Educating children in conflict zones: research, policy and practice for systemic change – a tribute to Jackie Kirk*.
7 Moorosi and Bush, 'School leadership development in Commonwealth countries: learning across boundaries', 2011, 59–75.
8 Moorosi and Bush, 'School leadership development in Commonwealth countries: learning across boundaries', 2011, 72.
9 Brooks and Normore, 'Educational leadership and globalization: toward a glocal perspective', 2010, 52–82.
10 Brooks and Normore, 'Educational leadership and globalization: toward a glocal perspective', 2010, 74.
11 Gainey, 'Crisis management's new role in educational settings', 267–274; Whitla, *Crisis management and the school community*.
12 Smith and Riley, 'School leadership in times of crisis', 2012, 57–71.
13 Özgüven and Öztürk, 'Effects of basic earthquake awareness education to given primary school students', 2006, 1–6.
14 Aydın, 'The perceptions of primary education eighth grade students towards "earthquake": a phenomenographic analysis', 2010, 801–817.
15 Smith and Riley, 'School leadership in times of crisis', 2012, 57–71.
16 Schoenberg, 'Do crisis plans matter? A new perspective on leading during a crisis', 2005, 2–6.
17 Whitla, *Crisis management and the school community*.
18 Weick and Sutcliffe, *Managing the unexpected: resilient performance in an age of uncertainty..*
19 Nader, Pynoos, Fairbanks, and Frederick, 'Children's PTSD reactions one year after a sniper attack on their school', 1990, 1526–1530.
20 Masten, 'Global perspectives on resilience in children and youth', 2014, 6–20.
21 Southwick, Bonanno, Masten, Panter-Brick and Yehuda, 'Resilience definitions, theory, and challenges: interdisciplinary perspectives', 2014, 1–14.
22 Coombs and Holladay, Communication and attributions in a crisis: an experimental study of crisis communication', 1996, 279–295.
23 Luthar, Cicchetti and Becker, 'The construct of resilience: a critical evaluation and guidelines for future work', 2000, 543-562.
24 Cefai, 'Pupil resilience in the classroom', 2004, 149–170.
25 Norris, Byrne, Diaz and Kaniasty, 'The range, magnitude, and duration of effects of natural and human-caused disasters: a review of the empirical literature', 2001.
26 Schwartz and Perry, 'The post-traumatic response in children and adolescents', 1994, 311–326.
27 Hofler, 'Psychological resilience building in disaster risk reduction: contributions from adult education', 2014, 33–40.
28 Pfefferbaum, 'Posttraumatic stress disorder in children: a review of the past 10 years', 1997, 1503–1511.
29 Klingman, 'School-based intervention following a disaster'.
30 Vogel and Vernberg, 'Children's psychological responses to disaster', 1993, 470–484.
31 Yule and Williams, 'Post-traumatic stress reactions in children', 1990, 279–295.
32 Benvenuto, Di Genova, Nuzzaci and Vaccarelli, 'Scala di Resilienza professionale degli Insegnanti prima validazione nazionale', 2021, 201–218.
33 Palmer, *The courage to teach: exploring the inner landscape of a teacher's life*.
34 Vernberg, La Greca, Silverman and Prinstein, 'Prediction of posttraumatic stress symptoms in children after Hurricane Andrew', 1996, 237–248.
35 Scali, Gandubert, Ritchie, Soulier, Ancelin and Chaudieu, I. 'Measuring resilience in adult women using the 10-items Connor-Davidson Resilience Scale (CD-RISC)'.

36 Seery, Holman, and Silver, 'Whatever does not kill us: cumulative lifetime adversity, vulnerability, and resilience', 2010, 1025-1041; Nuzzaci and Marcozzi, 'Fattori di rischio scolastici e abbandono della percezione degli studenti: il progetto internazionale ERASMUS KA2 ACCESS', 2019, 48–68.

37 Oliva, Murdaca, and Nuzzaci, 'Fattori individuali e contestuali nel *burnout* degli insegnanti', 2014, 99–120.

38 Vanderbilt-Adriance and Shaw, 'Protective factors and the development of resilience in the context of neighborhood disadvantage', 2008, 887–901.

39 Winje and Ulvik, 'Confrontations with reality: crisis intervention services for traumatised families after a school bus accident in Norway', 1995, 429–444.

40 Wolmer, Laor and Yazgan, 'School reactivation programs after disaster: could teachers serve as clinical mediators?', 2003, 363–381.

41 Luthar and Brown, 'Maximizing resilience through diverse levels of inquiry: prevailing paradigms, possibilities, and priorities for the future', 2007, 931–955.

42 Ungar, 'A constructionist discourse on resilience: multiple contexts, multiple realities among at-risk children and youth', 2004, 342.

43 Brunetti, 'Resilience under fire: perspectives on the work of experienced, inner city high school teachers in the United States', 2006, 812–825.

44 Day and Gu, 'Challenges to teacher resilience: conditions count', 2013, 22–44.

45 Brunetti, 'Resilience under fire: perspectives on the work of experienced, inner city high school teachers in the United States', 2006, 813.

46 Vogel and Vernberg, 'Children's psychological responses to disaster', 1993, 470–484.

47 Wolmer, Laor, and Yazgan, 'School reactivation programs after disaster: could teachers serve as clinical mediators?', 2003, 363–381.

48 Nuzzaci, 'Patrimoni locali, identità e linguaggi: educare "ai e con i" beni culturali e ambientali in aree ad elevata fragilità', 213–229.

References

Aydın, F. '"Earthquake" Perceptions of primary education eighth grade students: a phenomenographic analysis'. *Turkish Studies International Periodical for the Languages, Literature and History of Turkish or Turkic* 5 (3) (2010): 801–817.

Brooks, J.S. and Normore, A.H. 'Educational leadership and globalization: Literacy for a glocal perspective'. *Educational Policy* 24 (1) (2010): 52–82.

Brunetti, G.J. 'Resilience under fire: perspectives on the work of experienced, inner city high school teachers in the United States'. *Teaching and Teacher Education* 22 (7) (2006): 812–825.

Cefai, C. 'Pupil resilience in the classroom'. *Emotional and Behavioural Difficulties* 9 (3) (2004):149–170.

Coombs, W.T. and Holladay, S.J. 'Communication and attributions in a crisis: an experimental study of crisis communication'. *Journal of Public Relations Research,* 8 (4) (1996): 279–295.

Delors, J. *Learning: the treasure within. Teport to UNESCO of the International Commission on Education for the Twenty-first Century.* Paris: UNESCO, 1996.

Gainey, V.S. 'Crisis management's new role in educational settings'. *The Clearing House,* 82 (6) (2009): 267–274.

Gordon, N., Farberow, N.L. and Maida, C.A. *Children and disasters.* New York, NY: Brunner/Mazel Inc. 1999.

Gu, Q. and Day, C. 'Challenges to teacher resilience: conditions count'. *British Educational Research Journal* 39 (1) (2013): 22–44.

Hofler, M. 'Psychological resilience building in disaster risk reduction: contributions from adult education'. *Journal of Disaster Risk Science,* 5 (1) (2014): 33–40.

Kirikkaya, E.B., Çakin, O., Imali, B. and Bozkurt, E. 'Earthquake training is gaining importance: the views of 4th and 5th year students on Earthquake'. *Procedia – Social and Behavioral Sciences,* 15 (2011): 2305–2313.

Klingman, A. 'School-based intervention following a disaster'. In *Children and disaster,* edited by Conway F. Saylor, pp. 187–210. New York: Plenum Press, 1993.

Leeder, J. 'Teaching without schools: Haiti after the earthquake'. *Professionally Speaking,* 2010. Accessed 15 June 2022 http://professionallyspeaking.oct.ca/september_2010/features/haiti.aspx.

Lepore, S.J. and Revenson, T.A. 'Resilience and posttraumatic growth: recovery, resistance, and reconfiguration'. In *Handbook of posttraumatic growth: Research & practice,* edited by Lawrence Calhoun and Richard G. Tedeschi, pp. 24–46. Mahwah, NJ: Lawrence Erlbaum, 2006.

Liu, Q., He, F., Jiang, M. and Zhou, Y. 'Longitudinal study on adolescents' psychological resilience and it impact factor sin 5.12earthquake-hit areas'. *Journal of Hygiene Research* 42 (6) (2013): 950–954.

Luthar, S.S. and Brown, P.J. 'Maximizing resilience through diverse levels of inquiry: prevailing paradigms, possibilities, and priorities for the future'. *Development and Psychopathology, 19*(3) (2007): 931–955.

Luthar, S.S., Cicchetti, D. and Becker, B. 'The construct of resilience: a critical evaluation and guidelines for future work'. *Child Development* 71 (3) (2000) 543–62.

Masten, A.S. 'Global perspectives on resilience in children and youth'. *Child Development* 85 (1) (2014): 6–20.

Moorosi, P. and Bush, T. 'School leadership development in Commonwealth countries: learning across boundaries'. *International Studies in Educational Administration* 38 (3) (2011): 59–75.

Mundy, K. and Dryden-Peterson, S. (eds). *Educating children in conflict zones: research, policy and practice for systemic change – a tribute to Jackie Kirk*. New York: Teachers College Press, 2011.

Nader, K., Pynoos, R.S., Fairbanks, L. and Frederick, C. 'Children's PTSD reactions one year after a sniper attack on their school'. *American Journal of Psychiatry* 147 (11) (1990) 1526–1530.

Neilsen, L. *Literacy for living: What literacy means in the lives of three adults.* Portsmouth, NH: Heinemann, 1989.

Norris, F.H., Byrne, C.M., Diaz, E. and Kaniasty, K. *The range, magnitude, and duration of effects of natural and human-caused disasters: a review of the empirical literature,* 2001. Page no longer available http://www.ncptsd.org/facts/disasters/fs%5frange.

Nuzzaci, A. *Competenze riflessive tra professionalità educative e insegnamento.* Lecce-Brescia: Pensa MultiMedia Editore s.r.l., 2011.

Nuzzaci, A. 'Patrimoni locali, identità e linguaggi: educare "ai e con i" beni culturali e ambientali in aree ad elevata fragilità.' In *Individui, comunità e istituzioni in emergenza. Intervento psico-socio-pedagogico e lavoro di rete nelle situazioni di catastrofe,* edited by Stefania Mariantoni and Alessandro Vaccarelli, pp. 213–229. Milano: FrancoAngeli, 2018.

Nuzzaci, A. and Marcozzi, I. 'Fattori di rischio scolastici e abbandono della percezione degli studenti: il progetto internazionale ERASMUS KA2 ACCESS'. *Giornale Italiano della Ricerca Educativa – Rivista Italiana di Ricerca Educativa* 12 (23) (2019): 48–68.

Benvenuto, G., Di Genova, N., Nuzzaci, A. and Vaccarelli, A. 'Scala di Resilienza professionale degli Insegnanti prima validazione nazionale'. *Educational, Cultural and Psychological Studies* 23 (2021): 201–218.

Öcal, A. 'The evaluation of earthquake education in the elementary school social studies courses'. *Journal of Gazi Educational Faculty* 25 (1) (2005): 169–184

OECD. *Protecting students and schools from earthquakes: the seven OECD principles for school seismic safety.* Paris: Secretary-General of the OECD, 2017.

Oliva, P., Murdaca, A.M. and Nuzzaci, A. 'Fattori individuali e contestuali nel *burnout* degli insegnanti'. *Giornale Italiano della Ricerca Educativa* 7 (12) (2014): 99–120.

Özgüven, B. and Öztürk, C. 'Effects of basic earthquake awareness education to given primary school students.' *Turkish Journal of Disaster,* 1 (1) (2006): 1–6.

Palmer, P. *The courage to teach: Exploring the inner landscape of a teacher's life.* Wiley: San Francisco, 2007.

Pfefferbaum, B. 'Posttraumatic stress disorder in children: a review of the past 10 years'. *Journal of the American Academy of Child & Adolescent Psychiatry* 36 (11) (1997): 1503–1511.

Reardon, R.M. 'Elementary school principals' learning-centered leadership and educational outcomes: implications for principals' professional development'. *Leadership and Policy in Schools* 10 (1) (2011): 63–83.

Ross, K.E. and Shuell, T.J. 'Children's beliefs about earthquakes'. *Science Education* 77 (2) (1993): 191–205.

Rutter, M. 'Psychosocial resilience and protective mechanisms'. In *Risk and protective factors in the development of psychopathology,* edited by Jon E. Rolf, Ann S. Masten, Dante Cicchetti,

Keith H. Nuechterlein, and William S. Weintraub, pp. 181–214. Cambridge: University Press, 1990.

Scali, J., Gandubert, C., Ritchie, K., Soulier, M., Ancelin, M-L. and Chaudieu, I. 'Measuring resilience in adult women using the 10-items Connor-Davidson Resilience Scale (CD-RISC). Role of trauma exposure and anxiety disorders'. *PLoS ONE,* 7 (6) (2012): Article e39879.

Schoenberg, A. 'Do crisis plans matter? A new perspective on leading during a crisis'. *Public Relations Quarterly* 50 (1) (2005): 2–6.

Schwartz, E.D. and Perry, B.D. 'The post-traumatic response in children and adolescents'. *Psychiatric Clinics of North America* 17 (2) (1994): 311–326.

Seery, M.D., Holman, E.A. and Silver, R.C. 'Whatever does not kill us: Cumulative lifetime adversity, vulnerability, and resilience". *Journal of Personality and Social Psychology* 99 (6) (2010): 1025–1041.

Smith, L. and Riley, D. 'School leadership in times of crisis'. *School Leadership and Management: Formerly School Organisation* 32 (1) (2012): 57–71.

Southwick, S.M., Bonanno, G.A., Masten, A.S., Panter-Brick, C. and Yehuda, R. 'Resilience definitions, theory, and challenges: interdisciplinary perspectives'. *European Journal of Psychotraumatology* 5 (1) (2014): 1–14.

Troman, G. and Woods, P. *Primary teachers' stress.* London: Routledge, 2001.

Ungar, M.A. 'A constructionist discourse on resilience: multiple contexts, multiple realities among at-risk children and youth'. *Youth and Society* 35 (3) (2004): 341–365.

Vaccarelli, A. and Mariantoni, S. *Children after a natural disaster: materials for educators and tearchers.(Velino for Children-Amatrice Heartquake 2016).* Milano: FrancoAngeli, 2018.

Vanderbilt-Adriance, E. and Shaw, D.S. 'Protective factors and the development of resilience in the context of neighborhood disadvantage' *Journal of Abnormal Child Psychology* 36 (6) (2008): 887–901.

Vernberg, E.M., La Greca, A.M., Silverman, W.K. and Prinstein, M.J. 'Prediction of posttraumatic stress symptoms in children after Hurricane Andrew'. *Journal of Abnormal Psychology* 105 (2) (1996): 237–248.

Vogel, J.M. and Vernberg, E.M. 'Children's psychological responses to disaster'. *Journal of Clinical Child Psychology* 22 (4) (1993): 470–484.

Weick, K.E. and Sutcliffe, K.M. *Managing the unexpected: resilient performance in an age of uncertainty.* San Francisco, CA: Jossey-Bass, 2007.

Whitla, M. (ed.) *Crisis management and the school community.* Melbourne: ACER Press, 2003.

Winje, D. and Ulvik, A. 'Long-term outcome of trauma in children: the psychological consequences of a bus accident'. *Journal of Child Psychology and Psychiatry* 39 (5) (1998): 635–642.

Wolmer, L., Laor, N. and Yazgan, Y. 'School reactivation programs after disaster: could teachers serve as clinical mediators?' *Child and Adolescent Psychiatric Clinics of North America* 12 (2) (2003): 363–381.

Yule, W. and Williams, R.M. 'Post-traumatic stress reactions in children'. *Journal of Traumatic Stress* 3 (2) (1990): 279–295.

20

Intercultural relations and community development
Education in L'Aquila among earthquake and COVID-19 emergencies

Alessandro Vaccarelli and Silvia Nanni[1]

Starting with the data in the report '*Immigrati e italiani dopo il terremoto nel territorio aquilano*' ('Immigrants and Italians after the earthquake in the territory of L'Aquila'), which was published in 2010,[2] one year after the earthquake of 6 April 2009 that involved the Italian city of L'Aquila and 56 neighbouring municipalities, reflections on the social and educational needs that have marked out the population of L'Aquila, both of Italian origin and of other nationalities, became a focus of interest. Our research specifically looked to include, in a broader perspective, the needs of both the autochthonous and the immigrant populations and aimed to investigate some relevant issues related to multicultural coexistence after such a catastrophic event: what degree of coexistence has developed, as a result of this event, between autochthonous inhabitants and immigrants?

The qualitative and quantitative research, cofinanced by the European Union and the Italian Ministry of the Interior,[3] stressed that immigrant citizens who had experienced the same tragedy were weaker, more exposed and less protected than the Italian population.[4] It also showed that some competition dynamics, mainly caused by the housing crisis, had led to subtle attitudes of hostility and intolerance towards the immigrant population. More than 10 years after that tragic event, we now aim to present an overall picture from a social pedagogical perspective, which encompasses political and welfare choices about the development of the sense of community and territory, as both physical and psychological space of coexistence. Have these choices really supported projects based on welcoming, integrating and respecting differences from a truly intercultural perspective? The goal here is to draw up a first assessment at a historical moment in which the previous local emergency has been followed by a global emergency – the one linked to the spread of COVID-19.

The extraneousness of the catastrophe

> Foreigner: a choked-up rage deep down in my throat, a black angel clouding transparency, opaque, unfathomable spur. The image of hatred and of the other, a foreigner is neither the romantic victim of our clannish indolence nor the intruder responsible for all the ills of the polis. Neither the apocalypse on the move nor the instant adversary to be eliminated for the sake of appeasing the group. Strangely, the foreigner lives within us: he is the hidden face of our identity, the space that wrecks our abode, the time in which ourselves, we are spared detesting him in himself.[5]

Everyday language, even that conveyed by the media, does not always consider the depth and the long history of words for neutral objects in denoting meanings that never change, especially in processes of social categorisation – given once and for all, visible in their consistency and, therefore, *true and solid*. Let's examine here the term 'catastrophe'. In the midst of modernity, with the Lisbon earthquake of 1755, that term began to take on the meaning of annihilation, deterioration of the state of things, but also the meaning of transformation, indicating a leap from one order to another, a sudden change of direction, radical and irreversible upheaval. In this regard, 'the catastrophe is not only a traditional figure of destruction and annihilation, but also a powerful symbol of transformation'.[6] The verb *strépho*, from which the word 'catastrophe' derives (in addition to *kata*) has, among its various meanings, those of: 'to "turn" in the sense of "turning the rudder", changing course, or "turn the gaze", "rotate the pupils", changing the panorama'.[7] Modernity therefore presents the catastrophe as a dynamic 'figure', in which the event or the rupture, the point of no return, the twist, changes the course of things and lays the foundations for the – unexpected and human – search for new balances and future scenarios. The catastrophe, therefore, becomes the space and time of human formation, indeed it gives form (in the meaning of the German term *Bildung*) to a subject who is no longer the same as before and who tries, between pain and resilience, to rise from his destiny: for the individual it may represent a bet on one's own project of life and on one's own role as a citizen; for society it could represent the assumption of new perspectives such as prevention, risk culture, cooperation and peaceful coexistence, or even respect for the environment.

In contraposition to this view, which some might define as 'romantic' or 'sweetened', but which is, in any case, implied in the general perspective of the human sciences, there is another way of narrating it – that is the realistic way, which takes into consideration the worst social logics in which a catastrophe occurs, logics that are made stronger and more extreme by crisis situations and lack of resources. If, on one hand, in agreement with Schenck,[8] the Lisbon earthquake of 1755 gave strength to Enlightenment thought, on the other it was an opportunity to propose once again the logic of divine punishment: the Portuguese have behaved badly – so the Jesuits admonished – and God has sent his scourge on Earth.

If catastrophes today expose global problems and imbalances, by strengthening a certain political and scientific culture that sets problems in the frame of human rights and in the paradigm of reconjunction between the subject and the environment, the 'shock economy'– or disaster capitalism – finds in them the opportunity to do business, to destabilise institutional systems, to privatise public goods – including education – as happened during Hurricane Katrina in New Orleans, by sowing the seeds of a dystopian future increasingly marked by inequalities and imbalances.[9] We can add that, if in the past the catastrophe represented – even in the religious conception – part of the human experience, the world of today, richer than ever – and the disbelief we feel towards the COVID-19 pandemic proves it – considers it a foreign body, always postponed in time and space.

Narrating the realism of the catastrophe would mean delving into many different aspects that it is not possible to consider analytically here. We will therefore examine only some of them. If we consider the theme of otherness and diversity, the catastrophe becomes a scenario in which we not only perceive a deep extraneousness inherent in our experience (I am extraneous in front of it and it is extraneous in front of me, laying me completely bare), but one that also pushes us to seek what we do not want to be – 'strangers to ourselves', as Kristeva[10] describes it – in the stranger close to us.

In the contest of European history, and with reference to ancient time, both paganism and Christianity deal with the theme of divine punishment in view of faults that can only be expiated through the experience of catastrophe. God or the gods punish cities, societies, communities, but these often reorganise themselves internally in the most meticulous search of those who may have primary faults: most of the medieval chronicles, as Piccinni[11] states, expressly detect in human sins the cause of the plague that decimated the European population and recall lynching actions against non-Christians – for instance, the pogroms against Jewish people – instigated by groups of flagellants around Europe. Fault represents a key theme: a constant that reappears, in a more blurred way, even when the general climate changes, and when secular conceptions open the way for a rational vision – within the new concept of 'risk culture' – the natural scientific and technical prerequisites, in order to formulate explanations and orient human behaviour towards preventing and facing adverse situations. However, once again the catastrophe becomes *altera* or other – the one who is different from the crowd, the one who belongs to a minority, the stranger in the sense of 'strange' and extraneous, and thus participates, internally, to define its own otherness. The fault seems to remain, in the collective perceptions, as a legacy that continues to fulfil – *super tempora* (over time) – psychosocial functions that are classically categorised within the scheme of the 'scapegoat'. This scheme activates when a stressed population pours out its frustrations on minority groups, thus reducing its internal tension and projecting it towards an external target that is never the real cause of the problem. Let us consider what happened to Chinese communities in Italy during the COVID-19 emergency. To date we have anecdotal but highly significant data: hate speech on social media, aggression, denigration and actions of segregation.[12] And it has become apparent, in the context of an earthquake like that of L'Aquila, that situations of collective stress, mostly managed in line with the principles of the shock economy, have exacerbated competition for access to resources and triggered feelings of intolerance and hostility against the immigrant population.

A small multicultural city hit by an earthquake

Relations between Italians and immigrants

Between before and after the 2009 earthquake in L'Aquila, the conditions for the coexistence of these two worlds changed radically. Before 6 April they substantially moved in parallel ways and crossed each other only superficially in everyday life, inhabiting the social reality according to rules that hardly encouraged meetings and relationships. After 6 April, the two worlds unavoidably overlapped, inhabiting the same spaces: tent cities, hotels, barracks, the newly constructed CASE (*Complessi Antisismici Sostenibili Ecocompatibili*, or sustainable and eco-compatible anti-seismic complexes), sharing the same tragedy and the same problems. However, they were interacting within a psychosociological dimension – that of post-trauma – which tended to develop, in a bipolar way, the willingness to meet and the temptation to clash, as well as to sharpen the social tension.

From the very first days in the tent cities, the world of social volunteering met a series of needs that the immigrant population expressed implicitly or explicitly, especially those most vulnerable from a linguistic point of view, who could not understand the various bureaucratic procedures related to emergency assistance or the renewal of residence permits. Besides these needs, there was the cohabitation problem forced by the crisis: stories of rapprochement and exchange, distrust and hostility.[13]

The same volunteers who continue to intervene in emergency contexts and observe the dynamics between Italians and immigrants constitute a coordinated group of associations called Ricostruire Insieme (rebuilding together), financed by The European Fund for the Integration of Third-Country Nationals. Thanks to this fund, they have carried out research and opened an information centre for immigrants, as well as an intercultural centre aimed at facilitating meetings and relationships,[14] thus laying the groundwork to address the problems of reception, integration and conflicts in the post-emergency phase.

The research described in this chapter involved a sample of 403 adult citizens of immigrant origin and a sample of 981 adult citizens of Italian origin. Both groups were given two questionnaires to investigate attitudes, perceptions and relationship experiences resulting from the earthquake. Later interviews[15] enriched the results through qualitative data.

The experience of living together in tent camps or in hotels on the Abruzzo coast was an opportunity to get to know each other, to feel united by the same fate, to cry the same tears and live with the same uncertainties, but it was also a terrain of hostility and intolerance, as the examples quoted below demonstrate:

- 'In the tent city, for the distribution of products we had to wait for the Italians first.'
- 'Sometimes in tent camps, Italians came first, and then the immigrants. The citizens of L'Aquila in the camp wanted to be privileged over immigrants.'

- 'After the earthquake, it was said that we immigrants took the houses, the benefits ... I did not take anything.'
- 'In the tent city I used to give a hand (serving lunches) and some women were bothered that I was there working hard and, by the way, they didn't help.'
- 'In Piazza d'Armi [one of the locations of tent camps], at mealtime, they said to us to go back to our country ... not everybody, just a few people.'

The heroic phase and the honeymoon phase that characterise the first phases of disaster[16] allow feelings of solidarity to emerge, along with a strong sense of community and partial optimism. However, these turn quickly into feelings of uncertainty, disillusionment and fear for the future (disillusionment phase). The hunt for looters who burgle destroyed apartments or take advantage of the distribution of goods like food, clothing and personal hygiene products immediately pointed an accusing finger at immigrants; the right to assistance was perceived as a prerogative of the Italians and, therefore, undermined by the presence of immigrant families. Long-awaited housing allocations became a cause of tension and implicit conflict for the displaced. Those who had lived under tents felt they had priority over those who stayed in hotels; owners of destroyed houses felt they had priority over those who rented them; many Italians felt that immigrants should be queued up and actually be excluded from the housing allocation.

> It's just because I have a bit of culture and I know very well that it's not their [migrant families'] fault, but frankly these [politicians] may make you become racist.

The person quoted is an elementary school teacher, who had seen her housing needs frustrated due to not being allocated a prefabricated house and thus resented the inclusion of immigrant families on the same housing allocation lists. Although this inclusion was a fair choice made by the administration, it has to be read in the context of whole intervention and emergency response. The CASE project had a strong impact on public opinion and involved particularly onerous economic choices, but has housed no more than fourteen thousand displaced people, and has, at the same time, distorted social networks and urban structure. With regard to the CASE accommodation, over 50 per cent of the Italian citizens contacted for this research believe that it is right to give priority to Italians over immigrants, while more than 30 per cent believe that post-earthquake policies have given more importance to immigrants than to autochthonous inhabitants. All this while the media kept presenting the image of a city rebuilt and citizens fully satisfied with their needs. It is important to remember that, after the earthquake of Amatrice in 2016, right-wing nationalists had the opportunity to argue, at a national level, and using the slogan 'Italians first!' that the failed reconstruction of Amatrice was due to policies around reception of immigrants and refugees saved in the Mediterranean.

In this context, a counter-narrative on emergency and catastrophe needs to be built through the commitment of social forces in the field – such as those that, in the case of L'Aquila, led to the birth of Ricostruire Insieme – and through sciences such as pedagogy, which have much to say and do towards building more inclusive, participatory and thus better cities and societies.

The earthquake effects

Intercultural pedagogy and participation

The above-mentioned qualitative research[17] identified the needs of the immigrant population after the earthquake of 6 April 2009 and investigated the relationships between different cultures, namely between autochthonous and immigrant citizens. It emerged that Italian citizens of L'Aquila and immigrants have many needs and priorities in common, but there is also a significant gap that comes from the impact of immigration on a social, economic and practical-bureaucratic level, as if the effects of the trauma resulting from the migratory background had been experienced more strongly. In many cases, in addition to material necessities there were also immaterial needs such as sharing, proximity and participation.

The earthquake has, in fact, highlighted the problem of cohabitation that, as a result of the restoration – or even construction from scratch – of many urban and social spaces, has increased the chances of encounter and clash between the autochthonous and immigrant populations. The sense of frustration has definitely encouraged forms of discrimination and conflict. These have on one hand disadvantaged immigrants, and, on the other, misled the Italian citizens in the search for valid and adequate strategies to solve individual and collective problems.

In this case, the laissez-faire produces, as the research results reveal, 'ingroup' and 'outgroup' dynamics, mechanisms of defense and search for a scapegoat,[18] episodes of discrimination and racism that certainly should not lead to stereotyping the Italian population of the 'crater' [the areas struck by the earthquake] as racist *tout court*.[19]

This shows that it is necessary to coordinate and direct institutional actions – from local authorities to training centres and schools – and the activities of associations towards an intercultural and participatory planning approach. This should focus on advocacy processes,[20] dialogue and integration,[21] and so-called 'humanist' and 'economicist' social inclusion,[22] thus promoting opportunities for exchange and knowledge. The path from that terrible seismic event towards an integral and 'competent' sense of community is still long and tortuous, and requires a process of 'learning by doing'.

Intercultural education, defined by the Council of Europe in 2008 as one of the six pillars of the 'new Europe', still struggles to be recognised as a 'transversal social area'. In this sense, intercultural pedagogy could really assume a role of governance, coordination, collection and connection of procedures, strategies, studies, experimentations and social reflections.

The top-down management approach to the post-earthquake period by the government in office at the time, and the lack of involvement of the population in decisions concerning their housing, weighed especially on immigrant communities who had already experienced exclusion in terms of participation. Despite the timely construction of the CASE accommodation and MAP (*Moduli Abitativi Provvisori*, or temporary housing modules outside the town) to house those with a destroyed or condemned home in the Municipality of L'Aquila and surrounding territory, the whole community has been completely cut off from any kind of choice and decision about their future.

So, what happens to a territory, a social group or a community when participation is precluded?

> Throughout the [vast] world, we are witness[es] every day, and in varying degrees, to the excruciating spectacle of the simple man/ everyman crushed, humiliated, adapted and transformed into a spectator, remotely controlled by the power of myth ... which, turning against him destroys and humiliates him.

If the notion of community is problematic in its more general sense, it becomes even more complex in crisis situations. The earthquake distorts its meaning, not only on an individual level, but also on a collective one. The earthquake erupts into the life of a community, breaking the bonds between individuals and between groups. If we try to focus on the image of a displaced person, we feel a sense of anxiety deriving from the severing of the bond between the person and their territory, their social reference points and, therefore, their community. There are ambivalent links between disasters and communities: if the earthquake initially binds survivors together and strengthens the sense of community, once the danger has passed, the true sense of community can give way to mere individualism.

Educating through experience: a pedagogical challenge

What should be highlighted and developed here is John Dewey's idea that experience, if meaningful, whether painful or pleasurable, generates learning and offers the opportunity to think about what has been experienced.

Dewey explains how a meta-reflection on learning processes and valorisation of education is essential in relation to the lived, practiced experience. Every experience, both made and undergone, modifies those who act and those who suffer and, at the same time, influences, whether one likes it or not, the quality of the experiences that follow. Hence the 'principle of continuity' whereby each experience receives something from those that preceded it, and in some way changes the quality of those that will follow. Therefore, the experience allows the growth of the human being, with regard to their ability to interact positively with the world. This is the 'principle of growth': the environment modifies the living beings by posing problems to them – and they, in turn, act 'on' and 'in' the world, changing it. In the learning spiral, we reach Dewey's third dimension of experience, the one linked to the 'principle of interaction'. The experience is fulfilled not only inside the person but also by virtue of a transaction between the individual and the environment. As he explains, the human being cannot enter into a process of experience without putting themself into play, because they are a single subjectivity present in the world, able to act on things and modify them, and ultimately change them.[23]

According to the leader of American pragmatism, experience actively engages our perception and emotionality in the organism–environment interaction, and therefore in reality. In this view, the experience is constantly based on a negotiation between the ideas we have and the facts we come into contact with, in a sort of constructive dynamism.[24]

The first important consideration is that life develops in an environment, not only in it, but also because of it, interacting with it. No creature lives under its own skin; its subcutaneous organs are means to connect with what exists beyond its body, and to which it must conform, by adapting and defending itself, in order to live … Every need, such as the desire for fresh air or for food, is a deficiency that denotes a temporary lack of adequate adaptation to the surrounding environment. However, it is also a demand, a reaching out to the environment to fill the gaps and restore adaptation by establishing at least a temporary balance. Life itself consists of phases in which the organism loses the pace with the surrounding things and then returns in unison with it.[25]

In Dewey's perspective, temporary balance and social order are not determined by rules imposed from above or from outside but rather by the individual and collective awareness, by the reflexivity and responsibility that allow the human being to become, first of all, aware of the problems within their own context, and then, to try to solve them. The educational challenge is still that of encouraging the development of anyone living in a democracy within a learning society, that is a society based both on an intergenerational, widespread education which is life-long, life-wide and life-deep, and on a full awareness of ethical and civil responsibility, in order to limit differences and increase solidarity and collective social participation.

Meeting places: territory and community

It is necessary to orient educational action towards recognition and enhancement of the so-called 'interstitial spaces', namely those places that stand between: between before and after, between fullness and emptiness, between people. If a number of individuals live isolated from one another within certain spatial boundaries, they immediately fill the place next to them with their own substance and activity, but between them there is an empty space, or in other words a 'nothingness'. Yet, when they enter into reciprocal relations, the space between them seems filled and animated. Mutual interaction converts what was previously empty into something meaningful for us.

Zygmunt Bauman warns us about the danger of the opposite, namely the effects produced by the art of non-meeting. This happens when the other is placed in the background and does not participate preeminently, thus producing a progressive desocialisation of space, transforming it into a kind of blank space in which every kind of interaction and involvement appears to be interrupted.[26]

Our interstitial spaces can represent a possibility of growth and citizenship when they become places for meeting and living together, and thus [part of] a territorial network. The term 'territory' refers to an anthropological conception of the space lived in by individuals, groups and communities. In a social pedagogical approach, it is particularly necessary to take into account educational components and actors, in relation to the very close link between culture and territory.[27]

The latter should not be considered, then, only as a physical space in which the educational intervention takes place: it must be borne in mind that its characteristics also determine the structure and organisation of any training initiative. In other words, the educational intervention is based on the specific characteristics of the single territory.[28] The territory defines, therefore, not only spatial, social and anthropological dimensions, but also pedagogical aspects, since its inhabitants give rise to processes of knowledge and direct experience of activities, solidarity, positions and social bonds in relation to other individuals.

> A collectivity can be defined as a community when its members act reciprocally and in relation to others who do not belong to the same collectivity, by more or less consciously prioritising the values, norms, customs and interests of the collectivity, considered as a whole, over the personal interests or those of their own sub-group or other collectivities; that is when the awareness of common, although indeterminate interests, the sense of belonging to a positively evaluated socio-cultural entity to which people adhere affectively, and the experience of social relations involving the totality of people, become in themselves factors of solidarity.[29]

Twelve years after the earthquake and during the ongoing COVID-19 pandemic emergency, interculture, inclusion, participation and education are still the major challenges in the city of L'Aquila.

Notes

1 Although the essay in its entirety is the result of the collaboration of the two authors, introduction, section 1 and 2 can be attributed to Alessandro Vaccarelli and sections 3, 4 and 5 to Silvia Nanni.
2 Vaccarelli, 2010, 2011.
3 Title of the Project: *Centro informativo per l'immigrazione*, proposed by *Ricostruire Insieme*. European Union, Ministero dell'Interno (Ministry of Interior), *Dipartimento per le Libertà Civili e l'Immigrazione* (Department for Civil Liberties and Immigration), European Fund for the Integration of Third-Country Nationals.
4 In the research study, questionnaires, with closed and open answers, were used together with interviews for two target cohorts: Italian nationals and immigrants, with the aim of better understanding issues relating to the perception of the migratory phenomenon and the quality of relations with immigrants. The questionnaires allowed comparison of results for significant variables as well as comparative analysis of responses of two reference populations. Moreover, it allowed independent study of the two samples, each for its own specificity. Taking part in the study were 981 Italian citizens and 403 immigrants. The questionnaire for immigrants sought to understand what effects the earthquake had on their living conditions. The questionnaire for Italians investigated the effects of the earthquake on daily life.
5 Kristeva, 1998, 1.
6 Tagliapietra, 2014, p. XVIII
7 Tagliapietra, 2014, p. XVIII.
8 Schenck, 2010.
9 Klein, 2007.
10 Kristeva, 1998.
11 Piccinni, 1999.
12 https://www.huffingtonpost.it/entry/cuneo-una-ragazza-costretta-a-scendere-dal-bus-sei-cinese_it_5e382eecc5b69a19a4b33479 Accessed 3 February 2020.
13 Alaggio, Masciovecchio, 2010, 3–5. Accessed 10 May 2021.
14 Vaccarelli 2010.
15 Twenty interviews were collected in total, from 10 Italian citizens and 10 foreign nationals,
16 Sbattella, Tettamanzi, 2013.
17 Vaccarelli, 2010.
18 Ulivieri, 1997.
19 Vaccarelli, 2010, 104, Italian quote translated into English.
20 Fiorucci, 2004.
21 Cambi, 2006; Genovese, 2003.
22 Nanni, 2019, 230–238.
23 Cecchi, 2014.
24 Cecchi, 2014.
25 Matteucci, 2012, 40, Italian quote translated into English.
26 Bauman, 1996.
27 Tramma, 1999.
28 Tramma, 1999.
29 Tramma, 1999, 17–18, Italian quote translated into English.

Bibliography

Alaggio M. and Masciovecchio G. 'Ricostruire insieme e le azioni progettuali'. In Vaccarelli A. (ed.), *Immigrati e italiani dopo il terremoto nel territorio aquilano. Ricerca sui bisogni sociali, educativi e sullo stato della convivenza* 3–5. L'Aquila: Ricostruire insieme , 2010. Accessed 14 June 2022 http://www.ricostruireinsieme.it/wp-content/themes/multichrome/images/pdf/immigrati-e-italiani-dopo-il-terremoto_def.pdf
Bauman, Z. *Le Sfide dell'etica*. Milano: Feltrinelli, 1996.

Calandra, L. (ed.). *Territorio e democrazia. Un laboratorio di geografia sociale nel doposisma aquilano*. L'Aquila: L'Una, 2012.

Caldarini, C. *La comunità competente. Lo sviluppo locale come processo di apprendimento collettivo. Teorie ed esperienze*. Roma: Ediesse, 2004.

Cambi, F. *Incontro e dialogo. Prospettive della pedagogia interculturale*. Roma: Carocci, 2006.

Cappa, F. (ed.). *John Dewey. Esperienza e educazione*. Milano: Raffaello Cortina, 2014.

Catarci, M. and Fiorucci, M. *Intercultural Education in the European Context: Theories, Experiences, Challenges*. Farnham: Ashgate, 2015.

Cecchi, D. *Il continuo e il discreto. Estetica e filosofia dell'esperienza in John Dewey*. Milano: FrancoAngeli, 2014.

Crespellani, T. *Terremoto: evento naturale ed evento sociale*. Conferenza tenuta al Festival Scienza – L'alfabeto della Scienza – V Edizione, Cagliari, 2012.

Fiorucci, M (ed.). *Incontri. Spazi e luoghi della mediazione interculturale*. Roma: Armando, 2004.

Freire, P. *L'educazione come pratica della libertà*. Milano: Mondadori, 1973.

Freire, P. *Pedagogy of Freedom: Ethics, Democracy, and Civic Courage*. Maryland: Rowman & Littlefield Publishers, 2000.

Fukuyama, F. *La fine della storia e l'ultimo uomo*. Milano: Rizzoli, 1992.

Gasparini, G. *Sociologia degli interstizi. Viaggio, attesa, silenzio, sorpresa, dono*. Milano: Mondadori, 1998

Genovese, A. *Per una pedagogia interculturale*. Bologna: Bononia University Press, 2003.

Isidori, M.V. and Vaccarelli, A. *Pedagogia dell'emergenza. Didattica nell'emergenza. I processi formativi nelle situazioni di criticità individuali e collettive*. Milano: FrancoAngeli, 2013.

Klein, N. *The Shock Doctrine: The Rise of Disaster Capitalism*. Toronto: Knopf Canada, 2007.

Kristeva, J. *Strangers to Ourselves*. New York: Columbia University Press, 1998.

Latouche, S. *La scommessa della decrescita*. Milano: Feltrinelli, 2009.

Alaggio, M. 'Gioacchino Masciovecchio Ricostruire Insieme e le azioni progettuali'. In Vaccarelli A. (ed.), *Immigrati e italiani dopo il terremoto nel territorio aquilano. Ricerca sui bisogni sociali, educativi e sullo stato della convivenza*. L'Aquila: Ricostruire insieme, 2010.

Matteucci, G. (ed.). *John Dewey: arte come esperienza*. Palermo: Aesthetica, 2012.

Nanni, S. *Educazione degli adulti, sviluppo di comunità, pedagogia critica. Angela Zucconi e il Progetto Pilota Abruzzo*. Milano: FrancoAngeli, 2018.

Nanni, S. 'Il rischio come possibilità educativa: dallo "spazio interstiziale" alla comunità'. In Stefania Mariantoni S., Vaccarelli, A. (eds) *Individui, comunità e istituzioni in emergenza. Intervento psico-socio-pedagogico e lavoro di rete nelle situazioni di catastrofe*, 230–238. Milano: FrancoAngeli, 2018. Open access: ojs.francoangeli.it.

Nanni, S. 'L'approccio "umanista" contro i rischi vecchi e nuovi di esclusione sociale: riflessioni pedagogiche'. In Isidori M.V. (ed) *La formazione dell'insegnante inclusivo tra vecchie e nuove emergenze educative*, 144–154. Milano: FrancoAngeli, 2019.

Piccinni, G. *I mille anni del Medioevo*. Milano: Mondadori, 1999.

Sbattella, F. and Tettamanzi, M. *Fondamenti di psicologia dell'emergenza*. Milano: FrancoAngeli, 2013.

Schenck, G.J. 'Dis-astri. Modelli interpretativi delle calamità naturali dal medioevo al Rinascimento'. In Matheus M., Piccinni G., Pinto G., Varnini G.N. (eds) *Le calamità ambientali nel tardo medioevo europeo: realtà, percezioni, reazioni*. Firenze: University Press, 2010.

Tagliapietra, A. (ed.). *Sulla catastrofe. L'illuminismo e la filosofia del disastro*. Milano: Bruno Mondadori, 2004.

Tramma, S. *Pedagogia sociale*. Milano: Guerini Scientifica, 2010.

Ulivieri, S. (ed.). *L'educazione e i marginali: storia, teorie, luoghi e tipologie dell'emarginazione*. Firenze: La Nuova Italia, 1997.

Vaccarelli, A. (ed.), *Immigrati e italiani dopo il terremoto nel territorio aquilano. Ricerca sui bisogni sociali, educativi e sullo stato della convivenza*. L'Aquila: Ricostruire insieme, 2010. Accessed 15 June 2022 http://www.ricostruireinsieme.it/wp-content/themes/multichrome/images/pdf/immigrati-e-italiani-dopo-il-terremoto_def.pdf

Vaccarelli, A. 'La pedagogia interculturale tra emergenze sociali e rapporti interdisciplinari'. In Mariani, A. (ed.) *25 saggi di pedagogia*. Milano: FrancoAngeli, 2011.

Index

Page numbers in italics are figures; with 't' are tables; with 'n' are notes.

Abbey of Sant'Eutizio (Preci, Italy) *207*
Abruzzo (Italy) 31–2, 32t, 33
Acoustical Society of Italy (AIA) 221–2, 223
Act on the Development of Tsunami-resilient Communities 74
active museums 292
Agenda 2030 (UN) 283–4
Amorin, Analía 154
ANFE (Associazione Nazionale Famiglie Emigrati) 180, 185
apps, communication 261, *261–2*, 263–4
AQ99.it 186
Arendt, Hannah 109
Argentina 148–52, *151–2*, 154
Asensio, Raul 129
Autodesk 123D Catch 183

Barrio las 250 viviendas del IIPV (General Roca) 150
Basilica of San Benedetto (Norcia) 271
Basilica of Santa Maria di Collemaggio (L'Aquila) 13, 18–21, *21–4*, 182
Bauman, Zygmunt 337
Benedetto da Norcia, San 271
Benedictine order 271, 272, 273
Black Lives Matter 108, 290–1
Bohle, M. 214
Bononcini, Laura 177
Botanic Gardens Network 290
Brambilla, G. 221
Bredekamp, H. 238
Broad (gallery, Los Angeles) 289
Brooks, J.S. 318
Building Maker 180, 182
Bush, T. 318

Cage, John 220
Caracas (Venezuela) 142–6, *143–4*, 153
CASE project (*Complessi Antisismici Sostenibili Ecocompatibili*) 35, 95–8, *96–7*, 175, 332, 333–4, 335
Castellucio (Italy) *207*, 269, 271–2, *272*, 273, 275, 278, 279
Castilla Park (Lima) 128–9

catastrophe (term) 329–31
Celestine V (Pietro Angelerio) (Pope) 19
chabolas 142–3, 153, 154
Chinese communities, and COVID-19 331
chowks 159
City Planning Act (Japan) 66–7, 74
Click Days, L'Aquila 177–9, *178–9*, 185, 186
climate change 4, 7
Climate Disaster Resilience Index (CDRI) 68
collaboration/cooperation
    institutional 35, 37t, 213
    Japan 49, 55–6, *56*, 57, 60, 78, 189
    L'Aquila 19–21, 25
collective-type disaster public housing, Japan 57–9, *58*
Come Facciamo *176*, 177, 187
'commoning' 126–9
communication
    and museums 292
    risk and disaster 2, 4, 5, 37, 37t
    Italy 210–12
    Japan 71, 73, 75–9, 80, 265
    Kyoto 250–65, 253t, 254t, *255–62*, *264*, 265
community recovery 2, 30, 32–3, 35–6, *36*, 37, 37t
Comprehensive National Land Development Act (Japan, 1950) 66
condominium staircases (Caracas) 145
Consortium of Agricultural Commons 276
continuity principle 336
coping strategies 319, 320, 323
CORONA study 38–40, *38–9*
COVID-19 1–2, 6–7
    and Chinese communities 331
    CORONA study 38–40, *38–9*
    and education 316–17, 319–20
    India 156–7
    Italy 88, *88*, 210–14, 230, 283–92
    Japan 189–201, 194t, 195t, *196*, 196t, *198*, 199t
    and public spaces 108, 109, 111, 118, 157–68, *159–63*, *165–6*
    Latin America 141, 145
    Lima 123, 125
    Shahjahanabad 157–68, *159–63*, *165–6*
Crooke, Elizabeth 292

cultural heritage 15
  reconstruction
    Italy 206–10, *207–8*
    L'Aquila 17–18, 187
    Norcia 268–79, *270*, *272–3*
    see also museums

Deltaplano 277
De Micheli, Paola 206
Dewey, John 302, 308–9, 336–7
Di Crescenzo, Graziano 184
digital divide 309
Dilenschneider, Colleen, 'People trust
  museums more than newspapers' 291
Disaster Relief Act (Japan, 1947) 54
disaster risk management 63
  Italy 203–15, *205*, *207–8*
  Kochi (Japan) 64, 70, *70*, 73, 75, 79–80
displacement
  identity 6, 313–23
  people
    Italy 29, 34–5, 97, 208
    Japan 45, 47
Diver S City LAB 221
diversity 330
divine punishment 330–1
Drobeck, Nicole 180
Dryden-Peterson, S. 317

earthquakes 29, 40, *314*
  Italy 94, 173–4, 204–6, *205*, 275–7
  Japan 47, 48, 250–1, 263
  Lisbon (Portugal) 329–30
  Peru 125, *126–7*
  see also Great East Japan Earthquake
    (GEJE); Kyoto; L'Aquila; Norcia
education
  and experience 336–7
  Italy 211–12, 299–309, 301t, *305–7*
  intercultural pedagogy 334–6
  teacher training 313–23
educational poverty
  defined 302
  L'Aquila 299–309, 301t, *305–77*
educational risk management 321
El Barrio Julián Blanco, Petare (Caracas)
  142–6, *143–4*, 153
elderly
  loyalty to native places 207
  vulnerability 45, 49, 189–201, 194t, 195t,
    196, 196t, *198*, 199t
El Paraiso complex (Lima) *130*
Emidio di Treviri 276, 277, 280n13
Emilia Romagna (Italy) earthquake 29, 32t,
  33, 40
Enarson, E. 192
encounter, places of *see* places of encounter
Enomura, Y. 263
Errani, Vasco 205
European Framework for Action on Cultural
  Heritage 17–18
exhibitions
  Fa' la cosa giusta! (Do the right thing!)
    284–8
  Great Exhibition of 1872 (Lima) 125

'L'Aquila, 6 aprile 2019. Ricordo. Memoria.
  Futuro' 237, 240–2, *241*, 246–7
experience, and education 336–7

Facebook, L'Aquila 3D 177–9, *178–9*
fairs *see* exhibitions
Fa' la cosa giusta! (Do the right thing!) 284–8
famines 191
Faraone, Matteo 184
Faro Convention on the Value of Cultural
  Heritage for Society 15
favelas 146–8, *146*
'15-minute city' 112
flexibility, urban 111
Fonticulano, Pico 86–7, *86*
França, Elisabete 147
Freedberg, D., *The Power of Images* 238
freedom of information 210
Friends of Parks 138n14

Gabriel, Mariya 20
GAMeC (Gallery of Modern and Contemporary
  Art, Bergamo) 288, 289
gender, vulnerability 189–201, 194t, 195t,
    196, 196t, *198*, 199t
General Law for National Cultural Heritage
  (Peru) 129
General Roca (Argentina) 148–52, *151–2*, 154
geoethic approach 212–13
Gibran, Kahlil, *The Prophet* 213
Gilmore, Abigale 128
Gombrich, E.H. 238
Google 183–4, 186
  Google Earth 177, 180, 182, 186
  Google Maps 175–6, 182, 186
  Google Policy team 177
  Google Street View 184
Gordon, Rob 30, 35–6, *36*, 37
Grande Aquila project 95, 97
Great East Japan Earthquake (GEJE) 45–7
  gender and age vulnerabilities 189–201,
    194t, 195t, *196*, 196t, *198*, 199t
  Iwate prefecture 46, 54–5, 55t, 189, 190
  Miyagi prefecture 51, 54, 55, 55t
Grillo, Roberto 240–2, *241*
growth principle 336
Grupo de Innovacìon Educativa 'Aretè' 300
Guide (OECD/ICOM) 292
Gumbrecht, H.U. 239
'Gutenberg Galaxy' 237

Habermas, Jurgen 108
Hanshin-Awaji Earthquake 47, 48
Harvey, David 128
  The Rebel Cities 109
Haveli Rai Ji (Roshanpura) 162–4, *162–3*
Hello L'Aquila 184, *184*
heritage
  Lima 123, 129–36, *130*, *132*, *134–5*
  Norcia 268–79, *270*, *272–3*
heritage assets 283–92
Hiratada, Hirose 192
Huaca Fest (Lima) 124, 129, 131–6, *134–5*
huacas 124–5, 129–31, *132*
Hypr3D 183

identity 2–3, 5, 15
  displacement 6, 313–23
  L'Aquila 11, 14–15, 19, 25, 87–8, 97, 100, 302
  and soundscape 219, 227
  see also heritage assets; landscape
IGP Lentil Farmers Association 278
immigrant citizens see intercultural relations
Inca Road (Peru) 131, *132*, 133, *134*
India 156–68, *159*, *159–63*, *165–6*
Infobox *182*, 183
informal settlements
  Latin America 141–55, *143–4*, *146*, *149*, *151–2*
  New Lima 124–5
information see communication
innovation, community 30
intangible heritage, defined 268–9
interaction principle 336
intercultural relations, and L'Aquila 328–38
International Association for Promoting Geoethics 213
International Council of Museums (ICOM) 292
interstitial spaces 337–8
Ishinomaki (Japan) 47, 50–9, *51–3*, *56*, *58*
Italy
  disaster risk management 203–15, *205*, *207–8*
  earthquakes 94, 173–4, 204–6, *205*, 275–7
  public spaces 107–10
  toolkit for analysis and design 110–13, *113*, 113–14t
  see also Abruzzo; Castellucio; L'Aquila
Iwate prefecture (Japan)
  COVID-19 197–9, *198*, 199t
  GEJE 46, 54–5, 55t, 189, 190

Jacobs, Jane 153
Jahan, Shah 158
Japan
  COVID-19 189–201, 194t, 195t, *196*, 196t, *198*, 199t
  public reconstruction 45–7
  disaster public housing 48–54, *49*, *51–3*
  temporary housing 54–9, 55t, *56*, *58*
  spatial planning for tsunami risk 62, 79–80
  Kochi 63–4, *64*, 68–71, *69–72*, 73–4, 77–9, *79*
  and urban resilience 62–3, 65–8, *65–7*, 71–2, *72*
  see also Great East Japan Earthquake (GEJE); Kyoto
Joerin, J. 63, 68

Kawakita, Jiro, *Idea Method* 193
Klein, Naomi 300
Kochi (Japan) 63–4, *64*, 68–71, *69–71*, 73–4
  model for resilience 77–9, *79*
Kristeva, J. 330
Kyoto (Japan) 250–65, 253t, 254t, *255–62*, *264*
KYOTO Trip+ (app) 264

La Grande Fabbrica delle Parole (the great word factory) 285
landscape, Norcia 268–79, *270*, *272–3*

L'Aquila (Italy) 11–15, *14*, *21–4*, 25, *26–7*, 29, 173–4
  Basilica of Santa Maria di Collemaggio (L'Aquila) 13, 18–21, *21–4*
  building resilience 17–18
  education 299–309, 301t, *305–7*
  history and landscape 13–14, *14*
  and intercultural relations 328, 331–8
  photography 235–47, *241*, *244–6*
  public spaces 107, 115–18, *115*, 116t, 117t, 304
  reconstruction planning 16–17, 32, 32t
  and social media 173–87, *176*, *178–82*, *184*
  social reconstruction 33–4, 36, 38–41, *38–9*
  community spaces 85–100, *86–93*, *95–100*
  soundscapes 222–31, *223–7*, *229*
laws see legislation
Lefebvre, Henri 128
legislation
  Act on the Development of Tsunami-resilient Communities (Japan) 74
  City Planning Act (Japan) 66–7, 74
  Comprehensive National Land Development Act (Japan, 1950) 66
  Disaster Relief Act (Japan, 1947) 54
  General Law for National Cultural Heritage (Peru) 129
  Italian 110, 321
  Nankai Earthquakes Countermeasures Special Act (Japan, 2013) 77
  National Spatial Planning Act (Japan) 74
  Public Housing Act (Japan, 1951) 48, 50
Legnini, Giovanni 206
lentils, and Castellucio 271–2, 273, 275, 278
Lima (Peru) 123–9, 124, *126–7*, 135–6
  Huaca Fest 124, 129, 131–6, *134–5*
  pre-Hispanic sites 129–31, *130*
Lisbon, earthquake 329–30
literacy 315–16
Living Testimony, Otsuchi's GEJE victims 190–7, 194t, 195t, *196*, 196t, *198*, 199–201, 199t
Los Angeles County Museum of Art (LACMA) 289

M9 Museo 289
McCullough, M. 220
McLuhan, M., 'Gutenberg Galaxy' 237
The Mad Pixel Factory 182
mahallas 158–9, 164, 167–8
'Manual 10: Recovery' (Emergency Management Australia) 30
MAPs see temporary housing, L'Aquila
Maranga Archaeological Complex (Lima) 129, 131, *132*, 133, *135*
marcita meadows (Norcia) 272, *273*, 274–5, 278
Marone, E. 214
Masedu, F. 34
Mateo Salado complex (Lima) 131, *132*, 134, *134*
Matos Mar, J. 124
MAXXI (National Museum of 21st Century Art) (L'Aquila) 25, 85, 89, *89*
MiBACT (Ministry of Cultural Heritage and Activities and Tourism) 209–10

INDEX   **343**

Michigan, museums 290
Mitchell, W.J.T. 237, 238
Miyagi prefecture (Japan) 51, 54, 55, 55t
Moorosi, P. 318
Mundy, K. 317
museums
    and COVID-19 288–91
    and Fa' la cosa giusta! 286–8
MUSPs (Modules for Provisional School
    Use) 302
MUVE Fondazione Musei Civici di Venezia 290
'My City' project (L'Aquila) 300–1, 301t

Nagai, Y. 264
Nankai Earthquakes Countermeasures Special
    Act (Japan, 2013) 77
Nankai Trough tsunami 78
National Culture Policy (Peru) 129–31, 136–7
National Gallery (Singapore) 290
National Spatial Planning Act (Japan) 74
New Lima (Peru) 124–5
Nicolò, Simone 180
Noi L'Aquila 182–3, *182*, 187
Norcia (Italy) 268–79, *270*, *272–3*
Norcia Proloco Association 271, 271–2
Normore, A.H. 318
Nussbaum, Martha 308

Oldenburg, Ray 123
Onna (near L'Aquila) 85, 95, *95*, 98–100,
    98–100
Organization for Economic Co-operation and
    Development (OECD) 292
Otero, Rubén 154
otherness 330, 331
Otsuchi (Japan) 189–201, 194t, 195t, *196*,
    196t, *198*, 199t
'Outdoor Training and Citizenship' project
    (L'Aquila) 302

Palazzo Ardinghelli (L'Aquila) 25
Palazzo Carli Benedetti (L'Aquila) *91*
Palazzo dell'Emiciclo (L'Aquila) *27*, 90, *90*
Pallasmaa, J. 219
Palmerini, Goffredo 177
Palmer, P. 321
Pancini, Marco 177
pandemic *see* COVID-19
Panofsky, E. 238
Paraisópolis (Sao Paulo) 146–8, *146*, *149*,
    153–4
participation 201
    Italy, L'Aquila 32, 32t, 33, 176, 184–5, 187,
        210–12, 224–5, *225*, 334–5
    Latin America 128, 153
pavements (Caracas) 145
Perceived Sensory Dimensions (PSD) 220
Perdonanza Celestiniana (L'Aquila) 18–19
photography
    L'Aquila 235–47, *241*, *244–6*
    see also Click Days
Piccinini, G. 331
Pirondi, Ciro 154
places of encounter 283–92
Pontificia Universidad Catolica del Peru
    (PUCP) 129, 131, *132*, 134, *134–5*

privacy 37t, 153
Probabilistic Risk Assessment approach 203
Proctor, Nancy 289
Prosperococco, Massimo 184
PTSD (post-traumatic stress disorder) 34
Public Housing Act (Japan, 1951) 48, 50
public spaces 107–10
    L'Aquila 115–18, *115*, 116t, 117t, 304
    photography 240–2, *241*
    Latin America 140–1
    informal settlements 141–55, *143–4*, *146*,
        149, *151–2*
    Lima 123–9, *126–7*, 135–6
    Huaca Fest 131–6, *134–5*
    pre-Hispanic sites 129–31, *130*
    toolkit for analysis and design 110–13, *113*,
        113–14t
public sphere 108–10, 112, *113*, 118–19, 153

QR codes 264, *264*
quality of life (QOL) 33, 34–5
#quarantineculture 288, 291

rain chains (*kusari-doi*) 228–9
Reach Culture H2020 269
regulation *see* legislation
Repetto, Alice 182
residual spaces 141, 145, 147, 153
resilience
    CORONA study 38–40, *38–9*
    and Kochi 77–9, *79*
    and Norcia 268–79, *270*, *272–3*
    training teachers for 315, 319–23
Ricostruire Insieme (rebuilding together) 232,
    334
risk awareness 4
    Italy 214
    Japan 62, 63–7, *64–6*, 71, 80
    see also Kyoto
risk education 210, 316, 318
risk management *see* disaster risk
    management; educational risk
    management
roof terraces, Roshanpura 165–6, *166*
Rosati, Claudio 287
Roshanpura (India) 160, *160*, 164–6, *166*
rural heritage 271–2, *272–3*

safe bases 308
safe spaces 127, 136, 228
    disaster 125, 258, *258*
San Benedetto Abbey (Norcia) *208*, 271
San Bernardino (basilica church, L'Aquila) 14,
    229, *229*
San Francesco Solano Indicates an earthquake
    (Giovanni Battista Tinti) (painting) *314*
San Salvatore, Castelluccio (Norcia) *207*
Santa Scolastica plain 272, *273*
Sao Paulo (Brazil) 146–8, *146*, *149*
Schafer, R.M. 219
Schenck, G.J. 330
security 145, 153
Sen, Amartya 309
Seneca (Lucio Anneo Seneca) 94, 213
Sennett, Richard 110
SFIDE (La scuola di tutti) 285

Shahjahanabad 156, 157–68, *159–63*, *165–6*
Shaw, R. 63, 68
Showa Sanriku tsunami 191
SketchUp 180, 182, 183, 186
social inclusion 167, 308, 335
social learning 62, 71, 78, 79, 80
social media 210, 289
    L'Aquila 173–87, *176*, *178–82*, *184*
    and museums 292
social networks 7, 34
social reconstruction 6, 20, 29–41, 32t, *36*,
    37t, *38–9*
    and physical reconstruction 31–3, 32t, 40
    strategies 37, 37t
'Solo posti in piedi. Educare oltre i banchi'
    (standing places only – educating
    beyond desks) project 304
soundscapes 218–22
    L'Aquila 222–31, *223–7*, *229*
sponsorship, L'Aquila 185–6
symbolic values 15

teachers, training for resilience 315–23
technology
    apps 261, *261–2*, 264–5
    digital divide 309
    and education 315
    and museums during COVID-19 288–90
    QR codes 264, *264*
    see also social media; soundscapes
temporary housing
    Italy
    L'Aquila 95–6, *95*, 97, 98, 99–100, 232, 335
    Norcia 278
    Japan 54–9, 55t, *56*, *58*
Terre di mezzo (publishing house) 285
territory 337–8
thematisation 108–9, 243
'third places' 123, 125, 126, 129, 131, 137
3D modelling 186
    L'Aquila 180–6, *180–2*, 185

Toma Las 250 casas (Argentina) 148–51,
    151–2, 154
tourism
    and disaster information *see* Kyoto
    and touristification 276, 278, 279
tsunamis 78, 190–1
    Otsuchi evacuation 192–3, 197, 201
    spatial planning for tsunami risk 62, 79–80
    Kochi 63–4, *64*, 68–71, *69–72*, 73–4,
    77–9, *79*
    and urban resilience 62–3, 65–8, *65–7*,
    71–2, *72*
Twigg, J. 68

UNESCO, Representative List of Intangible
    Cultural Heritage of Humanity 19
United Nations, *Agenda 2030* 283–4
University of L'Aquila 19, 29, 174, 180, 185,
    304
    hall of residence *91–2*, 92
urban heritage 271, 279
U.S. Indian Ocean Tsunami Warning System
    Program 68

Vittorini, Marcello 85
vulnerability
    age 189–201, 194t, 195t, *196*, 196t, *198*,
    199t
    and gender 189–201, 194t, 195t, *196*, 196t,
    198, 199t

Walker, Charles 125
waste management 167, 168
wellbeing 33, 34, 290
    and education 299–309, 301t, *305–7*
Welsch, W. 219
women
    and residual spaces 147–8
    and security 153
    see also gender
word clouds, L'Aquila 306–8, *307*
Wraith, Ruth 35–6, *36*

Lightning Source UK Ltd.
Milton Keynes UK
UKHW051548201222
414218UK00012B/152